Reich and Nation

Reich and Nation

THE HOLY ROMAN EMPIRE AS IDEA AND REALITY, 1763–1806

John G. Gagliardo

INDIANA UNIVERSITY PRESS • BLOOMINGTON AND LONDON

This book was brought to publication with the assistance of
a grant from the Andrew W. Mellon Foundation.

Library of Congress Cataloging in Publication Data

Gagliardo, John G.
Reich and nation.

Bibliography: p.
Includes index.
1. Holy Roman Empire—History—1648–1804. 2. Holy
Roman Empire—Constitutional history. I. Title.
DD193.G33 943'.05 79-2170
ISBN 0-253-16773-6 1 2 3 4 5 84 83 82 81 80

CONTENTS

For all those spirits, ever near to me,
who helped so gently and so well along the way,
but especially for Beda, Granddad, Uncle Arthur,
and Ozzie.

Introduction

If boundary lines drawn on maps, together with the sheer number of peoples and territories they embrace, could by themselves confer political power, then the Holy Roman Empire of the German Nation would certainly have ranked as a giant among the European states of the eighteenth century. With a population of some 35 million souls toward the end of the century, the Empire sprawled across the middle of Europe, encompassing lands which stretched from Switzerland, the Dolomites, and the Adriatic in the south to the North and Baltic seas in the north, and from the northeastern border of France in the west to the frontiers of Poland and Hungary in the east. In spite of the reference to "German Nation" in its full, formal title, the Empire did not include some German-speaking peoples such as the East Prussians and German-speaking Swiss and Alsatians;[1] but while its boundaries had shrunk considerably since the heyday of the Hohenstaufen emperors in the twelfth and thirteenth centuries, it remained to the end of its days in 1806 a supranational Empire, including not only Germans (the overwhelming majority), but also Italians, Flemings, Walloons, Czechs, and some Slavs.

Apart from its size, population, and location in the heart of Europe, the Empire was adorned with a grandiose historical mystique—vague and imprecise, yet in some ways still compelling for many Europeans, especially Germans, as late as the eighteenth century—according to which it was the living and legitimate successor of the ancient western and Christian Roman Empire as renewed by Charlemagne and his successors. By virtue of this historical dignity, its head laid claim to formal precedence over all other monarchs of Europe—a claim which was honored by the authors of most formal treatises on monarchy and diplomacy in their discussions of the hierarchy of European princes.

The domination of Europe which these characteristics suggest should have belonged to the Empire did not. Indeed, the Empire had for centuries been afflicted by a kind of creeping paralysis that increasingly denied it, regarded as a single state, a significant active role in shaping even its own destiny, much less that of Europe as a whole. Its component territories, jealous of their own independence, proved unwilling or unable to cooperate in common enterprises except in the most fitful and reluctant way, even for the defense of the whole of which they were parts. On the other hand, attempts of the Emperor to revive or give greater central direction to a single imperial polity were resisted by the princes who governed the numerous lands of which the Empire was composed as encroachments on their privileges. Indeed, every major landmark of the constitutional history of the Empire since the Middle Ages, from the Golden Bull of 1356 to the Final Recess of the Imperial Deputation of 1803 and the final collapse of the Empire only three years later, was characterized by formally or informally increased restrictions on the powers of the Emperors, decreased limitations on the powers of the component territorial princes, or both. And virtually every European war in which the Empire or its major components were involved ended with some kind of territorial or political compromise of the integrity of the Empire.

The Peace of Westphalia of 1648, in particular, put the constitutional seal on the centrifugal political developments which had plagued the ideal of imperial unity for so long. Especially important in this connection were, first, the institutionalization of the role of France and Sweden as guarantors of the imperial constitution, with all that implied for gratuitous future interference in German affairs; and, second, the formal recognition of the right of member states of the Empire not only to maintain their own military forces, but also to conduct independent negotiations with foreign powers and to conclude alliances inside or outside of the Empire. The reservation that such alliances were not to be directed against the interests of Emperor or Empire was the pious hypocrisy which justified the grant of what amounted to independent foreign policy to all the territories of the Empire. Severely crippled as it henceforth was to be in all operations, foreign or domestic, which depended upon its ability to act as a single political unit, the importance of the Empire to Europe began to fade rapidly, while the diplomatic interest of all powers in its more important component states as essentially sovereign entities—Austria and the larger Electorates in particular—increased proportionately.

The diminished significance of the imperial union as a distinct state in continental affairs after 1648 has been reflected in most of the historiography of Europe over the last hundred years or more, in which the Empire in its last century and a half has either been condemned for its ineffectiveness, vilified for its stubborn and malignant refusal to give up the ghost earlier than it did, or else simply ignored in favor of attention to the history of various of the territories which survived it, as if it no longer existed at all after Westphalia. Without going into detail, suffice it to point out that the influential Prusso-German historical school of the late nineteenth century roundly condemned the Empire as an Austrian device, supported in devious ways by the German archenemy France, whose effect was to prevent the German national unification that was finally realized only under the superior political and spiritual leadership of Prussia. Even historians in other countries at the same time and later, under the pervasive nationalistic assumption that the formation of the modern nation-state was the last and highest stage of a process commanded by Providence itself, also tended to see the Empire as little more than a stumbling block to the progress of national political purification. The unmistakable impatience with the Empire revealed by such historians was matched in others by a no less unfavorable, if also good-humored, contempt for it, reminiscent of the frequent eighteenth-century ridicule best typified in the famous aphorism of Voltaire. But whereas they at least paid some attention to it, the average history student of today, especially the American student, may well see the last mention of the Empire after the Peace of Westphalia in his textbooks limited to the confirmation that it was neither holy, nor Roman, nor an empire.

Since the end of World War II, however, there has been an almost startling revival of interest among professional historians of several countries in the history of the Empire, especially after 1648. There are at least two basic reasons for this renewed interest. The first, especially strong in Germany because of the disastrous defeat of 1945 and the subsequent partition of the country, arises from a profound questioning of the entire course of German history in the modern period, which has resulted not only in an ongoing elucidation of the reasons for the fatal developments of the twentieth century, but also in an exploration of the various political alternatives the German nation had faced at various times in its history. Second, however, associated with this questioning, and not limited to German historians, has been a fundamenal reevaluation of the normative value of nationalism itself, especially the integral nationalism of the last century or so, as an adequate or appropriate foundation for a political order that can guarantee or even be compatible with the interest of the peoples of the world in freedom, security, and peace. In light of these considerations, the Empire has had a double appeal as an object of study: first, because it represented for hundreds of years the only viable political organization that embraced essentially the entire German nation; and second, because it was based on a constitution which, without precluding the development of a

national consciousness, specifically rendered impossible (or at least extremely unlikely) the development of a monolithic state power that could
be dangerous to the freedom of its own peoples—as that was conceived at
the time—or to the independence and integrity of other countries.

Let it be said here that no historian, recent or otherwise, has attempted
to prove that the Empire in its later years either was or could have been
a success as a competitor for power on the international scene. It has universally been regarded as so structurally deficient in this respect after 1648,
and so seriously further weakened by the growth of the Austro-Prussian
dualism after 1740, that even its survival in the jungle of interstate rivalries
of its last days has never been advanced as a serious historical possibility.
Instead, what has been at issue is the question of whether the Empire
served any legitimate and valuable functions in its final period of existence—whether, in fact, it was a functioning reality at all, something its
detractors have essentially denied. Among a number of recent works which
might be mentioned, two in particular have sought to show what remained
of the political reality of the Empire in the eighteenth century. The more
important of the two, in view of its comprehensive treatment, is the magis-
terial opus of Karl Otmar Freiherr von Aretin, *Heiliges Römisches Reich,
1776–1806* (2 vols., Wiesbaden, 1967), who on the basis of an astonishingly
impressive bibliography reveals that the consciousness of being part of an
imperial structure was still a very important factor in the policies of German territories large and small right up to the dissolution of the Empire
in 1806. This work, now essential to any study of the later Empire, is to a
degree complemented by the more recent book of G. Benecke, *Society and
Politics in Germany, 1500–1750* (London and Toronto, 1974), which con-
centrates on an earlier period, but has the virtue of demonstrating by a
detailed examination of the County of Lippe the continued dependency on
and support of the imperial nexus on the part of many smaller princes.
Both studies, in illuminating the nature and operations of the Empire by
means of analysis of the actual policies of the states of which it was composed, have made important contributions to revising the traditional picture of the Empire as but a dead formality, devoid of significant political
meaning and activity except as a function of the individual policies of its
larger territories regarded as essentially sovereign states.

This book sets itself a somewhat different task, however. It will attempt to explore and analyze the currents of opinion on which the German
consciousness of the Empire was based in the later eighteenth century—a
time of serious and recurring problems for the Empire which amount to a
period of almost permanent crisis in its final decades. Whatever historians
may eventually conclude about the extent of the life that still animated
imperial politics in this time, there is no question that the Empire was
very much alive as an idea and as an object of study, debate, and discus-

sion in Germany. This discussion extended far beyond the studies, classrooms, or courtrooms of those whose professional careers were intimately involved with the analysis, teaching, or practice of imperial public law. Their works, to be sure, though often abstruse in the extreme, helped to keep alive and to define the supraterritorial importance of imperial institutions, and have recently been examined in detail by the American historian Hanns Gross.[2] But the participants in this discourse on the Empire also included intellectuals and men of affairs of greatly varying interests all over Germany, whose opinions were aired in books, periodicals, and pamphlets of many different kinds. All these men knew that the Germans in some sense constituted a nation, and they knew that the Holy Roman Empire was the only political bond that tied that great and diverse nation together. For them to think in national political terms, if they were to do so at all, was therefore unavoidably for them to think about the Empire.

This study will examine their thinking about it: what it meant to them, both as an ideal and as a reality; what it needed by way of alteration, strengthening, or reform; how they justified it, anachronistic though it appeared in many of its features; and how they compared it to other states. From this examination will emerge conclusions suggesting that the internal political vitality found in the late Empire by the revisionist work of Aretin, Benecke, and others, was backed up by strong currents of public opinion for which the imperial structure was far more than merely a symbol of an ancient and noble tradition. If the judgment of G. P. Gooch that the Empire "perished unwept, unhonoured, and unsung"[3] may be taken as representative of the older view which held that no one really much cared about the Empire in its last years, then this book must also be considered revisionist, for it will show that in many quarters the Empire was regarded as the living guardian of a set of fundamental values rooted in and protected by its constitution, and that the widespread concern for its preservation was more than a mindless dedication to a "German habit," as the historian Klaus Epstein has dubbed the Empire.[4] As the imperial structure became visibly more flimsy under the repeated blows of misfortunes created by internal and external pressures, it was subjected to a scrutiny unmatched in its history, from which resulted analyses and proposals that are instructive of the nature of German national political consciousness in general in the final period of cosmopolitanism, on the eve of the national movement of the nineteenth century.

Before launching into the description of the structure and constitution of the Empire in the eighteenth century, it may be appropriate to make some remarks about the primary sources that form the chief basis for this study. Certain of their characteristics—especially the anonymity of many of them and the obvious partiality of many others whose authorship is known—present potential problems which should be recognized. Anonymity of published works, one of the curses of the scholar who works in printed literature dealing with questions of public policy, especially political ones, in the early modern period, can result from any one of several causes. Most obvious is the desire of authors to escape the wrath of civil authorities for the expression of officially disapproved opinions in jurisdictions where censorship was maintained with varying degrees of severity to prevent just such occurrences. In these cases, neither the correct place of publication nor the printer would normally be identified either, both because of the possibility that the author could be tracked down through one or the other, and because the printer was himself liable to prosecution. In other instances, a writer might wish to disguise his authorship of a publication because he was known to have a material interest in the views he was expressing, whether personal or by virtue of his employer or profession; an individual whose work was known to be that of a paid or at least self-interested polemicist could scarcely avoid the necessity of defending himself against charges of prejudice in public debate, whether such charges were justified or not. Finally—and this applies mostly to articles in journals—simple oversight or carelessness on the part of an editor or printer could result in the publication of anonymous essays, even in cases where the author might wish his name known or at least not care if it were known. On the other hand, since some of the lesser-known periodicals, in particular, were almost entirely composed by their editors alone, it is sometimes justified to assume that any article not specifically ascribed to another source, whether named or not, is the work of the editor himself. In any study of opinions, of course, the problem of anonymity is a serious one primarily because it does not permit direct inferences to be drawn between the self-interest of the writer and the content of his expressed views, and thus obscures the important question of bias. Fortunately, the names of a considerable number of authors whose anonymous works are involved in this study have been learned and disclosed in the *Deutsches Anonymen-Lexikon* and in other scattered sources; and where biographical data on these authors is available, it has been possible to suggest connections between their lives or careers and their published opinions on issues.

Beyond this, however, even confirmed bias in an author need not vitiate the value of his views in a study of public opinion. All societies, after all, consist of interest groups of many kinds, and a work such as this, in dealing with opinions, intends precisely to find out what those interest groups with respect to a particular set of issues were, how strong they were, what separated them from each other, and what they had in common. The partiality of authors to one or another point of view is therefore actually an indispensable requirement for meaningful research on this topic. Furthermore, the deliberate utilization of an argument for purposes of converting others to one's own point of view, or of confirming them in already similar positions, does not detract from the inherent legitimacy of the argument as indicative of the genuine convictions of its author. Nor does it mean that his arguments are his alone; indeed, the very desire to publish can be stimulated by the realization that the reasoned expression of a given point of view can give focus and effect to a body of opinion that is already in existence, but is also general and imprecise—waiting, as it were, to be given form and direction. Finally, the fact that a particular author is known to have been paid to publish certain opinions because they were favorable to the interests of his employer does not necessarily mean that the opinions were the result of his pay. On the contrary, the very opposite was often true: The pay was the result of opinions already sincerely held. Friedrich Carl von Moser, whose work will be discussed later on, is only one of many examples of this truth. He was employed by the Austrian court to publish views favorable to the Emperor's interest, but those views were commensurate with others which he had published earlier and independently, and which became the reason for Vienna's approach to him in the first place. It is a simple but important fact that the variety of opinions on imperial and other issues was sufficiently great among potential employers in the politically fragmented Germany of the eighteenth century that no competent polemicist who did not wish to compromise his beliefs in order to make a living would have far to look for a paymaster and a press conformable to his own convictions.

ACKNOWLEDGMENTS

I would like to express my gratitude to several institutions whose assistance greatly facilitated the preparation of this study. The University of Illinois at Chicago Circle awarded me a summer research grant which made it possible for me to spend the time in Germany assembling the vast majority of primary sources for this work. While I was in Germany, the library staffs of the Herzog August Bibliothek in Wolfenbüttel and the Bayerische Staatsbibliothek in Munich, in particular, were uncomplainingly helpful in many ways. Boston University awarded me grants-in-aid for microfilming much of the sources obtained abroad, as well as for the final preparation of the manuscript, and granted me through two sabbatical leaves the time free of teaching and other academic obligations without which the book might never have been completed. The interlibrary loans department of Mugar Library at Boston University, and especially Mr. Geoffrey Curran, have my most profound thanks for their patience and always good humored assistance in procuring hard-to-find sources. Thanks, too, to my typist, Mrs. Pauline Shannon, who labored valiantly and well through a difficult handwritten manuscript. Finally, my chairman, Sidney

Burrell, and my other colleagues in the History Department at Boston University have been a source of constant encouragement through the years in which this study was taking shape. To them, as well as to my family and friends, and especially to Jay Corrin, I have incurred debts of a sort unpayable in any ordinary sense, but which I trust this offering may in some small measure redeem.

Boston, Massachusetts   JOHN G. GAGLIARDO

Reich and Nation

Part I

THE HOLY ROMAN EMPIRE IN
THE EIGHTEENTH CENTURY

CHAPTER ONE

The Territories of the Empire

O F ALL THE BURDENS the modern student of the Holy Roman Empire must bear, surely none is more oppressive and frustrating than the bewildering complexity of its territorial composition and its formal constitution. This is no doubt one reason why imperial history, as such, has virtually disappeared from modern European history textbooks, and German history of the last several centuries is dealt with instead largely in terms of those territories such as Austria and Prussia which were ultimately destined to become "modern" states in a sense that the Empire was not. In view of the political paralysis which crippled both internal and external operations of the Empire for so many of the last centuries of its existence, it comes as an almost intolerably annoying paradox to students used to dealing in the tidier categories of the modern nation-state that such a feckless political aggregate should possess such a complicated and intricate body of constitutional and public law.

In fact, however, as will become apparent in the sequel, the imperial constitution was complex precisely because the relations it regulated not only were, but were intended to be complicated. The slowness of operation, if not exactly an intended result in itself, was at least generally accepted as the reasonable price to be paid for the result that *was* intended: the protection of an elaborate and interconnected series of legal and political relationships, which had evolved over centuries, had made their way into public law, and had achieved general and formal recognition as a status quo through the commitments of the Peace of Westphalia and the measures taken to implement them in subsequent years. In 1648, the territorial rulers large and small—like their ancestors—had struggled through periods of ferocious sporadic warfare which had on occasion devastated large parts

of the Empire, and whose causes and duration were at least in part traceable to the quarrels of members of the Empire among themselves. Now
they wanted not only peace, but arrangements whose character would
assist in the organization and institutionalization of a peace commensurate
with their rights as they understood them. This would be done, if necessary, through as painfully detailed and voluminous a body of public law as
was required to take account of *all* the forces of actual or potential discord
or invasion of their rights as they could presently see.

Even from these brief comments, it should be clear that the formal
constitution of the Empire must be understood in at least the degree of
detail required to convey the essential correspondence of its character
with the purposes of those who were governed by it and who sustained it
through express or tacit consent. In a peculiarly important sense, the Empire really *was* its constitution; and this fact was clearly understood by the
great teachers and commentators on German public law in the later seventeenth and the eighteenth centuries, whose massive, multivolume compila-
tions and interpretations of the subject were objects of awe to German
students in their own day, if also the butt of jokes to many contemporary
Europeans, and monuments to futile *Gelehrtenschreibsucht* to many modern historians. Fortunately, however, because present purposes require an
understanding of only the major territorial units, institutions, procedures,
and relationships which defined the essential character of the Empire in
the last century or so of its existence, and which formed much of the
vocabulary of those publicists and others whose thoughts are the basis of
this study, it is unnecessary to approach the level of detail even of some
recent and relatively brief explications, let alone the overwhelming minutiae of the *Staatsrechtslehre* of two centuries ago.[1] Some details can be
omitted from the following general description, even though they will
have to be included and explained in later chapters in connection with
material to be presented there.

The territorial composition of the Empire in the eighteenth century,
in the most technical sense, must be judged according to the number of
separate territories governed by distinct authorities which were defined
as "immediate" (*unmittelbar*) to Emperor and Empire—authorities not
legally answerable in the exercise of their legitimate governing rights except to the constitutional supremacy of the Empire itself. The possession
of this imperial immediacy (*Reichsunmittelbarkeit*) granted a constitutionally unique form of territorial authority known as *Landeshoheit,* which
carried with it nearly all the ingredients or attributes of true sovereignty,
but was legally distinct from it, and was everywhere in Germany admitted
to be so. By the standard of those who were "immediate," which is an arti-
ficial and grossly misleading one in some ways, the Empire must be said

to have consisted of over 1,800 territories, ranging in size from quite large states, such as Austria, Bohemia, Bavaria, Brandenburg, Saxony, and Hanover, to tiny estates of only a few square miles or less. The vast majority of these territories lay in western and southwestern Germany, while the north and east consisted of relatively larger and more compact territories— a circumstance which, in combination with certain political orientations, led some contemporaries to refer loosely to the former areas as *Reichsland,* revealing the connection between territorial fragmentation and the general conception of the Empire which had already anchored itself in the German mind.

THE ECCLESIASTICAL PRINCIPALITIES

Broadly speaking, all the territories may be broken down into four categories. First, there were the ecclesiastical states, ruled as distinct principalities by prince-prelates of the German Catholic Church, including the heads of religious orders, such as the Knights of St. John and the Teutonic Knights, who bore clerical titles ranging from archbishop through abbot to prior. These were the successors of the ecclesiastical officials who had once been granted wide secular governing powers as vassals and agents of the medieval Emperors, but who had succeeded in asserting much the same degree of independence from direct imperial control of their territories as had the secular vassals in the course of the later Middle Ages. In the eighteenth century, as earlier, these ecclesiastical rulers governed their territories, which lay mostly in southern and western Germany, with essentially the same political powers as those of any secular prince, and at the same time had a purely ecclesiastical oversight of districts which did not necessarily coincide with the political boundaries of their states. Unlike the secular princes, however—and this is a major difference—they entered upon their office not by hereditary succession, but by virtue of elections conducted by a permanently constituted council, composed mostly of lay nobles whose number varied considerably from one ecclesiastical territory to another, but it tended to increase with the size of the territory. Known as the Chapter (*Kapitel*), this body participated in various ways in the administration and government of the territory, with powers whose exercise in general tended to depend on the attitudes and force of personality of the ecclesiastical ruler himself. Its influence was always greatest, however, at those times when the death of the reigning prince made the election of a successor necessary. Since the rulership of an ecclesiastical territory, especially one of the larger ones, conferred a degree of power and influence in the Empire, it was a prize coveted by many, among them some families that ruled large secular territories. Bribery and other forms of influence were therefore common features of the elections of ecclesiastical rulers. This opportunity for enrichment, together with the more important fact that membership in a Chapter always conferred a decent income of some sort, helps to explain why seats in Chapters were in considerable demand among members of the imperial nobility, especially the Imperial Counts and Imperial Knights and their sons, who formed a substantial proportion of their membership.

As exclusively political leaders, who relegated their religious duties to suffragan bishops and spiritual councils composed of clerics and theologians, the ecclesiastical princes themselves were possessed of the same general powers of government within their territories as were the secular princes in theirs. Since these varied among the latter, primarily according to the extent to which they were successfully restricted by traditional rights and privileges of other corporations within their lands—the nobility, the towns, and so on—so they also differed within the ecclesiastical territories. Earlier impositions of restrictions on the ecclesiastical princes by the Chapters through the device of the so-called Electoral Capitulation (*Wahlkapitulation*)—a list of promises extracted as a formal condition of election—were stopped in 1695 by a decree of Pope Innocent XII, which was confirmed three years later by Emperor Leopold I. The degree of autocratic authority that could be attained by any particular ecclesiastical prince depended partly on his own personality, resolution, and policy and partly on the resources available to him. In general, the smaller ecclesiastical principalities simply did not have the wealth or population to encourage much in the way of political ambitions, while in both small and large territories the absence of hereditary considerations (the consequence of the elective nature of the office) sometimes stifled the dynastic interest which was an important stimulus to ambition among secular princes. On the other hand, when some of the larger secular dynasties which played politics with the ecclesiastical principalities were able to secure the election of younger members of the family to an ecclesiastical rulership, it was common for the policies of that state to be coordinated with those of the secular dynasty, thus injecting what amounted to a dynastic interest into the policies of the ecclesiastical prince. The Habsburg Emperors were occasionally successful at this game, as were even more notably the Bavarian Wittelsbachs. Some lesser families, too, such as the Schönborns, though devoid of a large secular base, were well represented in ecclesiastical rulerships through several generations, producing a sense of family pride and a measure of continuity in policy.

The political orientation of the ecclesiastical rulers is explained largely by their constitutional position. Since their claim to rulership rested on their election to a Catholic ecclesiastical office, they naturally opposed the forces of Protestantism in the Empire; by its doctrines, and without the guarantees of the imperial constitution, their states could be secularized in exactly the same manner as had a number of bishoprics and other ecclesiastical states before 1648. On the other hand, since both temporal and spiritual power were united in their hands, the ecclesiastical princes also opposed undue interference in their affairs by Rome, and tended to support a kind of episcopalism, based on the history and traditions of a semi-distinct German Catholic Church (*Reichskirche*), which assured them approximately the largest degree of autonomy which was still commensurate with the imperial constitution and their adherence to the universal Catholic Church. A further consideration was that most of the ecclesiastical states were small and lacking in power; indeed, even the largest of them could not compare in power to the largest secular states. Like many of the smaller secular states, therefore, they were not in a good position to defend themselves militarily against the possible expansionism of their large secular neighbors. What all this meant, in practice, was that the ecclesiastical rulers tended to find their strongest support in the guarantees of the imperial constitution itself, in whose history and provisions the independent existence of their states was unassailable. Their chief ally in this was the Emperor himself, whose Catholicism, rejection of excessive interference from Rome in the Empire as well as in his own hereditary lands, and desire to limit the growth in autonomy and power of the large secular states within the Empire, led him to become the champion of a constitutional status quo designed to preserve as much of his power and influence in the Empire as possible.

While a fairly close community of interests between Emperor and ecclesiastical states was therefore certainly the rule over the century and a half between the Peace of Westphalia and the secularization of those states in 1803—that is, virtually until the end of the Empire itself—it was not without exceptions. Apart from the serious problems created between the two by a number of actions of Joseph II, especially in the 1780s, the most obvious breach was between the Emperors and the several ecclesiastical states of the Rhineland and Westphalia, which were ruled by members of the Wittelsbach family from the later sixteenth century until the middle of the eighteenth, a period in which Bavaria took up an anti-imperial, pro-French position, an ambitious policy which actually put it and its satellite ecclesiastical states at war with the Emperor at various times. It must be repeated, however, that such examples of lack of cooperation, or of outright hostility, were exceptions to the more usual tradition of mutual support between Emperor and ecclesiastical states.

THE SECULAR PRINCIPALITIES

A second group of territories, accounting for a much larger proportion of both land area and population of the Empire than the ecclesiastical states, were the secular principalities. These were governed by members of the high nobility, by hereditary succession within the ruling family, who bore titles ranging from king (Bohemia) through duke, count, landgrave, margrave, and so on, down to simply "prince." The disparity in size between the largest and smallest of these territories was even greater than that of the ecclesiastical states. Their internal constitutions, furthermore, displayed an enormous diversity of forms and great differences from time to time and place to place in the degree of autocratic authority effectively exercised by the ruling prince himself. All, however, were to some extent limited by the existence of corporate bodies possessed of traditional rights and privileges which no ruler could ignore wholly and consistently. In most territories, the landed nobility, towns, and (in Catholic territories especially) the clergy had formal rights of representation in a territorial diet (*Landtag*), through which it was possible to exercise some influence on princely policy, especially in matters of territorial finance.

To explain the varieties of political orientation of the secular principalities within the Empire would be to write a history of the Empire itself, which is not our concern here. One generalization that would hold up reasonably well for the last five centuries of the Empire's existence, however, is that the territorial rulers, as jealous of the position of their states within the Empire as they were of their position within their own territories, opposed very stubbornly all actions of the Emperor which seemed to increase his powers, whether formal or real, within the Empire, and to support any interpretation of the imperial constitution which restricted his powers in favor of those imperial institutions, in particular the Imperial Diet (*Reichstag*), in which they participated directly, and therefore controlled.

Even this generalization, however, must allow partial circumstantial exceptions. For example, during the period of the Reformation and the religious wars up to 1648, most Catholic secular princes cooperated with the Emperor against the political and military challenges of German Protestantism, unquestionably contributing to a considerable temporary increase in the Emperor's power. Here, too, however, the exception proves the general validity of the rule, for as soon as the threat of Protestant domination of Germany was eased, the more important Catholic princes abandoned their relatively full support of the Emperor and his policies, and backed off into a more cautious position, which signaled a solidarity with their fellow Protestant princes at least on the ultimate question of the power of the Emperor relative to that of the princes. Both Charles V in the early 1550s and Ferdinand II in 1630 discovered to their chagrin that there was a definite and rather low limit to their ability to employ defense of the faith, even among their coreligionists, as a prop for their attempts to increase the Emperor's real powers within the Empire. And while religious differences continued even after 1648 to form an element of discord within the Empire, it is safe to say that among the secular princes those differences never again approached the position of a primary influence on their policy toward each other or toward the Emperor.[2]

Another fairly safe generalization about the political orientation of the secular states is that the intensity of devotion among them to the legal forms and observances of the Empire and its constitution, as well as to the idea of the Empire as a single community, tended to be in inverse proportion to the size and power of the territories themselves. This is particularly true of the last century and a half of the Empire's existence, a period which witnessed not only a shrinkage in the total number of independently ruled territories,[3] but also a distinct change in the dynastic self-consciousness of the rulers of the larger territories, whose resources permitted them to begin to forge some of the political, economic, and military foundations of modern states, if still on a very modest scale. The rulers of the smaller territories observed these developments with a considerable degree of trepidation, which was certainly not altogether unjustifiable given the long history of large and small territorial violations within the Empire. Caught between their traditional opposition to the monarchical pretensions of the Emperor, on the one hand, and the potential expansionist ambitions of their larger neighbors on the other, most small secular states sought refuge behind a strict status quo constitutionalism which offered a protection for their existence which their own power could not. Unable realistically to impute any political role or significance to themselves except within the imperial nexus, they were forced to a defense of the Empire as a matter of self-justification. Even here, of course, there were exceptions. Where family or personal relations between the ruling dynasties of a small and a large state were quite close, or where particularly unfavorable geopolitical circumstances made acceptance of a relationship of clientage advisable, small states could make common cause with the larger, and thus appear relatively indifferent to the common bond of the Empire.

As for the large secular states after 1648, a common textbook picture has them developing more or less steadily toward a position of increasing hostility or at least indifference toward Emperor and Empire. There are certainly many elements of truth in this picture, but they should not be exaggerated. In the period from 1648 to 1740, for example, though with some notable exceptions, the larger states, like the smaller, did their duty in the military defense of the Empire, especially against France, and they did so in spite of occasionally strong reservations about the extent to which the Habsburg Emperors in some of these wars might be serving their own dynastic interest rather than that of the Empire. Furthermore, their participation in the ongoing political business of the Empire—at the Imperial

Diet, for example—was no less responsible than that of the ecclesiastical or lesser secular principalities, though the relative inactivity of the Diet through much of this period hardly made it a good measure of anyone's responsibility.

It is true, however, that the more grandiose self-image of the rulers of larger states (which was deliberately inflated by the diplomacy of anti-Habsburg foreign interests) tended to weaken the idea that their own prestige and significance lay chiefly in their character as princes of the Empire, and instead encouraged them to regard themselves as powers of almost European importance. This self-image was reinforced by concentrating on the organization of internal space for the purpose of achieving a greater degree of self-sufficiency, which was made possible by the greater resources of the larger states. In some cases, a ruler's ties to the Empire might also be weakened by a significant foreign orientation. In some instances, this was the result of the simultaneous possession of a foreign title which took precedence over the imperial one. The Electors of Saxony, for example, were also Kings of Poland from 1697 to 1763, and often tended to regard Saxony largely in terms of the troops and money it might provide to support the Polish throne. The Electors of Brandenburg were also sovereign kings in Prussia, which lay outside the Empire, and, like the Emperors who were also Kings of Hungary, were sometimes accused of subordinating their imperial obligations to their concern for their dynastic interests outside the Empire. The political realities, however, were far more complicated than this accusation, left to itself, might suggest. An interesting reverse case is that of Hanover, whose Electors were also Kings of England after 1714. The continued lively interest of both George I and George II (1714–60) in the affairs of Hanover and the Empire led to charges in England that the interests of the King were taking second place to those of the Elector. And while George III after his accession to both titles in 1760 showed practically no further interest in Hanover, his virtual abandonment of the government of the Electorate to a kind of regency council actually resulted in an increase in the Hanoverian government's sense of involvement in and concern for the imperial bond, making this large state one of the more active or "patriotic" members of the Empire in its last years. The Electors of Bavaria, finally, while not possessed of a foreign crown, became virtual clients of France for three quarters of a century beginning in 1670, thus giving them also a significant and sometimes decisive foreign orientation for that period.

THE IMPERIAL CITIES

A third group of territories, accounting for probably less than two percent of the population of the Empire, and even less of its territory, were the fifty-one so-called Imperial Cities (*Reichsstädte*). These, too, were immediate to Emperor and Empire, and were governed for the most part by exclusive and often self-perpetuating patrician oligarchies, which varied in the extent to which they represented the views and interests of their constituent populations from moderately to hardly at all. These were located almost entirely in western Germany, especially the southwest, and like the other territories of the Empire, their size varied considerably. Since the political authority of the city normally extended to a certain rural territory around the city itself, some of them—like Nürnberg, Ulm, Rothenburg, Bremen, and others—were larger than some of the smaller ecclesiastical or secular principalities, and had something of the character of city-states. Others, by the eighteenth century, as victims of fundamental changes in the geography of commerce stretching back to the sixteenth century, as well as of the baleful effect of wars since that time, had sunk to the level of mere villages. On the whole, economic developments since the end of the Middle Ages had not been kind to the Imperial Cities, and the vast majority of them were in economic and financial distress. The unfortunate economic results of the Empire's political fragmentation were at least as visible in the Imperial Cities as in any other small territories, subject as they were to the tolls, duties, and other revenue-generating devices of the territories surrounding them, which acted as restrictions on the movement of goods and therefore also on the production of goods.

Some cities, however, had not only managed to maintain their prosperity, but even to increase it. This was true of coastal cities such as Lübeck, Bremen, and Hamburg, but especially the latter two, whose location west of the Danish peninsula allowed them to assume a steadily growing importance as middleman between interior Germany and the seafaring states of western Europe. A few others were able to develop or preserve a measure of economic importance based on special local or regional services. Frankfurt am Main, for example, maintained throughout the eighteenth century considerable importance as a regional financial center. These, however, were isolated bright spots in an overall picture of stagnation which was relieved only by a slight general increase in economic activity toward the end of the century.

Extremely proud of the distinction which raised them to a legal and constitutional position in the Empire entirely different from that of cities and towns which were subordinate to some other ecclesiastical or secular territorial authority, the Imperial Cities were among the most loyal supporters of the Emperor and the constitution of the Empire. These alone, after all, were the guarantors of their special status in an age when some of the more powerful secular princes, in particular, had begun to regard these cities as annoying enclaves of special privilege on or within their borders, whose existence as independent entities barred them from achieving the fullest possible economic and political integration of their own territories. Boundary and other legal disputes between Imperial Cities and adjoining princes were common, and served to make the cities more aware of their dependence on imperial institutions for their protection.

The particularly close connection between Emperor and Imperial Cities was evident not only in the cities' preservation of elaborate ceremonial observances of the death of a reigning Emperor and the accession of his successor which went well beyond the practice of other territories, and in their payment of not inconsiderable sums of money to the Emperor at the ceremony of homage, but also in their special relationship to the so-called Aulic Council (*Reichshofrat*), one of the two supreme courts of the Empire and the one which was under the direct control of the Emperor. The Council's competence included supervision of the internal constitutions and the public finances of the Imperial Cities.[4] Whether on appeal from within the cities or on its own initiative, the Aulic Council was empowered by the Emperor to establish investigative commissions to look into the composition and the actions of city governments and their fiscal situation and policies, as well as to order changes in the cities based on the recommendations of these commissions. This power was in fact employed on numerous occasions to attempt to settle political quarrels between the governing magistrates and the citizens of the cities, as well as to improve their overall fiscal and economic viability. Imperial intervention of this kind was not continual, but was frequent enough to provide observable evidence of the strong ties between the Imperial Cities and the central organs of imperial government. The Imperial Commissioners who appeared on the streets of the cities may not have been greeted with universal enthusiasm by the municipal governments; but that they were able to appear at all, and that their presence was not vigorously protested as it was in even very small principalities where serious abuses in public finance made imperial investigation necessary, is convincing proof of the affinity between Emperor and cities, which persisted to the very end of the Empire.

THE IMPERIAL COUNTS AND KNIGHTS

A final group of territorial authorities comprised the families of the Imperial Counts and Knights (*Reichsgrafen* and *Reichsritter*). As in the case of the ecclesiastical principalities and the Imperial Cities, almost all of these families lived on lands scattered in profusion throughout western and southwestern Germany. There were some 170 families of Imperial Counts, and slightly over double that number of Knights' families. Together, the number of distinct territories they governed approached 1,600–1,700, of which the vast majority were the tiny estates of the Knights. As territorial authorities, all were immediate to Emperor and Empire, as they were for themselves personally even if they did not actually possess territory to which immediacy applied. A fundamental distinction between Counts and Knights lay in the fact that whereas the former, like the princes and Imperial Cities, were possessed of *Reichsstandschaft*—that is, the status of Estates (*Stände*) of the Empire, with the right to participate as a group in the government of the Empire through membership in the Imperial Diet—the latter were not. By way of compensation for this, on the other hand, the Knights were also not subject to the duties of *Reichsstandschaft,* including its financial obligations. They tended to define their responsibilities to the Empire in terms of a feudalized obligation to the Emperor, including personal service and strictly voluntary financial offerings (so-called *Charitativ-Subsidien*) paid to the Emperor himself in time of war.

The effective rights of territorial lordship—*Landeshoheit*—applied as fully to the Imperial Counts and Knights as to any prince. Indeed, since the Lilliputian size of their territories almost forbade the formation of the territorial diets which were a common feature of larger states, they were permitted a degree of personal authority over their handful of subjects which was in some respects more complete than that of more powerful princes. On the other hand, their abject powerlessness as individuals, which was recognized by all in spite of the ludicrous occasional posturing of some of them, had well before the eighteenth century led to attempts to provide individual protection through association. As early as 1512, the Imperial Counts of the Wetterau district formed an association (*Grafenkollegium*), with its own coordinating Directory and a provision for periodic meetings of the members. This organization was imitated in succeeding decades by Counts from Swabia, Franconia, and Westphalia, so that a total of four such Colleges were formed, and continued their existence until the end of the Empire.

Not surprisingly, however, in view of their exclusion from the Imperial Diet and from the formal regional organizations of the Empire, the Circles (*Reichskreise*),[5] which were essentially restricted to those who possessed *Reichsstandschaft*, it was the Knights who went furthest in the development of a group organization. By 1577, the Knights had grouped themselves into a total of fourteen administrative districts, called cantons, which spanned three Imperial Circles. At the head of each canton was established a managing Directory consisting of a Director (*Direktor* or *Ritterhauptmann*) elected for life, several Councillors, and a number of juridical consultants, along with the clerical personnel necessary to administer the chancellery and archives attached to each canton. These Directories performed some very important services for their members, especially in facilitating the procedures for settling quarrels among the Knights themselves, or with others, including legal representation at the two su-

preme courts of the Empire. They were empowered to levy taxes on the
Knights and their subjects, and could act to prevent the shrinkage of the
territorial base of the Knights as a group by utilization of the so-called
Retraktrecht, which permitted them to repurchase Knights' land which
had been sold to a buyer who was not a Knight within three years of the
date of the original sale. Further, the right to send and receive diplomatic
representatives and to make foreign alliances, which technically belonged
to the Knights individually as part of their *Landeshoheit,* was in fact
exercised almost exclusively by the Directories. The cantonal organization
was essential to the collective political visibility of the Knights within the
Empire. The Directories, which also corresponded with each other across
cantonal lines and which alternated in the exercise of overall supervision
of all Knights as a General Directory (*General-Direktorium*), conferred
a certain sense of group solidarity on the members that would otherwise
have been lacking, and with the legal expertise the Directories were able
to buy and maintain with the collective funds of the Knights, they were
able to convey some of that same sense of solidarity to the various constitutional bodies of the Empire before which the Knights' interests had to
be represented.

As a group consisting of families and individuals whose territorial
base was the least impressive of all the immediate lordships of the Empire,
and who were therefore wholly devoid of material means for the defense
of their own position within the Empire, the Imperial Counts and Knights
must also be reckoned among the most stubbornly loyal supporters of the
imperial constitution, as well as of an interpretation of it which posited a
relatively strong position for the Emperor within it. This orientation was
reinforced by certain inescapable economic imperatives. By the eighteenth
century, it had become customary for the landed property of Counts and
Knights to be bequeathed intact to a single heir, in order to avoid a fragmentation of estates so excessive as to deny an adequate income to the
possessors. This meant that income-producing positions of some kind
outside the estate had to be found for the other direct heirs. In Catholic
families, two quite frequent sources of employment were the Imperial
Court itself and the ecclesiastical principalities. It had long been common
for the Emperor to choose substantial numbers of Counts and Knights for
his service, whether in administrative, diplomatic, or military capacities;
whereas a lengthy tradition of employment in the ecclesiastical states,
whether as officials or as members of the Chapter, had provided a living
for generations of Counts and Knights, and had always held out at least
the chance of elevation by election to the rulership of the principality. In
both cases, powerful immediate individual reasons for loyalty to the Emperor among Counts and Knights were thus added to historical corporate
ones. Direct employment by the Imperial Court is self-explanatory, while

the generally pro-imperial orientation of the ecclesiastical princes tended to impose the same interests and attitudes on their officials and employees.

Protestant families of Counts and Knights—a distinct minority—of course had no chance of employment in the Catholic ecclesiastical states, and were second choice to Catholics in the Emperor's employ as well, though by no means totally excluded from it. Consequently, while some of their members were able to find employment in the almost wholly elee-mosynary Protestant religious foundations of northern Germany, a considerable number—proportionately almost certainly greater than among the Catholics—entered the service of one or another secular prince, usually Protestant but not always so.[6] To the extent that the employees of princes shared their opinions and orientations, and to the extent that the princes were unfriendly or indifferent toward the Emperor or the imperial constitution as forces which in some way threatened their definition of their own *Landeshoheit,* it can be said that the positions of such Counts or Knights represented something of a departure from the ordinary loyalties of their class.[7] Where it existed at all, however, this difference was characteristically one of degree rather than of kind, since the active opposition of princes to Emperor or imperial institutions was almost always expressed as opposition to particular policies at given moments rather than as hostility to either in principle, thus making a choice in matters of basic principle unnecessary for their employees. In fact, many members of the imperial nobility in the service of secular princes found it possible to maintain both territorial and imperial loyalties to the end.

For his part, the Emperor regarded the Imperial Counts and Knights as his "own" nobility in a special sense that was denied the princes. And while he was in a position to do much for them, they were also in a position to render him services beyond the employment he may have afforded them in his own government or army. It must be remembered that the Imperial Counts, as Estates of the Empire, did participate in the deliberations and votes of the Imperial Diet, as well as in the affairs of the Imperial Circles; and that while the Imperial Knights were denied such participation, they, along with the Counts, could make their influence felt through their membership in the Chapters of the ecclesiastical states as well as in the rulership of those states to which some of their family members were elected. In these ways, even the Knights achieved a political representation in imperial affairs which exceeded their very small territorial power, and which could be employed to the advantage of the Emperor.

CHAPTER TWO

The Imperial Constitution

L IKE THE CONSTITUTIONS of virtually all states large or small before the
end of the eighteenth century, that of the Holy Roman Empire did
not consist of a single document, however long, drafted in a few weeks,
months, or even years by men of a single generation. It was the cumulative
product of a centuries-long history, in which the slow and unspectacular
growth of unwritten practices into habits, and of these into "traditions,"
took their place alongside formally enacted and celebrated statutes, peace
treaties, written and unwritten promises, assurances, and oaths to form a
vast and complicated body of public law. Never subjected to formal col-
lation or codification except in the privately initiated works of scholars
and teachers of public law, the imperial constitution, so defined, was vague
and even contradictory in many particulars. Attempts have been made by
modern scholars to cut through some of the complexities of the constitutional law of the Empire by identifying a relatively small number of
enactments, which, taken together, would sum up at least the major relationships and practices that defined the Empire in law. Thus, Conrad
Bornhak calls attention to nine laws, or series of legal agreements, which
he terms "the organic constitutional laws of the Empire." Stretching back
to 1220, these include, among others, the Golden Bull of 1356, the Eternal
Peace of 1495 and its associated reforms, the Treaty of Passau of 1552 and
the Religious Peace of Augsburg of 1555 which grew out of it, the Peace
of Westphalia of 1648, the Electoral Capitulations since 1519, the Peace
of Teschen of 1779, and the Final Recess of the Imperial Deputation of 1803.[1]

While a scheme such as this represents a simplification that must not
be allowed to obscure the real complexity of the constitution or the importance of that complexity for the history of the Empire, it is nevertheless

16

true that these laws have a special importance from at least three points of view. First, some of them actually instituted changes or reforms which were to have considerable significance for the future of the Empire. Second, others of them amount to a summation and a consecration of institutions or practices which had evolved over time to the date of the enactments, but without the formal recognition which they now received in them. Finally, taken as a group, these laws were the ones most frequently cited by contemporaries, including the experts, in their attempts to explain the constitution or to use its provisions in argumentation, thus indicating their assignment of a certain "organic" importance to these laws.

For an understanding of the institutions and operations of the Empire adequate to present purposes, it is unnecessary to review the provisions of these laws in detail. A more useful explanatory device can be provided by a schematic review of the fundamental institutions of the Empire as they existed and functioned essentially unchanged for a century and a half following the Peace of Westphalia. These will be grouped under five headings: the Emperor, the Diet, the Courts, the Circles, and the Army.

THE EMPEROR (KAISER)

The Supreme Head of the Empire (*Reichsoberhaupt*) was the Emperor. It had been established for centuries that this office was an elective one. And while there were almost no formal restrictions on eligibility for the office, in a practical sense it was clear not only that the dignity of the position, as well as its functions, required a candidate to possess high noble status, but also that he govern directly a dynastic state or territory with sufficient resources as to confer weight and power in the execution of imperial tasks. Furthermore, while no specific law excluded the possibility of the election of a Protestant, the special relationship of the Emperor to the German Catholic Church rendered this eventuality unlikely, and in fact no Protestant ever evinced a serious interest in the imperial office. These factors certainly help to explain why the candidate of the House of Habsburg, the House of Austria, as the prince governing the largest and most powerful single group of territories within the Empire, was raised to the office in every election but one from 1438 until the end of the Empire in 1806.[2] What may thus appear to be an almost heritable quality of the imperial crown within the Habsburg family, though strictly forbidden in imperial law, was reinforced in the last centuries of the Empire's existence by the common practice of choosing the successor to the imperial dignity during the lifetime of the reigning Emperor; elected and crowned as "Roman [or German] King," he assumed the title and powers of Emperor immediately upon the death of his predecessor.[3] The willingness of the Electors to perform this favor is traceable not only to bribes, preferments, or concessions they could and sometimes did receive from a reigning Emperor or his successor, but also to a legitimate fear of the possible consequences of interregnum, which in all monarchies was a potential source of mischief and turbulence.

The Electors to whom the choice of Emperor fell, as well as the legal forms of the election itself, had been determined by the so-called Golden Bull of 1356, which was regarded as one of the fundamental laws of the Empire. According to its terms, the Archbishops of Mainz, Cologne, and Trier, as well as the King of Bohemia, the Duke of Saxony, the Count Palatine of the Rhine, and the Margrave of Brandenburg were to hold the title of Elector, in addition to such others as they might bear. Since the head of the House of Habsburg was also the hereditary King of Bohemia, he claimed the right to vote for himself. Over the centuries, some changes in the composition of the College of Electors took place. Thus in the early 1620s, the electoral title was removed from the Count Palatine and transferred to the Duke of Bavaria, but was restored to the former in 1648 by the creation of a new Electorate, without prejudice to that of Bavaria, thus increasing the number of Electors to eight. And in 1692, the House of Braunschweig-Lüneburg (Hanover) was granted a ninth Electorate. The number changed again in 1777–78, when the extinction of the direct Wittelsbach line in Bavaria caused that electorate to fall to the head of the elder branch of the family, the Elector Palatine; legally barred from possession of two electoral titles or votes, he assumed the Bavarian title (by now the older of the two), thus reducing the number of Electors to eight once again. It remained there until 1803, when it was again increased.

The powers of the Emperor had been steadily eroded over the centuries, and while the office always retained great moral prestige and dignity, powers of true monarchical sovereignty had long since been stripped from it. Apart from the various restrictive formulas contained in laws passed by the Imperial Diet with the assent of the Emperor, the most severe limitations on the Emperor's power were those contained in the Electoral Capitulations, the solemn promises extracted from the candidate for the throne by the Electors as the condition of his election. First imposed on Charles V in 1519, the promises simply grew in number with every succeeding Emperor, until. in 1711, the whole list of them was ceremoniously enacted into formal imperial law, but without prejudice to the ability of the Electors to add new promises in the future. The tendency of nearly all important limitations on the Emperor's authority was toward the strengthening of the concept and the reality of *Landeshoheit*, the essentially unhindered exercise of the attributes of sovereignty in both internal and external affairs by the immediate Estates. This meant, in effect, that the actual governmental powers of the Emperor virtually stopped at the borders of each immediate territory; or, putting it another way, that those powers applied only to matters which affected the Empire as a whole, or to all the individual states in common, as well as to quarrels of immediate rulers of whatever rank among themselves. Even these powers, for the most part, had to be exercised with great circumspection, entailing not only a strict observance of existing law but also the prior consent of important constituencies within the Empire.

Since the formal legal bond of Empire was still derived in principle from the feudal nexus, all territories within the Empire were ultimately traceable to fiefs granted by the Emperor, who in this capacity was therefore also the Supreme Feudal Lord (*Oberster Lehensherr*) of the Empire. This feudal relationship was honored at least in theory by the territorial lords of the Empire almost to the very end, if in an increasingly insouciant and mechanical way, and conferred certain rights on the Emperor, most of which had sunk to the level of mere ceremony. He did, however, possess the right to depose territorial rulers for breach of feudal contract, or to order them punished for offenses against public order, the criminal laws, and so on. Such proceedings were understandably rare, and were undertaken against even the smallest Imperial Knight only after the individual's behavior had established him as so thoroughly odious both to his subjects and his peers that an imperial action could be undertaken without risk of offending the sacred principle of *Landeshoheit*. Still, such proceedings did occur virtually until the end of the Empire.

The feudal law of the Empire also entitled the Emperor to grant titles of nobility, as well as elevations in rank of persons and territories. This was a restricted entitlement, however, since it had long been recognized that this right could be employed to the considerable political advantage of the Emperor. Thus, for example, no grant of nobility to a person not immediate to Emperor and Empire could be made without the consent of his (immediate) territorial lord; nor could new Electorates be created without the consent of the Council of Electors, nor any grant of princely rank conferring *Reichsstandschaft* be made without the consent of both the Council of Electors and the Council of Princes. Other limitations at lower levels of rank existed as well. Similarly derived from the feudal law was the right to grant the status of academy and university to educational institutions throughout the Empire, and to give validity to the academic degrees conferred by them.

The Emperor also had special rights with regard to ecclesiastical matters in both Protestant and Catholic confessions, but especially in the latter. Apart from decayed rights stemming from the medieval conception of the Emperor as the protector of the entire western Christian Church, including the right to reject an elected Pope and to call a general church council —rights which for good reason went unused in the last centuries of the

Empire's existence—the Emperor could still approve or reject the publication of papal pronouncements within the German church; appoint commissioners with a right of disqualification at the election of German archbishops, bishops, and abbots; and request most religious foundations to grant one prebend or its equivalent to individuals named by the Emperor. As with so many old formal rights, these went almost entirely unexercised for political reasons, the benefits of using them being considered less important than the protests and complaints they inevitably occasioned within the Empire.[4]

As part of his reserved or prerogative rights in matters of law and justice, finally, the Emperor had powers with respect to the appointment of members of the two imperial supreme courts, pardon from the judgments of those courts, the granting of power to territorial rulers to deny their subjects the right of appeal from territorial to imperial courts (*privilegium de non appellando*), and the conferral on individuals of the right to be accused and judged only at the highest courts of the Empire, that is, at one of the imperial courts. He also had a host of lesser rights regarding such matters as protection of patents and copyrights, supervision of the book trade, the conferral of the postal monopoly in the Empire, and so on. While these rights, individually or collectively, were not of sufficient importance to provide a really meaningful constitutional power base for the Emperor, they could be used on a selective basis to purchase particular political advantages at given moments.

Like his constitutional powers, the income derived by the Emperor from the imperial office as such had by the eighteenth century been reduced to a variable but always inconsiderable sum. Part of it came from ceremonial and almost entirely voluntary gifts of the imperial Estates on the occasion of the election or coronation of an Emperor; part from taxes or quasi-taxes on some Imperial Cities as well as on Jews in Frankfurt and Worms; and part from other sources such as fines assessed in gold by the imperial courts, payments attendant to the granting of nobility or elevation of rank to individuals, feudal assessments for the reconferral of some imperial fiefs, especially in Italy, and the voluntary gifts of the Imperial Knights during wartime—the *Charitativ-Subsidien*. This income was not adequate to cover even the ordinary costs of imperial administration, let alone the extraordinary costs occasioned by war or other crises. With absolutely no right of general taxation within the Empire as part of his prerogative powers, the Emperor consistently had to support his office by reliance on the income of his own hereditary lands. This, in turn, meant that no prince of the Empire without substantial dynastic resources could realistically hope to carry the financial burdens of the imperial office. The reign of the one non-Habsburg Emperor of the eighteenth century, Charles VII of Bavaria, illustrates the point. Even without the disastrous war in which he involved Bavaria, the expenses of imperial office by themselves would almost certainly have bankrupted the Bavarian state had his three-year reign not been ended by his early death in 1745. In view of the great financial and political liabilities of the office, not the least of which would have been the hostility of the Habsburgs themselves, no other eighteenth-century German prince was foolish enough to entertain very seriously the notion of becoming Emperor.

THE IMPERIAL DIET (REICHSTAG)

The Imperial Diet was the advisory and legislative body of the Empire as a whole, as well as a court of final appeal from the judgments of the two supreme courts. Composed of the delegates of those territorial lords who were entitled to be represented in it, it was this body which gave the meaning to the famous and almost mystical formula "Emperor and Empire" (*Kaiser und Reich*), intended to convey the sense of a kind of co-equal responsibility of head and members for the preservation of harmony of a single body, a higher unity within diversity. Except for those few, essentially unimportant matters left to the Emperor as part of his reserved or prerogative rights, it was only the statutes and determinations duly enacted by this body and confirmed by the Emperor that bound the entire Empire to a single observance in law. As contemporary usage had it, "Imperial law breaks territorial law" (*Reichsrecht bricht Landesrecht*).

The Diet could be convoked only by the Emperor. Before the mid-seventeenth century, it had been called together at irregular intervals, generally to consider matters of immediate and pressing concern. Following the Peace of Westphalia, however, the obvious discomfiture of the Emperors with the limitations imposed on them by that peace led to a growing fear among the princes that the Emperors, in order to escape the surveillance of the Diet, functioning as a sort of policing agency for the terms of the peace, might at some point decide never again to convoke a Diet. Consequently, when Emperor Leopold I in 1663 found himself compelled to convoke the Diet in Regensburg to request imperial assistance against the Turks, the delegates, after disposing of current business, refused to disband. From that year until the end of the Empire in 1806, the Diet remained in permanent session, thus earning for itself the entirely appropriate name of "Eternal Diet." Among the results of this permanency were, first, that whereas the Diet had once convened in a number of different cities, the city of Regensburg now became its permanent seat; second, that the already common tendency of the territorial lords to represent themselves by means of delegates rather than in person became universal, as did the Emperor's practice of exercising his functions through representatives; and third, that attendance at the sessions of the Diet became quite sparse, both

because most of the daily business was trivial and because many territories, including some fairly large ones, which had once been quite willing
to underwrite the costs of representation when the Diet met only irregu-
larly and for relatively short periods of time, proved unwilling to do so
for the permanent sessions of the Eternal Diet.

The Diet consisted of three councils, or colleges: the Council of Electors, the Council of Princes, and the Council of Cities. The Council of
Electors (*Kurfürstenrat or -kollegium*) was composed of the representatives of the Electors. The chairmanship of this council fell to the Elector
of Mainz, who as Archchancellor of the Empire was first in dignity among
the Electors, just as they were first in dignity among all the princes of the
Empire. Though its constitutional position as one of the three deliberative bodies of which the Diet was composed was not essentially different
from that of the other two, it enjoyed not only a greater prestige than
they did, but also a special relationship to the Emperor, who frequently
consulted it informally on a wide range of matters, thus giving it on
occasion the appearance of an executive committee for the Diet. This
special relationship developed partly from its size, which meant that it
was relatively easy to convene, but more importantly from the fact that
its members were, after all, the most notable princes of the Empire, who,
moreover, controlled a significant number of votes in the Council of
Princes. And while the other councils sometimes resented what seemed to
them to be an arrogation of a constitutionally unsanctioned power by the
Electors, their feelings did not alter the political realities on which the
situation was based.

The second council, the Council of Princes (*Fürstenrat* or *-kolleg-
ium*), had a rather complicated organization. It was divided into two
basic groups: the temporal or Princes' Bench (*weltliche* or *Fürstenbank*),
which technically included all the non-Electoral secular principalities entitled to representation in the Diet; and the spiritual or Prelates' Bench
(*geistliche* or *Prälatenbank*), comprising the ecclesiastical principalities.[5]
Not all territories represented on either bench had the same voting rights.
There were a total of one hundred votes in the Princes' Council. From
the temporal bench, sixty principalities had the right to a full vote, known
as the *Virilstimme;* but the seventy-four Imperial Counts who were entitled to representation on the temporal bench exercised their votes collectively according to the four bodies (curias) to which they were individually
assigned, each of which had but one full vote, known in this case as a
"curial vote" (*Kuriatstimme*). Similarly, thirty-four principalities of the
spiritual bench had the *Virilstimme,* while some twenty-four lesser prelates were grouped into two curias (the Swabian and the Rhenish), each
of which had one *Kuriatstimme.* The picture presented here is simplified
in some ways, if complicated in others, by the fact that some princes con-

trolled more than one vote. The right to vote rested essentially on a territorial entitlement, not a personal one, with the result that when a given
prince acquired new territories, whether by virtue of secularizations (mostly prior to the eighteenth century), or by inheritance through the extinction
of collateral lines, which could happen anytime, he also acquired their
voting rights in the Diet. Figures from the eighteenth century show that
Brandenburg controlled no less than eight votes; the Palatinate and Hanover six each; and Bohemia, Baden, and Mecklenburg three each, thus
reducing the sixty votes of the temporal bench to a more realistic total of
thirty-seven.[6] The significance of all this becomes even clearer when one
considers that a number of princes with full votes also participated in the
voting of the Imperial Counts through territorial possessions which were
entitled to membership in those curias; and that of the princes specifically
mentioned above, the first four were also Electors, with seat and vote in
the Council of Electors!

The Council of Cities comes last in two respects: It was not even formally recognized as a legal component of the Diet until 1648; and it represented territories that were collectively far less significant politically and
in every other respect than the first two. It was composed of two subgroups, or benches, with fourteen cities in the Rhenish bench and thirty-
seven in the Swabian. Each bench debated certain matters separately,
usually according to the area affected by the matter at hand, while other
concerns could be debated by both benches together. While here, as in the
other two councils, a simple majority of votes was supposed to commit the
entire council, in fact, the number of delegates on hand was frequently
so small that no effective decisions could be reached at all.[7]

The Diet as a whole met under the majesty of the Emperor himself—
who, however, like the members, was represented by officers named by
him. These were the so-called *Prinzipalkommissar* and, in his absence, the
Konkommissar; their job was to communicate the Emperor's requests and
proposals to the Diet, and to convey its decisions to him for his consideration. These responsibilities were channeled through the office of the Imperial Archchancellor, Mainz, who through his designated official acted
as a kind of chairman for the Diet. He received and approved the creden-
tials of the delegates to the Diet, as well as those of ambassadors sent to
it by various foreign states; he put into legal form all items to come before
the Diet; and he drew up and controlled the agenda (to which items could
be submitted not only by the Emperor and members of the Diet, but also
by private persons or corporations, and even foreign states) except insofar
as the Diet reserved to itself the right to alter it.

Actual voting was done not by the Diet as a whole, but within the
three councils of Electors, Princes, and Cities separately, where a simple
majority in each carried the vote. A vote of two of the three councils gave

a decision binding on the entire Diet. Where disagreements between the councils existed as the result of early deliberations, a procedure known as *Co-* and *Re-Relation*— discussion and compromise between the councils, essentially—was employed to achieve agreement. The practice was for the Council of Electors and the Council of Princes to do this between themselves first. If they in fact agreed, they would approach the Council of Cities for its approval; but even if the Cities dissented, of course, the agreement of the first two could be presented as a decision of the Diet. Technically, the Council of Cities since 1648 could cast a deciding vote in case of disagreement between the other two. In fact, however, this was simply never permitted to happen. By unwritten understanding, either the first two councils did reach agreement, or the matter was simply never formally voted on, and therefore dropped altogether. Formal decisions of the Diet were communicated to the Emperor, who could respond to them in several ways: by approving through ratification, in which case they became law; or by ignoring or refusing ratification, in which case they died; or by sending them back for suggested amendments, in which case the whole legislative procedure was repeated.

In addition to the division of the Diet into three voting bodies, another important distinction was observed between the Protestant and Catholic members of the Diet, all of whom were organized regardless of the voting council to which they otherwise belonged into the so-called *corpus evangelicorum* (Protestant) and *corpus catholicorum* (Catholic). These had arisen as informal groupings for mutual defense and assistance during the age of confessional struggle, but had achieved formal constitutional recognition only at the Peace of Westphalia. This division was significant in two respects. First, it corresponded increasingly after 1648 to a certain broad difference in the political orientation of the members of each body, in that while the Catholic group consisted largely of ecclesiastical and small secular principalities whose sympathies lay with the idea of a strong imperial bond, involving a relatively effective position for the Emperor, the Protestant group was dominated by the larger dynastic secular states, whose active jealousy of their own independence made them cool towards Empire and Emperor.[8] Second, after 1648 this difference could also be translated into political action by the two groups by virtue of a constitutional provision that permitted decisions of the Diet to be arrived at by these bodies as distinct entities rather than in the usual three voting councils. In this case, decisions were made through a process of negotiation and agreement between the two rather than by majority vote. Technically, this procedure, known as *itio in partes*, was supposed to be possible only when proposals directly or indirectly affecting matters of religion were at stake—thus revealing the origins of the provision as rooted in the desire to prevent the imposition of confessional views on the Protestant minority by the Catholic majority. The division was required, however, whenever the unanimous vote of one of the two bodies called for it. Since it was relatively easy to find some kind of religious implication in almost any proposition which could properly come before the Diet, it became increasingly common in the eighteenth century for votes on all important matters to be taken in this way. Indeed, by the last third of the century, even the appearance of a religious reason as the basis for the procedure had been abandoned as unnecessary.

Because until 1803 Catholic majorities existed in both of the two most important councils of the Diet, the procedure of *itio in partes* was initiated exclusively by the Protestants. But this had little to do with problems arising from differences in religious conviction as such, which were of steadily declining importance after 1648. Only the unique connection of the German Catholic Church with the political life of the Empire, primarily through the existence of the ecclesiastical states, made it possible for the two *corpora* to persist as political factions almost until the end of the Empire. The self-interested devotion of these states to the constitutional balance of 1648, which was increasingly threatened in theory and reality by the elaboration of territorial sovereignty in the large secular states, virtually guaranteed their leadership of a party at the Diet dedicated to the preservation of the status quo. Similarly, to the extent that the balance they defended, and the ideas on which it rested, were perceived as already too restrictive of territorial sovereignty by those rulers whose states were strong enough to justify or stimulate the concept of self-sufficiency, those rulers were sure to become adherents of a kind of "party of movement," working toward at least an evolutionary redefinition of the status quo in which their own freedom would be increased at the expense of the common bonds of the constitution. In this sense, the *corpus evangelicorum,* while tightly knit enough to guarantee the loyalty even of those of its own members—for example, the Protestant Imperial Cities and Imperial Counts—whose political interests hardly corresponded in all particulars with those of the large secular states, also represented the long-term policy of large Catholic secular states better than did its Catholic counterpart—a fact not altogether lost on rulers such as the Elector of Bavaria.

These considerations help to explain why the Imperial Diet was never able to carry out, or indeed even seriously to approach the task set for it by the Peace of Westphalia: a reform of the Empire which would at the same time take into account its history since the time of the Reformation and provide an effective basis for future cooperation within an improved structure. The contradictory interests of Emperor and Estates, and of the latter among themselves, prevented enactment of almost all important proposals, and indeed eventually led to an unconscious but real operational redefinition of the very nature of the Diet. By the middle of the eighteenth century at the latest, the original high advisory, deliberative and legislative functions of the Diet had gone essentially unused for so long, and had been buried under such a mass of accusations, recriminations, and debates over trivia, that the entire body had taken on the aspect of a permanent and usually sleepy congress of diplomatic delegates, in which the chief concern was to see to it that as little as possible was done, and with as little rapidity as possible. As a congress of diplomats, the advancement or protection of particular interests took precedence over the advocacy of the general good, and it is difficult to escape the impression that the hand- ful of delegates normally present in Regensburg, when they were not entertaining or being entertained in the occasionally sumptuous residences their governments maintained, or simply wandering aimlessly about in the halls and conference rooms of the Diet itself, spent most of their time watching each other very, very closely.

It is true, of course, that even by this at least partial redefinition of its character, the Diet still served as important function as a forum for the peaceful exchange of opinions and negotiations; within a single imperial system it was, after all, still the only real German national forum. It is also true that real crisis could revive interest in and increase both atten- dance and the tempo of activity at the Diet—as during the long period of Louis XIV's wars—and could result in some reasonably effective measures for common imperial defense. But even these represented less new legis- lation than enablements on the basis of old. And it is this absence of new legislation representing new directions that says the most about the inac- tivity of the Diet. It has long been common for historians to point to the Imperial Guild Ordinance (*Zunftordnung*) of 1731, revised in 1772, as the only major piece of imperial legislation passed in the entire eighteenth century; no serious challenge to this judgment is likely to appear.

THE IMPERIAL COURTS (REICHSGERICHTE)

The two imperial supreme courts, the Imperial Cameral Tribunal (*Reichskammergericht*) and the Aulic Council (*Reichshofrat*), may be regarded as the third and last institutional pillar of the imperial consti- tution. Together with Emperor and Diet, they tended to define "The Em- pire" for many Germans—as in the formula variously attributed to Johann Jacob Moser and Johann Stephan Pütter, by which the Empire was said to be "visible" only at Vienna (the Emperor and the Aulic Council), Regensburg (the Diet), and Wetzlar (the Cameral Tribunal). The courts bulked very large in the political literature as well as in the scholarly treatises written about the imperial constitution, both because they more than any other were the agencies which by their work defined and upheld the laws of the Empire on a day-to-day basis, and because their very existence provided the ultimate proof that the essence of the Empire lay in its character as an association founded on law.

The Imperial Cameral Tribunal was founded in the late fifteenth century as part of a general imperial reform movement which, among other things, was one of the stages in the reduction of the Emperor's power in favor of the Estates. Dissatisfied with the irregularities and partialities of the previous system by which the Emperor had dispensed justice, the Diet of Worms in 1495 forced on Emperor Maximilian I the creation of a permanent supreme court, presided over by a person of high noble rank chosen by the Emperor and representing his personal authority, and containing a number of judges (*Assessoren*), originally sixteen, some of whom were chosen by the Emperor, others by the Electors, and the remainder by the other Estates. The costs of the Cameral Tribunal were to be defrayed partly by fees and partly by a general tax (known as *Kammerzieler*) levied differentially on the Estates of the Empire according to a fixed formula, and paid twice a year. Over the following three centuries, the number of judges legally authorized for the court by the Diet fluctuated considerably. The Peace of Westphalia authorized a total of fifty, and also specified parity in the numbers of Protestant and Catholic judges; this figure was never attained, and was formally reduced to twenty-five not long after. In fact, the number of judges never exceeded eighteen, and sank as low as five, until reforms instigated by Joseph II after his accession in 1765 once again confirmed the authorized total of twenty-five, all of whom actually were appointed and began work in the early 1780s.

Almost from the moment of its establishment, the Cameral Tribunal fell behind in its work load. This was not just the result of the very slow written procedures to which the court was committed, but also of a chronic understaffing that was itself the result of persistent underfunding. In spite of several adjustments over the years in the statutory yield of the *Kammerzieler*, many imperial Estates paid them late, or not at all, or in less than the required amounts. The result was a backlog of cases that grew from generation to generation; the often-cited figure of 60,000 unprocessed cases in the early 1770s gives some idea of the problem.[9] Almost from the beginning, the Diet had provided for the periodic visitation of the Cameral Tribunal by deputations carefully chosen from the membership of all three of its voting councils, which were supposed to observe conditions at the court and to make proposals for changes and improvements. Like almost everything else in which the Diet was involved, however, proposals for visitation could easily become enmeshed in political wrangling, with the result that visitations were infrequent, but might last for years when they did occur. The last visitation, which began in 1767 and lasted for nearly a decade, would probably not have occurred at all had Joseph II not insisted that since a visiting deputation constituted a court in itself, in that it could hear cases and appeals from the Tribunal during its official life, it was therefore a right of the Emperor, not of the Diet as such, to institute it. It is also an irony that the Empire collapsed at just the moment when the changes brought about in the operation of the court in the wake of this visitation resulted in such greatly improved a conduct of business as to enable the court for virtually the first time since its founding to handle its case load on a current basis.

The jurisdiction of the Cameral Tribunal was in many cases the same as that of the other supreme court, the Imperial Aulic Council. This concurrent jurisdiction was no accident. In agreeing reluctantly to the establishment of the Cameral Tribunal, Maximilian I had specifically reserved to himself as Emperor a continuing authority as supreme judge within the Empire. With no intention of permitting his judicial authority to be exercised exclusively by a court as far removed from his immediate presence as the Cameral Tribunal was, he moved almost immediately (1498) to establish a new body in Vienna with judicial powers comparable to those of the Cameral Tribunal. This was the Aulic Council, whose existence and functions were essentially permanently fixed by 1559. Apart from its obviously closer connection with the Emperor, the major difference between the Aulic Council and the Cameral Tribunal was that the former functioned not only as a court, but as a kind of advisory council for the Emperor in all matters pertaining to the Empire, as well as a commission to exercise certain prerogative powers of the Emperor with regard to feudal matters, as well as to investigate the constitutional and fiscal affairs of various territories of the Empire, especially the smaller secular states and the Imperial Cities.

The Aulic Council was composed of two groups of councillors (*Reichshofräte*): the Lords' Bench (*Herrenbank*) taken from the nobility, and the Learned Bench (*Gelehrtenbank*) drawn from the legal community. All were appointed by the Emperor, and their commissions, unlike those of the judges of the Cameral Tribunal, expired at the death of the Emperor. Also unlike the Cameral Tribunal, which was broken up into subgroups called senates for the actual conduct of business, the Aulic Council sat as a single group. Presided over by the Imperial Vice-Chancellor (appointed by the Elector of Mainz in his capacity as Imperial Archchancellor), its members were paid from fees or fines, as well as by healthy subventions from the dynastic revenues of the Emperor. The number of councillors varied slightly from time to time, but was normally twenty-four. Pressures similar to those which had resulted in confessional parity among the members of the Cameral Tribunal after 1648 were acknowledged by Ferdinand III in 1654 only to the extent of appointing a fixed number of six Protestants to the Aulic Council. While the members could be appointed from anywhere in the Empire, a greatly disproportionate number—about two-thirds—were taken from Austria itself.

The volume of judicial business at the Aulic Council, in terms of the number of new complaints and cases, was even greater than that of the Cameral Tribunal, and only the greater informality of procedure permitted at the former allowed it to dispose of cases with a rapidity that in some degree mitigated the severity of backlogs. Even so, untreated cases piled up in numbers sufficient to create a stream of laments that attracted the attention of the young and always reform-happy Joseph II, whose efforts to speed up the operations of the Aulic Council were not crowned with total success, but did effect palpable improvements, which were probably more the result of threats and browbeating of the councillors than of procedural changes.

The juriscompetence of the two imperial supreme courts was complicated not only by concurrent jurisdiction in a number of areas, but also by exclusions which could be granted by the Emperor, whose own dynastic lands, it should first be noted, were almost in their entirety excluded from the possibility of appeals to either of the imperial courts. Other territories of the Empire could receive a similar exclusion through the famous device of *privilegium de non appellando* (privilege of not appealing), which in effect prohibited the subjects of the territorial ruler to whom this privilege was granted from appealing to the imperial courts beyond the verdicts of the highest territorial courts. This privilege was coveted by the German rulers not only because it was a mark of prestige and an attribute of territorial sovereignty, but because it closed off their judicial systems from the rest of the Empire, thus making possible the achievement of the kind of integration, in this respect at least, which the more ambitious of them were attempting to bring about for the whole of their administrations. Virtually all the more important territories received the privilege, either limited or unlimited, from the sixteenth to eighteenth centuries, frequently as the result of political deals struck with the imperial court.[10] Technically, even the unlimited privilege did not abolish the right of subjects to appeal to the imperial courts in cases where legal recourse to territorial courts was allegedly denied, or where judicial verdicts were nullified through non-implementation. This special jurisdiction of the imperial courts could not be made effective against the larger territories, however, which forbade their subjects to make use of it. Indeed, in a sense the entire history of the *privilegium de non appellando* parallels the history of the growing self-sufficiency of the larger territories of the Empire, and constitutes a recognition that matters of justice, like all others, were inevitably responsive to the realities of political power.

The Cameral Tribunal had exclusive jurisdiction in cases where breach of the *Landfrieden* was charged against any territory immediate to Emperor and Empire—that is, where one territory was charged with taking hostile coercive action against another in violation of the terms of the Eternal Peace of 1495, which required settlement of such quarrels by ju-

dicial means. The Aulic Council, on the other hand, had exclusive jurisdiction in cases pertaining to the prerogative rights of the Emperor, the
feudal nexus, and criminal accusations involving the immediate Estates
of the Empire. In virtually all other matters, the two courts had concurrent
jurisdiction, meaning simply that plaintiffs entitled to use them could
choose either. Thus, either could be employed as a court of first instance
in civil cases in which immediate Estates were involved in quarrels
among themselves or with the subjects of other immediate Estates, and in
the second instance as a court of appeal from the highest territorial courts
for the subjects of immediate Estates, insofar as jurisdiction was not limited by the *privilegium de non appellando*. Either could also act as a court
of appeals from certain lower imperial courts in southwestern Germany,
which were the insignificant remainders of a time long past, as well as
from the so-called *Austrägalgerichte,* which were essentially temporary
courts of arbitration set up at the request of immediate Estates to whom
the procedure was available as an alternative to the generally more expensive and time-consuming recourse to one of the supreme courts.

Since the Emperor had only the power to pardon from judgments of
the imperial supreme courts, the only legal recourse from their verdicts
was to the Imperial Diet, and then only in certain cases involving specific
interpretation of imperial laws or cases where religious bias could be alleged. This right of recourse to the Diet was unquestionably abused in
most of the cases actually brought before it, providing merely another
example of the influence of politics in matters of justice.[11] The execution
of judgments of the imperial courts against mediate persons was left to the
territorial rulers whose subjects they were; and against immediate Estates
to the executive officers of the Circles within which their territories lay.
Needless to say, executions against large and powerful territories or their
protégés were never carried out. Compliance with judgments among the
small Estates was usually voluntary; the will to coerce even them was lacking except in individual cases where a ruler's outrageous or perverse behavior made him an object of universal loathing.

Because of the differences in their origins, the way their personnel
were chosen and paid, and their somewhat differing procedures and scope
of operations, the Cameral Tribunal and the Aulic Council had strongly
contrasting images in the Empire almost from the moment of their establishment and right down to the end of the Empire. The Cameral Tribunal
had the reputation as that of the "Empire's (or Estates') court," and the
Aulic Council that of the "Emperor's court." In particular, it was generally
felt that the Aulic Council had a strong penchant for protecting both the
dynastic and constitutional interests of the Emperor, and that its members
were therefore interested parties in many of the cases they tried. Its more
informal and oral procedures merely fortified this impression among those

who had it. It was also accused of religious bias by the secular states, most of which were, after all, Protestant. Given the fact that religious parity of its members was never achieved or indeed even attempted, and that the Aulic Council did, admittedly, have administrative and supervisory functions stemming from its character as a sort of state council for the Emperor in strictly imperial affairs, it is not difficult to see why many people might find an incompatibility or a conflict of interest between these functions and those of a supposedly impartial court of law. Although most charges of religious partiality were probably groundless, there was nevertheless a strong tendency for the more powerful and Protestant territories to use the Cameral Tribunal, while the less powerful and Catholic ones inclined toward the Aulic Council. This tendency admits of many exceptions, however; the *very* small Protestant territories—those of Imperial Counts and Knights, for example—were at least as likely to go before the Aulic Council as the Cameral Tribunal, while the Imperial Cities, with their special relationship to Emperor and Aulic Council, did so almost uniformly. Conversely, some of the largest territories (particularly Brandenburg-Prussia and Hanover in the eighteenth century), far from supporting the Cameral Tribunal as a judicial counterweight to the Aulic Council, attacked its activities as part of a whole imperial system they found constraining, with the certainly unintended result that its judges for a time became noticeably more friendly to the Austrian interest.

What is really rémarkable about the imperial courts, however, is that on the whole, and in spite of the maddening slowness and considerable expense attendant to their conduct of judicial business, as well as of the frequent charges of partiality hurled at them from various quarters, they preserved a high reputation in the Empire as the ultimate institutional guarantors of the imperial constitution. The political conciliations and arrangements which were very much a part of the operations of the Aulic Council may seem redolent of corruption to the student of today, as no doubt does the strange practice known as *Sollicitieren* (solicitation) in the Cameral Tribunal, a device whereby some litigants could obtain priority of attention to their cases by the court through a cash payment. On the other hand, it must not be forgotten that the Aulic Council was, after all, an administrative and constitutional court, among other things, and that many of its decisions necessarily had political implications and results which were expected and even demanded by the litigants themselves. As for the Cameral Tribunal, the practice of solicitation was probably about as good as any other method for determining which cases to deal with first from overfull dockets which could not be fully cleared off in any event. Furthermore, not all solicitations were admitted, while some that involved very small payments, or indeed none at all, were accepted, indicating an honest attempt to come to grips with real priorities. In both courts, a distinct

receptivity to the urgency of cases involving immediate human misery can
be confirmed.

There is no question that the imperial courts did introduce a measure
of order into the complicated political and constitutional arrangements of
the Empire, and that within the bounds set by political realities they also
protected the small against the transgressions of the great. While it has
been usual for historians to insist on the limits of the effectiveness of the
courts, it has perhaps not been sufficiently emphasized that the very existence of such bodies, as well as the generally high reputation enjoyed by
them and their judgments in wide segments of public opinion, created a
kind of legalistic climate almost everywhere in the Empire, and this climate helps to account for the observance of specific judgments of the courts,
as well as of legal forms in general, even among rulers who had the raw
power to ignore them if they chose to do so.

THE IMPERIAL CIRCLES (REICHSKREISE)

The so-called Imperial Circles were simply districts into which the
Empire was divided for the purpose of distributing certain legal, administrative, financial, and military obligations which, in the absence of an
effective imperial central government, could not be carried out in any other
way. The first six Circles came into existence in 1500 as part of a short-
lived scheme for the reorganization of the executive functions of the Empire, and their original function was simply that of nominating members
to a new executive council (the *Reichsregiment*). After the collapse of this
experiment, the Circles were found to be a convenient mechanism for the
nomination of those members of the recently created Imperial Cameral
Tribunal who were not named by the Emperor or the Electors, and therefore remained in existence. By 1512, furthermore, it had become clear that
some effective means had to be created for the local execution of the judgments of the Imperial Cameral Tribunal, and especially of judgments arising from breaches of the Eternal Peace. In that year, therefore, the Imperial
Diet not only authorized the reorganization of the Empire into a total of
ten Circles, but required each Circle to elect a Captain (*Kreishauptmann*,
later *Kreisoberst*), to whom the task of military execution of judicial verdicts was to be entrusted.

The troubling question of how the various territories of each Circle
should be called together for this purpose was removed in 1522 with the
institution of the so-called Prince-Conveners (*kreisausschreibende Fürsten*). For each of the original six Circles (the Franconian, Swabian, Bavarian, Upper Rhenish, Westphalian, and Lower Saxon), two of the most
prestigious princes—one ecclesiastical, one temporal—were named to this
office. The ecclesiastical prince had the additional title of Director (*Kreis-*

direktor), while the temporal prince now usually became Captain as well (except that in Circles formally designated as religiously mixed, and where both Prince-Conveners were Catholic, a third, a Protestant prince was chosen as Captain). In the four newer Circles (the Austrian, Burgundian, Electoral Rhenish, and Upper Saxon), where the question of the relative rank or prestige of princes was solved by the absolute predominance of one territory at the time of the creation of the Circles (Austria in the first two, Mainz and Saxony in the last two), only one Prince-Convener was named, who also assumed the functions of Director and Captain.

The Circles themselves had a rough, if rather strangely laid out, geographical coherence. Their membership did not correspond exactly with that of the Imperial Diet, since the Circles reserved to themselves the determination of membership, thus including here and there some individuals who were not entitled to participation in the Diet, and excluding a few who were; but the correspondence was fairly complete, since the Circles included all important Estates, and, like the Imperial Diet, excluded all Imperial Knights. The entire Kingdom of Bohemia and the Duchy of Silesia (which had belonged to Bohemia until its loss to Prussia in the eighteenth century), it should be noted, belonged to no Circle and were not subject to the obligations the imperial constitution imposed upon Circle members. With the exception of the four newer ones, each Circle also developed over the years constitutions and administrative organizations, which were determined largely by their own experience. The newer Circles, precisely because of the absolute preponderance in them of one prince (or, in the case of the Electoral Rhenish Circle, because of the mutual jealousy of the no fewer than four Electorates it embraced), found no need to organize a structure to facilitate the cooperation of numerous territories of medium or small size, and therefore retained an existence which was more formal than real.

Among the duties of the Prince-Conveners was that of presiding over the assemblies of the members of the Circle, which they themselves convoked. One or two of these Circle Diets (*Kreistage* or *-versammlungen*) met on an annual basis, but most met much less frequently. Some, like the Swabian, were organized into benches in almost as complex a way as the Imperial Diet, except that all voting was done in plenary session, with a majority vote deciding, and there were no curial votes, only full ones. The Circle Diet was empowered to pass legislation on a wide variety of matters of common concern to its members. In this sense, it was intended to address itself to the amelioration of local and regional problems far more than was the Imperial Diet, whose legislative competence was properly limited to objects of Empire-wide concern. Some of the Circle Diets made far greater use of their powers than others; common objects of legislation included the building of roads and bridges, control of beggars, con-

struction of prisons and workhouses, and regulation of the coinage. The
Swabian, Bavarian, and Franconian Circle Diets even held occasional
common sessions in the eighteenth century to work more effectively on
problems such as these across Circle boundaries. The Circle Diets could
also authorize taxes with which to pay for their programs, and had certain
responsibilities with respect to the apportionment among their members
of imperial troop levies and their expenses.

In those Circles where an active sense of cooperation between the
members was developed and maintained over a period of time, a fairly
sophisticated administrative machinery for the accomplishment of common
tasks came into existence. The two Prince-Conveners headed the executive body, or Directory, which normally included a few other Estates of
the Circle as well, and to which were attached a secretariat or chancellery,
archives, and offices for the syndics and secretaries of these bodies, as well
as for accountants and controllers of the coinage (*Münzmeister*). As chief
executive officers of the Circle, the Prince-Conveners represented it in its
external dealings with other Circles as well as with the Imperial Diet and
the Emperor, and were responsible for carrying out in their Circle all
applicable laws and decisions of the Empire, including the general injunc-
tions to peace and order and, so far as possible, the composition of quarrels
of the Estates with each other or with their subjects. In his capacity as
Captain, the temporal Prince-Convener supervised the formation and provisioning of the Circle army and, in conjunction with the Diet, nominated
the generals and lesser officers who commanded it.

The amount of political activity demonstrated by the Circles varied
from considerable to literally none at all. The reasons for the inactivity of
the four newer Circles have already been discussed. Of the remaining
Circles, only the Swabian, Franconian, and to a much lesser extent the
Bavarian showed much consistent interest in peacetime in organizing attention to various issues and problems of public life. In time of war, on the
other hand—meaning here primarily war formally declared by the Empire
(*Reichskrieg*)—almost all of the so-called "anterior" (*vorderen*) Circles
(the Swabian, Upper Rhenish, Electoral Rhenish, and to some extent also
the Westphalian and Franconian) showed a heightened degree of activity
related more or less exclusively to the urgent need to organize resistance
to the military threat posed by neighboring France. The long periods of
war with France under Louis XIV, and again in the Revolutionary era,
did much to revitalize all the Circles, including those where Diets had
not been held for years. By 1801, however, the Burgundian, Electoral Rhenish, and Westphalian Circles had virtually been destroyed through territorial losses to France, and the remainder demonstrated no vigor in the
short time left to them. In general, the tendency of the larger territories
toward greater independence and self-sufficiency weakened their sense of

involvement in the Circles as it did in the Empire as a whole, and resulted either in deliberate attempts to evade financial and other responsibilities or at best in a cooperation which was at once minimal and reluctant.[12] The smaller territories of the Empire, on the other hand, showed a measure of devotion to the Circles and a willingness to bear the burdens of a sincere cooperation within them that was consistent with their greater regard for the imperial constitution as a whole. In this respect, then, the edifice of Empire rested most heavily on the weakest of its pillars.

THE IMPERIAL ARMY
(REICHSHEER OR -ARMEE)

By the eighteenth century, the principle had long been established that the Empire as a whole had the obligation to provide the military means necessary to implement the declarations of war which the Emperor, with the concurrence of the Imperial Diet, was constitutionally empowered to issue on behalf of the whole Empire. [13] In view of the permanent tension that characterized relations between the Emperor and the princes, however, and in view of the obvious connection between military might and the realities of political power, it should come as no surprise that questions relating to the formation and organization of an imperial military force were among the most touchy with which the Empire had to deal. One possibility had never seriously been entertained in modern times: that the Empire should make available to the Emperor either the funds or the troops for any sort of permanent or standing imperial army under his undivided command. Such a proposal was tantamount to the political suicide of the princes, and they knew it.

On the other hand, no one disputed the right of the Emperor to maintain an army of his own, supported by the resources of his dynastic lands, but with some rights of recruitment within the Empire itself.[14] In the sixteenth century, most wars fought by the Habsburg Emperors were in fact fought with the resources of their own family lands, exceptions being formally declared imperial wars against the Turks, for which the Imperial Diet made specific, short-term grants of funds and troops from the member territories. In the early seventeenth century and during the Thirty Years' War, when no *Reichskrieg* was ever declared, military cooperation was based almost entirely upon specific treaties arranged between Emperor and princes, and the latter among themselves. The first imperial war after the Peace of Westphalia was declared against the Turks in 1663, and was followed in 1674 by the first of a series of declarations of war against the expansionistic France of Louis XIV.

The experiences of the first war against Louis, together with the increasing conviction that more wars were likely to come, resulted in the imperial legislation of 1681 which, in confirming some earlier laws and revising others, fixed the structure for the military constitution of the Empire thereafter. The basis for the legislative deliberations of 1681 was the so-called Imperial Register (*Reichsmatrikel*), which had been drawn up and adopted by the Diet of Worms in 1521 as part of an early effort to come to grips with the military needs of the Empire. This Imperial Register of 1521 set a specific number of troops—4,000 cavalry and 20,000 infantry—as the base figure by which future contributions would be determined. Known as the *Simplum*, imperial grants of troops would henceforth be expressed as fractions or multiples of this number—a *Duplum*, *Triplum*, and so on. At the same time, the Register specified the amount of money necessary to support these troops: reckoned at ten florins per horseman and four florins per footman each month, the monthly total came to 120,000 florins. This amount was known as a "Roman Month" (*Römermonat*), and the financial contribution voted by the Diet for military purposes was henceforth expressed in multiples of this base amount. When the monthly support for a horseman was increased to twelve florins in 1541, the total of a single Roman Month rose to 128,000 florins. It should be noted, however, that troop authorizations and Roman Months were voted separately, in no necessarily proportionate relationship.

The laws of 1681 raised the total number comprised by the *Simplum* to 12,000 cavalry and 28,000 infantry. They also directed that both troop and financial contributions voted by the Imperial Diet be broken down and apportioned according to a specific formula to the ten Circles, which were in turn responsible for distributing these totals among their members through their own Circle Registers. Several adjustments in the amount of the Roman Month also occurred in subsequent years, the last of them in 1776 when it was determined that each obligated member of the Empire should pay 125 percent of the 1521 total, due to intervening monetary inflation. In fact, however, even with this adjustment, the Roman Month now yielded slightly less than half of its 1521 total because of temporary or permanent abatements which could be granted to individual members by Circle Diets or the Imperial Diet.[15]

The Roman Months, regardless of how many might be voted, were usually the smallest part of the total contribution an individual prince or ruler had to make toward the costs of a *Reichskrieg*. Regardless of their origins, in later years the Roman Months were intended to cover only the costs of the Imperial Army regarded as a whole—that is, payment of the imperial commanding generals, the general staff, couriers, spies, engineering materials of various kinds, and so on.

For the rest, the individual territories not only had to make contributions to a special fund (the *Kreiskasse*) to cover expenses arising from the war which were common to the Circle as such, but also had to bear the

entire cost of the salaries, equipment, and daily provisioning of the contingent of troops which they were obligated to raise. The Imperial Army,
which was composed of literally scores of contingents of widely varying
size, was paid, dressed, trained, and equipped differently in kind and in
quality. The Swabian Circle, for example, which according to the *Simplum*
was to contribute 1,321 horse and 2,707 infantry, was forced to spread the
responsibility over a total of ninety-three Estates! In addition to the abatements in assessments for the Roman Months, however, it was also possible
for some territories, especially small ones, to apply for permission to com-
mute their troop contributions either wholly or in part into cash payments
instead; known as *Reluitionen,* these moneys would go to other territories,
which were then supposed to furnish extra men.

Some territories, of course, had standing armies of their own of a
respectable size; but if these armies participated in an imperial war, they
normally did so on the basis of separate treaties with the Emperor, whose
dynastic interests in a particular war (the War of the Spanish Succession,
for example) might be so compelling as to force him to find military assistance from within the Empire that went well beyond the efforts authorized
by the Diet. As Emperor, he was of course in a position to grant numerous favors for this assistance to the territorial rulers who gave it; but the
latter were not thereby relieved of their ordinary legal obligation to supply
contingents to the Imperial Army if an imperial war had been declared.
The chief burden of fighting a *Reichskrieg* almost always fell upon the
dynastic lands of the Emperor himself, which normally supplied as much
in the way of troops and money as the rest of the Empire put together.
This fact more than any other accounts for the survival of the right of passage of the Emperor's troops through the territory of the Empire—a privilege essential to the Habsburgs' defense of their dynastic lands in the
Austrian Netherlands. It also accounts for the permissions granted to the
Emperor to recruit for his own army in certain areas of the Empire outside his dynastic lands, including the five "forward," or western, Circles
(the Swabian, Upper and Electoral Rhenish, Franconian, and Westphalian), as well as the Imperial Cities of the Lower Saxon Circle and the
ecclesiastical principalities of the Bavarian.

As one might expect, the command structure of the Imperial Army reflected in full measure the distribution of rights and powers that characterized the rest of the imperial constitution and government. Company
and battalion officers were named at the Circle level, often as the result
of negotiations between territorial authorities that were conducted slowly
and with difficulty because of mutual jealousies and misplaced pride. Overall leadership of the army, however, belonged to the Emperor himself, who
usually chose not to exercise it in person, and therefore named Imperial
General-Field Marshals (*Reichs-Generalfeldmarschälle*) as his supreme

representatives. One of them had to belong to the *corpus evangelicorum*. The other highest offices included Imperial Masters-General of Ordnance (*Reichs-Generalfeldzeugmeister*), Generals of Cavalry (*Generale der Kavallerie*) and Lieutenant General-Field Marshals (*Generalfeldmarschalleutnante*). There was also a General War Commissar (*Generalkriegskommissar*) and a Quartermaster-General (*Generalquartiermeister*). Some of these men were able and indeed distinguished officers and field commanders; others were political appointees with little enthusiasm and even less ability. Technically, the conduct of military operations was supposed to be supervised by an Imperial War Council (*Reichskriegsrat*) chosen by Emperor and Empire under observance of the principle of religious parity. In fact, though this Council was sometimes named, it seldom functioned, and the actual conduct of operations usually fell to the Austrian Court War Council (*Hofkriegsrat*), whose participation, though specifically forbidden in the Emperor's Electoral Capitulation, was a virtual necessity to any coordinated war effort. Necessity also rendered nugatory another of the Emperor's electoral promises not to billet imperial troops on any territory of the Empire without a complicated prior series of consultations. Multiple complaints on this score were a common feature of any imperial war.

Apart from the relatively recent custom of keeping some of the highest general officer positions occupied even in peacetime, the only really permanent military facilities of the Empire as such were the fortresses of Kehl and Philippsburg on the right bank of the Rhine, the occupation of which had been abdicated to the Empire as a whole by France in the late seventeenth century. Garrisoned thereafter chiefly by troops from the Circles within which they lay, their gradual history of decay, especially after the 1730s, says much about the reluctance of the Estates to be burdened with extraordinary military expenses, particularly in peacetime. After the Imperial Diet in 1753 refused an urgent request of the Emperor to provide funding for renovation and garrisoning of the two fortresses, both were evacuated by their Circle garrisons—Kehl in 1754, Philippsburg in 1772.[16]

As the foregoing sketch should indicate, the military constitution of the Empire was at least as complicated and cumbersome as all other public institutions of the Empire. Like them, too, it reflected with considerable accuracy and detail the intricate regulation and balance of the power relationships that defined the operations of imperial government. This is above all true with respect to the stubborn and incorrigible refusal of the Estates to permit the construction of a military force which had even the remote chance of adding permanently to the strength of the already existing dynastic forces of the Emperor. Nor was any of the more powerful princes interested in a standing army of any kind which, while requiring substantial annual outlays from him, would not be responsive to his individual command. The result was an imperial military machine whose wheels were intended to turn very infrequently, and then only when danger to the Empire had become so palpable as to be undeniable—practically speaking, only after violation of some part of the Empire's territory by military action had already occurred. Seven *Reichskriege* were declared between the Peace of Westphalia and the end of the Empire, and every one of them had the character of joining wars already underway. Even when the wheels of the war machine, rusty.after long disuse, did turn, they did so slowly and under full observance of the constitutional rituals prescribed for them.

In evaluating the procedures that invariably resulted in a painfully slow-motion mobilization of the Imperial Army, however, it should not be forgotten, first, that those procedures were designed less for efficiency than to ensure a just and equitable distribution of the burdens of war among the territories of the Empire; and, second, that in an age when military operations were still characterized by siegecraft and very limited mobility,\the dangers of slow mobilization were not as great as they were later to become. Procedures for mobilization predicated upon an army whose purpose was almost wholly defensive, as that of the Empire was, therefore did not have to be very rapid. It is probably true that the Empire was spared some serious defeats and territorial losses in the late seventeenth and early eighteenth centuries by factors extrinsic to the quality of the Imperial Army, chief among which was the availability of strong and determined allies who relieved some of the military pressure from France. And certainly it is true that the subsequent record of the Imperial Army in the eighteenth century—the disaster it suffered at the hands of Frederick II of Prussia in 1757, for example, as well as its essentially ineffectual efforts against France in the wars of the Revolution—was anything but enviable. Still, it is at least arguable that in the first example the Imperial Army was facing one of the most distinguished field commanders of the entire century, and a much admired German prince to boot; while in the latter case, it faced an entirely new kind of war for which neither it nor any other army in Europe was prepared. It is probably also necessary to distinguish between the more practiced and proficient leadership of the dynastic standing armies and the often untutored and unexercised officership of the Imperial Army, at least at the secondary level, shot through as it was with parade-ground heroes and uniformed nonentities. After all, the same German soldiers who under German leadership were so often mocked as worthless in later eighteenth-century Europe, had formed the backbone of the great victories of Prince Eugene, the Duke of Marlborough, and other great commanders at the beginning of the century.[17]

CHAPTER THREE

The Nature of the Empire

THE INSTITUTIONS, PROCEDURES, and relationships which made up the imperial constitution in the century and a half after the Peace of Westphalia made the Holy Roman Empire into the strangest and most peculiar political body of its time in Europe. Even in an age when all states and their constitutions, as results of a long and differentiated process of historical evolution, presented a picture of government which was anything but neat and simple, the Empire was in a class by itself. The object of reverence to many, as well as of both genuine curiosity and a kind of good-humored ridicule to others who lived both inside and outside of it, it was also the cause of considerable frustration to political theorists who had to attempt to understand it and to make it understandable to others.

Before the middle of the seventeenth century, most scholars and commentators on German public law found it necessary to attempt to force the imperial constitution to fit certain forms of government established by classical (chiefly Aristotelian) political theory. They were joined in this by polemicists who had axes to grind for the Emperor, for one or another prince of the Empire, or even for a foreign power, whose interests would be served by emphasizing the preponderance of monarchical over aristocratic elements in the constitution, or vice versa. Nor did such attempts to categorize the form of government of the Empire ever cease altogether. In the years after the Peace of Westphalia, however, a fundamentally new approach to the understanding of the Empire emerged, and was to gain strength among scholars for the last century or more of the Empire's existence. At the risk of oversimplification, this approach may be said to have involved an abandonment of the preoccupation with the form of government of the Empire, and the adoption of a historical and descriptive method which sought to emphasize the evolution of the various institutions and practices of the Empire in their relationship to each other, as well as their present interaction, in order to give a picture of the Empire which was more operational and practical than structural and theoretical.

The political philosopher Samuel Pufendorf (1632–94) is usually regarded as the first major figure to move in this new direction. In his *De Statu Imperii Germanici*, published in 1667 under the pseudonym Severinus de Monzambano, Pufendorf concluded that the Empire did not fit any of the traditional categories of states, even in their corrupted forms, and that it was "an irregular state-body, much like a monster."[1] With this often-cited phrase, he struck a mighty blow at earlier theorists who had ignored the realities of the imperial political scene in order to force their own classical definitions on the constitution. Yet while Pufendorf was ultimately able to accept the Empire, regarded as an irregular commonwealth, as a distinct category of polity, he was never comfortable with it logically. Troubled by the impossibility of locating an undivided sovereignty in either the Emperor or the territorial rulers, he finally characterized Germany as a state in a midpoint of degeneration between true monarchy and a *systema civitatum,* that is, a kind of organized federation in which the members are equal and sovereign, subject to a common jurisdiction only in such matters as had been reserved to that jurisdiction by specific original agreement. In declaring the present constitution to be in a continuing process of decline, Pufendorf gave voice to a conviction that this system of polity was inherently unstable, and while recognizing that no return to monarchy was possible, believed that an end to this irregular state of affairs could come only through the breakup of the Empire into fully sovereign and independent states, or through deliberate negotiations which would eventuate in a true *systema.*[2] On the other hand, such solutions were theoretical constructs, intended at best for an indefinite time in the future; in the meantime—and Pufendorf gives no evidence that he considered this to mean anything but a long time—the best solution to prevent what amounted to a state of permanent constitutional crisis from destroying harmony within the Empire entirely was to encourage the growth of stability in the status quo by safeguarding the legal rights of all the members of the Empire. Pufendorf thus reduced the chief problem of the Empire in his time to self-preservation against the forces of internal disruption, which could best be accomplished by the strengthening of a conception of the Empire as a legal order rather than as a true state with externally directed goals.[3]

While Pufendorf's rejection of earlier attempts to make the imperial constitution conform to one or another classical model represented a giant step toward a more realistic appraisal of the Empire, it is nonetheless true that even he remained strongly hostage to an imperative for logical classification that influenced his view of the Empire as a "diseased" structure.

By contrast, the two most prolific and influential scholarly writers on German public law of the eighteenth century, Johann Jacob Moser (1701–85) and Johann Stephan Pütter (1725–1807) shied away from the problematics of such classifications, and showed remarkably little interest in any kind of general reform of the Empire or its institutions. Moser declared forthrightly the great difficulties of talking about the form of government of the Empire, since the phrase "form of government" implies a short but sufficient concept of the manner in which a state is governed, who has the most to say in it, and how this government compares with those of other independent states; whereas the government of the Empire was simply too unique and complicated for any short description: "Germany is governed in German, and indeed in such a way that no school word or a few words or the mode of government of other states are suited to make our kind of government comprehensible."[4] Moser not only questioned the importance of the whole problem of forms of government, but believed that too serious an attempt to solve it could be harmful; once someone got it into his head that a particular form was the correct one, he might attempt to draw conclusions from it that would be disadvantageous to the rights and prerogatives of the Emperor or of the Estates as they actually existed, and thus throw an apple of discord into the constitutional balance between the two.[5] And unlike Pufendorf, Moser liked the constitution of the Empire as it then existed, precisely because it represented a good balance of government between Emperor and Estates; indeed, it corresponded better than any other to the divine order, in which no force existed without a counterforce.[6] This constitution was not without weaknesses, some of them serious; but this was no obstacle to making Germany a happy state if both parties wanted it that way. Moser saw the reality of the Empire, in its public law, as consisting of the sum total of its positive laws, each of which had to be understood not in relationship to some preexisting concept of constitutional form, but in its own historical origin and its subsequent evolution as part of a growing corpus of law. For him, the accurate description of the way the Empire operated in relation to these laws was tantamount to a definition of the Empire.[7]

Moser understood that practical politics had a strong and often determining influence on constitutional life, but he also believed that the patterns of interaction laid down by laws already in existence could in fact serve the cause of unity. To the extent that the tendentiousness of earlier treatments of the public law of the Empire had obscured that fact, Moser sought to remedy it by as precise and objective a description of the constitution as possible, feeling that widespread ignorance of the relationships and remedies prescribed by existing law was a hindrance to their observance. For him, then, exact knowledge of the constitution would tend to strengthen its unifying elements. This does not mean that Moser was entirely unprepared to make criticisms of the constitution, or to suggest remedies for its deficiencies. But as a jurist, he was always wary of abstract political theorizing, while at the same time he recognized that the really basic problems of the Empire lay much less with law than with policy, and that the latter was unlikely to be changed by even the most well-meaning public proposals of private persons such as he. This helps to explain why he never showed much interest in imperial reform, and even in his criticisms restricted himself largely to generalities. He did, however, generously declare himself willing to elaborate reform proposals on request—if indeed presumably only on that of a political figure of some importance—and at the end of his life he even expressed regret that no one had ever really asked him to do so.[8]

Johann Stephan Pütter, while very much like Moser in his desire to avoid a categorization of the form of government of the Empire which could be construed as a bias in favor of either Emperor or Estates, was even more inclined than the latter to accept the present condition of the Empire, and its territories, without criticism.[9] He saw in the public law of the Empire simply a juristic, not a political, system. It was entirely in keeping with this view that the only reforms he ever solicited had to do with the cumbersome operations of the imperial courts, which for him represented functional rather than structural defects.[10] Pütter also avoided all attempts to reduce the sense of the constitution to a few basic or directing principles; for him, it was a legal order (*Rechtsordnung*) which had never been constructed according to a conscious plan, but had simply evolved as the result of the particular concerns of particular times into the complexity it now was.[11]

Whatever their differences on particular issues, Moser and Pütter were wholly representative in several ways of the currents of formal imperial public law doctrine of their age. Both accepted the constitutional system as it existed; neither proposed structural changes of any significant kind. Both believed it to be an essentially good system; neither had answers for its obvious operational problems that went much beyond the hopeful notion that things can be made to work, and work well, if people really want them to. It is as much as anything else in this judgment, which recognized that the ability of the Empire to act positively was dependent upon the active good will of its components, that both Moser and Pütter reveal the real meaning the Empire had taken on for most of those who lived in it by the eighteenth century. An active public policy for the common good of all of Germany was no longer truly expected from the imperial system —or if it was, it was as the exception rather than the rule. The rule was expected to be inaction, or at most action to preserve and support the constitutional status quo that was defined, essentially, by the Peace of Westphalia. If a Moser and a Pütter, in the absence of all positive thrust in imperial legislation, could still declare the system a good one, it was because they, with most others, thought of the *essential* purpose of the Empire in negative terms: the prevention of disturbance of a beneficial condition already arrived at.

That beneficial condition can most succinctly be described as one of an almost exquisite manifold balance, whose integrity was protected by the most imposing edifice of public law imaginable. The chief weights and counterweights of the balance are clear enough: Emperor against Empire, Protestant against Catholic, Electors against princes, large territories against small, ecclesiastical states against secular states, and even mediate against immediate subjects of the Empire. To be sure, since the theoretical potential of the Empire for positive action was not limited to the preservation of these balances, neither Moser nor Pütter nor any other "classical" teachers of public law were prepared to describe the imperial system merely as a balance-of-power system; indeed, their continuing commitment to the idea that the Empire, its peculiarities notwithstanding, was a true state, could not permit them such a description. Sovereignty within the Empire, though hopelessly divided and scattered, existed; the supreme headship of the Emperor was undoubted, as was the common subjection of all Estates to the constitution—even if the real meaning of both of these was not altogether clear or precise. Still, the notion of multiple constitutional balances runs at least as a strong undercurrent throughout the writings of Moser and Pütter, not to mention those of less distinguished publicists and commentators of the eighteenth century, where the concept of the Empire as a system of political balances frequently emerges quite explicitly.

The increasing acceptance of this concept in the eighteenth century can ultimately be ascribed to the initially unintended results of the Peace of Westphalia. It must be remembered that the terms of that peace were not supposed to weaken, much less destroy, the constitution or government of the Empire as such. Rather, they were at least partly intended to create favorable conditions for future imperial reform by assuring the various interested parties positions of such security as were necessary to permit them to approach negotiations for reform in good faith. As time passed, however, and serious discussion of reform never really got underway, the political balances established as a floor for imperial renovation increasingly hardened into a permanent part of the law itself, and to such an extent that they came to be accepted as the chief raison d'être of the constitution, whose other provisions existed simply to protect them. This classic confusion of means with ends was of course confirmed by developments after 1648 in the larger territorial governments, whose growing strength gave them practical reasons to insist that any meaningful imperial reform would constitute a breach of the semiautonomy granted them at Westphalia. The irony, then, is that a peace which was made part of the constitution in order to facilitate imperial reform ended up by becoming the chief barrier to it.

The balances established at Westphalia hamstrung the political operations of the Empire so badly over the long run as to paralyze it; capable at best of responding sluggishly to overt military threats from the outside, the Empire after 1648 was never again to function to any significant extent as a real supraterritorial government. Unable to see political movement where, to all intents and purposes, none existed, it is wholly understandable that political and constitutional commentators would begin to reformulate their entire concept of the Empire. One recent historian, in attempting to correct what he regards as excessively harsh modern judgments of the Empire, has suggested that in its last years it should properly be regarded as a *Rechtsordnung*—a legal system; and since a *Rechtsordnung* "will always understand the cultivation of power as something secondary," it should not be judged according to the imperatives of power, by which it would indeed appear rather feckless.[12] While this is doubtless true, it must also be said that the Empire became simply a *Rechtsordnung* precisely because it no longer had the ability to cultivate power; that was something it had lost both to foreign powers and to its own larger territories. Consequently, when the Mosers, Pütters, and their ilk abandoned investigation of the form of government of the Empire and concentrated instead on the juristic details of the constitution, it was because they recognized, if only tacitly, that while the Empire might still theoretically possess the form of a state, it had all but ceased to have the attributes of a state—one of which was, in fact, the ability to cultivate power. If there was a single purpose of this *Rechtsordnung* that the Empire had become, it was probably to guarantee peace in Germany (and therefore to some extent in Europe as a whole) by protecting the intricate and interconnected balances referred to above. For nearly one hundred years after Westphalia, it performed this function reasonably well, and a certain amount of pride in the Empire as a *Friedensordnung*, [13] a peace-preserving order, was not altogether unjustified among those who sought to bring out the redeeming features of the imperial system.

Unfortunately, however, the terms of the Peace of Westphalia which had established the political balance in Germany also contained the seeds for its future disturbance. The vastly expanded prerogatives of territorial supremacy (*Landeshoheit*) which it conferred meant that a consistently pursued policy of dynastic self-strengthening in any of several larger territories could, over time, produce something resembling modern states whose power would be greatly disproportionate to that of the vast majority of the other imperial territories—not only absolutely, but also relative to the conditions obtaining at the time of the Peace of Westphalia. This is in fact what gradually occurred after 1648. Spurred on by both foreign example and the iron necessities of reconstruction following the Thirty Years' War, several states developed standing armies and increasingly sophisticated civil administrations, which began to transform their relationship to the Empire. The most striking early example is probably that of Bavaria, whose ruling family attempted as early as the late seventeenth century to play the role of at least a second-rate European power in alliance with France against Emperor and Empire. This did not appear excessively serious, however, since the political situation in Germany subsided back into balance once the wars with France were over. Not even by the second quarter of the eighteenth century, therefore, did the growth of territorial sovereignty in Germany seem to pose any real or immediate threat to the integrity of the Empire and its constitution; the *Friedensordnung* remained essentially intact.

This situation was to change drastically and permanently as the result of a chain of events which began with the sudden and wholly unexpected attack by Prussia on the hereditary lands of the House of Habsburg in 1740.

Part II

THE IMPACT OF INTERNAL
DISCORD, 1763–90

CHAPTER FOUR

Healing Wounds: F. C. von Moser
and the German National Spirit

IT IS UNNECESSARY, for present purposes, to retell the story of the mid-century wars between the Houses of Habsburg and Hohenzollern by which the energetic and ambitious King of Prussia, Frederick II, propelled his originally not very considerable hereditary lands into the ranks of the European great powers, in large part at the expense of Austria. Whether as German wars—in which character they are known as the Three Silesian Wars (1740–42, 1744–45, and 1756–63)—or as parts of the larger European and colonial conflicts known as the War of the Austrian Succession (1740–48) and the Seven Years' War (1756–63), their outlines are too well known to require restatement here. Since the focus of this study is the German Empire itself, however, and since these twenty-three years of turbulence and territorial change profoundly affected—in fact, largely determined—the subsequent internal history of the Empire virtually until its extinction, it will be useful to review some of the major events and results of these wars from the standpoint of their influence on the shaping of political attitudes toward the Empire and of the political configurations which resulted from those attitudes.

First and most obvious, these wars demonstrated once again that the ideal of imperial unity between head and members, as well as between members among themselves—an ideal strengthened, on the whole, through the long period of imperial cooperation in the wars against Louis XIV as well as by the quarter-century of peace which followed them—could not bear up under the pressure of any real political crisis within Germany itself. Austria and Prussia were the chief German antagonists in these wars, of course, but most of the other larger territories and not a few of the smaller as well had chosen sides—and not always the same one—at various

49

times during the hostilities. While few of these states had suffered permanent damage as a result of their participation in the Austro-Prussian quarrel, the wars proved expensive for nearly all, and at least a few of them had been for a time rather badly bruised and battered—for example, Bavaria in the early 1740s and Saxony through much of the Seven Years' War. The result, following 1763, was a kind of political disarray within the Empire, in which exhaustion and mutual suspicions combined to produce a condition resembling multiple isolationism which, while wholly unlikely to recreate the active military and political confrontations of recent years, was equally inimical to a revitalization of imperial cooperation on any broad basis. Neither Prussia, whose meteoric rise to political prominence and whose growing image as a military "barracks-state" had produced real anxiety in many German courts in spite of widespread personal admiration for its great king, nor Austria, whose alliance with Russia and especially with France during the Seven Years' War had merely reinforced traditional fears of Habsburg designs on Germany in many quarters, was capable of inspiring the sort of confidence that could attract and keep friends. At the same time, however, no lesser state was disposed to offend either of the German giants, so that the Empire for some years after 1763 fell into a sort of quiet and polite, but also watchful, anarchy in which the desire of the territorial princes to cooperate even for the most peaceful purposes was no greater than their inclination to become involved once again in adventures of the mighty such as those of the recent past.

Second, the results of the wars had altered the traditional political balance of the Empire in complex ways. Prussia, by a determined and successful defense of its original conquest of the Habsburg Bohemian province of Silesia, had raised itself to a position of power that was entirely novel in the modern history of the Empire. This was not a position of equality with Austria, as most contemporaries well recognized; indeed, Frederick II himself and his ministers, as well as all their immediate successors, knew better than most that the favorable outcome of the wars had resulted from a lucky combination of circumstances at least as much as from their own efforts, and that by most of the criteria then employed to measure the power of states, Prussia was not really to be compared with any of the traditional great powers of Europe. Prepared to accept the diplomatic advantages conferred by Prussia's suddenly increased visibility on the political map of Europe, these statesmen nonetheless recognized that the surest way to preserve Prussia's newly won reputation was to avoid having it tested—especially during the long period of economic rehabilitation made necessary by the unusually destructive Seven Years' War. This did not mean that Frederick or his successors were unwilling to consider new territorial gains; it did mean, though, that future acquisitions—as in the partitions of Poland—would almost certainly not be attempted except by diplomatic means involving little or no risk or great-power confrontations.

Within the Empire itself, Prussia's primary concern after 1763 was the preservation of its title to Silesia—a wholly defensive goal, which was unlikely to call forth much in the way of either diplomatic or military initiatives in the absence of any threat to that title. On the other hand, in spite of a momentary thaw in Austro-Prussian relations symbolized by the friendly meetings of the young Emperor and Austrian coregent Joseph II with Frederick II in 1769 and 1770, Prussia was bound to regard any actual or potential increase in Austria's influence in Germany as a danger to its own position. And here was the novelty of the Austro-Prussian dualism as far as the Empire was concerned: there had now grown up for the first time on German soil a state which, while not sufficiently mighty to wrest the imperial crown from the possession of the Habsburgs, nor even desirous of doing so, was yet powerful enough to organize an anti-Austrian opposition party within the Empire as its own creature—an opposition party, that is, whose goals would inevitably be shaped by the particularistic political interests of its Prussian leader rather than by the traditional interests suggested by the old slogan "German liberty." That motto, to be sure, had in the past served as the basis for many conflicts between the Emperor and the Estates, and had weakened the power of the Empire regarded as a single state. But it had never excluded the notion that the Empire as a whole still had a single interest, even if its meaning had to be continuously redefined in ways that occasionally brought hostility between head and members. The mid-century wars, however, had resulted in the emergence of a German state which no longer saw itself as confined to the traditional context of imperial politics; it now perforce had interests that transcended those of a mere German Electorate, and it had to alter its perception of the role of Austria from that of the greatly limited elective head of the German Empire to that of a direct great-power competitor. With this alteration came a change in the way Berlin regarded the Empire itself, which eventuated in the insight that while Prussia had indeed become a European state, its continuing membership in the Empire could provide it with one base from which to seek allies against the Habsburgs. This would inevitably have to be done in the name of the preservation of the imperial constitution, of course, but would in reality have virtually no purpose beyond that of advancing or safeguarding Prussia's special interests.

Since the Habsburgs, as a European great power in their own right, had long since appreciated the advantages they could derive from the imperial Estates as allies in the service of their dynastic interest, it was to be expected that this traditional policy would again suggest itself as a useful expedient in their rivalry with Prussia. And while it is certainly far too strong to say that the Habsburgs had always defined their imperial duties exclusively in terms of the utility of the Empire to their dynastic interest, it is nonetheless true that events since the outbreak of the first Austro-Prussian war in 1740 had added new reasons to older ones for Vienna to reappraise its position vis-à-vis the Empire in the harsh light of political reality. The loss of the imperial crown to the family during the short but traumatic reign of the Bavarian Charles VII (1742–45) and the insouciance or outright hostility of much of the Empire during the whole War of the Austrian Succession were two such reasons; so was the uselessness of the Imperial Army to the Austrian cause after Vienna had succeeded in goading the Imperial Diet into a declaration of war against Prussia in the Seven Years' War. Together, they had greatly weakened the Habsburgs' estimate of the worth of the imperial crown, and hence also their sense of responsibility to the Empire. These factors, added to the constantly diminishing real powers of the crown since the end of the Thirty Years' War— a trend which Charles VII, in his eagerness for election, had considerably accelerated—and the preoccupation of the Habsburgs with their slow but increasingly successful work of molding something resembling a modern state out of their diverse dominions, led Vienna inexorably toward a more and more nakedly utilitarian and self-interested definition of the Empire, the terms for which were increasingly laid down by dynastic raison d'état alone.[1]

By the time Joseph II became sole ruler of the Austrian inheritance in 1780, memoranda had begun to circulate in Vienna containing at least indirect hints that it might be to Austria's advantage to give up the imperial office. Joseph himself was probably less appreciative of the crown than any of his predecessors or successors. As a young man, he had learned most of what he knew of the imperial constitution from one of his tutors, Christian August von Beck, a man who was convinced that the Empire was soon going to fall apart, and who suggested the advisability of Joseph's separation of himself, his hereditary lands, and a new imperial title from the Empire before the collapse occurred. From this teaching, Joseph was persuaded that the Empire deserved little consideration against the much more important task of the centralization and modernization of the Austrian state, and on at least one occasion indicated his willingness to lay down the imperial crown in return for specific political advantages for his hereditary lands.[2]

In fact, however, neither Joseph nor his two successors abdicated the imperial dignity until Francis II was literally forced into doing so in 1806. In the rivalry that had become established between Austria and Prussia, the crown could still be useful to Austria in a number of ways, just as Prussia's electoral and princely rank within the Empire could be valuable to it. The rest of the Empire, of course, was to be caught in the middle, reduced as it finally was to a mere object of competition between the two German great powers. While it is true that the baleful implications of that rivalry for the Empire did not begin to become fully realized until both powers started to cast about actively in Germany for partners and allies in the question of the Bavarian succession just after the mid-1770s, it had required no very special powers of insight to recognize that the Empire since 1740 had become the theater for a new and serious struggle with the gravest implications for the fragile imperial constitution and the delicate balances it had consecrated.[3]

By the end of the Seven Years' War, some public-spirited Germans had become convinced that the propaganda of the two German combatants and the hotly debated question of the rectitude of the one or the other had obscured the much more important and serious general result of their antagonism: the weakening of imperial unity as prescribed by the venerable formula of concord, *Kaiser und Reich*. Among those who actually tried to do something to call their fellow Germans back to a sense of their common destiny and imperial responsibility, one stood out well above the rest. Friedrich Carl von Moser (1723–98), the son of the well-known public lawyer Johann Jacob Moser, published a modest work entitled *Concerning The German National Spirit* in 1765 and thereby touched off an extraordinary controversy in the public press that is very instructive of the currents of opinion about the Empire at the beginning of the last four decades of its existence.

The younger Moser had acquired a sound and thorough knowledge and appreciation of the imperial constitution through his studies at Tübingen as well as through his own father's work, and no evidence indicates that his early views differed much from the rather common picture of the Empire as a political system balanced between two religious parties and two principles of government (the monarchical and the aristocratic), in which a certain amount of conflict between Emperor and Estates was both a natural and a healthy thing. The opinions he had expressed about the Seven Years' War in the work which first made him famous, *Der Herr und der Diener* (1759), were certainly consistent with this view. A firm Protestant of Pietist bent, Moser was favorably inclined toward the German policy of Frederick II of Prussia, whom he saw as the leader of a Protestant counterweight to Catholic Austria. The war itself, for him, had nothing of the character of a European conflict, but only of an imperial one, in which one heroic Estate was pitted against an Emperor whose political and religious intolerance, abuse of power, and reliance on foreign assistance had made war a necessity for the protection of the imperial order.[4] As little as two years later, however, Moser's views had changed somewhat. While his personal admiration for Frederick remained as great as ever, and he continued to believe that the war was beneficial in working against an Austria whose efforts had recently been inimical to the Empire, he also had come to recognize that the war had more to do with sheer power than with religion or freedom, and that Frederick, too, was contributing his share to the destruction of imperial unity.[5]

As he retreated from his pro-Prussian position, Moser tried to distinguish between the concepts "patriotism" and "love of fatherland," in order better to define his own position; the latter, he wrote in his *Beherzigungen* of 1761, while inborn and natural, was also a result of prejudice and habit, and carried too many overtones of self-interest, so that the attempt to define a patriot as one who loves his fatherland would merely demonstrate that there were as many "patriots" in Germany as there were different (and often opposing) interests. Moser's German patriot, however—the patriot he himself wanted to be—was the man who looked to the well-being of the whole of Germany, not just to the advantage of his particular "fatherland" within Germany. Yet, as the Prussian professor and man of letters Thomas Abbt pointed out in a review of *Beherzigungen,* Moser nowhere said anything about the interest that all subjects of all the German princes were supposed to have in common. If there was to be an imperial patriotism rather than a merely territorial one, Abbt suggested, then Moser would have to be more specific about the all-German interest this patriotism was to serve. The criticism was a fair one, and appears not to have been lost on a Moser who at this very moment was in the process of abjuring his Prussian loyalties, but without yet having found a new political direction. His retreat from political themes in writings published between 1761 and 1765 is probably indicative of a period of reflection and search for the very interest to which Abbt's critique had referred.[6]

The event which began Moser's conversion to a new position was the ceremonious election and coronation of the future Joseph II as Roman King in March and April of 1764. Moser attended the festivities in Frankfurt, and there had conversations with a number of Austrian officials, including the Imperial Vice-Chancellor Colloredo, who made a determined effort to win the sympathies of the already well-known publicist by candidly admitting Austria's past mistakes to him, and explaining the present and future course of Vienna's policy in ways designed to gain his support. Like many Germans outside of Prussia who really wanted to be able to look to Vienna for the leadership of the Empire, Moser was susceptible to this frank and open approach, and perhaps flattered by it as well. Once he could believe that Austria's Catholic zeal, in particular, would be curtailed—a belief much strengthened by his extremely favorable impressions of the young and reform-minded Joseph—it was not difficult for him to relocate his political confidence in Vienna. This was obviously recognized there, for in October 1764 Colleredo authorized the Austrian minister

Count Pergen to approach Moser to enter Austrian service as a publicist in the imperial cause, as well as to pass along information within the Empire that might be of interest to the Emperor, or to the House of Habsburg. This proposal, accompanied by the offer of an annual pension of 1,500 Gulden, was laid before Moser in December and immediately accepted. While Moser had thus become virtually a Habsburg agent—even a spy of sorts—within the Empire, this conversion cannot be judged by twentieth-century standards of political conduct; it is certain that he himself did not look at his new employment in the light of any sort of espionage, and perceived nothing shameful in it. While there were, to be sure, elements of naivete and credulousness in his political positions throughout much of his life, these were more the result of benevolent but often excessive hopes than of any hypocrisy, whether conscious or unconscious; he was not the kind of man to enter the service of any cause in which he did not sincerely, if sometimes almost too wholeheartedly, believe.[7]

The first fruits of Moser's reorientation were soon forthcoming. On December 20, 1764, he handed Count Pergen a plan for a "purification of the national spirit," which called for the foundation of a historical and political journal with the title *The Friend of the Fatherland* (an early model for the periodical *Patriotisches Archiv für Deutschland,* which Moser actually did establish twenty years later), as well as for a systematic attempt to shape public opinion through the publication of enlightening pamphlets and flyers on various public questions at moments of critical political decisions. The journal never got off the ground in this period, though Moser went to work almost immediately, also in December, on a short exhortation entitled "New Year's Wish for the Imperial Diet at Regensburg," where he called upon the representatives of the German territories to regard this moment, following a long and destructive war, as the dawn of a new era for Germany, in which a genuine and exact observance of the laws of the Empire could form the basis for a general improvement beginning at Regensburg.[8]

Far more important than this brief piece, however, was the much longer book Moser published in mid-1765—a work on which, together with his earlier *The Master and the Servant,* much of his public reputation was to rest for many years to come. *Concerning the German National Spirit (Von dem Deutschen national-Geist),* though published anonymously, was quickly recognized as Moser's own; it was read very widely, and was reviewed and discussed by the most famous critics and in the best-known periodicals of the time.[9] Moser began by contrasting what the Empire was theoretically supposed to be (a noble and unified, if also diversified, realm) with what it was in reality (a disunified object of robbery and mockery for its neighbors, strong enough to tear itself to pieces but too weak to prevent anyone else from doing so). He then went on to lament the general ignorance of and indifference to imperial law, the religious hatred which divided German from German, and the combination of incompetence and partiality with which those responsible for teaching the imperial constitution went about their wholly inadequate work.[10] He reserved his sharpest criticisms for the "spirit of independence" that had seized the larger princes of the Empire as a consequence of their development of special interests, making them indifferent or hostile to their fellow princes as well as to the Empire as a whole. By defining "the common good" exclusively in terms of their own narrow and immediate self-interest, they helped to make or interpret permissive general laws for the whole Empire that encouraged each territory to believe itself entitled to legislate independently of all others, even in matters that were clearly of general concern. In this *sauve qui peut* atmosphere, Moser warned, there also existed the danger not only that larger Estates might attack and absorb the smaller with impunity, but also that foreign powers, under the pretext of preserving the same "German liberty" which served the larger German states so well as a mask for their naked self-interest, might once again attempt to subject the Empire to their influence.[11]

The correction of this state of affairs, according to Moser, required no changes in the laws or institutions of the Empire; the problem, after all, lay not in the constitution but in the fact that the national spirit, which animated it, had evaporated, giving way to a provincial spirit instead. Moser was not unappreciative of the positive effects of Germany's political fragmentation, which permitted a cultural diversity he regarded as a unique benefit of the country's constitution; but that fragmentation had to be balanced or offset by a common, overarching national spirit, acting as a kind of moral cement, if it was not to become a source of abrasions and conflicts that could ultimately destroy the whole. The problem, then, was how to restore that lost national spirit and make it politically effective once again. To this end, Moser proposed a reformation in the teaching of public law (*Staatsrecht*), especially at the institutions of higher learning. Believing as he did that the constitution of the Empire, where it was taught at all, was badly presented, and by teachers whose position as civil servants to their various rulers all too frequently gave them a personal stake in emphasizing the permissive and particularistic elements of the constitution over those which bound all Estates to a common national duty, he felt that if the young men who were to become the future diplomats, officials, and advisors of the German princes were educated to respect the national and patriotic principles of the constitution, then in their later careers they would tend to facilitate greater cooperation among their princely employers. An even more immediate strengthening of national spirit could be achieved, said Moser, if princes could be moved to appoint capable and impartially patriotic individuals to important official posts right away.[12] In the end, therefore, Moser's solution to the problem of imperial disunity boiled down to the necessity of changing the attitudes of individuals and groups toward the imperial nexus and their relationship to it. This was less a matter of laws than of the spirit that alone could give force to laws; it was, in other words, a matter of "good, honest, earnest will," the instrument by which the "lords and chiefs" of the German fatherland had to be moved by the true patriot "to want what they ought to want."[13]

In the veritable explosion of reviews and commentaries to which the publication of Moser's book gave rise, one fundamental critical theme predominated: an unwillingness to accept Moser's restriction of the term "national spirit" to a particular set of political attitudes and opinions and, specifically, to those which involved the relationship of the individual Estates to the Empire or Emperor. Justus Möser, the highly respected Osnabrück official and publicist, criticized Moser for dealing only with "political intrigue" (*Staatsintrigue*) and the courts of the German princes in his work. These had little to do with the nation or with its true interest, as Möser understood them, and he suggested that Moser might more accurately have entitled his work "The Spirit of the German Courts."[14] Möser's belief that the term "nation" had to include a much broader range of people and ideas than those assigned to it by Moser was echoed by two other of the latter's critics. Friedrich Carl Casimir von Creutz, a high-ranking official in the Landgraviate of Hessen-Homburg, a philosophical freethinker, and something an enemy of Moser's father, not only argued that the concept "nation" was related primarily to the original language of a people (by which criterion he therefore included the Danes, Swedes, Dutch, and Swiss, among others, as part of the German nation), but also that the subjects of the German princes would have to be directly involved in the political processes of the Empire, as they were not, for Moser's equation of "German nation" and "German Empire" to be acceptable.[15] Johann Jakob Bülau, the city clerk of Zerbst and author of the most detailed direct response to Moser's work, also refused to accept Moser's implied equation of "German national spirit" with "the spirit of the imperial constitution." Bülau's concept of national spirit was the broadest of all—a universal cultural one, which embraced all the characteristics that distinguished one people from another. His idea of an adequate treatment of the German national spirit would have required of Moser the almost impossible task of writing what amounted to a cultural history of mankind to show where the German people fit into it at various times, how they changed, how they differed from each other, and so on. Like Justus Möser, Bülau thought Moser's book mistitled; its narrow focus on the need for political unity of the Empire suggested that it might better have been called "Concerning the Duty of Submissiveness of the German Imperial Estates to Their Emperor."[16]

At the base of these various responses to Moser's work was a double concern. First, that in addressing himself exclusively to the princes of Germany, but in a book supposedly dealing with the German national spirit, Moser was forgetting the interests of the vast majority of Germans who were not princes—the peasants, artisans, burghers, provincial rural nobility, and so on. In this respect, what almost all his critics said or implied was simply that he offered nothing new; that in failing to pinpoint the true national interest in which *all* Germans could partake, he gave no answers, no solutions to the confusion in which the Empire found itself.[17] Second, there was concern that in his emphasis on imperial cooperation, Moser unknowingly might actually be preparing the way for a further oppression of the already downtrodden German peoples. Any high degree of cooperation between the territorial rulers themselves, or between them and the Emperor, far from creating better or freer conditions for the people, might instead simply reinforce, by agreement, the absolutist tendencies of all princes, and lead to the extinction of that variety in the political constitutions of the various German states which presently assured the Germans at least some measure of choice between different kinds of governments. The very division and disarray which Moser condemned were therefore a guarantee against the monocratic despotism of an all-powerful Emperor or the oligarchic one of a group of princes who might use their influence to assault the rights and liberties of all Germans by means of uniform and tyrannical imperial laws. Bülau, for example, openly declared that while the picture of powerful Estates thumbing their noses at the legitimate judicial authority of the Emperor was a disturbing one, it was to be preferred to the abuse of that same authority by an arbitrary Emperor, and that, all other things being equal, the introduction of an imperial despotism was more to be feared than the anarchy of one or more of the opposing Estates.[18] Creutz, for his part, flatly denied the basic premise of Moser's argument, namely, that a common national political belief or orientation (Moser's *National-Denkungsart*) was either necessary or desirable, and asserted that Germany was freer in measure as its division into more and more small civil societies or states increased.[19]

In spite of these criticisms, however, most of Moser's reviewers paid him the compliment of recognizing the honorable and patriotic intentions that underlay his efforts, and appeared particularly impressed and pleased that he was at least trying to deal with the question of patriotism at the national or imperial level rather than at the more usual provincial one—indicative, perhaps, of a growing sense that too many writers were abusing the word "patriot" by applying it even to individuals animated by a devotion to their own territory so selfish and exclusive as to involve callous disregard or outright hostility for all others.[20] Heartened by the interest his work had obviously awakened, and encouraged by the apparent public approval of his intentions, at least, Moser plunged ahead in a publicistic campaign that now began to take on something of the character of a crusade. A major part of his new zeal seems to have been the result of personal discussions with Joseph II, whom he met in Vienna in January, 1766, while delivering the good wishes of the Landgrave of Hessen-Kassel to the newly crowned Emperor. Moser's favorable earlier impressions of the young Habsburg were enormously strengthened in these meetings, and he became an enthusiastic partisan of Joseph. His high esteem for the character and personality of the new Emperor tended to deepen and legitimize his previous conviction that the imperial office should enjoy a new respect in and a stronger leadership of the Empire, and in 1766 he rushed into print with two books which voiced these beliefs more emphatically than ever before. The first, *Reliquien*, was a rather discursive work, and is important largely because of its numerous and thinly veiled attacks on Frederick II of Prussia and his policies. In view of the praise Moser had lavished on Frederick in *Der Herr und der Diener* in 1759, it is understandable that some of his readers began to wonder whether he knew where he stood, or what he wanted, or even to suspect him of having abandoned the impartiality and objectivity on which he himself had so vigorously insisted.[21]

Unfortunately, Moser's second work of 1766 did nothing to allay such suspicions, and indeed seems to have convinced many people that he had become an all-out Austrian partisan. *Was ist: gut Kayserlich, und: nicht gut Kayserlich?* in which Moser not only summarized the constitutional history of the Empire in the previous two and a half centuries in such a way as to show that the Estates had stubbornly and persistently assaulted and weakened imperial law and the legitimate rights of the Emperor, but also placed virtually all blame for the present disarray of the Empire on the princes and their political egoism. Beginning with the reigns of Maximilian I (1493–1519) and Charles V (1519–56), and with the first Electoral Capitulation imposed on the latter, Moser tried to demonstrate that the Estates, frequently with the help of the German archenemy France, had steadily limited the powers of the Emperor as a way of escaping their duties and responsibilities under imperial law. By the time of Leopold I's reign (1658–1705), the princes, now in possession of territorial armies raised partly by French subsidies, were able to force the Emperor, who needed their help against the Turks and the rapacious Louis XIV of France, to treat with them as semisovereign lords rather than as the vassals they were in law. From that time on, the drive of the princes toward political autonomy behind the shields of "German liberty" and *Landeshoheit* had been pursued with increasing vigor and success.[22]

Moser admitted that an important distinction existed between the dynastic interests of the Habsburg family and the strictly imperial interest of the head of that family as German Emperor; to be *gut österreichisch* (a good Austrian), as he put it, was something far different from being *gut Kayserlich* (a good imperialist). He also acknowledged that on occasion the Austrians themselves had unfortunately failed to recognize the distinction, but vigorously denied that Vienna had consistently dragged the Empire into wars which served only its dynastic goals; such a charge ignored the fact that the Empire had freely voted to join these wars because it recognized that a truly imperial interest was at stake in them, said Moser, and those who made allegations such as this were engaged in a deliberate and malicious attempt to damage both the House of Habsburg and the empire by insinuating that it was impossible to be *gut Kayserlich* without also being *gut österreichisch*.[23]

While Moser was prepared to recognize the division of the Empire into two major parties as more helpful than harmful to the general interest, he also insisted that no special alliances were needed to maintain the balance of these parties; the security of each lay in the precise and jealous observance of the fundamental laws of the Empire itself, which would give to both the common interest on which peace, harmony, and an undisturbed progress could be based.[24] For this to happen, however, some very real changes in attitude would have to be brought about. In particular, most servants of the German princes, whether in ministries, at the courts, or in the universities, would have to stop regarding themselves as employed solely for the purpose of limiting or calling into question all the rights of the Emperor and making his office as difficult and inadequate as possible. A minister or councillor was certainly bound to look after his prince's interests, Moser wrote, but he was equally bound to observe the imperial laws that regulate the relations between Emperor and Estates, while academicians and other learned men who write and lecture for public consumption could have no excuse before their fatherland and their own consciences for lying or distorting the truth.[25]

The critics handled this work considerably more roughly than Moser's earlier ones. Even the most favorable one, while approving Moser's general position that an Emperor with more than merely ceremonial attributes was necessary to Germany and that a greater degree of harmony between head and members would be a desirable thing, felt that Moser was far too uncritical toward the past policies of the Habsburgs and was disinclined to accept his notion that discord between Emperor and Estates was an aberration in the history of Germany, a deviation from the unity and harmony that Moser supposed to be the norm for the German national spirit.[26] Other reviewers were less gentle, finding in the book's evident partiality for the Austrian side its Achilles' heel. Justus Möser did not like it; neither did the enlightened and influential literary group centered around Friedrich Nicolai and Moses Mendelssohn in Berlin, in whose journal *Allgemeine deutsche Bibliothek* both of Moser's newest works were belatedly discussed in 1769. The reviewer, Johann August Eberhard, a private tutor in Berlin at the time, attacked Moser on several grounds. He raised objections to Moser's implication that every inhabitant of the Empire either could or must have but one interest and one imperial fatherland, an idea that Eberhard regarded not only as absurd in itself, given the political conditions created in Germany since the Thirty Years' War and, more recently, the Seven Years' War, but also as destructive of civil order insofar as it encouraged the subjects of imperial princes to adopt a so-called "imperial interest" over the heads of or even against the policies of their own territorial rulers. He also expressed the fear that a revival of imperial sentiments along the lines proposed by Moser would lead toward the reintroduction of a feudal regime in which, in particular, the beneficial rise of a propertied middle class would be halted and then reversed, throwing its members back into the feudal slavery it had taken them so many centuries to escape. The strengthening of the Emperor's office might also bring with it a return to religious uniformity, said Eberhard—a prospect that could only be regarded with horror by the enlightened.[27]

Moser made one last effort in this period to answer his critics and to define a position that so many of his early readers had clearly found elusive and imprecise. He chose to do this in a rambling book of over 400 pages entitled *Patriotische Briefe,* which he published (again anonymously) in 1767 specifically as a commentary on Bülau's answer to his work on the German national spirit of 1765. Bülau, in common with Moser's other critics, had questioned whether there really was such a thing as a German national spirit, and had asked Moser to define the single national interest from which such a spirit might arise. Moser now tried to do just that. In every political constitution, regardless of its composition, he wrote, there must be a great and general thought which is central to it, and which encompasses the true or at least presumed national interest; when this thought insinuates itself into the consciousness of the entire people, and becomes their common belief, it becomes their national spirit. In Germany, this thought always had been and still was *freedom*. From it had arisen that multiple balancing of rights which is the German constitution; imperial law, therefore, did not create the German national spirit, but was a product of it. Yet Moser hinted that the imposing edifice of imperial law that had grown up over the centuries had for many people eventually obscured the spirit from which it had originally sprung and which it was intended to serve. For this reason, he was not able to define the national spirit in terms of the thoughts, convictions, and sentiments which all Germans, irrespective of position, now *did* have regarding the German constitution, but only as those which they *ought* to have.[28]

As in earlier works, Moser's position was that the Estates, in their jealous guardianship of their "German liberty," had come to interpret the constitution too exclusively in terms of its protection of their individual self-interest, forgetting that another and equally important part of its purpose was to safeguard a common German freedom that did not necessarily coincide with the self-interest of particular territories as their rulers chose to define it at any given moment. Liberty and license are different things, Moser seemed to suggest, and the laws and institutions of the Empire were intended to establish and guarantee the former, not the latter. The Emperor, the imperial courts, the Diet, and so on, were essential ingredients of a balance designed precisely to protect freedom by restricting license. To do this, however, all had to be permitted to function as the laws intended that they should. This principle explains why Moser, though not opposed to reforming the constitution, also did not want it to go very far: partly because of his fear that in the present situation reform would probably tend in the direction of division rather than greater unity, but also, and more importantly, because he believed it unnecessary. Adequate laws conferring adequate powers on the various agencies of imperial government were already on the books, and all that was really required was that those agencies not be kept from operating according to the exact prescription of the laws.[29] This was particularly urgent in the case of the Emperor, whose powers, though quite limited, were sufficient as long as he was allowed to exercise them, particularly in his supreme judicial capacity.[30] Defending himself vigorously against Bülau's accusation that patriotism, for him, meant nothing more than submissiveness of the Estates to the Emperor, Moser insisted that it really meant simply "Give to the Emperor what is the Emperor's, and give[the Estates] what is [theirs]."[31]

Sensitive as he doubtless was to earlier charges that he had so far offered little more than the vaguest and most general sort of suggestions for improving the operations of the Empire as a basis for an increased public confidence in it, Moser in this work seems to have strained to produce a few specific proposals to satisfy his critics. These ranged from already shopworn recommendations for improving the quality of personnel of the Imperial Cameral Tribunal and reinstating annual visitations of it to hints that the territorial map of Germany might be rearranged to bring about a geographical separation of smaller from larger territories, presumably in order to protect the former from the latter and to permit the smaller princes to pursue "patriotic" policies without fear of retribution from the more selfish rulers of the larger states.[32] Moser even toyed briefly (and rather idly, as he himself admitted) with the idea of a national representa-

tion for the "Third Estate" in Germany, whose delegates might constitute
a sort of lower house in the Diet, providing a permanent repository of national spirit that could act to assist and encourage Emperor and Estates in
the execution of their patriotic duties.[33] Ideas such as these were not likely
to convince anyone that Moser's vision of a revitalized Empire had become
any more concrete or realistic than it had ever been. As the last of the above
proposals demonstrated, his emphasis remained essentially where it had
always been—on the necessity for reawakening and tapping the national
spirit, in whose absence no reform of laws or institutions could ever be
effective, and in whose presence no reform was necessary. This represented
the simplest of solutions to the Empire's confusion, perhaps, but also one
of the most difficult to carry out. And while constantly preaching the need
for good will, Moser himself, in the end, could find no way to create that
good will where it did not exist, and could only hope that every German
prince would someday by himself perceive that even his own self-interest
demanded a patriotism in which the laws and tribunals of the Empire,
and even its Supreme Head, were recognized as essential to his own well-
being and freedom.[34]

The *Patriotische Briefe* was Moser's last excursion into serious political
writing for a long time; indeed, until the early 1780s he did very little
writing at all. This did not mean that he had lost interest in his national
and patriotic cause, which he continued to ponder and about which he was
to write at some length again later in his life. He does appear to have felt,
however, as he wrote in the preface to *Patriotische Briefe,* that the important concerns he had wanted to bring before the public had now been
published, widely disseminated, and thoroughly reviewed and discussed
in the important books and journals, so that his readers could now make
up their own minds; his own part, for the moment, was finished.[35] It is
also highly probable that Moser had come to question whether the hopes
and plans he cherished for Germany could ever be realized. He may have
tried to pass his literary efforts of the 1760s off to himself and to others as
a largely intellectual exercise—setting up straw men, as it were, or sending
up trial balloons merely to test the political mood of Germany. But his
personality was really incapable of that sort of detachment; always passionately committed to the positions he publicly advocated, he could not
help but have been sharply disappointed by the generally negative critiques
of his works, as well as hurt by the almost vicious attacks on his personal
integrity a few of them contained.[36] Moser's Germans, it seemed clear,
were simply not yet ready to be converted into patriots.

If anything else were needed to complete Moser's retreat from public
political debate, it was supplied by his acceptance of a rather highly visible
post in Austrian service. In April 1767, Joseph II conferred on him the title
of Aulic Councillor, and in August he took a Protestant seat on the

Learned Bench of the Aulic Council. From this position, in spite of his own inalterable conviction of his impartiality, it would obviously be difficult for Moser to retain any credibility as an objective commentator on issues of imperial politics. Even more important, however, was his growing awareness that the same skepticism and indifference to his imperial ideal he had experienced throughout Germany were also to be found in the Austrian Court. Now resident in Vienna, Moser became much better acquainted with Joseph, whom he saw almost every day. Slowly, he began to see the predominance of dynastic interests in Joseph's policies, and while he never ceased to regard himself as loyal to the Emperor, he began to take independent positions in his work that came as an unpleasant surprise to the young Emperor. In one case, for example, charged with investigating the status of the ecclesiastical foundations of Trent and Brixen, Moser concluded that they were immediate Estates of the Empire rather than the taxable feudatories of the County of Tyrol Joseph had wanted them shown to be. Joseph, while praising Moser for the sophistication of his work, also rejected his conclusions, and entrusted the further elaboration of the subject to another and presumably more predictable Councillor. On another occasion, Moser joined with a number of his colleagues in opposing various changes in the Aulic Council proposed by Joseph in 1768–69. Believing that any revitalization of this body ought to come from within itself, founded on a lofty conception of its imperial responsibilities, Moser seems to have feared that Joseph's reforms would convert it into nothing more than a tool of the House of Austria.[37]

Increasingly chary of a man whose opinions he could not control, and who was also a well-known publicist, Joseph apparently concluded that he had to neutralize Moser by getting him out of Vienna. This he did, in early 1770, by appointing him administrator of the imperial County of Falkenstein. Moser, himself not terribly happy in the disappointing political atmosphere of Vienna, took up the new job gladly, and with his usual energy tried to clear up the mismanagement that had characterized the earlier administration. In Falkenstein, it was not long, however, before his reforming efforts ran afoul of vested traditional interests, whose protests eventually brought him into a degree of official disfavor in Vienna. Denied the opportunity for a personal hearing before Joseph himself, Moser petitioned for removal from his position in early 1772; when his request was granted soon thereafter, he left imperial service altogether.[38] Under these unhappy circumstances ended Moser's direct association with Vienna, the city which only a few years before he had almost ecstatically described as "the true patriotic church" and "The new political Jerusalem." Many years later, looking back on this period of high hopes and passionately committed efforts on behalf of German unity, an older and wiser Moser wrote the epitaph of his own imperial dream: "Twenty and some years ago, I too did missionary work (*den Missionarium*); in Berlin they cursed it and in Vienna they laughed about it. Interest is the God of the world."[39]

By the time Moser penned these words in 1790, of course, he had even stronger reasons for doubting that imperial unity would ever be realized than those which had led to his withdrawal from public debate more than two decades earlier. To be sure, he could easily have confirmed that self-interest ruled the world simply on the basis of the reception accorded his writings published in the 1760s. The hostility toward the Emperor and the suspicion of Vienna's policies and intentions, as well as the stubborn defense of the politically anarchic status quo of the Empire, which marked the vast majority of responses to those writings, would have made clear to even the most naive observer of the German scene that the particularistic self-interest of the German territories had no use for greater imperial unity. But there was nothing remarkable about that in an Empire in which quarreling and mistrust between Emperor and Estates had long since become almost a definitive component of its constitution, and if Moser was at all surprised, the surprise can only have been caused by the vehemence with which it was asserted by his critics, not by the mere fact of its assertion.

What may seem more remarkable, in view of the intensity of the recent conflicts between Austria and Prussia, is how little that dualism made its way into the controversy surrounding Moser's works, in which the basic lines of disagreement were still determined by the traditional and more general dualism of Emperor and Empire. Even for Moser, who shared with most other Germans of the day the belief that the sudden prominence of the Hohenzollerns was a transitory phenomenon that would in all likelihood disappear with the death of Frederick II, the Prussian challenge to Austria was merely the latest example of the by now familiar drive for greater independence on the part of the territories, no different in kind from many other episodes of the last several hundred years. In all this, of course, Moser was quite mistaken, and that was to be demonstrated by a series of occurrences beginning just a few years after he left Vienna and which culminated in the establishment of the so-called League of Princes (*Fürstenbund*) in 1785—an event which no longer left any doubt that the Empire was faced with an internal crisis different from and in many respects more ominous than any it had faced before.

CHAPTER FIVE

Wounds Reopened: Background
and History of the League of Princes

THE LAST GENERAL and explosive issue of imperial politics before the period of external challenges inaugurated by the French Revolution and Napoleon was the formation of the League of Princes (*Fürstenbund*) in 1785.[1] In shorter general histories of Germany, this association of imperial princes is usually dismissed with relatively cursory treatment as simply the last, and successful, attempt of Frederick II of Prussia to block the desires of the House of Habsburg to expand and consolidate its territorial holdings in the Empire, thereby increasing its dynastic strength and its ability to influence events in Germany and in Europe as a whole. This interpretation, which finds in the League merely a diplomatic tool for the achievement of Prussian goals, is in fact not too different from that of Frederick II and his advisors, and their immediate successors, who resolutely resisted all hints and suggestions from lesser members of the League that it be something other than an association for the defense of the constitutional and territorial status quo. The short history of the League, which came to an end in 1790 when a reconciliation between Austria and Prussia removed its raison d'être from the standpoint of its chief member, supports the contention that the League was significant largely as an episode in the Austro-Prussian dualism.

While it is almost certainly true that the chief accomplishment of the League was the wholly negative one of preventing any significant alteration of territorial relationships within the Empire—a goal achieved as much by the mere fact of the League's existence as by its actions, which were few—the formation of such an association was regarded by many Germans as an almost revolutionary act, whether for good or for ill. Immediately, it touched off an intense public controversy, which ultimately involved issues that transcended the confines of the Austro-Prussian dualism and produced a kind of general introspection on imperial constitutional affairs—the last such introspection produced by strictly native events before the storm from the West was to impose even more drastic and profound reasons for self-examination. Since this public debate reveals a great deal about the picture Germans had of what the Empire was, or ought to be, in a political sense, and what kinds of values it did, or ought to, represent, the League of Princes, which sparked the debate, has an importance for the historian that transcends its own immediate political intent.

That specific intent, of course, was to prevent the absorption of Bavaria by Austria, an action that Austrian statesmen had been weighing as a possibility for quite a long time—as far back, indeed, as the late seventeenth century. There was an obvious appeal to the idea; Bavaria was a large territory, directly contiguous to the Austrian hereditary lands, whose possession could anchor Habsburg power and influence in the German-speaking lands of the Empire more solidly. In addition, since the political ambitions of the Bavarian Electors from the late seventeenth century onward had converted Bavaria into an outpost of French influence on Austria's own borders—a situation which could, and did, turn downright dangerous in time of war—it was in Austria's strategic interest to secure her Bavarian flank through annexation. At no time was annexation by sheer conquest a very serious possibility, even when Bavaria was overrun by Austrian troops in wartime, simply because the Empire itself, whatever its feelings about the betrayal of imperial interests by a maverick Bavaria may have been, would not have permitted it. The alternative to conquest was exchange, and on several occasions formal and informal proposals to exchange all or part of Bavaria for outlying possessions of the Habsburg family— Naples, the Austrian Netherlands, or territories to be reconquered from France, for example—were bandied about, though nothing came of them.

Soon after the middle of the eighteenth century, following the loss of Silesia to Prussia in the War of the Austrian Succession and the failure to recover it in the Seven Years' War, there was a general feeling in Vienna that a means had to be found to strengthen Austria's position in Germany. Adding to the malaise at the Austrian court in these years was the extremely unsettling fact that in several territories of the Empire, the childlessness of aging rulers held out the prospect of territorial successions which could threaten the Austrian position. Two of these territories, the Margraviates of Ansbach and Bayreuth, were ruled by members of the Hohenzollern family, whose most famous representative now sat on the Prussian throne in the person of Frederick II. While these territories were not large, they had a combined population of over 400,000; and since they lay to the north and the west of Bavaria, they were really within the Austrian zone of influence in southern Germany. In 1769, Karl Alexander of Ansbach assumed possession of Bayreuth upon the death of its previous ruler, Friedrich Christian, thus combining the two territories in personal union. While the exact disposition of the two Margraviates at the death of Karl Alexander was not certain, Prince Kaunitz and other Austrian statesmen knew that a Prussian claim to both was a very real possibility. The prospect of two strong Prussian outposts in southern Germany was understandably disturbing to the Austrian court.

Even more worrisome, however, was the situation of the two main branches of the Wittelsbach family. By the mid- to late-1760s, it seemed increasingly likely that neither Maximilian III Joseph of Bavaria (1727–77) nor Karl Theodor of the Palatinate (1724–99) would produce legitimate heirs. Their own cognizance of this led them to conclude a series of family treaties in 1766, 1771, and 1774 which together provided for the succession of the survivor to the inheritance of the other, so that for the first time in four and a half centuries all the main territorial holdings of the House of Wittelsbach would be united. Since neither had an heir, however, this raised the further possibility that the combined Wittelsbach holdings might one day fall to a third prince whose own territorial possessions would be added to the united Wittelsbach inheritance. From the standpoint of the Austrian court, this possibility had several ominous aspects. In the first place, it would mean the creation of a new state whose total resources could raise it to a position of power in the Empire second only to that of Prussia and of Austria, which could compete with Austria on a very strong footing for influence in those Rhenish and southwestern German areas that had long been the preserve of the Emperor. Second, given the history of antagonism between Austria and Bavaria, as well as the always watchful hostility of Prussia, there was the horrifying possibility that a future Hohenzollern-Wittelsbach alliance could attempt to repeat the imperial experiment of 1742–45 by securing the election of a now much stronger Wittelsbach to the imperial throne, followed, perhaps, by a genuine drive to exclude Austria entirely from the affairs of the Empire.

It is of course true that the long reduced real value of the imperial crown, together with the growing concentration of Vienna on the economic, political, and administrative development of the Habsburg dynastic lands and the steady reorientation of her foreign policy away from the west and toward the east and southeast, had diminished Habsburg interest in the imperial crown over the years. But its utility at least as an adjunct to dynastic policy was not so inconsiderable as to suggest that its benefits should be ignored completely, much less abandoned to a possibly hostile interest. With such new considerations added to the by now almost inveterate desire to acquire Bavarian territory, Prince Kaunitz as early as 1764 had suggested that Austria begin to prepare a policy for the Bavarian succession, which in effect would permit as much acquisition of Bavarian territory as circumstances might allow. By the end of 1772, Joseph II had decided that on the event of the death of Maximilian III Joseph without heirs, he would employ the device of claiming most of Bavaria for the Habsburgs as lapsed fiefs of either the Empire or of the Kingdom of Bohemia, and he specifically instructed the Austrian minister in Munich to begin to prepare the political and diplomatic ground for this action.[2]

By the mid-1770s, interest and apprehension about the Bavarian succession was general throughout the Empire, though there was no reason to expect the immediate demise of either of the Wittelsbach princes, the eldest of whom turned fifty in 1774. Prussia's early policy toward the eventuality of the succession vacillated between alternatives of dealing with Austria, agreeing to her acquisition of all or part of Bavaria in return for her acquiescence in Prussian expansion (at the expense of Saxony, for example); opposing any Austrian acquisitions while expanding her own territory; or taking the completely conservative line that any Austrian interference with the terms of the Wittlesbach succession was a threat to the stability of the whole Empire, a violation of the sanctity of treaties, and an invasion of the inheritance rights of all imperial Estates. By September of 1775, however, Frederick II had essentially decided on the last of these alternatives, which was to remain his public position on the Bavarian question to the end of his life.[3]

Since the summer of 1777, a representative of Karl Theodor had been in Vienna discussing with Austrian officials terms under which the Elector Palatine might acquiesce in an abdication of Bavarian territory to Austria if and when he succeeded to the Bavarian inheritance. The Elector's readiness to negotiate over Bavaria was due partly to his own personal dislike of the country, which he regarded as uncouth and unenlightened, and partly to his conviction that in the face of Austria's determination to have something out of the succession there was no real possibility of entering upon it whole. Even more important was his fear of Prussian designs on the Duchies of Jülich and Berg on the lower Rhine, which he would rule undisturbed during his own lifetime, but whose future thereafter was uncertain. The specific concession which Karl Theodor's representative was soliciting from Vienna in 1777 was an Austrian guarantee of the heritability of these duchies, though a much larger project for the future was adumbrated in these discussions as well. This was nothing less than a possible exchange of all of Bavaria for the Austrian Netherlands. Karl Theodor was fully aware of earlier Austrian interest in such an exchange, and there is every reason to believe that this always remained the real heart of his intentions, the more so because the recent Wittelsbach family treaties had expressly recommended the exchange as long as it could be accomplished with appropriate advantage to the family interest.[4]

In late December 1777, while these negotiations were proceeding with no real sense of urgency, Maximilian III Joseph of Bavaria died unexpectedly. Surprised and dismayed, Kaunitz recognized immediately that it was impossible to proceed with the earlier plan to incorporate most of Bavaria as lapsed fiefs, if only because the necessary preparation for such an action in the rest of the Empire, including especially Prussia, was very incomplete. But it was also necessary to move quickly if anything were to be had, lest delay provide the opposition a chance to gather strength and ultimately impose endless negotiations from which Austria might conceivably emerge with nothing. Consequently, a hastily drawn-up treaty was forced upon Karl Theodor's representative on January 3, 1778, and was subsequently ratified by the Elector himself. By this agreement, whose acceptance by Karl Theodor was made a condition for future (and presumably more promising) negotiations about the disposition of the Bavarian inheritance, the Elector's succession to Bavaria was recognized by Austria, subject to his abdication to Austria of nearly all of Lower Bavaria and the district of Straubing. Other clauses held out the prospect of further Austrian acquisitions in Bavaria in exchange for minor Austrian territories in southwestern Germany and perhaps elsewhere. Austrian troops began to occupy the promised Bavarian territories on January 16—the very day the Elector's ratification reached Vienna.

Frederick of Prussia was caught as much by surprise as anyone else by the sudden death of the Bavarian Elector. Immediate military action was out of the question for several reasons, not the least of which was the necessity for Frederick to find out just where the political and diplomatic support for his opposition to the Austrian coup was to come from. Nor, while doing this, was he above listening with considerable interest to Austrian proposals for compensations to purchase his support not only for what had already happened, but for even more extensive Austrian acquisitions. By June, however, Frederick's virtual paranoia about the dangers of any Austrian expansion—as well as the fact that he was too deeply mired in his own public propaganda to be able to keep any credibility for the future if he now participated in the same game he had self-righteously been condemning for some time—resulted in the breakdown of negotiations and a Prussian resolve to resort to arms.

By this time, war was not as risky a proposition as it might have been earlier. For one thing, both Saxony and Mecklenburg had claims on the Bavarian inheritance, and took sides with Prussia almost immediately. For another, the heir-presumptive to Karl Theodor's entire inheritance, Duke Karl August of Zweibrücken, had been persuaded to protest the

January treaty at the Imperial Diet, and to appeal to Prussia for help, thus giving Frederick at least such appearances of righteousness as were necessary to neutralize the rest of the Empire. Finally, Austria's evaluation of the policy that would be adopted by foreign powers proved disastrously wrong: France, technically an ally since 1756, not only declared that her alliance with Austria did not apply to the present circumstances, but secretly encouraged Karl August's opposition to the January treaty—thus revealing the very real limits of the recent diplomatic friendship between Bourbon and Habsburg. Catherine II of Russia, whose energies the Austrians supposed were too fully occupied in a war with the Turks to allow her to take any active interest in supporting her Prussian ally, made it clear that she would not be indifferent to Austria's attempts to strengthen herself through the acquisition of new territories in Germany, although she also informed Frederick that she was unwilling to intervene against Austria in this affair without being called upon to do so by a clear majority of the Estates of the Empire—a condition which Frederick, in spite of his best efforts, was unable to satisfy.

Armed hostilities began with the invasion of Bohemia by Prussian troops in early July, 1778. Characterized by elaborate jockeying for defensive positions and by only the most cautious offensive thrusts, this War of the Bavarian Succession was one of the more dumdrudge wars of the eighteenth century, in which neither side regarded the possible gains as worth a major military effort. It is also clear that both sides from the beginning expected a diplomatic solution to be forthcoming fairly soon. The two hostile powers had direct and indirect diplomatic contacts throughout the war, which were without results, and both showed some willingness to attempt a mediation through the Imperial Diet or at least the Council of Electors. The failure of such attempts, due not only to procedural problems but also to the usual factional quarrels, and the mingled suspicion and fear of both Austria and Prussia on the part of so many Estates led finally to the grudging acceptance of a plan originally proposed by Maria Theresia for a mediation by France and Russia. France, which had shown itself friendlier to Austria's interest once war had actually begun, made threatening noises about joining Vienna in the war if Prussia rejected this plan. While the Empire as a whole was not delighted by the prospect of inviting foreign states to meddle in its affairs—and this was especially the case with regard to Russia—the acceptance of this mediation by the two German great powers was all that was needed.

Three days after an armistice of March 7, 1779, between Austria, on one side, and Prussia and Saxony, on the other, negotiations were begun in the town of Teschen in Austrian Silesia. The final treaty was signed on May 13. By its terms, the earlier agreement between Austria and Karl Theodor was nullified; Austria gave up all claims to the Bavarian inheritance, but was allowed to keep a small strip of eastern Bavaria, the so-called *Innviertel*, with some 80,000 inhabitants. Prussia's rights of eventual succession to the Margraviates of Ansbach and Bayreuth were confirmed. Saxon claims to the Bavarian inheritance were to be satisfied chiefly by a cash payment from Karl Theodor, while those of Mecklenburg were bought off with the grant of the *privilegium de non appellando* to its Duke by Joseph II. The Peace of Teschen also expressly restated the validity of the terms of the Peace of Westphalia, and since the treaty was subsequently confirmed by the Imperial Diet and formally guaranteed by the two foreign mediators, it meant that Russia had joined France and the now unimportant Sweden as guarantors of the imperial constitution, with all that could bring by way of future opportunities to influence the Empire's destiny.

The political complacency into which the Empire had lapsed after the Seven Years' War had been abruptly and severely shaken by the events of the Bavarian succession and the war it caused. Among other things, it had served to focus attention on the uncomfortable fact that the peace of the Empire seemed to rest too largely with the two German rulers whose power, so wholly disproportionate to that of the other imperial Estates, enabled them to pursue egoistic policies which, while affecting the Empire, were formulated essentially without regard to imperial interests or desires. The first stirrings of the movement that led to the formation of the League of Princes in 1785 arose from the conviction of a number of lesser princes that their own liberties needed to be protected by an association. Although the suspicions and fears of most princes were originally directed almost equally at Austria and Prussia, the ideas for such an association gradually began to carry a much more pronounced anti-Austrian complexion. This stemmed partly from the good will Frederick II reaped through not claiming immediate territorial compensation at the Peace of Teschen, which lent credence to his self-proclaimed role as a selfless protector of the imperial constitution. But it was even more the result of the actions of the restless Joseph II, especially after the death of his mother and coregent in 1780 removed certain restraints on his policy.

Three events in particular created an increasing sense of real alarm in the Empire. The first was the successful attempt of Joseph to have his youngest brother, Archduke Max Franz, elected coadjutor bishop of Cologne and Münster in 1780. This action not only guaranteed the succession of a Habsburg to an Electoral throne, but seemed to suggest a more active Austrian policy for the future in the occupation of other ecclesiastical thrones. Combined with not altogether groundless rumors that had been floating about for some years to the effect that Austria would not be averse to a general secularization of the ecclesiastical states, especially if a way could be found to assure their rulership to members of the Habsburg family, the election of Max Franz took on something of the aspect of an Austrian offensive within the Empire.

While all princes shared some misgivings about this matter, the ecclesiastical princes were the most alarmed. They were soon to become even more disturbed by a second matter, namely, Joseph's decision to reorganize the diocesan divisions of Austria proper. Because of the peculiar history of the German Catholic Church, certain German ecclesiastical princes—notably the Archbishop of Salzburg and the Bishop of Passau—administered dioceses which included some Austrian territory, and even conferred princely powers in some particular enclaves. Joseph, who not only wanted to have all his lands free of foreign ecclesiastical influences as a prerequisite to the full subordination of the church to the state in Austria, but who also regarded the traditional diocesan boundaries as inefficient for the spiritual mission of the church, fell to quarreling with Salzburg as early as the mid-1760s, and by 1782 had virtually stripped it of its previous ecclesiastical rights in Austria, which were then awarded to complaisant Austrian bishops instead. In Passau, the death of the reigning bishop in 1783 led immediately to an Austrian denial of the further exercise of diocesan rights by Passau in Austria, and even to the temporary confiscation of such wealth and goods belonging to the bishop and the Chapter as lay within Austria's borders. These measures, unsupported by imperial law and redolent of a friendliness to the general idea of secularization, could only be regarded with horror by all ecclesiastical princes, whose prelatic rights frequently extended to territories over which they did not hold temporal power, and which in some cases provided a significant proportion of their income.

These actions, on top of the recent Bavarian unpleasantness, not only gave rise to further rumors of Austrian intentions to lay claim to other inheritances in the future (Württemberg, for example), but also cast a new and ominous light on even the most ordinary and ongoing business of the Imperial Aulic Council, which found itself accused more frequently than usual of arbitrary encroachment on the rights of the Estates, of attempting to impose credit and debit commissions on various territories in order to influence their policy toward Austria, and so on. What made all of this appear especially sinister, however, was a third ongoing circumstance: the paralysis of the Imperial Diet as a deliberative body between 1780 and 1785, which resulted from a procedural quarrel over the question of whether a Catholic or a Protestant should cast the curial vote of the Westphalian Imperial Counts. It speaks for the growth of suspicion against the Habsburgs that the blame for the crippling of the Diet was generally laid at Austria's door, though Prussia in fact was at least as much to blame. Nonetheless, since this squabble prevented the Diet from debating other matters, it was commonly held to be part of an Austrian plot to prevent the presentation of complaints against the Emperor. Even in non-German affairs, Joseph seemed to be doing his best to confuse his friends and vindicate his enemies. His treatment of the Dutch in 1782 in successfully but harshly insisting on their evacuation of barrier fortresses in the Austrian Netherlands, which they had occupied since the wars of Louis XIV, and his much more serious project of 1784 to break the Dutch blockade of the Scheldt, a right which had been guaranteed to the Dutch at Westphalia and reconfirmed in later peace treaties as well, strengthened the prevailing impression of the Emperor as an aggressor—even with his ally, France.

Finally, there was Joseph's resurrection of the Bavarian question. The Peace of Teschen, while dashing all hopes for Austrian acquisition of Bavaria through unilateral measures, had reconfirmed all the Wittelsbach family treaties, within which was provision for the exchange of Bavaria under favorable conditions. Fully aware of this, Joseph had concluded in the early 1780s that the time was ripe to approach Karl Theodor with new terms for an old idea—the exchange of Bavaria for the Austrian Netherlands. From the Emperor's standpoint, the most important single external diplomatic barrier to this idea was the opposition of Russia, which had been so clearly demonstrated in 1778–79. By showing a friendlier attitude toward Russia's expansion at the expense of the Turks, Joseph was able to contract an alliance with Catherine II in 1781, which not only broke the back of Prussia's only foreign alliance, but held out the prospect of Russian assistance for Joseph's plans in Germany. From late in 1782 on, Joseph began to push in earnest for the Netherlands-Bavarian exchange, a project which reached its final form in late 1784 with the promise of a royal title for Karl Theodor as "King of Burgundy" with a continued seat on the Council of Electors, after the completed exchange. After some initial resistance based on Joseph's intentions to hold back some portions of the Netherlands as compensation for a proposed secularization of Salzburg and Berchtesgaden, or perhaps as inducements to secure French agreement to the Bavarian exchange, Karl Theodor agreed to the project. Having obtained Catherine II's agreement to the plan by his benign acceptance of Russia's conquest of the Crimea in late 1783 and early 1784, Joseph now secured the good offices of the Russian diplomat Romanzov who, acting as an agent for Vienna and Munich, began to apply pressure on Karl Theodor's heir, Karl August of Zweibrücken. France, significantly, refused throughout to give a definite commitment in favor of the exchange.

From Frederick II's standpoint, Prussia's position was becoming steadily more problematical. He himself had no foreign allies, while the Emperor had succeeded in creating at least the appearance of the old and extremely dangerous three-power alliance that had nearly destroyed Prussia in the Seven Years' War; and there were rumors that this reconstructed alliance was merely awaiting the aging monarch's death before launching an attack on Prussia. While there was in fact no substance to such rumors, and Frederick himself discounted them, it was obvious that Austria's planned expansion into Germany was a grave threat to Prussia's security, and that support had to be found to stop it. It was at this point, early in 1784, that Frederick and his advisors made the firm decision to achieve that support in the form of a league within the Empire.

Frederick based his belief in the successful formation of such a league on the continuing interest that had been shown in some form of association among many of the medium-sized and smaller territories of the Empire for some time, but especially since 1778. Territories as large as Baden, Hessen-Kassel, and Braunschweig, and as small as Sachsen-Weimar, Sachsen-Gotha, and Anhalt-Dessau, and not excluding such significant ecclesiastical states as Mainz and Würzburg-Bamberg, had at one time or another discussed plans for leagues of imperial Estates. These plans had gotten nowhere, partly because of disagreements over the form and purposes of such an association arising from the differing circumstances of each state, and partly because of the basic dilemma posed by recognition of their need for a protection that their own power could not provide, along with their simultaneous fear of becoming political dependents of any state, such as Prussia, which would be strong enough to offer that protection.

For a long time, Frederick was as hostile to the idea of Prussian leadership of an association of small states as were the rulers of those states themselves. In the situation of 1784 and 1785, however, he needed an alliance that could prove effective in terms of real power against the specific danger represented by the Bavarian exchange scheme. The smaller states, while aware of a potential danger to themselves in the Bavarian affair, had a much more numerous list of fears and grievances which suggested that their objective in association involved reforms designed to strengthen the Empire and its institutions against the tendency of *any* force within the Empire—whether Emperor or some other overmighty prince—to disturb the balance as they understood it, that is, an *effective* balance which did not preclude evolutionary developments to their own advantage. With no real interest in the Empire except insofar as it could be deployed against Austria, Frederick judged his immediate needs in terms of power, and in the actual construction of his league turned to two states which had real advantages to offer in that respect: Hanover and Saxony. Hanover, in addition to its own resources, offered the further benefit of a connection, if only a loose one, to England; while Saxony, like Hanover an Electorate, was a considerable territory with a strategically important geographical position vis-à-vis Austria. Thus, the original three members of what has come to be known as the League of Princes were the Electors of Brandenburg, Hanover, and Saxony.

Neither Hanover nor Saxony, it must be said, was eager to join. The latter, which since the War of the Bavarian Succession had withdrawn into a loudly proclaimed neutrality between Prussia and Austria, had to be forced into joining by a Prussian declaration that not to do so would be regarded as an anti-Prussian act. Hanover, meanwhile, while agreeable to the principle of an association to defend the imperial constitution, had long regarded Prussia with as many misgivings as Austria, and, like many of the smaller states, wanted to avoid appearing merely anti-Austrian. Recognizing that this would be the inevitable result of membership in any league which Prussia not only joined but actually initiated, she nevertheless saw herself as having no real choice once Prussia began to push her urgently into a commitment. Not surprisingly, however, a number of subsequent signatories among the lesser Estates of the Empire chose to join the League through Hanover rather than Prussia, thus signaling their desire to be identified as supporters of the constitution rather than as friends of Prussia or enemies of Austria.

The eleven public articles of the treaty of association signed by the three Electors on July 23, 1785, committed all of them to the preservation of the imperial system according to existing law, to mutual cooperation at the Imperial Diet, to oppose all innovations and arbitrary actions, and, in short, to protect all imperial institutions and the legitimate territorial and legal rights of all Estates of the Empire collectively and individually—and to do all this by constitutional means. It also provided for acceptance into the League of all Estates, regardless of religion, which shared these intentions and purposes. Two "secret" articles, however, were appended: One listed a specific group of princes who were to be invited to join, and the other expressly committed the original signatories to oppose with forceful measures not only the present Bavarian exchange project, but any similar project in the future, as well as all secularizations and partitions—even if such changes had the voluntary agreement of all participants. A third and final, "most secret" article laid out the military obligations of the three allied princes in case armed force had to be employed. The treaty also stipulated a common policy for the three courts in the election of a Roman King, the drafting of an Electoral Capitulation, and the creation of any new Electorate.

In the months and years that followed the signing of the original treaty, a number of medium-sized and small territories joined the League, including a few who waited until Frederick William II succeeded Frederick II on the throne of Prussia following the latter's death in August of 1786. Not all were asked to subscribe to the secret articles, and few did. Braunschweig, Baden, Hessen-Kassel, and the two Duchies of Mecklenburg were the most significant secular principalities to join, but their membership did not represent the real shock to the Austrian court that came when the Elector of Mainz, Friedrich Karl von Erthal, added his name to the list, and was followed in this not long thereafter by his coadjutor, Karl von Dalberg. As Archchancellor of the Empire, Mainz had a constitutional position second only to that of the Emperor; and as the most prestigious of the ecclesiastical princes, his membership meant not only that the League had opened up that group of states which were traditionally staunch allies of the Emperor, but that Mainz might use its influence to attract other ecclesiastical members, thus threatening to expand the League to include a majority of the Estates of the Empire. In fact, this did not happen. Only a handful of ecclesiastical states attempted to join through Mainz, most of the rest preserving a careful neutrality. Furthermore, with such larger territories as Palatinate-Bavaria, Württemberg, Hessen-Darmstadt, and Oldenburg remaining out of it, the League never really came close to embracing the whole Empire.

It is probably an exaggeration to say that the League of Princes by itself blocked the Bavarian exchange scheme. The increasingly negative attitude adopted by France had already rendered the project somewhat dubious by early in 1785; the League then tipped the scales definitively against it. Except for the flurry of diplomatic activity within the Empire attendant to the formation and expansion of the League, however, which did force Austria to divert her energies into attempts at political countermeasures for some time, the League accomplished far more by the sheer fact of its existence than by anything it did. Not even the most starry-eyed among those who saw in the League an opportunity to bring some badly needed reform to the Empire and its institutions believed that this was very likely to happen while Frederick II lived; his indifference toward the Empire and his iron control of the League meant that its role would be limited strictly to the defensive, conservative purposes for which he had established it. Reform-minded princes such as Karl Friedrich of Baden, Friedrich Karl of Mainz, Franz of Anhalt-Dessau, Ernst of Sachsen-Gotha, and above all Carl August of Sachsen-Weimar, had higher hopes for Frederick William II, who as crown prince of Prussia had expressed sentiments favoring a stronger imperial nexus. Indeed, for about a year and a half after he began his reign, Frederick William listened with apparent interest and respect to various proposals for imperial reform through the League, including a grand project for a general congress of the members of the League. This initially favorable attitude changed gradually, however, partly as the result of the advice received from his own ministers, and partly because of resistance to imperial renovation on the part of the other two original signatories; Hanover began to play dog in the manger with any reform movement of which it was not the leader, while a timorous Saxony continued to oppose the utilization of the League for any purpose that might create further hostility in Vienna.

By late in 1788, though communications concerning the possibilities of imperial reform still flowed back and forth between some members of the League, it had become increasingly clear that nothing was likely to happen. Two other events of that year, furthermore, had contributed to undermine the belief of the more powerful members of the League, especially Prussia, in the need for such an association at all. One was the involvement of Austria, allied with Russia, in war with the Turks; the campaigns of this war went badly for Austria almost from the beginning, and served not only to divert her attention from German imperial affairs but also to demonstrate weaknesses which made the threat she had seemed to pose for the Empire appear less real. The other was a treaty of alliance between England and Prussia, signed in August of 1788, by which Prussia undertook to send an Army of Observation into Holland to support the stadholder William V of Orange against strong internal elements which opposed his policies, and which were supported secretly by France. Frederick William II supported William because he was his brother-in-law; England supported him because William persisted in a pro-English policy which was repugnant to the rest of his countrymen. The success of the Prussian military action in late 1788 not only increased Prussia's faith in her own strength, but revealed weaknesses in French policy and resolve that reduced estimates of the assistance France could bring to her ally Austria. The Anglo-Prussian treaty, meanwhile, had in itself achieved the one thing that Prussia had needed since 1781, and for which the League of Princes was in large measure a second-class substitute: an alliance with a great power.

For all these reasons, then, Prussia no longer found it a matter of much urgency to cultivate the League. Nor, for that matter, did some of the other members much object to her neglect by this time. Not altogether happy with the strong Prussian flavor of the League to begin with, they became increasingly more dubious about the whole enterprise as the weakness of Austria and the greater strength of Prussia became more obvious. Prussia's unconcealed attempt in late 1789 and early 1790 to utilize for her own selfish purposes her contribution to an armed intervention in the Bishopric of Liège that had been mandated by the Imperial Cameral Tribunal as an imperial execution against rebels there gained her much ill will among her allies in the League. While a last flicker of cooperative purpose can be glimpsed in the efforts of the four Electoral members of the League to formulate a common policy in the imperial election of 1790 that was made necessary by the death of Joseph II in February of that year, their failure to reach agreement provides proof that the real reasons for the association had long since faded away. Indeed, even before the election of Leopold II in September 1790, Berlin and Vienna had begun a slow process of at least partial reconciliation, the first fruit of which was the Convention of Reichenbach of July 1790. Perceived now as essentially superfluous by Prussia, which also had no intention of letting it live on under the leadership of any other state, the League of Princes now simply suffocated in its own inactivity and purposelessness.

CHAPTER SIX

The League and the Constitution

To THOSE WHO TEND to think of the League of Princes exclusively as an episode in the Austro-Prussian rivalry, the considerable contemporary literature released upon the German public in the wake of the formation of the League will probably appear somewhat puzzling in certain ways. It is, for example, often difficult to classify the numerous books, pamphlets, and articles in which the League was discussed as specifically pro- or anti-Prussian or pro- or anti-Austrian, even when, as is true in the overwhelming majority of cases, the position of approval or disapproval taken with respect to the League itself is clear and decisive. This characteristic, of course, is partly explained by the nature of the League and the manner in which it came into existence. First, Prussian statesmen, who clearly did see the League as an instrument of a particularistic policy directed exclusively against Austria, would have found it impossible to attract allies had its purposes been cast in this way. Second, desirous neither of offending Austria more than circumstances required nor of serving the exclusive dynastic interest of a state with a power in northern Germany as potentially threatening as was that of Austria in southern Germany, the other imperial princes who considered joining the League would be reluctant to do so except under a banner which denied that the League was directed against anyone in particular and at the same time affirmed an intention of benefit to everyone. Not surprisingly, therefore, the public formula of concord under which the union was born and expanded was as an "Association for the Preservation of the Imperial System."

The integrity of this formula as expressive of their general goal was insisted on with virtual unanimity by those who wrote in favor of the League. The tone was set by Christian Wilhelm Dohm, an official in the

Prussian Foreign Ministry and the author of the best-known early defense of the League. Dohm had written a short history of the affair of the Bavarian succession in 1779, while still teaching in an academy in Kassel; this work was regarded with high favor in Berlin, and he was invited to take up a joint position in the archives and Foreign Ministry, the latter of which became permanent in 1783.[1] Personally involved in the planning which led to the formation of the League, he was commissioned by Frederick II to write in defense of it. His book appeared in 1785 in the form of a refutation of one of the earliest and strongest tracts composed against the League by the Imperial Knight Otto von Gemmingen.[2] "The German League," wrote Dohm, "is directed absolutely against no person, but solely against things, to wit, against violation of German freedom and encroachment on the rights and possessions of the Estates"; it was an "obviously legal, reasonable, defensive association," whose purpose was "simply defense and preservation of the present condition of things."[3] Other writers took their cues from this position, including a reviewer of Dohm's book, who spoke approvingly of the League's intention to preserve peace and the Empire,[4] and the author of another attack on Gemmingen's treatise, who argued that the League was not established against Emperor and Empire, or the Eternal Peace, or the imperial constitution, but only against the possibility of the disruption of these, and for the preservation of the existing constitution.[5]

The desire to emphasize the positive and constitutional goals of the League rather than its negative and political ones, however, did not mean that writers were afraid to point to Austria as the offending state whose specific policies had created the necessity for the League. A relatively impartial author could refer unabashedly and rather good-naturedly to the tendencies of the House of Austria toward the establishment of "universal monarchy," forgive an *Austrian* patriot for defending those tendencies, yet argue in favor of the *German* patriot who must approve the League because it preserved the imperial constitution.[6] Even the well-known historian Johannes von Müller, whose *Darstellung des Fürstenbundes* (1787) was at once the most famous and detailed defense of the League,[7] while aiming a sharp and lengthy critique at recent policies of the Habsburgs and hinting darkly at an Austrian drive toward universal monarchy, insisted on the impartiality of the purposes of the League. Like its other proponents, he emphasized that the League was not directed for or against persons, but only for the law and against enemies of the law. It named neither a particular state nor person, and related not to any given fact, but only to possible cases. Müller clearly controverted the facts in asserting that the League was not opposed to any specific undertaking—the secret articles committed the members to oppose the Bavarian exchange, after all—and certainly was at least guilty of self-deception in stating that the

League was neither a Prussian construction nor even an association of other Imperial Estates with Prussia, but entirely an association of Estates among themselves. He probably also went well beyond what other defenders of the League would have been willing to say when, after pointing out that the League was an expression of the general imperial duty to maintain the constitution, he piously concluded that such a union stood as much for the lawful rights and reputation of the Emperor, and of Austria, as of any other Estate.[8]

While such high-minded presentations of the purposes of the League probably helped to calm the fears of some of its prospective members, and certainly proved their utility in evoking a favorable judgment of the League from even such a timid and unpolitical soul as Johann Stephan Pütter,[9] the essential practical goal for which it was initially established was everywhere recognized as the prevention of the expansion of Austrian power and influence, centered very largely (though not exclusively) around the issue of the Bavarian exchange project. This issue, in turn, was cast as a problem of balance of power, both for the Empire and for Europe as a whole. Here too, however, the argument against Austria, while pursued vigorously, was put in terms which impugned the morality of Austrian policy very little. Dohm's work is a good example. Defining Germany as a free state in which the exercise of supreme power was divided by laws and tradition, he found it entirely natural for each participant in the exercise of that power to attempt to extend its rights and sphere of competence beyond what was assigned to it by the constitution. While Austria was presently engaged in precisely such an attempt—as indeed it had been throughout its entire history—it should not therefore be construed as an insult to tax its Emperors with trying to do what it was only a part of human nature to do.[10] Human nature, however, also dictated that those German states which did not want to be overwhelmed by an overmighty Austria combine to protect themselves, thus bringing into the German system the benefits of the same balance-of-power principle that, according to Dohm, had proved so beneficial to the European states-system as a whole. He admitted that the phrase "balance of Germany" was a relatively new one; but his own acceptance of it indicates his belief that it had virtually become a part of the German, or imperial, constitution.[11]

Interestingly enough, the aged Johann Jacob Moser in one of his last, anonymously published works, and for all his devotion to the traditional multiple balances of the constitution, was not only able to accept this new term, with its idea of a simple balance, but even called it specifically a balance between Austria and Prussia.[12] Dohm, however, was unwilling to do this. He insisted that Prussia, with respect to territory, resources, and population belonged only to the medium-sized powers of Europe, and that her earlier spectacular victories against superior power were the result of various special circumstances that were unlikely to recur in the normal course of events. From this he derived not only the necessity for Prussia to ally herself with other smaller powers in order to balance off larger ones, but also the impossibility of Prussian agreement to any scheme for the overthrow of the imperial constitution and the subjection of the Estates of the Empire. Regardless of any advantages proffered to Prussia, said Dohm, the advantages reserved by Austria to herself in any such scheme would be even greater, and would ultimately result in an imbalance even more unfavorable to Prussia.[13] The benefits of Dohm's arguments to Frederick II are obvious. By presenting Prussia as less than a great power, and needful of allies, and by demonstrating that it could not serve Prussia's interest to reach a compromise with Austria involving even a partial partition of the Empire between the two—a possibility actively feared by many people in Germany even before the War of the Bavarian Succession—he sought to assuage fears and reservations that might work against expansion of the membership of the League. Dohm's presentation was not pure propaganda, however. As suggested earlier, abundant evidence indicates that in this period and for many many years thereafter, Prussian statesmen in fact and for good reasons did not think of Prussia as a first-class great power, and although Frederick II certainly toyed with ideas involving partition of the Empire (some of them proposed by Austria), he rejected them on a number of well-considered grounds, not the least of which was precisely that Prussia could not realistically expect gains greater than or even as great as those which Austria would be likely to carry away from any agreement.

Specific arguments against the Bavarian exchange project followed two patterns. The first, which attempted either to challenge the legality of the exchange or to make the case that the value of the territories to be exchanged was unequal in favor of Austria, and that Karl Theodor therefore ought not to entertain the notion of such a bad bargain, was not taken very seriously by anyone. Any allegation that a voluntary exchange would be illegal was flimsy if not downright absurd in an age when such exchanges were, and for centuries had been, accepted as routine. The attempt to set a value on the territories involved in the proposal, on the other hand, rested on statistical estimates which were dubious not only in themselves because of the primitive state of the art, but also because they were susceptible to a partisan manipulation in which figures more or less gratuitously asserted by one side could be more or less gratuitously denied by the other.[14] Pro-League attempts to utilize both arguments, that is, to show that the exchange was illegal *because* it lessened the value of the traditional Bavarian Electorate—as an inheritance as well, presumably[15]—were of no particular significance, either.

One of the implications of the above positions, of course, was that the exchange should be opposed on the grounds that Austria's resources in population, land area, and income would be increased relative to those of other existing states. To this extent, it was a balance-of-power argument, albeit a primitive one. This line of reasoning was dismissed by Johann Jacob Moser, who also introduced the main terms on which the second pattern of argumentation, a more sophisticated balance-of-power approach, was henceforth to be conducted. Starting from a hypothetical situation in which a future Prussia had attained the same strength as Austria, Moser projected a Prussian takeover of neighboring Saxony based on an exchange of territories voluntarily agreed to by both. As long as a true equivalency in the exchange existed, so that the quantity of power possessed by Prussia was not greater, he wrote, one would suppose that there would be no problem with this arrangement, and that even the other European powers could be brought to agree to it. Not so, said Moser; the calculation of power within the Empire was more complicated than this simple scheme suggested. The basic issue here would be that of preventing Prussian supremacy in the Empire, and the problem would be that *there was no real equivalent for Saxony*.[16]

What Moser was really saying through this device, of course, was that there was no real equivalent for Bavaria; that the balance of power within the Empire was not simply a matter of sums of square miles, people, and money; and that Austria, by any sophisticated reckoning, would be gaining a decisive strategic advantage in Germany regardless of the actual equivalencies of the territories involved in the proposed exchange. Dohm spelled it out in greater detail. By giving up the Netherlands in exchange for Bavaria, Austria would escape the necessity of having to defend the former against France. Expensive and difficult to defend, the Netherlands had traditionally acted as a kind of hostage against the possibility of the growth of excessive power in Austria. The acquisition of Bavaria by Austria, furthermore, would deprive France of one of her natural and historic allies in the Empire, whose geographical position made it possible in time of war for French troops to make a direct approach to the borders of Austria proper. The exchange would therefore alter the balance of power between France and Austria in the latter's favor. Since France was a guarantor of the imperial constitution, the effects of this for the Empire were obvious, and the exchange ought not to be permitted.[17]

While for Moser and Dohm the balance of power in the Empire was the most immediate concern, both were careful to place this "inferior" balance in the wider context of the European states-system. Indeed, Moser's rather brief commentary on the Empire was preceded by a much lengthier treatment of the principles of the European balance designed not only to serve as an introduction to the German issue but also to point out that while a permanent condition of jealousy and suspicion between states might seem unpleasant and distressing, it was in fact a necessary means of self-defense, creating a natural mechanism of rivalry which protected peace and prevented the oppression of one people by another.[18] Dohm, too, by emphasizing the geographical centrality of the Empire in Europe, tried to link the balance of power in the former to the peace of the latter, and thus to insist that all the cabinets of Europe had a stake in the success of the League.[19]

As clear and pointed as the views of Moser and Dohm were, the real burden of the balance-of-power argument fell to the penetrating mind of Johannes von Müller. Müller had worried about the whole idea of partitions and the possibilities they opened up for the growth of preponderant power in Europe since the partition of Poland in 1772, and as early as 1774 had expressed some suspicion that Austria might be considering annexation or partition of his native Switzerland. His growing fear of Austria was eased somewhat by Prussia's actions during the crisis over the Bavarian succession, and he began to hope that Frederick II might become a self-conscious protector of the European balance against Austrian attempts to overturn it—a view that he held consistently thereafter, in spite of a momentary lapse in the early 1780s, when he wondered whether Frederick might not yield to the temptation to agree with Austria on some kind of partition in Germany.[20] Müller had a profound conviction that small states were inherently more likely than large ones to encourage freedom in both a political and a cultural sense. This view, developed out of his own Swiss background as well as from the opinions of the French philosopher Montesquieu, led him to approve the concept of "German freedom" as it was expressed in the political fragmentation of the Empire— a fragmentation which was protected only by the balance of power in the Empire. The same balance, however, also protected the peace and freedom of Europe as a whole. With a total of some 600,000 troops in the various states of the Empire, said Müller, the balance and freedom of all of Europe, and indeed the well-being of the whole human race depended on the question of for whom and for what the Germans might fight, and whom they might follow.[21] The subjection of this enormous aggregate power to the will and direction of any single state would invariably lead toward the establishment of a universal (European) despotism, and was a prospect so fearful to Müller that he regarded an intervention in German affairs by her neighbors, especially France, as entirely justified and acceptable to prevent its realization. Indeed, under such circumstances it was the duty of imperial princes to ally themselves with and render military aid to a foreign protector of their freedom.[22]

On the other hand, Müller believed strongly that it would be in the best interests of all for the Germans to protect the balance of power in the Empire without foreign intervention or assistance—that, indeed, the Empire must protect its own balance to prevent such intervention. His one great reservation about the Peace of Westphalia was that it had preserved the constitution of the Empire only with the help of foreign powers. He was also very much aware that, as in the example of Louis XIV, the role of protector of German freedom could be abused in such a way as actually to threaten the balance of power in Europe. "It is not enough, for European freedom," he wrote, "that the imperial constitution exists; the Germans themselves must be strong enough (to guarantee) this."[23]

The means to do this lay in association, a principle whose efficacy for the defense of freedom he extolled in the pages of the periodical *Deutsches Museum* in July 1786,[24] as well as throughout his major treatment of the League of the following year. He sought to prove that alliances of princes were devices regularly resorted to throughout the history of Germany, that their effects had been generally beneficial even when the intentions of individual members had sometimes been selfish, and that refusal to join such associations when the need for them was clear was cowardice to oneself and treason to mankind.[25] In the present situation, the League of Princes represented for Müller a combination consciously created to uphold the balance principle, with the further advantage that it was an exclusively German association.[26] It is arguable that Müller would ideally have preferred that Prussia not have to be a member of the League, or at least that her leadership of it not be quite so patent; but he was realistic enough to know that the inner solidarity and cohesion required of any association intended to preserve the balance could be given only by a prince powerful enough to protect the other members, with their assistance, but not so powerful as to carry out the overall purpose alone. In the period in question, that could only be the King of Prussia.[27]

The specific arguments launched by Müller against the Bavarian exchange generally followed lines earlier laid down by Dohm. He brought out in detail the potential growth of Austrian power in both relative and absolute terms; the dangers to which France would be subjected, with the implications of that for peace and stability; the legitimate fears of the imperial Estates about the threat of the Emperor's hegemony in Germany, and so on. To these older arguments, however, he added an interesting new one, which had perhaps been hinted at by J. J. Moser earlier, but not developed. Should the exchange be executed, the new "King of Burgundy" (i.e., the transplanted Karl Theodor), receiving all the exemptions for his territory that Austria had previously enjoyed, would not be subject to the jurisdiction of the imperial courts, would thus not see himself encouraged to observe imperial law, and might attempt to make inroads against existing rights and territories of such ecclesiastical states as Lüttich (Liège), Trier, Cologne, and others. Furthermore, since this Burgundian border would be even less defensible against French attack than it had been under the Austrians, who could at least call on military assistance from the other Habsburg territories, the Burgundian king would probably find it necessary to ally with either France or Austria.[28] In either case, his interest in the Empire, as such, would be reduced to almost nothing.[29] What Müller pointed out here, in effect, was that the Bavarian exchange would result in a net loss to the Empire of one large territory from among those that truly were "the Empire"—that is, non-Austrian (and perhaps also non-Prussian) Germany. Bavaria would now be part of Austria, while the new Kingdom of Burgundy would at best regard itself as independent and at worst be a tool of one of the great powers. Whichever path Burgundy took—every one of which had a considerable likelihood for altering the balance of power—the Empire itself would be weakened.

The counterattack of the anti-League forces was no more exclusively based on what can clearly be regarded as pro-Austrian sentiments than the pro-League writings were based solely (or even largely) on pro-Prussian feeling. The issues were simply too complicated for that. It is true, however, that just as a general suspicion of long-standing Austrian policies can be detected in many defenses of the League, so also can a distrust of Prussia and her motives be found in many early attacks on the League. Some of this, of course, was quite deliberate and virtually official. When Johann von Pacassi, a teacher of public law in Vienna, justified Austria's desire to acquire Bavaria on the grounds that Prussian territory now encircled Austrian lands in the north "like a sickle," and that Austrian expansion would help to check that of Prussia, thus giving the entire Empire a greater security,[30] he was no more writing as a private person than was Dohm, an official in the Prussian Foreign Ministry, writing for the other side the year before.

But one did not have to have an official post in Austrian service to dislike Prussia, or to give voice to the suspicion that the League of Princes was merely another Prussian device to further her selfish interests in the Empire. As a public argument, furthermore, and depending on how it was employed, this had at least two advantages: It struck at a very sensitive point in the League's formation and structure—the relationship between Prussia and the lesser members; and it had the effect of answering in kind the tendency of pro-League writers to criticize Austria as a state whose interests, divided as they were between territories which lay inside and outside the Empire, could never assure the degree of devotion to the welfare of the Empire that would characterize a completely German imperial state.[31] Otto von Gemmingen tried to draw a distinction between the general interests of the Empire and the particular ones of the King of Prussia, suggesting that the latter, based on the conquest of Silesia, required the king to grasp whatever opportunity presented itself to awaken mistrust of Austria and to weaken her. Judged by the standard of how much territory Austria had lost since the days of Charles V, and how much Brandenburg had gained—and usually by force rather than legally—Gemmingen then asked his readers to make up their own minds about which power represented the greatest danger to the Empire.[32] Like Gemmingen, Christoph Ludwig Pfeiffer, an official in the Imperial City of Heilbronn, was incensed at the lesser German princes for allowing themselves to be gulled into joining what he regarded as a purely Prussian union directed against the Emperor, as if the latter were not just as much a part of the Empire as they. He insisted that a distinction be made between the Electorate of Brandenburg and its fully sovereign associates, Prussia and Silesia. The fact that the last two, which lay outside the Empire, were also governed by the ruler of the first, should not mislead anyone into supposing that they were all the same thing, wrote Pfeiffer, and no prince of the Empire should believe that his imperial obligations included assisting Electoral Brandenburg or the "Kingdom of Prussia-Silesia" to establish and maintain a balance of power in Germany.[33]

The influence of arguments such as these, or at least of the considerations which underlay them, cannot be dismissed as unimportant. Prussia's growth to great-power status as the result of the two mid-century wars and the first partition of Poland in 1772 had altered dramatically the terms of the traditional balance of rights and powers contained in the formula *Kaiser und Reich,* and had created profound reservations in the minds of many German princes about Prussia's relationship to the Empire.[34] While it is true that there was never any real expectation that the League would embrace anything approaching a majority of the Estates of the Empire, it is also true that a number of princes who were invited to join refused to do so; and while a simple unwillingness to be committed, arising from sheer timidity, accounts for part of this, suspicion of Prussian motives cannot be discounted. Max Franz, the Elector of Cologne, Joseph II's own brother, at one time gave some consideration to joining the League out of concern about the Emperor's policies, but in the end refused to do so, largely because he could not be convinced that it was not simply a Prussian tool.[35] Even one of the most active spirits in the League, Carl August of Weimar, was unhappy about the way the League came into existence, and specifically expressed reservations about the membership of courts whose interests were not restricted solely to the Empire—a comment clearly directed more against Prussia than Hanover, which enjoyed the reputation of a "patriotic" imperial Estate among the smaller princes. According to Carl August no one in the Empire trusted Frederick II, who was generally believed prepared to compromise with Joseph the moment an acceptable proposition—for compensation, presumably—was offered to him.[36]

The attempts by its opponents to discredit the League by impugning the intentions of its leader, Prussia, were really only the cutting edge of a much more important kind of argument, one which reveals a fundamental difference in the approach of pro- and anti-League groups to the very political nature of the Empire. An important key to this anti-League approach is its refusal to accept as the chief issue for debate the argument which bulked largest in the writings of the proponents of the League— the balance-of-power argument. The implications of the Bavarian exchange (or indeed of any or all of Emperor Joseph's policies) for the balance of power either in the Empire or in Europe as a whole played a remarkably small role in anti-League writings. It appeared in far fewer than one might expect, and with a few exceptions was treated perfunctorily when it did appear. In the works of those whose orientation was truly pro-Austrian, this may be explained partly by the fact that the exchange project as official Austrian policy had all but been shelved even before the formation of the League, and therefore did not have to be defended. But even for them, and certainly for those whose opposition to the League was not purchased by the Austrian court, a better explanation lies in their rejection of the very premise that a balance of power within the Empire along the lines suggested by the League's defenders was either necessary or desirable, with the implication that any league established for such a purpose was therefore itself either unnecessary or actually harmful.

The most explicit attack on the balance-of-power principle came from Christoph Ludwig Pfeiffer, who supposed that the purpose of the League was the preservation of a balance of power in Germany as the means of maintaining the present imperial system, but who stated flatly that the basic constitution of the Empire rested on very shaky ground indeed if in fact it was now to be power rather than laws which guaranteed it.[37] Gemmingen echoed the thought indirectly in asserting that the greatest advantage of the Empire could be achieved only through "the largest possible agreement of all members among themselves as well as with their Supreme Head, [with] the strictest observance of the fundamental laws of the Empire and a permanently effective power for their preservation."[38] Neither Pfeiffer nor Gemmingen was prepared to accept the notion of a "balance of Germany," which suggested a principle not formally recognized in the imperial constitution. This stand against a chief purpose of the League, as expounded by its own defenders, could count on some real support within the Empire. When Dohm admitted the relative novelty of the term "balance of Germany," he could as well have said that it was regarded as an extremely dangerous one in many quarters. Odious to those who believed in a strong Emperor because it suggested that his legitimate powers of overlordship were somehow shared by Prussia, the phrase was also offensive to the rest of the imperial Estates except Prussia because it hinted at the necessity of a choice of dependency on one or the other of the great German powers.[39] This is what Gemmingen was referring to when he spoke of the tendency of the League to undermine the imperial

system through limiting the freedom of some individual Estates, weakening the reputation of others, destroying the constitution, and profoundly
insulting the integrity of the foreign guarantors of the constitution.[40]

In this kind of critique, then, the ability of the League to fulfill its
own stated purpose, that is, the preservation of the imperial system, was
denied because the principle on which it relied as the means for doing
this—the balance of Germany—was itself not only an innovation, but also
destructive of the traditional system. One author, following this argument, concluded after a lengthy analysis that the League of Princes might
actually be an illegal association, since the imperial constitution did not
provide for associations of Estates as a means of legal remedy against the
Emperor, even in cases where the latter might himself be acting contrary
to law. Legal recourse was available through other channels—the Diet,
for example—and these should be employed instead. Furthermore, it was
a presumption on the part of the League to set itself the task of protecting
the imperial system, since that duty was constitutionally reserved to the
Emperor. As a legally dubious association of members of a state whose
efforts were directed against their ruler, the League was weakening the
sacred bond between ruler and subject, and represented a political evil
whose effects could be particularly severe in a state such as the Empire,
where the bonds of unity were already very weak. Particularly concerned
that the oppositional stance of the League could further reduce the effectiveness of execution of judgments of the imperial courts, and thus lead
to a further collapse of the whole system of imperial justice, this writer
concluded simply "that an association of imperial Estates directed against
the Imperial Court for any reason is contrary to the true interest of the
German Empire."[41]

The idea suggested above, namely, that the constitutional position of
the Emperor was the real target of the League, was common among its
opponents, some of whom were convinced that this association was simply
the latest device of a group of territories which for generations had been
striving to throw off even the last formal appearances of subjection to
Emperor and Empire. One author suggested that the specific occasion for
the formation of the League was the fear among Protestant princes that
Joseph II's enlightened religious measures might someday lead to a unification of the various Christian churches in Germany. Since some of these
Protestants, and especially the King of Prussia, had found in the *corpus
evangelicorum* a convenient constitutional device by which to pursue their
true political goal—independence from the imperial nexus—they feared
the progress of mutual religious understanding, and to prevent it had
now attempted, by means of the League of Princes, to turn even the
Catholic Estates against the Emperor. If these attempts were successful,
and the Emperor was reduced to "an inactive simulacrum," then the long-

term goal of some of the imperial princes would be realized: a "formal anarchy" in the Empire, which, while benefiting a few of them, might end in the destruction of the imperial system.[42]

A specific scenario for that destruction was sketched out by Otto von Gemmingen, who projected the possibility that the House of Austria, weary of all the burdens and contradictions of a constantly less rewarding imperial office, might decide to renounce the crown and its obligations and to join her erstwhile enemies in a partition of the Empire from which her high constitutional responsibilities had heretofore deterred her.[43] To the objections of a pro-League polemicist that this would be unlikely, because Austria would be subject to the ordinary constitutional restraints applicable to any imperial Estate even if she did give up the crown, C. L. Pfeiffer held out the prospect of a complete Austrian withdrawal from the Empire. He supposed that the Empire might then be subjected to a Prussian Emperor, and he painted a dark picture of German weakness in the event of enemy attack while an unconcerned Vienna sat on its hands.[44]

For all of the real or imagined issues which resulted in the charges and countercharges so far discussed, the early debate over the League of Princes was in fact dominated by an almost universal uncertainty about what the League would actually mean to the Empire. That was due to the supposition that its significance would ultimately emerge through what it did—that is, that its activities and accomplishments, whether negative or positive, would constitute its real definition. And since the League during the period in which the literature so far discussed appeared (1785–86) was concerned almost entirely with recruiting members rather than with developing particular policies, it is not surprising that writers in this period dealt more with what the League *might* do than with what it had done or was doing. In the event, they might have spared themselves the effort, since the League subsequently did almost nothing and exhausted its political purpose virtually at the moment of and through the fact of its establishment. It is uncertain whether, as one historian has suggested, this was due chiefly to the death of Frederick II only a little more than a year after the formation of the association,[45] or whether it was the result of an early understanding of the three original Electoral members that the League was to have essentially a reactive rather than an active character. What is quite certain, however, is that some supporters and members of the League had very high hopes indeed for it as a vehicle for an active policy of imperial reform, and that the failure to realize such a policy was due primarily to the lack of interest in or hostility to reform on the part of the larger courts, led by Prussia.

By all odds, the central and leading figure of the small group which saw in the League an opportunity to renovate the Empire, or at least to remedy some of its worst operational deficiencies, was Duke Carl August of Weimar. During the War of the Bavarian Succession, Carl August had toyed with the idea of institutionalizing some form of understanding and cooperation among the smaller Estates not involved in the quarrel between Austria and Prussia, in order to protect their neutrality by creating a greater impression on the warring powers.[46] His interest in some sort of association continued into the 1780s, and he was deeply involved in discussions of one of the more serious proposals for a league of small- and medium-sized territories associated with the name of the Baden minister Wilhelm Freiherr von Edelsheim. Not altogether happy with the form and procedures of organization of the League of Princes as it was actually established, Carl August nevertheless had great respect for Frederick II and a particularly high regard for and confidence in the crown prince, Frederick William, and acceded not ·only to the public articles of the treaty in August 1785, but also to its "secret" and "most secret" clauses early in the following year.

As early as November 1785, Carl August initiated what was to become a long series of complaints about the failure of the larger courts, especially Prussia, to keep the smaller members of the League informed of its progress. His concern in this matter reveals not only his belief that the form the League seemed to have taken was not adequately reflective of its proper character as a *Reichsunion,* but also that its purposes were being defined too exclusively in the interest of the larger states.[47] At first, Carl August sought to remedy this deficiency by pressing the larger courts to ask for advice and counsel from the smaller members, and to encourage a sort of regular circular correspondence among all the members in order to create a stronger sense of unity and common purpose. By the spring and early summer of 1787, however, after the accession of Frederick William II in Prussia had emboldened him to assert his own views more strongly than would have been advisable while Frederick II still reigned, he had worked out with the Elector of Mainz a much grander plan for a general congress of the League, consisting of high-ranking representatives of as many of the members as possible; this body would deliberate the amelioration of imperial legislation, and make recommendations to the other German states through the medium of the Imperial Diet. How vastly significant Carl August believed such a congress could be as a means for reforming the Empire can be seen from his letter of November 2, 1787, to Karl von Hardenberg, later to be a famous Prussian minister, but at this time an official of the Duke of Braunschweig. The proposed congress, Carl August wrote, might not only improve the laws, but also the entire system of imperial justice, through arranging visitations for the courts; it could prepare responses for proposals which might come from Vienna; and it could provide a basis of unity from which to eliminate all kinds of discord from the Empire. Such "preparatory works," furthermore, would serve to speed up the operations of the Imperial Diet, since proposals brought before the Diet would already have been agreed upon at the congress. It would even be possible for the congress to negotiate with imperial Estates which were not members of the League in order to get their votes for legislation to be proposed at the Diet. Voting at the congress itself would be consistent with the idea of the League as a truly equal union, each member regardless of rank having one vote.[48]

While Carl August was exhausting himself in a flurry of correspondence and circuit-riding to various princely courts to push his plans for the congress, the conservative opposition to his proposals, as indeed to any conception of a purpose for the League which went beyond a very narrowly defined preservation of the existing order of things, began to harden. His erstwhile ally the Elector of Mainz, for example, who had probably never really intended to support the convocation of a full, formal assembly in any event, cooled rapidly to the idea of the congress when it became apparent that Carl August was deadly serious about both the equality of its members and its duty to bring real reform to the Empire.[49] At the same time, even some true supporters of reform hurt their own cause by their lack of realism. An excellent example is that of Karl von Dalberg, whose sincere devotion to the unity and welfare of the whole Empire was recognized in almost all quarters, but whose idealistic enthusiasms often led him into errors. One of the worst of these was an almost painfully sincere letter to Carl August, written a few months before his election as coadjutor bishop of Mainz, in which Dalberg expressed his desire to do as much good as possible, deplored the factional spirit (*Parteigeist*) which prevailed in Germany, and then voiced his hope "that the so excellent League of Princes might gradually become a union of the whole Empire and even of the Emperor." This astonishing notion of including the Emperor in the League, incredible in anyone who had the slightest political common sense, produced a predictable reaction. Carl August, obviously embarrassed, replied to Dalberg with remarkable restraint; referring to the latter's "project of general world improvement, which . . . sounds as nice as the perpetual peace of the abbé de St. Pierre, and may well be just as little realizable," he advised Dalberg not to make such wishes or plans public. Others reacted with less forbearance. Friedrich vom Stein, a Prussian diplomat to whom Carl August had felt compelled to send Dalberg's letter, responded by terming the latter's wishes "sentimental-political hogwash" (*sentimental-politisches Gewäsche*), and even called into question his qualifications for election to the coadjutor position. A few days later, Stein reported to Carl August that Frederick William II, to whom he had shown the Dalberg letter, had commented simply: "If we were all united, we would no longer need a League of Princes; but it is necessary because all of us can never be of one mind. . . ."[50]

While the Dalberg case was far from typical of the stance of reform-minded members and supporters of the League, it does point up one reason for the reluctance of many people to admit a reform function among the purposes of the League. Simply stated, to enter upon the path of reform was to open a Pandora's Box of unknown and potential problems. No one could really know where reform might ultimately lead. Even Carl August, who was far from a fantast in political matters, had projected an open-ended agenda of reform whose final effects on the Empire he could not honestly predict. Consequently, the decision to stay on known ground, even if it meant immobility, was not an unnatural one.[51] That decision was reinforced by the most concrete political considerations, not the least of which was that virtually any attempt by the League as a whole to adopt a reform policy ran the risk of appearing to be at the same time an attempt to take over the Empire. Indeed, even the convocation of a general congress of the League might be construed as the establishment of a kind of "anti-Diet." [52] This could in turn give the lie to the professed goal of preserving the imperial constitution, insult those princes who had not joined the League, and blunt the drive to recruit new members.[53]

Concerns such as these were of course primarily the property of the rulers of the larger states, who never got much beyond the idea of the League as a diplomatic instrument directed against Austria, and who therefore wanted to give the Habsburgs as little opportunity as possible to argue throughout the Empire that the League was an aggressive device threatening the status quo. But even lesser princes, including some who believed very strongly that the League could be a force for good in the Empire, were extremely cautious about appearances. Duke Ernst of Sachsen-Gotha, a very close ally of Carl August, at one point urged the latter to be certain that any steps toward reform be taken only with the strictest observance of legal forms. "The greater and more powerful," he continued, "can always transgress the constitutions and laws of the Empire unpunished, [because] they are protected by their beloved cannon law (*ius canonum*), which can be countered only with still stronger arguments. The less powerful, who find themselves unable to assert their rights with the sword . . ., can maintain these . . . only by gentler means and reasons, and for this a thorough knowledge of the constitution is indispensable. . . ."[54] Behind these comments lurked at least a hint of concern that overzealous reformers might be tempted by the intensity of their convictions and in the name of a higher cause into violations of the imperial constitution—the only shield of the weak against the mighty. In this worry may be seen the basis for at least a secret reservation against the cause of reform, even among those who favored it in the abstract.

As things turned out, no one needed to worry very much. Carl August, to be sure, continued throughout much of 1788 to receive encouraging letters about the future possibilities of the League from many quarters, including not only the eternally and naïvely optimistic Dalberg, but also from the Prussian court through the diplomat Stein and even the powerful Count Hertzberg himself. But the actual decision on the future of the League as an instrument for imperial reform had been reached early in 1788 by the two most important associated courts. In late January, the Prussian Privy Cabinet Ministry informed Frederick William II of its reservations about Carl August's proposals which, in their advocacy of reform, seemed to go beyond the real purpose of the League, which was simply the preservation of the old constitution. It advised not only against a formal congress of the League, but even against a circular letter as a means of communication among the members. With Frederick William's immediate adoption of this position, it became the official, if still secret, policy of the Prussian court.[55] By mid-April, the Electoral Saxon court had decided on much the same position, indicating its preference for using either the representatives at the Imperial Diet or simple bilateral correspondence of particular courts as the means of exchanging views within the League, and at the same time defining the goals of the League very narrowly within the framework of a purely defensive orientation.[56]

The growing pessimism about the possibilities of imperial reform through the League which characterized the attitudes of many of its once-hopeful supporters throughout 1788 was not the result of any official knowledge of these views, which were kept from them, but of the increasingly obvious intentional inactivity of the League's chief members. No one expressed the prevailing disappointment better than Johannes von Müller, whose reputation as one of the most vigorous and articulate early advocates of the League lent a special weight to his views. At the conclusion of his original defense of the League, Müller had hinted that a patriotic association of German princes, such as the League was, might be the mechanism by which the inertia and hesitation that prevented the improvement of the imperial constitution could be overcome. He did not develop any detailed proposals, saying that he did not wish to cloud the stated purpose of the League with others at that time; but he specifically admonished the League not to forget that if it was truly to serve the national well-being, it would do so not by reason of its existence but by virtue of its activity.[57]

It was precisely the lack of such activity which moved Müller in 1788 to publish a short but bitter indictment of the League designed to stir it to a new life and purpose. In contrast to his earlier work, which had taken as its main theme the Bavarian exchange and the general problems of the balance of power associated with it, Müller now asserted that if the League had no purpose other than that of maintaining the present status quo of territorial possessions in order to insure that Bavaria would have the good fortune someday to receive the Duke of Zweibrücken rather than Joseph II as its ruler, then it was really the most uninteresting political machination the Empire had witnessed in recent years. In other respects, too, the status quo which the League supposedly defended was hardly a laudable one, characterized as it was by insecurity of laws, justice, and rights, and by a notable lack of cohesion and national spirit.[58]

Müller admitted that he did not know the specific terms of the treaty which established the League, but believed that its original purposes should not in any case prevent it from becoming a positive force for good. While his own proposals remained fairly general, he, like Carl August, clearly thought that the essence of a strong imperial system lay in better laws, a more efficient judicial system, and a more vigorous and effective execution of laws and judgments. "Our Empire," he complained, 'is an ill-cohering, clumsy mass, where the strong do what they will, and the others not what they should; [whereas] we should have a well- and firmly organized state (Staatskörper), capable of its own self-defense."[59] To counter fears of where reform might lead, Müller tried to show that real improvements could be made in the Empire without in any way prejudicing the position of the individual princes themselves, whose thrones would always be safe if only because of the odiousness of anarchy to the German spirit. He ended his writing with the plea that "Something must [be done] for the Empire; the nation must be helped"; and he added a denunciation of the League for its inactivity: "We believed that there might be a tendency for something noble in the union. It almost seems we were wrong."[60]

Not all public opinion agreed with Müller, whose widely circulated call for the League to enter the lists of reform may actually have helped to stimulate the publication of several tracts whose authors wanted to hear nothing of a special association tampering with the imperial constitution. In one of these, the supposed "imperial patriotism" of the League was denounced as a mask for other, selfish intentions of its members, behind whose actions lurked nothing but an unjustified fear of the growth of Austrian power. The Emperor, for the safety of the Empire, ought to have the necessary power to defend it, and attempts to reduce his power below this level constituted not a defense of the constitution but its overthrow. In any case, this writer averred, the Empire already had enough power to preserve itself, "and the association of all members for common defense, for mutual protection, and maintenance of the whole body, is already so firmly joined in the constitution and in the laws themselves, that no new brotherhood of patriots, league, [or] sham association is needed." He emphasized the Electoral Capitulation as a permanent and sufficient instrument for the protection of the rights and freedoms of both Emperor and Estates, and contented himself with the suggestion that it be frozen in its present form.[61]

A similar suspicion about the real purposes of the League emerged in 1789 in a long and thoughtful article in the *Staatswissenschaftliche Zeitung,* whose author tried to show that preservation of the status quo and preservation of the genuine imperial constitution were two very different things. If the League aimed at the former, it was bad, because whereas the constitution was supposed to provide for a true balance between monarchical and republican elements, time had tipped that balance considerably in favor of the republican, that is, the princes; to defend the status quo was therefore actually to defend a deviation from the real constitution. Not opposed to the idea of imperial reform as such, this writer nevertheless believed that the true constitution was a good one, and that its fundamentals ought not to be disturbed, and he specifically rejected the notion that either the Electors (by means of a future Electoral Capitulation) or the League ought to be the instrument of reform. The latter was an irregular association, with no legal status in the Empire, while the former had already arrogated to themselves, through the Capitulations, the power not only to make new laws but to interpret old ones. This power, however, properly belonged to the whole Empire, and should be returned to it. The Imperial Diet, as the constitutionally recognized legislative body of the Empire, should be entrusted with the task of drawing up not only a permanent Capitulation, but also a durable code of constitutional law (*Staatsgesetzbuch*) which would eliminate the ambiguity of earlier laws that had encouraged self-serving and divisive interpretations by different forces within the Empire.[62]

The proposed revitalization of the Diet was supported in numerous other writings, and represented a very conservative response to the dilemma posed by the recognition of the need for reform and the unwillingness to permit any single interest group to capture a reform movement for its own selfish advantage. The problem, of course, was how to see to it that the Diet could function as the active and effective legislative body it had not been for generations. One writer who had supported the League on the basis of what he had taken to be its real purpose of reactivating the Diet and facilitating its transaction of important business expressed a common conviction that no basic improvement could be expected unless the Diet returned to the practice of resolving issues through genuine floor debate rather than by votes of majorities which had been concocted in secret in advance of the introduction of issues to the floor.[63] It was suggested elsewhere that since the Electoral Capitulation required the Emperor to call a Diet at least once every ten years, it might be better if he did just that, rather than to confirm the present "living dead" Diet in the permanent session which had been its debilitating fate since 1663. Such a change might, among other things, encourage the princes to attend the sessions in person rather than through their delegates, which would in turn be likely to focus attention on issues of considerably greater importance than the minutiae which now crowded the agenda of the Diet.[64] With such weak and backward-looking suggestions as these, the debate over the League of Princes ended in the same atmosphere of unreality and futility that had enveloped the association itself.

CHAPTER SEVEN

The Imperial Office
and the Election of 1790

GRADUALLY, THE DISCUSSIONS surrounding the League of Princes had broadened from an originally rather narrow focus on the pros and cons of the Bavarian exchange scheme to include a constantly wider set of issues concerned with the nature of the Empire and its constitution, and the proper means of reforming both. But regardless of the general and specific differences of opinion that emerged among commentators and polemicists, the terms of their argumentation remained on at least one piece of common ground: The goal to be sought was the preservation of the general imperial system, however variously conceived. No matter how high passions for or against Austria or Prussia may have run, the possibility of a radical solution to the political problems of Germany through partition or secession found virtually no support. One reason for this, no doubt, is that both Austria and Prussia, but especially the latter, chose for their own good reasons to fight out their dynastic quarrel in this instance as Estates of the Empire rather than as European great powers. To do so meant binding themselves to terms acceptable to the allies each had to find within the Empire; and those terms clearly predicated the preservation of an imperial structure.[1] It meant, too, that even the most avid partisans of a purely dynastic policy on the part of either state would be unlikely to risk damaging its policies by open advocacy of any proposals which went against the goals to which it had publicly committed itself.

In reviewing the literature of the period it is a surprise therefore to find a lengthy and persuasively presented argument for what amounted to the abolition of the imperial bond altogether. Published anonymously in 1787, it bore the simple title: *Why Should Germany Have an Emperor?* Its authorship is still uncertain.[2] Obviously a devotee of the Enlightenment and a radical opponent of Catholicism, this author tended to see in the imperial nexus simply a remnant of the religious and political barbarism of a time long past, whose despotic and obscurantist influence had happily been broken in some territories of Germany by the Protestant Reformation. Professing to find absolutely no utility in the imperial constitution with respect to the political, military, moral, cultural, or economic affairs of Germany, he asserted that the greatest degree of enlightenment in his own time was to be found in those states where the *nexus imperii* was felt least; this was in Protestant states, where enlightenment was indeed growing in direct proportion to their effective independence from the imperial system. He dismissed most of the major institutions of the Empire—the Emperor, the imperial courts, the Diet, and so on—as either useless or harmful, and insisted that the only good ones were those which, like the *corpus evangelicorum,* in tending to neutralize the others kept them from doing the harm of which they were capable. In reality, he averred, the only reason why the imperial system had survived so long was precisely that its various organs were virtually without power to exert influence on the territories; had they in fact been able to do so, then that half of the Empire which consisted of relatively powerful states would long since have declared full independence, and the other half would have fallen under the domination of the Emperor. The very weakness of the Empire therefore accounted for its continued existence.[3]

It should be obvious, in spite of the title of the work, that what was at issue here was not just the question of whether Germany needed an Emperor. Even without one, the author fully admitted, it would be possible to have an imperial bond of some sort; indeed, given the worthlessness of the imperial dignity, this was virtually what Germany had now. But was there any point in any kind of association at all? Not really, said he. The whole notion of a federation (*Verbund*) of independent states presupposed a common interest more important than the private interests of every particular state. Since the only common interest of the German states was to preserve the Empire in order to protect their sovereignty and independence from the Emperor, that is, to use the constitution to get rid of the constitution, then the abolition of the latter would remove all future purpose of federation. But what about the protection supposedly afforded by the imperial bond to the smaller states? Here, the author, having already disposed of the Emperor's role, examined the Imperial Cameral Tribunal and the Diet and concluded that both were not only subject to procedural delays which crippled their effectiveness in all respects, but were also so profoundly subordinated to political considerations which had nothing to do with justice (or even law) that neither body could realistically be said even now to provide any protection for the small territories. This being the case, he was not inclined to worry much about the lesser states, assuming that whatever protected them now would continue to do so; and he even hinted that their full independence, in removing the expenses and harmful effects of their imperial ties, might result in better government. In any case, his overall conclusion was clear: The German states, happy now to the extent that they were ruled independently of the Emperor, would be happier still if the imperial bond were dissolved completely and if every ruler could govern freely without having to concern himself about his neighbors any more than political necessity might dictate.[4]

Of the various indignant responses to which the publication of this sensational and even horrifying point of view gave rise, one in particular stands out both for its content and because of the wide circulation it achieved. This was the work of the Imperial Knight, later Count, Julius von Soden, published anonymously in 1788 under the title: *Germany Must Have an Emperor*. Soden, at this time an official of the Margraviate of Ansbach and the Brandenburg ambassador to the Franconian Circle, made an important distinction at the beginning of his book in saying that he proposed to write as a German citizen (*Bürger*) rather than as one with allegiance to a particular state, since questions pertaining to the welfare of the whole Empire could properly be addressed only by one who felt himself to belong to the whole.[5] The significance of this distinction becomes clear in his subsequent division of the states of the Empire into three classes. The first consisted of those states which by virtue of their foreign possessions had in reality separated their German territories from the Empire by weaving them into a system of full sovereignty, and which had too much strength for the power of the Emperor to be effective against them. Prussia (Brandenburg) and Great Britain (Hanover) were mentioned as the only examples of this group of states. The second class consisted of medium-sized territories, powerful enough to restrict the effectiveness of the Emperor's power but not to cripple it altogether. The third group comprised all the smaller princes and Imperial Counts, Knights, and Cities, which were more or less fully subject to the Emperor. The utility of the imperial bond in preventing internal wars and providing remedy against violations of personal and property rights, according to Soden, while less apparent for states of the first class, was indispensable for those of the second and third classes, which therefore had a common German national interest not shared by the first.[6] Whoever regarded the Empire as a German could appreciate its benefits, Soden therefore suggested, while those (including his opponent, presumably) whose "foreign" states derived little or no advantage from it could not.

Soden's separation of the interests of the greatest states, above all, Prussia, from those of the rest of Germany, rested upon the criterion of power. The large states were powerful enough to defend their own rights, but the remainder were not. The Empire was a necessity to the latter precisely because, under the supervision of the Emperor as the supreme judge, it substituted a system of justice for a system of power. Without that justice, all territories of the Empire would be forced to flee for protection to one or another of the "great parties" of Germany, which could result in their subjection. That, in turn, could remove one of the great advantages of the present situation of Germany—its enormous diversity of states and rulers, whose peaceful competition was responsible for assuring greater freedom and for increasing enlightenment by various means, including the encouragement of large numbers of institutions of higher learning. Suggesting that true well-being lay in such things as these, Soden pointed out that the ranking of states by the criterion of happiness was frequently the reverse of the ranking by power, simply because the demands of power consumed energies and resources which could otherwise be applied to more humane pursuits. In thus linking a higher level of human happiness with an Empire implicitly defined as a system of justice, Soden answered strongly in the negative the great question raised by the proposals of his anonymous opponent, that is, whether the welfare of the nation as a whole would be increased or more widely diffused if it lost its Supreme Head and Judge.[7]

Soden also dismissed as a "phantom" the supposedly oppressive effects which the author of *Why Should Germany Have an Emperor?* ascribed to the imperial constitution and its agencies. He took the view that the powers and privileges of the Emperor were by no means entirely chimerical, and as restrictions on the sovereignty of territorial rulers they were capable of limiting only their power to do harm, not good; indeed, he challenged anyone to show any way in which even the greatest German states had been kept from increasing their own enlightenment and welfare by the existence of the imperial office. In defending the other two major institutional supports of the Empire, the Imperial Cameral Tribunal and the Diet, Soden took an unusual approach. Admitting that both were slow and cumbersome, and characterized by deficiencies of which only some were susceptible to correction without doing violence to the underlying intent of the whole constitution, he defended the value of both less in terms of their actions than in terms of the effects the fact of their existence had on the consciousness of the nation. The feeling and knowledge of the availability of an imperial judicial remedy not only gave the subject courage against the possible oppression and despotism of his ruler, but also acted as a rein on the ruler himself; while the Diet, as an assembly of the representatives of the whole nation, kept alive the idea of the German imperial system as a constitutional one, and therefore was "a shield of German freedom."[8] In this approach, the reliance on power and its ability to coerce obedience once again gives way to a system of justice, now conceived as a mental construct, a fixed state of mind, which compels obedience mystically and by inveteracy rather than by the utilization of force.

One of the most interesting aspects of Soden's work is that although he was a fierce defender of the Empire, he all but admitted that some states —the largest—no longer needed it. His argument that even Prussia and Great Britain received some guarantee and protection for their German possessions from the imperial nexus was almost an afterthought and must have sounded unconvincing even to himself.[9] But if these very few states did not need the Empire, all the others did; and while the bonds of the Empire were unessential to the former, they also could not hurt them, whereas the abolition of the constitution would bring disaster to the latter. His writing was therefore a plea for a differential understanding of the continuing efficacy of an Empire which no longer had a single unified interest. It was significant, too, that Soden's case for the integrity of the Empire rested so strongly not just on a moral idea, but one which had to be accepted by all, or nearly all, if it was to work at all; this amounted to a tacit recognition of the extreme fragility of an imperial structure that could not call upon power for its own defense.

As it happened, an opportunity to continue the lively debate over imperial issues to which the position of the Emperor was central, as in the two works previously discussed, came sooner than anyone had reason to expect. Emperor Joseph II died on February 20, 1790, in his forty-eighth year, inaugurating an interregnum which was not ended until late September of the same year when Joseph's younger brother was elected to the imperial dignity as Leopold II. This period of just over seven months was one of considerable ferment in Germany, and was characterized by much uncertainty and many rumors about the immediate future of the Empire. Not since 1745 had an interregnum occurred, because Joseph II had automatically stepped up to the imperial title from the position of Roman King he already occupied at the death of his father, Francis I, in 1765.

Much had happened in the Empire since 1745, including most recently the formation of the League of Princes, whose membership included four of the eight Imperial Electors. With the chance that just one more Elector —possibly Karl Theodor of Palatinate-Bavaria—could be won over to its side, the League might hope to control the coming election and place a non-Habsburg on the throne for only the second time in four and a half centuries. While this did not in fact happen, and Leopold won election easily and unanimously, a number of projects for a transformation of the Empire in the direction of emasculating the imperial office still further had been discussed by some members of the League in the few months following Joseph's death. One of these involved keeping the Imperial Diet in session during the interregnum, under the supervision of the so-called Im-

perial Vicars (Palatinate-Bavaria and Saxony), in order to control its
deliberations and prevent the Empire from interfering in a military strike
against Austria that Prussia was weighing in consequence of recent Habsburg foreign policy.[10] Another, toyed with only briefly, was the replace-
ment of the Habsburgs by the Palatinate-Bavarian Elector.[11] The only
scheme that came close to realization, however, was the plan to impose on
Leopold a new Electoral Capitulation, whose terms would truly have reduced the Emperor's powers to nothing and given nearly full sovereignty
to the princes. Only four of the eight Electors (Brandenburg, Hanover,
Saxony, and Mainz) could be brought to agree to such drastic terms, however, so that the Capitulation finally agreed upon by a majority, and subsequently accepted by Leopold, while still unfavorable to the Emperor's
interest, was much less severe than the original proposals. In all these cases,
representing the last attempt of the League to assume a decisive role in the
fundamental processes of the Empire, the disagreements and mutual suspicions between the members, which had begun to surface almost before
the ink on the treaty of association had dried, and which had deepened
in the meantime, prevented a cooperation adequate to produce any important result. While the crisis of this election year therefore passed without
bringing the real changes that some had hoped for and others had feared,
it too left a residue of published opinions concerning the contemporary
evaluation of the Empire.

Since the only ruling house outside of Austria that was rumored to
have both interest in and a chance at the imperial throne in 1790 was that
of Palatinate-Bavaria, it is not unnatural that the only major polemic of
that year that went beyond mere barking at the Habsburgs and actually
tried to rally support for someone else was written by an anonymous partisan of the Wittelsbach Karl Theodor. The entire argument of this author
was built on the double premise that Germany must have an Emperor,
but that it should not have a strong Emperor. The constitution of the
Empire, said he, simply did not seem to harmonize with a powerful Emperor; and he laid out in specific terms the same notion of a moral idea as
the only real cement of the Empire which had appeared more obscurely
in Soden's writing: "the stability and strength of the imperial system [and]
the preservation of the constitution rests not on a physical power, but
simply on the bond between head and members, on the mutual [and]
exact observance of the laws."[12] Insisting that the laws were "the only
protection" and "the general guarantee" of the rights of all, he went on to
demonstrate that because the system of law and justice in the Empire had
become so firmly institutionalized over time, a powerful Emperor had
become essentially superfluous to its operation. Since respect for the law
had long since become a habit among the princes, and since the imperial
courts and the Prince-Convenors of the Circles were entirely adequate as

the machinery for settling such quarrels as might arise, there was no longer much of a function for the Emperor in matters of internal security.[13] As far as external security was concerned, the Empire could defend itself by means of the Circles and such constitutional associations as the League of Princes. As long as the power and the wars of its Emperors did not provoke attacks from the outside, the Empire really had nothing to fear anyway, since the European balance to which Germany was so important made it a matter of concern to all great powers that the Empire be preserved.[14]

While the above arguments were supposed to prove that a mighty Emperor was unnecessary, the author hastened to assure his readers that the imperial office itself was quite necessary—that, indeed, a Germany without an Emperor would be in far worse shape than with a powerful and despotic one. In the latter case illegal designs could at least be opposed by the powerful Estates, while in the former the lesser states would find no help at all against the territorial ambitions of their larger neighbors. The solution to the problem lay in the election of an Emperor from the ruling house of a medium-sized territory which, furthermore, should have no possessions outside the Empire. The lengthy argument supporting this position boiled down to the view that a powerful Emperor with interests outside the Empire was likely not only to be distracted by those interests from fulfilling his obligations to the Empire, but also to be led by them into foreign entanglements in which he would quite naturally attempt to enlist the aid of the Empire, whose real interest, however, lay in not becoming involved. With such an Emperor, one could never be sure that his influence on the government of the Empire, the Aulic Council, and so on, was motivated by a general concern for the welfare of the Empire or a particular concern for the good of his house alone. A less powerful Emperor, on the other hand, whose lands were confined to the Empire, would not only be free of foreign temptation, but would also recognize that his election to the imperial office rested not on the claims of superior dynastic power but on the expectation of service to the Empire. This Emperor would be obliged to cleave closely to the Estates, since it was only their power that gave him his, and would not be tempted to violate imperial law, since that law was his entire entitlement to office.[15]

Apart from its advocacy of the House of Palatinate-Bavaria for the imperial throne—which was not specifically revealed to the reader until near the end of the work, after all the foregoing groundwork had been laid—one of the most interesting features of this book was its unusually strong emphasis on the need for a *German* emperorship, the persistent implication being, of course, that the previous Habsburg occupants of the throne were "foreign" by virtue of their accrued interests if not their roots. The author spoke of the advantages of a new regime in which "only honest German men" would surround the throne; wherein the actions of the Emperor would stem "not from foreign, but only German-patriotic sources"; where no foreign political or governmental principles would be grafted onto the constitution of the German Empire; and where, finally, Germany would receive "a genuinely German imperial government, constituted solely according to the constitution and the fundamental laws of the Empire." Not to be overlooked, too, were the advantages of an imperial throne located "not at the farthest removed and outermost frontiers of the German Empire, but in the heart of the state," where the smaller princes that were most needful of the Emperor's protection would be closest to him, and where "the protector and father of the Germans reigns in the bosom of the Fatherland."[16]

From the standpoint of its ultimate political purpose of course, this book might as well not have been written, since there was never a really serious possibility that Karl Theodor would be given the imperial crown. On the other hand, the Habsburg succession could no longer be regarded as automatic, either; the loss of the crown to the Bavarian Charles VII in 1742, as well as the Austro-Prussian antagonism, the genuine fears created by the policies of Joseph II, and the establishment of the League of Princes —all indicated that a transfer of the imperial crown to some other house was at least a possibility in 1790.

In a treatise written shortly after the election of Leopold II as an explanation of why a Habsburg had once again received the crown, the Prussian legation-secretary Johann Traugott Plant, following some of the same lines laid down in the previous work, made out a reasonable case for both Palatinate-Bavaria and Saxony as imperial houses. Recognizing that Germany needed a strong Emperor not only to give the necessary order to the complicated internal operations of the Empire, but also to defend the smaller states, especially in southern and western Germany, against their greedy neighbors both domestic and foreign, he yet insisted that the office did not require a hugely rich or mighty prince. He called on the guarantees of the constitutional structure itself, as well as the interest of foreign powers in the preservation of the Empire, to prove that neither the expenses nor the military might of the imperial office had to be very great, and concluded from this that Austria was not the only ruling house that might qualify for the imperial dignity. Saxony was large, rich, and powerful enough for it, and since the Elector was himself Catholic but at the same time the Director of the *corpus evangelicorum,* his elevation to the emperorship could lead to better relations between Catholics and Protestants in the Empire. Dresden, the capital of Saxony, also recommended itself as the capital of the Empire because of its beauty and its central location. The case for Palatinate-Bavaria was weaker, since its debts were greater and its internal organization not as good as Saxony's; but even Munich would be better than Vienna as a capital.[17]

For all these considerations, however, Plant regarded the election of Leopold II as both appropriate and natural. The long tradition of Habsburg rulership had conferred a familiarity and experience with the imperial office which lent a high degree of efficiency to the conduct of imperial affairs, while the manifold connections of the Habsburgs to other European states through marriage and diplomacy provided a degree of protection for the Empire from many sides. The personal characteristics and abilities of Leopold himself were a factor in his election, Plant surmised, but so was the lack of an alternative candidate who could give reason to suppose he might be any better for Germany. In spite of the dynastic ambitions of earlier Habsburg Emperors which had led them into actions contrary to the interests of the Empire, there were no important political reasons against the choice of an Austrian, especially since his powers were closely restricted by the Electoral Capitulation. There were, however, good political reasons not to deny the crown to the Habsburgs, among which Plant cited the by now almost familiar argument that an Austria angered by exclusion from the imperial throne might actually make an alliance with the Turks to attack Germany, or at the very least withdraw her German lands from the Empire, an action which could encourage other rulers to do the same, resulting in the dissolution of the entire imperial system.[18]

Dire prognostications such as these were important not because they were common or widely believed, for which there is no evidence, but because they do reflect the sense of deep concern about the future of the imperial crown that pervaded the interregnum. The anonymous booster of the Palatinate-Bavarian candidacy had concluded his presentation with the assertion that Leopold would find the union of the imperial crown with his own dynastic crown a burden, and that he really did not want to be Emperor at all.[19] This judgment was not founded on any specific knowledge of Leopold's personal intentions, of course, but there were some strong circumstantial reasons for believing that Austrian interest in the crown might be at an all-time low. It was fairly common knowledge that many advisors at the Austrian court had long since revised downwards their evaluation of the dynastic benefits to be had from the imperial crown, and Vienna's apparently declining interest in the office had recently been emphasized in the not altogether unfounded rumors that Joseph II had been prepared to divest himself of the imperial dignity if that would help to effectuate the Bavarian exchange. Added to this was the fact that Austria had been involved in a constantly more serious complex of foreign and domestic crises in Joseph's last years, which by the time of his death presented a picture of such confusion and desperation as to cause anyone to wonder whether the new head of the dynasty would be willing to accept the added responsibilities of the emperorship.

This concern came to the fore in a number of ways, virtually all of which stemmed from the general conviction that Austria must continue to occupy the imperial throne. Persuading the Habsburgs themselves to want the crown was apparently the motivation of one writer who, after insisting that Germany's political economy made a guardianship by a strong Emperor an absolute necessity, went on to praise the German nation and its numerous contributions throughout history in order to prove that Germany was worthy of Austria, and that the effort and expense of acquiring the imperial crown were justified.[20] J. T. Plant, too, had tried in a very long and detailed commentary to show that the crown still carried many tangible benefits for the Emperor, and how many advantages the House of Habsburg in particular had derived from it throughout its history.[21]

A very different tack was taken by another publicist, an obviously confirmed partisan of Austria, who seems to have regarded it as his task to persuade the Electors and the rest of the Empire that it was entirely safe to elect a Habsburg, since the real assets of the imperial office were so small that election to it would add little to the dynastic power of whoever held it. He complained that the long lists of the Emperor's powers drawn up by publicists and teachers of public law who had no practical knowledge of imperial operations were misleading, and that even those experts who knew better, insofar as they belonged to "the system of the counter-party," had an interest in exaggerating the Emperor's power "in order thereby to maintain the self-consciousness, mistrust, and jealousy of the Estates against the imperial court." Yet even he admitted that the crown could confer considerable influence in the Empire, if one behaved with moderation and circumspection, and concluded that it was a desirable prize for any German state "which requires no greater power [i.e., than it already had] for its own preservation in the European balance." He made much of the prestige of the imperial crown as the foremost in Europe, but also believed that it was only the reputation of the House of Austria which had given it that prestige, and that no other German house would be likely to maintain it.[22]

Apart from the quite general agreement that the imperial crown should remain with Austria, there was also a widespread conviction that the powers of the Emperor should not be limited any more than was already the case, and even that they should be increased. This conviction was typically expressed in the form of criticism of the Electoral Capitulation, which was held to be not only excessively restrictive to the point of making impossible the discharge of the legitimate duties of the Emperor, but also in itself unclear, equivocal, and self-contradictory in many of its articles.[23] Insofar as the problem presented by the Electoral Capitulation was perceived as relating exclusively to its own inherent deficiencies, or to its restrictions on the Emperor's power, the obvious solution was simply to rewrite it—perhaps, as one author suggested, as a truly permanent document whose provisions could neither be expanded nor reduced in the future.[24]

The position taken by Karl Friedrich von Kruse, however, hints strongly that a larger constitutional issue was involved in the attack on the Capitulation. Kruse, a widely-known and greatly respected senior official of the Principality of Nassau-Usingen,[25] attacked both the form and content of the Capitulation, which in its present form he regarded as simply unsuitable to be law in the Empire at all. More fundamentally, however, he found the very method of making law by means of Electoral Capitulations inappropriate. Through such a piecemeal, heterogeneous, and almost whimsical legislative procedure, "there must in the end appear a monstrous political structure (*Staatsgebäude*) which, because everything has been pushed out of joint, must finally collapse from the pressure of its own shapeless mass."[26] This statement must be linked to Kruse's uneasiness about the recent increase of "unions, cabinet cabals, private negotiations, and associations of particular German courts in matters which, according to the prescription of the laws, pertain to the whole Empire," and to his numerous and severely critical comments about the selfishness, excessive self-esteem, and lack of common spirit of the larger Estates. Taken together, all of these suggest that his real dissatisfaction with the Electoral Capitulation stemmed from his unwillingness to concede to the Electors what amounted to a special right of legislation for the whole Empire that was not only self-serving, but also simply did not belong to them by his understanding of the constitution.[27] This impression is strengthened by the general solution he offered: a new, general, and all-encompassing constitution (*Reichsgrundgesetz*) which would be drawn up by the whole Empire, and would spell out the rights, duties, and obligations of Emperor, Electors, princes, and all other Estates, as well as provide for the improvement of all institutions and practices contained in or relating to the constitution.[28]

The conviction that what was at stake in the interregnum was nothing less than the preservation of the historic constitution of the Empire emerged even more clearly and specifically in a thoughtful anonymous publication of 1789, whose author was much disturbed by rumors that a serious intention existed of continuing the sessions of the Diet under the Imperial Vicars, whose position would permit them to exercise the same power of assent to laws possessed by a reigning Emperor. Since the Vicars were themselves Electors and Estates, since they were in no mood to protect the position of the Emperor in the constitutional system, and since they were likely to be assisted in the Diet by a small group of powerful Estates which could control that body through their own client system, it was entirely possible that laws could be passed without the agreement or participation of an Emperor, which would alter the traditional balance between Emperor and Estates fundamentally and irretrievably in favor of the latter. That, however, would amount to the destruction of the constitution, and to prevent it this writer suggested that any deliberations of the Diet during an interregnum ought to be regarded as illegal.[29] The basic problem, as this author saw it, was that while the Peace of Westphalia had indeed created a truly and beneficially balanced constitution, half-monarchical and half-aristocratic, the monarchical half was constitutionally more susceptible to infringements by the aristocratic than the reverse. The Electoral Capitulation was the prime example of the legal means available to at least some of the Estates for this purpose, because it allowed the Electors virtually to prescribe laws by themselves. While he saw this as a clear contradiction of the principle that legislative power in the Empire should properly belong only to Emperor and Estates together, he did not dispute the legality of Capitulations, but instead pleaded that the powers of the Emperor not be reduced in them. At the same time, he suggested that laws never be passed without the participation of the Emperor, a proposal which could be realized by always providing a successor to the throne during the lifetime of a reigning Emperor through the election of a Roman King.[30]

The last two works discussed above are excellent examples of the mature and sober reflection on the problems of the Empire that had been produced by both the adventurism of Joseph II and the chief response to it, the League of Princes. It has already been shown that the League was regarded in some quarters with serious reservations even among those whose views would indicate that they were neither confirmed friends of Austria nor committed foes of Prussia, and that those reservations were based primarily upon a concern that the leadership of the Empire might simply be migrating from the hands of an extremely ambitious Emperor with strong dynastic interests into the hands of a few of the largest states of the Empire (especially Prussia), which also had their own dynastic axes to grind.[31] Rejecting with equal conviction the prospect of an Austrian and an Electoral dictatorship, they entrenched themselves behind the ancient formulas of unity—*Kaiser und Reich, Haupt und Glieder,* and so on—as the means of reaffirming the undoubted right of all Estates of the Empire to participate according to its constitution in shaping the destiny of that body.

The old and familiar fear of encroachment on the rights and freedoms of the Estates by the Emperor was still very real at the time the League of Princes was founded, and the popularity of the latter was unquestionably greatest at that very moment. As rumors of the possible adoption of a reformist role by the League began to circulate, however, and as Austria's internal and external problems increased, concern mounted that the Empire might be delivered over to a small clique of large secular states whose ambitions were no more compatible with the interests of the other Estates than were those of the Austrian *imperium*. In the midst of this uneasiness, Joseph II died, and it appeared that the League's time might finally and truly have come. Its opportunity for mischief, as seen by those who did not wholly trust it to begin with, had suddenly increased many fold, since there was no longer an Emperor to set bounds to it; worse yet, its Electoral members probably had it in their power, chiefly through the Electoral Capitulation, to reduce the imperial office to the point where an Emperor would never again be able legally and by virtue of the powers of the office alone to intervene against whatever selfish and destructive imperial policy the largest secular courts might agree upon among themselves.[32]

What resulted, around 1790, in the works of Kruse and others, was an unmistakable reaction in favor of the preservation of the powers of the imperial crown, together with a repeated insistence on the principle that the maintenance of the constitution was the business of the whole Empire, not of any single group of self-appointed reformers. Reform, to be sure, was almost universally solicited except, perhaps, by the hardest-headed ministers of the Austrian and Prussian monarchies, and even they would not admit their opposition in public. Reform, however, actually meant almost exclusively restoration, the reestablishment of a condition of unity and cooperation between Emperor and all Estates which was assumed (in part fancifully) to have existed at one time, but which was now rapidly and visibly dissolving in the face of a myriad of conflicting interests. Kruse, like many others, expressed a certain amazement that the imperial constitution continued to exist at all, and was forced to conclude that in the absence of the intrinsic clarity and wisdom of its laws, only a "true love of fatherland" among all members of the Empire could account for its survival.[33] He too, admitted that as things then stood, it was not the laws themselves, nor yet the constraints and restraints of effective power that held the Empire together, but only the moral bond of patriotism.

The tragedy is that the genuine reformers like Kruse also could rely on nothing besides the dubious force of a moral idea to get reform started. Some, indeed, had recognized that no reform was likely unless the moral idea could be harnessed to political power actually in being; but when they tried, as Carl August, the ever-hopeful Dalberg, and some other smaller princes did, to hitch their ideas to the vehicle of power, they discovered to their chagrin and frustration not only that real power had no need for imperial reform, but that they had become trapped inside the vehicle they had sought to use. With these considerations in mind, Dalberg's pious wish that the League might someday become an association of the whole Empire, embracing even the Emperor himself, sounds a bit less stupid. It at least had the advantage of recognizing that if a reform movement was ever to be successful, it would have to find a way to escape the pernicious pressures of the Austro-Prussian dualism, while at the same time maintaining access to sources of real political power. One possible solution was to expand the League's membership so greatly by the addition of members with a true concern for the improvement of the imperial system that their demands would gradually displace or neu-tralize the special and particularistic Prussian interests which had domi-nated the origins of the League. Prussia, eventually faced with the choice of accepting a redefinition of the goals of the League or of opposing it, thereby revealing the naked self-interest of her policy and isolating her-self from the rest of the Empire, would be forced to commit herself to a reform program whose main features were determined by her allies. With such a massive "patriotic" coalition in force, it would then be Austria's turn to face the choice of subscription or isolation—a choice which could result in but one decision.

It is doubtful that the somewhat superficial mind of the Coadjutor Bishop ever worked out implications such as these from his own position, the purely political naivete of which would not have been any the less even had he done so. Prussian statesmen knew quite well how to prevent any such scenario from developing, and in the event were never in the slightest danger of allowing the League to escape the narrow purposes they had set for it. By 1790, the friends of the old imperial idea had essen-tially only two practical choices, neither of which was very palatable. One was to accept a reform of the Empire along the lines which were rumored to be the basis for the policy of the League's Electoral members during the interregnum, namely, a drastic reduction of the Emperor's powers, with a corresponding increase in the territorial sovereignty of the princes —a policy whose results could at best hardly benefit the smaller states, but at worst could lead to territorial violations and even absorption of smaller territories by the large. The other choice was to admit that the theoretical unity of the Empire was a fiction, at least for the moment, and that the repugnantly innovative principle of a German territorial balance of power was in fact the only present means of preserving a status quo which, for all of its faults, was better than any realistically foreseeable alternative. In the situation of 1790, this meant standing up for the one of the two poles of power in Germany that appeared the weaker—Austria; and the means of doing so was to argue for the continuing importance of the Emperor in the constitutional structure, and against all attempts to reduce his already minimal powers any further.

Thus, on the eve of the massive political and military challenges which were to end with the destruction of the imperial constitution, the Empire presented to the world the picture of a house divided against itself, whose formal unity depended almost entirely upon the realities of a balance of power in which the condition of survival was immobility, a virtual paralysis of imperial political life. The ideal of a real unity of head and members was far from dead; indeed, it was to remain a very powerful current of public opinion until the end of the Empire in 1806. But there were limits to the ability of an ideal, by itself, to move events. The old issue of power remained intractable, and was inescapable for even the most patriotic and high-minded of rulers. One of these was Max Franz of Austria, the last Elector of Cologne, whose Habsburg blood in no way diminished his character as a genuine German patriot and guardian of the imperial constitution, even if this was not commonly recognized at the time. During the interregnum following the death of his brother Joseph II, Max Franz was himself proposed as the next Emperor in a short writing entitled *The Union of the Imperial Scepter with the Crozier: A Political Fantasy*. Published anonymously in Regensburg, this work apparently caused some sensation with its suggestion that because of their rivalry neither Austria nor Prussia should receive the imperial crown, and that indeed no secular principality at all should have it, since the temporal princes were too engrossed in their own territorial ambitions to care much about the Empire.[34] The idea of electing an ecclesiastical prince to the imperial office was an interesting and novel one, but as its own author acknowledged, it was indeed a political fantasy. Max Franz would certainly have been the first to recognize this, for nowhere more than in the ecclesiastical states was there a greater awareness of the tenuousness of political claims based solely on the power of ideas. Max Franz demonstrated this in a letter of this period: "We German princes," he wrote, "have only laws, treaties [and] formal and solemn promises to set against the power which disregards all of this; only morality can save us."[35] This comment, intended as a judgment on the present condition of the Empire, turned out to be prophetic of its future as well.

Part III

THE CHALLENGE
FROM ABROAD, 1790–97

CHAPTER EIGHT

Before the Storm: Contemporary
Reflections on the Imperial System

T HE LIVELY DEBATE over the imperial constitution that had been generated by the almost permanent sense of crisis within the Empire since the War of the Bavarian Succession continued into the 1790s, but was given a new focus which reflected both a lessening of concern for some old issues and an increasing concern over new ones. In particular, the intense preoccupation with specific constitutional and political problems arising out of the various facets of the Austro-Prussian dualism almost evaporated from public discussion for a few years. The reasons for this are understandable. On July 27, 1790, after lengthy and difficult preliminary soundings and negotiations, Austria and Prussia signed an agreement which resolved a series of outstanding disputes between them. Frederick William II of Prussia undertook not only to support the Habsburg candidate at the impending imperial election, but also to give up his support of rebellious elements in various of the Habsburg lands, especially Belgium and Hungary, which had so distracted the ailing Joseph II in his last days and had weakened the whole domestic and international position of the Habsburgs. The new ruler of the Habsburg inheritance, Leopold II, promised in turn to end Austria's war with the Ottoman Empire without any great acquisitions, and to compensate Prussia for any Austrian expansion which might occur.

This agreement, known as the Convention of Reichenbach, did not of course put an end to the rivalry of the two German great powers: Austria's continuing interest in absorbing Bavaria, which was hardly a secret in Berlin, was nearly as disturbing to Prussia as was the impending Prussian inheritance of the south German Duchies of Ansbach and Bayreuth to Austria. Deep reservations about the agreement had existed in the

117

chancelleries of both states. Both Hertzberg and Kaunitz had advised their respective masters against it, and the latter was to lose his influence after a long and distinguished career because of his views. Furthermore, the Austro-Prussian rapprochement was by no means greeted with universal delight throughout the Empire; on the contrary, the old fear of many lesser states of being pulled too tightly under the control of one or the other of the two great powers in their search for allies against each other was now transformed into an even greater fear that their cooperation might eventuate in an agreement for the actual partition of Germany between them.[1] Such concern, however, did not become a major object of attention in the public press, for which the Convention of Reichenbach and the subsequent unanimous election of Leopold II seem to have signaled a welcome respite from the recurrent constitutional crises, real or imagined, of the 1780s. Indicative of this respite was the virtual absence of mention of the League of Princes from discussions of the Empire after 1790—strong contemporary support for the view of many historians that Reichenbach more than any other single event marked the end of the League.

The stimulus for another kind of analysis of the Empire, one which sought to evaluate the relationship between the government it provided and the overall well-being of the peoples it embraced, is at least partly traceable to the outbreak and progress of the French Revolution. It is true that the flare-up of active hostility between Austria and Prussia over the Bavarian succession in 1777–78, and the chronic state of tension between them in the 1780s, had produced a general speculation on the future of the imperial structure, part of which was expressed in the form of general examinations of its strengths and weaknesses and its contribution to the welfare of those who lived within it.[2] The Revolution, however, gave a new urgency and immediacy to this kind of analysis, as indeed it did to the consideration of virtually all major questions of public life in Germany. In the early 1790s, before the seriousness of the French challenge to Germany had become apparent through military conquests, German interest in the Revolution centered largely around the internal changes occurring in France, the ideology which underlay them, and the possible implications of both for Germany. In the enormous literature that grew up around the scores of political and societal issues that could be made out of the unfolding revolutionary experience in France, only a relatively small part was devoted to the Empire as such. That is due primarily to the double level of political competence built into the imperial constitution, whereby the immediate responsibility for nearly all governmental decisions affecting the general population was vested in the territorial rulers by virtue of their *Landeshoheit*. Since the implications of the Revolution for alterations in the political or social relationships of individuals or groups applied primarily to this level, rather than to that of the Empire (i.e., the relations of the territorial rulers among themselves or between themselves as a group and the Emperor), it was natural that the primary focus of the ongoing ventilation of views about the Revolution would be on the territories rather than on the Empire.[3]

On the other hand, since it was a revolution whose initiators intended among other things to provide the country with a new national constitution, the French Revolution also invited evaluations of their own national institutions by the other peoples of Europe. In Germany, of course, the only national political bond which could be discussed in this context was the imperial constitution; and the early 1790s witnessed the publication of a fairly large number of examinations of the strengths and weaknesses, the benefits and disadvantages, of the imperial constitution. On the whole, the tone of these writings was more reflective than polemical, and few of them found either advantages or disadvantages in the constitution which were not at least partly balanced by examples of their opposite. This is explained partly by the extraordinary complexity of the constitution, which represented a peculiar compromise between so many different constitutional principles and governmental practices that it was almost impossible for anyone, regardless of his overall judgment, not to find in it things he liked and things he did not. Furthermore, while the number of writings containing analyses of the imperial constitution was very large, the patterns of praise and criticism of it were relatively few and remarkably consistent.

As far as its defenders were concerned, this consistency arose chiefly from certain basic assumptions about the purposes of government itself. These assumptions were not always made explicit, but in the most thoughtful works they were set out quite clearly as the basis for subsequent argumentation. In a lengthy treatise of 1790, for example, the Leipzig professor Christian Ernst Weisse, a former student of J. S. Pütter, sought to bring out the advantages of the imperial nexus which, according to him, had been obscured not only by the excessive preoccupation of publicists with the detailed nature of the union, but also by a general fear of insulting territorial rulers by praising an association which in certain ways restricted or modified their sovereignty. Admitting at the outset that most German and foreign evaluations of the imperial constitution were negative, Weisse ascribed this to a standard of judgment based solely on the criterion of external power—"the efficacy of the nation against other states"—whereas he proposed to examine the German constitution from the standpoint of an ultimately more important purpose: the preservation of civic freedom.[4] The rest of his book was devoted to a detailed analysis of the protections against violations of right afforded all Germans by the imperial constitution. This analysis amounts to what can fairly be called the standard political argument for the advantages of the imperial bond.

One aspect of the preservation of freedom, of course, is protection against foreign domination. Weisse's argument here was that the imperial union gave to each of its members a defensive guarantee which none would have as a fully sovereign and independent state. This protection was institutionalized in the Imperial Circles, and was further solidified by a general spirit of confederation which was not only permitted by the imperial bond but actually encouraged by it. Since the imperial guarantee was exclusively defensive, however, and applied only to the German lands of the members, it could never become an encouragement for individual territories to wage offensive wars that could invite retaliations and involve other territories against their will. He conceded, however, that the military institutions of the Empire, and indeed its whole machinery for dealing with overt foreign military threats, were far from perfect, and in his final argument seemed to suggest that the Empire's best defense lay in its contribution to the preservation of peace—this is, in helping to see to it that its admittedly deficient military defenses simply did not have to be tested in war. It did this through its crucial role in the preservation of the European balance of power. This role, however, could be played effectively only by the Empire regarded as a single entity. The individual territories, by themselves, had neither the requisite strength for self-defense nor the advantage afforded by the diplomatic guarantees of other European great powers, which had an urgent balance-of-power interest in protecting the integrity of the Empire as a whole, but not necessarily of any particular member of it. Again, therefore, the European balance provided a protection for the individual German states only insofar as they were members of a single body.[5]

The imperial association also provided protection against oppression at all domestic levels, according to Weisse. Feuding among the German states had been brought to an end through the existence of the supreme judicial powers which had their original source in the Emperor, and which protected not only the weaker against the stronger, but the stronger against leagues of the weaker. The imperial judicial system also provided the means whereby quarrels between individual rulers and their subjects could be settled peacefully, and set limits to despotic tendencies of rulers, as well as to their ability to alter their territorial constitutions unilaterally. Private citizens, too, were spared the effects of mutual violations of right by their ability to appeal their quarrels to the imperial courts. Weisse, indeed, professed to find in the judicial system one of the greatest advantages of the imperial constitution, but he admitted that the system was both slow and expensive. He also regretted the lack of a common civil code for all of Germany, but noted that the imperial tie offered at least the possibility for the construction of such a general code at some time in the future. Finally, Weisse pointed to the various assurances against religious oppression that were built into the imperial constitution, which had the effect of encouraging tolerance by permitting two or more religions to coexist in peace within the same community over a long period of time.[6]

Weisse's almost exclusive emphasis on the advantages of the associative bonds of the Empire is in some ways misleading. Writing at a moment of political crisis in the Empire, possibly in the interregnum of 1790, his primary concern seems to have been to counter those territorial forces whose divisive influence appeared to stem from an insufficient appreciation of the real benefits of the imperial nexus. In some ways, indeed, Weisse's work was about as good an answer to the anonymous author of *Why Should Germany Have an Emperor?* as had been that of Julius von Soden. But as Weisse himself made clear, the true excellence of the imperial system lay in its preservation of a multiplicity of states, which he called the first cause of the advantages Germany had above other European countries; indeed, of all the various directions of development the imperial constitution might have taken from the time of its origins, that from which the concept and reality of *Landeshoheit* had arisen was the best possible. Without *Landeshoheit,* he averred, Germany would probably still play the most glorious role of all European states, but the freedom of the Germans themselves would probably not have been as well assured as it presently was.[7] Basically, then, Weisse saw the laws and institutions of the Empire as supplements to the territorial constitutions; their function was to minimize the dangers and disadvantages of political fragmentation without destroying its benefits, and to assist in the preservation at all levels of the one value—civic freedom—which was most precious to the Germans.

It is important to recognize the extremely conservative nature of this defense of the imperial system, because for this period, at least, it was the typical defense—one which regarded any considerable movement toward either greater centralization of power or greater territorial autonomy as equally dangerous. In this view, furthermore, lies an assumption that the legitimate sphere of imperial authority did not extend further than was necessary to guarantee the fulfillment of the formally recognized legal obligations which bound all who lived within it. It neither had nor was expected to have any mandate or function for change, even in the direction of increasing the well-being of its members, and therefore, in this view, could not be judged as if it did. The Empire, in other words, was to set and enforce certain limits to the will of others, but was really to have no active will of its own. This was essentially the argument followed by Carl Friedrich Häberlin, disciple of Pütter, professor of law at the University of Helmstedt and later editor of the influential periodical *Staats-Archiv,* who in 1792 published a highly favorable treatment of the imperial constitution based on the sole criterion by which he thought any constitution should be judged: its contribution to the first and most important purpose of all civil association, namely, to live in peace and to enjoy one's honor and property.

Häberlin specifically rejected the increase and encouragement of well-being as a primary goal of government, regarding it as important but nevertheless incidental to the chief purpose of providing the security without which neither life nor honor nor any amount of property was safe.[8] Häberlin's approval of the constitution of the Empire, as his subsequent arguments demonstrated, was based squarely on the numerous checks it provided against the invasion of individual rights to life and property on the part of any political authority, whether imperial or territorial. The possibility of the development of monarchical tyranny by the Emperor was held at bay by the elective nature of his office, an ever-vigilant Imperial Diet, and the imperial judicial system, while any tendencies toward despotism among the territorial princes, insofar as they were not checked by representative institutions (*Landstände*) within the territories themselves, were discouraged by the avenues of appeal to imperial agencies, especially the courts, that were available to individuals.[9]

A somewhat unusual feature of Häberlin's evaluation of the imperial constitution was its explicit attempt to point out the advantages derived from the constitution by the ordinary citizen (*Bürger*) as opposed to the territorial princes. That, no doubt, was in part a response to the prominence of the issue of individual rights in the discussions of constitutions engendered by the Revolution in France. It was also based on the assumption, implicit also in the works of Weisse and many other publicists and commentators of the late Enlightenment, that the happiness of the individual was the highest good of society, and that the proper function of the state was limited to the protection of minimal conditions under which the individual could pursue a happiness whose content was determined by himself.

One of the clearest and most unequivocal statements of this philosophy of the state was produced at precisely this time by the young Wilhelm von Humboldt. His long essay on the proper limits of the efficacy of the state not only specifically denied to political authority any function of looking after the positive welfare of its citizens, but also set out a formula for the correct purpose of the state that corresponded exactly with Häberlin's defense of the imperial constitution: "the maintenance of security against external enemies as well as internal quarrels."[10] This was what Humboldt called the "negative" welfare of citizens, whose protection should be at once the absolute duty and the outer limit of state power.

Attempts of authority to increase positive well-being by collective measures tended to produce a false uniformity and to suppress the individuality of men, according to Humboldt. That, in turn, hampered the
achievement of the highest possible level of human happiness because that
level could only be defined in terms of wholly individual requirements.
Weisse, Häberlin, and many other defenders of the Empire understood
quite well what Humboldt meant when he insisted that "The constitution of the state and the national association (*Nationalverein*), no matter how closely interwoven they may be, should never be confused with
each other."[11] The latter was the dynamic framework within which man
achieved that ongoing development of his individual potential in which
his happiness truly consisted, and the former was to be only a protective
shield for it. Friedrich Meinecke has correctly interpreted Humboldt's
position as meaning that "the constitution should make itself felt as little
as possible, and the strengthened and expanded private interests of the
citizens should replace the activity of the state as much as possible. The
state should be as weak, not as strong, as it can afford to be."[12]

Almost all—and there were many—who in these years wrote in praise
of the Empire found in its guardianship of freedom, along the lines suggested above, its chief role and benefit. Thus, a certain Prussian War
Councillor Randel, writing in the *Deutsche Monatsschrift* in 1792, ap-
plauded the multiple balances specified in or encouraged by the imperial
constitution, including even the Austro-Prussian dualism and the League
of Princes, as responsible for discouraging oppression and for assisting
the growth of a spirit of fairness, lawfulness, and moderation throughout
Germany, all of which had in turn created a feeling of freedom and a
living belief in human rights.[13] Similarly, the famous author, dramatist,
and editor Christoph Martin Wieland saw the intentional unwieldiness
of the operations of the Empire as productive of fewer international complications and a greater domestic tranquility or, in other words, of both
external and internal security. It was that security, in turn, which laid the
firm foundation for progress toward well-being.[14] Public peace, the undisturbed enjoyment of individual property, and freedom of conscience—
general happiness, in short—also bulked large in the advantages conferred by the constitution as described by Karl von Dalberg in a writing of
1795.[15] In that same year, Günther Heinrich von Berg, an associate of
Pütter on the law faculty at the University of Göttingen, based his favorable assessment of the constitution almost entirely upon the restrictions
it placed on the arbitrary exercise of power at all levels and the protection consequently afforded to all against violations of their rights from
foreign and domestic quarters.[16]

By these evidences, then, the point is perhaps sufficiently made that
the defenders of the Empire started with the assumption of a very limited
responsibility for the imperial government, as indeed for all government

in general. Human progress, welfare, and happiness were not to be generated by state power, but by individuals or groups in their free interaction and cooperation with each other. The state was not to arrogate to itself the direction of this process, but was merely to guarantee the self-fulfilling community against disturbance from any source, and the state's power should be no stronger than the successful performance of this task required. The relative weakness of a constitution was therefore not necessarily a bad thing; indeed, it could be evidence of the moral strength of the society which created it, and for its admirers in the early 1790s the imperial government corresponded about as closely to the proper combination of functions and power as any political structure of its nature could.

This does not mean, however, that they did not worry about the operational deficiencies of the various agencies of imperial government. A wholly typical critique on this score was delivered by W.A.F. Danz, a professor of law in Stuttgart, who in a lecture of 1792 castigated the Imperial Diet for its legislative inactivity, the petty jealousies of its deputies, and its lack of common spirit; flayed the imperial courts for political partisanship and inadequate staffing and supervision which led to a lengthiness of judicial process so inordinate as to be the ruination rather than the remedy of many litigants; and condemned the Imperial Circles as inadequate to the execution of cooperative enterprises by reason of the conflicting interests and mutual suspicions of the territorial rulers they embraced.[17] Dalberg exhibited similar concerns, especially about the course of justice and, even more importantly, the whole process of execution of judgments;[18] and the same kind of worry and criticism appears in many other writings of the time.

Two remarks can be made about these criticisms. First, they pertained not so much to the integrity of structures as to the efficiency of their operation. As G.H. von Berg put it, in referring to the generality of critics of the Empire: "They criticize the constitution of the state, and mean the administration."[19] The structures—that is, the agencies or organs of imperial government, as well as the procedures prescribed for them by law—were perceived as adequate and appropriate; only their proper functioning was crippled.[20] Second, the inadequacies perceived in the imperial government were attributed explicitly or implicitly almost exclusively to human failings. Lack of awareness, neglect and inattention, petty jealousies, excessive and unenlightened self-interest, and the absence of a national or community spirit—all were implicated in the deficiencies of imperial operations, virtually every one of which could have been eliminated or at least mitigated by genuine observance of the spirit of the constitution, primarily on the part of the territorial rulers. Here again, then, the basic problem was seen as a moral one, and it could be solved only by moral means. This was usually formulated in terms of the reawakening of a national spirit, something it will be necessary to deal with at greater length later on.

Still, while all of the arguments so far presented have dealt with problems related to the imperial constitution in the narrower sense of the supraterritorial institutions and their procedures alone, it must not be forgotten that when men of this time spoke of "the German constitution," those institutions were only one part, and in many cases the lesser part, of what that broader and less legalistic term meant to them. The other part was that dispensation by which the Empire was divided into numerous virtually sovereign and semiautonomous states or territories—in other words, its political fragmentation. It should come as no surprise to learn that admirers of the constitution defended this fragmentation, and indeed, along with defense against foreign threats and its judicial role, regarded the guarantee of it as the most important function of the imperial constitution. Again, it was the true happiness of individuals, as the final end of society, which justified this judgment. Berg stated flatly that "The German citizen can ... live largely satisfied and happy, and that he can (is due primarily) to a constitution which created numerous states in Germany"; and Professor Danz insisted that "For the philosopher, for the true friend of humanity, for the cosmopolitan, it is no longer subject to doubt that for political associations the union of small states is the most desirable of all."[21]

Such assertions were based to some extent on prior philosophical convictions about the tendency of large monarchical states to encourage the growth of despotic government—a view strongly represented in the well-known writings of the French philosopher Jean-Jacques Rousseau among others.[22] According to such convictions, by which the dispersal of political authority conferred a greater degree of freedom and good government through a better representation of local interests, Germany was particularly fortunate. The historian Ludwig Timotheus Spittler believed in the "happy medium size" of the German states, combined with their loose association in an imperial union, as something which not only benefited the individual subject, but also assured the peace and freedom of what he called "the German states-system."[23] The argument was laid out in greater detail in an article of 1793 which contrasted France of the old regime to Germany. Written by Karl Leonhard Reinhold, a professor of philosophy at Jena and a collaborator of C. M. Wieland on *Der teutsche Merkur,* it pointed out that France had possessed a single and unlimited monarch with absolute powers which were protected by officials whose own self-interest, as royal employees, lay in maintaining undiminished the prerogatives of the crown from which they derived their own authority. The arbitrariness of government which resulted from the mindless execution of inflexible royal programs had gradually vitiated both the constitution and the administration and had ultimately produced a violent revolution by a people whose own govenment had failed to acquaint it with a reasonable balance of freedom and obedience. Germany, on the other hand, possessed a constitution which provided for multiple rulers who governed under a common law which restricted their own sovereignty with respect to arbitrariness, but which they gladly supported because of the guarantees it gave their thrones. Political revolution—that is, the attempted amelioration of the constitution by force, either by princes or subjects—was therefore presently impossible in Germany, whereas improvement by means of better insight and good will was encouraged.[24]

The contributions of political fragmentation to the freedom and welfare of citizens, according to contemporaries, were of several specific kinds. Freedom of the press, and of thought in general, was encouraged by the sheer difficulties of censorship across the boundaries of territories whose multiplicity guaranteed the existence at all times of at least some places hospitable to free thinkers and a free press. This same freedom worked retroactively to lessen tendencies toward oppression of other kinds by organizing the force of public opinion all over Germany against abuses and injustices wherever they might occur. The possibilities of good government in all territories were enhanced by the competition for the services of talented public officials produced by the existence of so many governments; such officials, if ill-treated, had the same alternative of simply fleeing to some more congenial territory that was available to all other citizens or subjects. As suggested earlier, the small size of most territories meant not only that the ruler could be approached in person by subjects with petitions and grievances, but that he could also become closely acquainted with them and their various circumstances, so that the laws and institutions for the regulation and encouragement of trade, industry, agriculture, the arts, and so on, could be matched to the realities of local circumstances better than in a very large state.[25] From this point of view, political fragmentation and *Landeshoheit* thus had the effect of making it possible for individual rulers to initiate beneficial reforms in their own states independent of the lethargy or misgovernment of the states surrounding them. It was also possible to argue, as one commentator did, that the evil effects of ill-considered or overhasty reform—for which many of the efforts of Joseph II served as an example—could be kept from becoming general by the same fragmentation, which prevented the extension of reform across territorial boundaries except by a process of voluntary acceptance based on the demonstrated merit of reform.[26] The same reasoning was used to suggest that the multitude of separate states protected the peace and order of the Empire as a whole by making it difficult for the various German peoples to unite for revolutionary purposes.[27]

Most of the other supposed advantages of Germany's political division can be lumped under the heading of "golden moderation" (*goldene Mittelmässigkeit*), a phrase given currency by Wieland in a very widely read and cited preface to Schiller's *Historischer Kalender für Damen* of 1792. Starting from the premise that the landlocked or continental (*mittelländische*) position of most German territories, together with other circumstances of geography, history, and climate, had set certain limits to the progress of German culture and well-being in comparison to some other areas of western and southern Europe, Wieland insisted that these same conditions had also produced a better distribution of the benefits of civilization throughout Germany than was true of those other areas. Fewer extremes of wealth and poverty, more and better distributed schools and universities, more opportunities for individual advancement in society, and a greater general expansion of enlightenment among the people— all these comprised that "golden moderation" of Germany which Wieland knew was a term of abuse in the minds of foreigners, but which he not only defended strongly but also attributed directly to the division of Germany into such a large number of small states of differing composition.[28]

Wieland's high reputation in the intellectual world undoubtedly gave the views he expressed in this and other similar writings a wider audience than would have been true of others, but he was by no means the only one who held them. His own collaborator K. L. Reinhold had expressed many of the same sentiments in an article of 1790 in *Der teutsche Merkur* which revealed an almost smug self-satisfaction with Germany's repose in contrast to the ongoing turmoil in France. Among all the European states, Reinhold opined, Germany was perhaps the most inclined to revolutions of the spirit, but the least inclined to political revolutions. That was the happy result of a constitution which protected the Germans against the worst of all ills of a state, namely, the excessive wealth of the few and the extreme poverty of the many, a circumstance which must infallibly lead to major disturbances. Reinhold, like many others, also called attention to the considerable benefits of not having a single capital city which, while providing a brilliant showplace for artistic and intellectual talent, might so dominate the cultural life of the nation as to suppress diversity and individuality. He admitted that Germany might have no golden age of literature such as that of Louis XIV in France or Queen Anne in England, but he believed that this was more than compensated for by the fact that there would also be no such age to outlive—that is, that slow and steady cultural growth was to be preferred to cycles of gold and iron ages.[29]

Reinhold's views were entirely consistent with an approach to German culture in general which had become increasingly prevalent among men of letters since the middle of the eighteenth century. Rooted in the so-called "German Movement," the real beginnings of which are to be found in the works of the poet and dramatist Friedrich Gottlieb Klopstock, this approach emphasized the cultural contribution the Germans could make to all of Europe by their special ability to master the whole realm of the arts and sciences and to become the leaders and teachers of Europe toward the highest goals of humanity. Repeated references to the advantages of the wide diffusion of schools, learning, and enlightenment in Germany are related to this sense of cultural mission, as is also the developing sense of the moral superiority of Germans over other Europeans.[30] Since this whole movement arose in part as a reaction against the cultural domination of France, it was natural that in establishing Germany's special cultural claims, France was used for purposes of comparison and contrast. Reinhold was fairly typical of a large part of the German *Gelehrtenrepublik* in his assessment of the French as a people whose refinement had eventuated in a sensuality which was destructive of true morality and knowledge and had led to luxury as a bad substitute. He contrasted this with German thoroughness or profundity (*Gründlichkeit*), which was as much favored by the nature of the German constitution as refinement on the French model was limited by it.[31] Similarly, the north German author Gerhard Anton von Halem compared the witty but shallow sophistication of the Frenchman to the modest, unassuming, and uncorrupted nature of the Germans, and suggested that Frederick the Great, as Germany's most praiseworthy son, had achieved his greatness less because of the quality of his thought, which was French, than because of his character, which was German.[32] These and many other similar evidences make it clear that praise of the overall level of enlightenment in Germany, which was attributed to the nature of the constitution itself, was not so much an attempt to establish a quantitative superiority of Germany over other countries with respect to the numbers of learned men as it was to establish a claim to moral superiority through the connection of character with widespread learning. In this sense, the German constitution was regarded as an essential precondition of the European-wide German cultural mission.

If one were to single out one general and basic point of disagreement between the critics and the defenders of the imperial constitution in the early 1790s, it would probably be on the issue of the significance of political fragmentation as a fundamental characteristic of the German political system. In most writings of authors favorable to the Empire, there was a kind of assumption of the coequal importance of imperial and territorial governments in the definition and assessment of the imperial constitution. In theory, at least, the benefits conferred by the whole system rested on a more or less exact balance between these two levels of government, upon which the welfare of all—Emperor, princes, and peoples—was predicated. And in spite of their own critique of the weaknesses of the agencies of imperial government, which could only stem from an at least tacit recognition that the sum of the influence of the territorial governments was in fact greater than that of the imperial government, they tended to construct their arguments on this theory of balance rather than on the reality of imbalance. The result was a judgment of actual conditions which often reflected purely logical deductions from theory as much as or more than empirical observations.

The critics, on the other hand, are distinguished by their emphasis on the realities of a constitution which for them had come to be defined by the considerable preponderance of the elements of territorial fragmentation over the bonds of imperial unity. For them, therefore, the question of the goodness of Germany's constitution reduced far more to the simple evaluation of the advantages or disadvantages of political fragmentation than was true for those who professed to find a real equilibrium still operating. One entry in the literary prize competition of the Mainz Academy at Erfurt on the problem of how to increase the devotion of Germans to the imperial constitution illustrates the point. After referring bitterly to the "sovereignty-swindle" of the territorial princes which over the years had reduced the powers of the Emperor to nothing and had all but collapsed the effectiveness of all other imperial institutions, its anonymous author went on to assert that the happiness and welfare of the individual German states rested on the nature of their particular domestic constitutions far more than on the so-called imperial constitution, and that a prize question dealing with how a territorial prince might make the constitution of his own land dearer to his subjects would be more useful than the present question, whose importance he denied, in effect, by refusing to answer it.[33]

One implication of this kind of perception of the real nature of the German constitution was that the benefits it conferred were not distributed very equally among different classes of persons. As the real masters of the land, the territorial rulers were in a position to get the most. Even K. L. Reinhold, in one of his writings favorable to the Empire, had admitted that the limits placed by the imperial constitution on the arbitrariness of rulers applied more to their relations with each other than to their relations with their subjects.[34] Another author devoted much of a very lengthy work to the demonstration that the overwhelming majority of Germans derived very few advantages from the present constitution of the Empire, most of whose blessings were limited to the princes and Electors. Particularly significant, in view of the importance attached by others to the protection supposedly afforded every German citizen by the imperial judicial system was his conviction that the power of territorial rulers to arrogate to themselves through the *privilegium de non appellando* a judicial competence that ought properly to belong to the imperial government had destroyed the most basic advantage that every German had a right to expect from the constitution—the protection of Emperor and Empire against injustice.[35] The thrust of arguments such as these was to attack the imperial constitution at what was indeed one of its weaker points, namely, the efficacy of its contribution even to the "negative welfare" of the non-noble classes of Germany—a contribution which was clear enough in theory and which was regarded by nearly everyone as desirable, but which was lacking in implementation.[36]

Once wedded to the position that the imperial government was essentially ineffective, and that the territorial princes collectively gave the constitution its true character, it was also possible to deny that most of the other benefits which were supposed to derive from the imperial nexus were in fact connected with it, or indeed that they existed at all. An anonymous Prussian citizen of obviously enlightened persuasion dealt with a number of such alleged benefits in the pages of the *Berlinische Monatsschrift* in 1792, partly as a direct answer to Wieland's earlier essay of the same year.[37] While conceding that most German territories enjoyed reasonably good government, he attributed this to a set of historical and other accidents and not to the imperial constitution, which offered no guarantee that widespread good government would continue. The constitution did indeed contain provisions by which bad rulers could be kept from illegal excesses, but the process of doing so took so long that a generation or more could pass before a wrong was righted. He regarded all statements concerning Germany's "golden moderation"—in fact virtually all comparisons of the well-being of Germans with that of foreigners—as essentially gratuitous and lacking in factual foundation. His own experience confirmed that there was an active enlightenment and a desire to spread useful arts in Germany, but he again refused to see this as a result of fragmentation. Enlightenment, like industriousness, springs up in a people by itself, he averred, and the only requirement of a constitution, or of rulers, is that they not place obstacles in the path of these self-generating qualities.[38]

In this respect, political fragmentation had one enormous drawback on which virtually all who wrote about the Empire were agreed: the obstacle it presented to economic growth, with all the consequences attendant to it. The most ardent admirers of the Empire had to admit that there was little to be said for it on this point. Within this group, indeed, Christian Ernst Weisse was unusual in trying to make any case at all for the economic benefits of the imperial association, and even he wound up in the dubious position of arguing simply that there was nothing in the imperial constitution that prevented economic cooperation on a national basis if the territories wanted it.[39] Others did not even bother to go this far. They either accepted the admittedly disadvantageous economic consequences of territorial fragmentation as one of the prices one had to pay for other kinds of benefits on which they chose to concentrate instead, or else followed the path taken by Wieland, whose "golden moderation" was in one sense nothing more than an attempt to substitute moral equivalents for the lack of material rewards in an essentially stagnant economy.

The economic criticism of Germany's constitution followed a predictable pattern, which can be summarized in a few basic points. First, political fragmentation was a great obstacle to trade, not only because it posed difficulties to the construction of a network of modern roads and canals across territorial boundaries and made uniform improvements in the navigability of interterritorial rivers hard to carry out, but also because it subjected commerce to frequent tolls and other types of transit taxes which, being added to the cost of goods, made them more expensive to the consumer and therefore lowered that demand on which all trade was based. Second, trade and industry were both hurt by the mercantilist measures adopted by the scores of German rulers in their attempt to maximize fiscal gain and at the same time maintain as great a degree of economic self-sufficiency as possible for their often tiny states. In imposing large customs duties on many goods, or forbidding the import of some altogether, these rulers lowered demand still further, and thus depressed both commercial and industrial sectors—all in the name of increasing governmental revenues and protecting home industries which would not have been viable in a freer economy, and which therefore had to be supported by grants of monopolies or other preferments whose effects were detrimental to the economy as a whole.[40]

A third criticism attacked a different kind of problem. One author, accepting Montesquieu's teaching that the principle of honor was the moral basis of monarchy, found that monarchy as a form of government was simply inhospitable to the spirit of commerce and industry. By establishing recognition by the monarch as the sole criterion of social status, it encouraged men who had made real contributions in commercial and manufacturing pursuits not only to abandon their valuable acquisitive activities in the search for titles and official positions which would confer a more "honorable" status, but to push their sons in the same direction as well, thus removing the most progressive and productive spirits from the economy. The agricultural sector suffered also, since even the landed noblemen under such circumstances could hardly wait to turn his estate over to the indifferent care of an overseer and hurry off to the court, "where he sells his freedom for a key or a star."[41]

To this argument that the ordinary tendency of any monarchy to siphon off its economically most aggressive souls was considerably strengthened by the sheer number of monarchically governed states in Germany, another critic added that the new and more "honorable" occupations into

which those souls had been redirected not only failed to contribute anything to society, but actually were harmful to it in that they comprised
a bloated official aristocracy which consumed huge sums of government
money without giving much in return. Specifically referring to an argument of Wieland that the numerous states of Germany provided employment for more learned and talented men than might a single state,
this author pointed out, first, that on balance large numbers of such men
were simply not desirable from an economic standpoint, and second, that
there would be no need for governments to provide a social security for
such "freeloaders" (*Kostgänger*) if the German constitution truly encouraged commerce and manufacturers and gave a social incentive to individuals to succeed in them. Frustrated by government policies which
reduced the productivity of industry by an excessive taxation rooted in
the necessity to provide support for hordes of bureaucratic supernumer-
aries, this critic believed that only a unification of national energies could
overcome the economic parochialism and destructive selfishness of the
present territorial system of political economy.[42]

For all its emphasis on the need for a more rational and progressive
economic policy, however, this article, like those discussed immediately
before it, was also a plea for the removal of obstacles which prevented one
large social group—the entrepreneurial middle class—from attaining social honor on its own initiative, side by side with the privileged classes.[43]
In the present scheme of things, upward social mobility for members of
this group was possible only through the abandonment of a socially more
useful activity in favor of a less useful one. Such a perverse situation was
deplorable, and to the extent that the preservation of a multitude of small
states encouraged the continuation of an economic stagnancy which did
not offer prospects and rewards to engage the permanent interest of talented men it had to be condemned. Again, therefore, an imperial constitution which was at least partly defined precisely in terms of preserving
territorial multiplicity was judged deficient because the benefits it conferred were very unequally shared by different classes of its inhabitants.

The correction of the economic ills of the Empire was regarded as
virtually impossible except on the basis of supraterritorial cooperation.
The abolition of tolls, the reduction or extinction of territorial import
duties, the abandonment of grants of monopolies, and even the forced
liberalization of guild membership in order to increase production and
lower prices—all these and other measures could in theory be undertaken
by individual princes. But it was recognized as unlikely, since unilateral
steps in the direction of freer trade in the midst of a jungle of mercantilist states would lead infallibly to individual ruin. Economic improvement
through general legislation in the Imperial Diet also appears not to have
had much backing. The reasons were spelled out in an interesting reform

proposal of 1791, whose author asserted that a complete unity of the Empire in economic matters was no longer possible because certain of the German states on the basis of their size and strength had developed special commercial interests which, in their view, did not permit them to make common cause with others. While this made an all-German economic system impossible, it was at least fortunate for the commercial interests of the rest of Germany that the two states which best fitted this category, Austria and Prussia, lay in the eastern part of Germany rather than in the west, where their control of the Rhine, Main, and Weser rivers would have created enormous difficulties for all other German states in trading with Holland, England, and France.[44]

This happy geographical circumstance made it possible for the author to suggest that all or most of the states of western Germany would do well to form an association for common economic improvement. The states should make of themselves a large free trade area, at least with respect to their own peoples, and adopt common legislation in regard to trade with other nations. Freedom of investment across state boundaries would be permitted, and mutual economic jealousy should be discouraged: As soon as a manufacturing enterprise in one territory distinguished itself by the quality and cheapness of its products, other states should not only refrain from competing with it, but encourage the sale of those goods at home. Sales of shares in all such enterprises would guarantee that the riches of one territory would soon enough become the riches of all.

Crowning this work of economic reform would be the creation of a permanent Deputation of Commerce (*Kommerzdeputazion*), which would not itself attempt to direct trade, but would be a deliberative and advisory body, making or examining plans for the abolition of hindrances to trade and enlightening the various associated courts to keep them from passing bad economic legislation. The deputation should be free of undue influence from any particular prince, should play no favorites with any industries or persons, and should not be regarded as a source of income or profit by any rulers. The seat of this new agency should be in a commercial center such as Frankfurt am Main, Aachen, or Cologne, but preferably in one of the last two, with their easier access to channels of overseas trade with England and Holland. Two unessential but beneficial guidelines for the membership and operation of the deputation were also suggested: First, that the only requirement for membership be that of having formally studied the economics of trade, so that nobles with no knowledge at all and merchants who had learned only "by routine" should not be members; and second, that no title or rank other than such as might be based on length of service would be allowed to affect the operations of the body.[45]

Several elements of these proposals are significant in the overall issue of contemporary evaluations of the Empire. First, while the idea of working to overcome a general imperial problem through regional association indicates a lack of confidence in the ability of the Empire to act as a unit, it also reflects the continuing belief that within certain limits the imperial nexus still provided a framework within which it was possible to arrive at meaningful cooperative improvements, and to do so without many of the difficulties which would attend negotiations between altogether sovereign states. The machinery of the Imperial Circles which was so often praised by the defenders of the imperial constitution, though only indirectly called upon by the author of these plans, was the most obvious structural example of the possibilities for accommodation to regional needs built into the imperial constitution.

Second, the explicit exclusion of Austria and Prussia from this economic reform, together with the author's admission that both already possessed what amounted to integral national economies of their own, was a considerable step toward narrowing the definition of the Empire to include only those states which were incapable of self-improvement or even survival except through association.[46] The economic case for a "third Germany" made out here reinforced the tendency toward the same kind of redefinition in political terms which had emerged in often rather vague ways in the argumentation about the League of Princes, and which was rapidly to become more explicit and self-conscious among observers of imperial politics as time went on.

Finally, this writer's emphasis on technical competence and bureaucratic equality between nobles and commoners in the membership of his Deputation of Commerce, combined with a veiled reference to the fact that all of Germany might derive benefits from this kind of equality, conveys a conviction that the monarchical-aristocratic makeup of German governments was indeed a chief obstacle to urgently desirable economic reforms. So, of course, was the political division of Germany. What was really at issue here, insofar as the imperial constitution was concerned, was that the constitution protected an aristocratic values-system, as part of the status quo, which was not only in itself inimical to the commercial spirit in certain ways, but which also made all forms of cooperation across territorial boundaries difficult. For representatives of the entrepreneurial middle class, it was not a question of asking governments to become active in their behalf, but to cease being active to their unique disadvantage; and as this writer shows, it could not be easy for them to defend an imperial system which by its structure not only permitted but even encouraged the latter kind of activity.

Besides its clear economic disadvantages, one other effect of political fragmentation was almost universally lamented among commentators of otherwise differing points of view. That was the blighting of a German national consciousness and sense of common purpose which was variously referred to as "national spirit" or "common spirit" (*Nationalgeist, Gemeingeist,* or sometimes *Gemeinsinn*). While religious differences, in particular, were usually implicated as one of the causes for what was everywhere conceded to be a deplorably low level of national spirit, the political division of Germany was almost always regarded as the prime culprit, since it was seen as responsible for creating, sustaining, or reinforcing nearly all particular differences between territories, not excluding the religious ones. The tensions and problems created by the conflicting policy interests of so many different and essentially autonomous territories had everywhere created a myopia which had eventually resulted in restricting the sentiments of patriotism almost exclusively to the territorial level. In a widely read article of 1793, Wieland remarked that while much had been taught him about various kinds of duties as a child, so little was said about any duty to be a German patriot that he could not now remember ever hearing the adjective "German" used to describe anything honorable. Admitting that a patriotism based on the principle *patria est ubi bene est* might exist in the various territories, he yet doubted very much that the connection between the well-being of particular territories and the maintenance of the general constitution of Germany, or even of any other part of the Empire, was perceived by the various peoples of Germany. The existence of provincial patriots was undisputed, "But German patriots, who love the whole German Empire as their fatherland, love [it] above all else, [who] are ready to make considerable sacrifices not only for its maintenance and protection against a common enemy, but also, when the danger is over, [for] its well being, the remedy of its defects, the promotion of its improvements, of its internal flourishing [and] its external reputation: where are they?"[47] Another writer echoed this thought in remarking simply that "One seeks the German in Germany in vain,"[48] while others actually spoke of the existence of a German "national hatred" (*National-Hass*), characterized by estrangement, mutual contempt, and the employment by the peoples of larger states of such phrases as "out there in the Empire" and "Imperials" (*Reichler*), indicating that their territorial pride prevented identification with the rest of the German nation.[49]

There were various reasons for contemporaries to regret the absence of a national spirit. One arose from the conviction of enlightened men of letters that the German cultural mission to Europe and the world had to be fulfilled within the framework of a cultural nation whose creation was hindered by a territorial fragmentation that did not permit the numerous individual contributors to see themselves as parts of a single national community. Justus Möser, the sage of Osnabrück, had remarked in a writing of 1781, which deplored the lack of a single German fatherland, that the

Germans had "at the most father-cities and a learned fatherland";[50] but what many of his fellow writers feared was that even this learned fatherland did not truly exist, and that it had yet to be created.[51] Wieland recognized that there was a relationship between the inability of many Germans to perceive a larger political nation beyond their own small territories and their similar inability to see themselves as part of a national cultural community, and in 1792 he proposed that some unspecified institutions of national scope (*National-Institute*) might be set afoot to work toward creation of a greater common national spirit. This would not require a union of the political leaders of the nation, which he recognized as difficult in any case; but it would imply some means of providing encouragement and opportunity for writers to work actively at creating a sense of national identification among all Germans. Writers, Wieland asserted, were the real men of the nation, because their audience was all of Germany, and it was up to them to preach the advantages of the German constitution and awaken that common spirit which alone could cut across the differences produced within the Empire by political and other divisions. In particular, he felt that the writing and execution of dramas based on German history was a good way to get a sense of common experience across to all classes of readers.

Johann Gottfried Herder was somewhat more specific and concrete than Wieland in proposing the establishment of a national German Academy. This organization was not intended to displace already existing academies and learned societies, because its purpose would be different from theirs: It would concentrate less on the cultivation of the arts and sciences generally than on a more practical spiritual and moral culture emphasizing the German language, German history, and everything else that belonged to the active philosophy of "national education and happiness." In suggesting that the original members of the Academy be chosen by the German princes from their own lands, and that subsequent members also be selected by them from lists of nominees supplied by the Academy, Herder obviously hoped to link political authority to this national cultural institution in order not only to increase the latter's visibility and to assure it of operating revenues—the princes were to set up a fund for salaries and other costs—but also to heighten the political common spirit of the princes through their cooperation in the establishment and ongoing life of an institution of national scope.[52]

Even more strongly than Wieland, Herder believed that the absence of a strong national spirit was a subjective rather than an objective problem. A German national spirit existed; what was missing was the general recognition that it existed. One does not—cannot—create a national spirit, which arises entirely from the common experience of a people. Since the diversity which characterizes any great people, and which is actually a part of its cultural identity, can sometimes obscure the greater unity which resides within it, it may be necessary to create a consciousness of the national spirit which a people would otherwise act out unself-consciously, thus robbing itself of the cultural perfection which the unification of its moral and intellectual forces could bring. To awaken this awareness, Herder, too, suggested the writing of a new German history. It was not to be a history of Germany as that term was ordinarily understood, however, but specifically a history of the German national spirit, in order to demonstrate by examples that Germany, in all classes of its people, had always had such a spirit, had one now, and must necessarily have one forever.[53]

Since the unity of national spirit solicited by the representatives of the *Gelehrtenrepublik* was a cultural unity which was to serve a German mission also defined in exclusively cultural terms, it is not surprising that political considerations played a very small part in the elaboration of the means proposed to achieve a stronger national spirit. If indeed many writers felt that political fragmentation contributed to the cultural parochialism of Germany, it did not follow for them that political unification was an appropriate means for producing cultural unity. Ludwig Wekhrlin was perhaps unique among authors of the time in his belief that a political concentration of Germany through monocratic government for the Empire was indispensable for the creation of a genuine common spirit.[54] Others, almost without exception, accepted the efficacy of moral and intellectual means to attain a goal which was itself moral and intellectual in nature. Wieland, for example, recognizing that his proposals to encourage the preaching of a national spirit were completely apolitical in character, made no apologies for this, but instead insisted that the moral conversion of hearts and minds might well produce surer, more powerful, and longer-lasting effects than formal or institutional measures that might be set afoot by the political leaders of the nation.

There is a temptation to assume that this lack of attention to the possibilities of greater political concentration as a means of achieving a stronger national spirit merely reflected a conviction that the political realities of the time forbade the entertainment of such an idea. In fact, it was more than that. It should not be forgotten that for all the evils ascribed to Germany's territorial fragmentation in learned society, the overall judgment of it was favorable. Wieland might be accused, as he in effect was, of trying to make a silk purse out of a sow's ear in telling Germans to be happy with their constitution merely because it consecrated a set of conditions which could conceivably be worse;[55] but the sincerity of Wieland's own views about the goodness of a constitution predicated on a multiplicity of states is beyond doubt.

Apart from the advantages of diversity and the diffusion of enlightenment attached to this multiplicity, there was also a widespread fear that a real political unification of Germany might tend to work against one

of the most frequently mentioned original and praiseworthy characteristics
of the Germans as a cultural community: their extreme openness to all
manifestations of human creativity, regardless of their place of origin—
their ability "to collect and utilize the treasures of knowledge from the
whole world, and thus to provide themselves with the most many-sided
culture."[56] This special ability, usually called "universality" (*Universali-
tät*) in writings of the time, was regarded as so important to the cultural
identity of the German that any circumstance which tended to lessen it
would have to be seen as destructive of the national character. The fear
that political unification could do just that was impacted into the frequent
condemnations of unified kingdoms possessed of great capital cities which
could tend to produce adherence to a single and exclusive cultural standard
admitting of no accruals; and the same fear explains the careful distinction made between "national pride" (*Nationalstolz*) and "national spirit,"
in which the former, seen as a degenerated form of the latter, produced
a weakening of receptivity to foreign cultures, a disinclination to take up
their good and useful products.[57]

What has been said should not be taken to mean that the cultural
cosmopolitanism of the German writers of this period made them indifferent to political questions altogether. Many genuinely hoped that the
creation and diffusion of national spirit would lead to a general relaxation
of political jealousies and an elevation of moral sensibilities that might
result in a greater willingness of territorial rulers to cooperate with each
other in enterprises of economic improvement, social welfare, and even
defense. But this simply was not of primary importance to them, and
their explicit approval of a present constitution in which such cooperation
was admitted to be all but impossible shows that they were prepared to
sacrifice the benefits of political unity to those characteristics of the constitution which, in their eyes, made it possible for the Germans to excel
in the most important areas of human creativity: morality and spiritual
culture. Their appreciation of the Empire was based on its benignant guardianship of a set of conditions within which the human spirit was free
to set and pursue its own goals; that freedom, seen as the essential underpinning of "German universality," was rooted in the political diversity
of the Empire, whose lessening was actually undesirable insofar as it
might bring with it a greater capability for political dictation of uniform
moral and cultural standards.

On the other hand, the sacrifice of political benefits did not have to
be a permanent one. For the German cosmopolitan, the building of a
nation was not a political process, but a moral one—the elevation to self-
consciousness of the already existing character of a people; once that had
occurred, then the spirit of politics would itself become national, so that
all the deficiencies present in the existing German constitution would be
overcome. The majority of commentators on the imperial constitution

did not ascribe the problems of its operation to imperfections in structures or laws but to the absence of a sufficient will to make them work. That will, however, would arise by itself as a natural by-product of the suffusion of the Empire with national spirit; *Nationalgeist,* in other words, would automatically engender *Gemeingeist.* In the meantime, while the constitution of the Empire may not have given much in the way of direct encouragement to the formation of a national spirit, and indeed probably hindered it in some ways, it also protected the cultural conditions and the civic freedom necessary to permit the "real men of the nation," to use Wieland's phrase, that is, the writers and intellectuals, to go about their patient work of heightening national awareness. Nor was there any reason to suppose for the future that the Empire would not be the best of all states once the expanded moral awareness of its multiple political leaders guaranteed that it functioned as its constitution intended that it should.

What distinguished many of the authors whose works were primarily critical rather than laudatory of the Empire in these years of the early 1790s was their impatience with those aspects of its constitution, and above all territorial fragmentation and the uncooperativeness it produced, which more or less absolutely prevented all who were not princes of politics or of letters from having any visible stake in the German system. The middle classes, for example, saw themselves connected to politics only through their fiscal exploitation by territorial princes, and had almost no reason to be concerned about the Empire as such, since it brought them no visible advantage. Their self-fulfillment, like that of the intellectuals and men of letters, lay in their professions; but unlike ideas, their freight wagons or barges could not easily overleap territorial boundaries. The economic critics of the Empire knew this. So did those who, like Günther Heinrich von Berg, worried about the ideological inroads of the French Revolution in Germany and the problem of awakening popular support for the constitution as a means of resisting them. Berg's conclusion that the real issue had less to do with popular dissatisfaction with the German constitution than with indifference to it is an interesting one, because it called attention to the fact that the constitution was invisible to the majority of Germans.[58] Unlike the French, the Germans could not defend their system because it was imperceptible as a system. An earlier writer had put the same thought more clearly and more bitterly: "There is then, to speak properly and truly, no common fatherland in Germany, and Germany, except in the compendia of public law, is no longer a single state." In such circumstances, love of fatherland was reduced to "simply an idea without reality."[59]

It is appropriate to close this discussion of the Empire and national spirit with the views of the man who had first created a sensation with his own plea for German national unity over a quarter of a century be-

fore. The aging Friedrich Carl von Moser, by his own admission stimulated to a renewed interest in the question of national spirit by Wieland's
comments in Schiller's *Historischer Kalender für Damen,* in 1792 repub-
lished a short pamphlet on German unity he had written in 1765, with
some new remarks added. In these remarks, Moser asserted that Germany
indeed had a national spirit, just as it had a wine- and beer-land—in every
little place a different wine or beer, and every five or ten years a different
spirit. He now questioned, however, whether a common spirit was really
desirable for Germany, and asked: "Does not the principle and means of
our preservation lie in the constant friction of forces, in the continual action and reaction of political alkali and acid?" He wondered whether it
might not be just as well to leave things the way they are for the next
hundred years, "until the ark in which so many small and large, clean
and unclean creatures are shut up together springs a leak and everyone
saves himself, or is gobbled up, as he is able or must be according to time
and circumstances."[60]

This bitterly pessimistic appraisal of the future of the Empire, so different from the exhortations of the younger Moser of the 1760s, has been
interpreted as the result not only of a steadily growing disappointment
with the political history of the Empire, but also of the French Revolution. The Revolution had indeed created a vital constitutional system
from the common spirit of the people, especially the middle class, but it
had also destroyed the social system of ranked estates which Moser wanted
to preserve, and had put popular sovereignty and the legal equality of all
citizens in its place. Perhaps, then, his own doctrines of national unity
based on contractual freedom, historical and natural rights, and so on,
had begun to appear somewhat dangerous to him. In any case, it is true
that the last few years of his life were characterized by a quiet, status quo
political conservatism which did not even venture as far as his father's
wish simply to reinstate the reality called for by the laws and traditions
of the Empire.[61] It even appears that this older and disenchanted Moser
may have concluded that it was in the basic nature of the German national spirit not to have a common spirit at all.

CHAPTER NINE

The Empire at War:
Military Problems and Proposals

B Y 1794–95, IT HAD BECOME clear that the challenge of the French Revolution to Germany had a direct military side which in the short run,
at least, was even more serious than the political and ideological implications which had helped to stimulate the controversy over the Empire's
peculiar constitution and the benefits or disadvantages it conferred on the
German peoples. Indeed, the beginnings of the final collapse of the imperial constitution are directly traceable to the outbreak of war between
the Austro-Prussian alliance and France in April 1792. The massive military power developed by the French Republic, and later Napoleon, not
only destroyed the European balance of power which was so important to
the protection of the territorial integrity of the Empire, but in doing so
it also disrupted the delicate balance of power within the Empire on which
the maintenance of its traditional constitution had so largely come to
rest. The war demonstrated the military weakness of the imperial structure, and also opened up both the possibility of and the necessity for
political changes that led irresistibly toward the reorganization of Germany in ways that made preservation of the Empire impossible.

The first phase of the war from its beginnings in 1792 until the Peace
of Campo Formio in 1797—the agreement which contained most of the
major elements of the reorganization which was not formally completed
until 1803—can be described without excessive detail for present purposes.
The policy of Austro-Prussian reconciliation, which had achieved its first-
fruits in the Convention of Reichenbach of July 1790, was continued by
the monarchs of both states, in spite of oppositional elements within their
own courts, and resulted in two subsequent agreements which helped to
set the stage for the beginning of war with France. The first of these,

the Convention of Pillnitz of August 27, 1791, produced a statement from both monarchs warning the French that events in their country were a matter of concern to all sovereigns in Europe, and proposed that if other states would contribute forces according to their power, Austria and Prussia would intervene to restore the compromised freedom of action of Louis XVI and to introduce a moderate constitution for France. While the concern of both Austrian and Prussian governments about the actions of the revolutionaries in France was real enough,[1] this agreement was not made in actual contemplation of action, since it was well known that England, without whose agreement no military steps could seriously be entertained, was opposed to intervention. Furthermore, once Louis had given his consent to the constitution drawn up for him by the National Assembly, the question of monarchical solidarity no longer seemed to be at issue, and Leopold II declared that cause for hostilities no longer existed.

The continued assaults of the Girondist faction of the new Legislative Assembly on the prerogatives of the French crown, as well as the Girondists' often open and strident republicanism, however, led to the conclusion of a defensive alliance between Austria and Prussia, whereby a mutual guarantee of possessions was exchanged, and a formal protest of the violation of German landlords' rights in Alsace was made. That alliance of February 7, 1792, also declared that any violation of the Empire's borders by France would be a cause for war. The Girondists, seeing in war a chance to trump their domestic opponents as well as to embarrass the king—whose wife, Marie Antoinette, was the sister of Leopold II—used the Austro-Prussian agreement to demand, through the Legislative Assembly which they controlled, that Austria not only disarm but also give up all alliances directed against France. This demand of March 1792 was refused by Francis II, who in the meantime had succeeded his father on the throne, and the French, carefully distinguishing between Francis II as German Emperor and as King of Bohemia and Hungary, declared war on him in his latter capacity alone, as well as on Prussia, on April 20.

The war did not, therefore, begin as a *Reichskrieg,* but as a war of one European great power against two others. And in spite of some Austrian attempts in the spring of 1792 to propagandize the war as a defense of the Empire against French aggression, it is clear that at the outset both Austria and Prussia intended to fight a war of conquest in which all gains would be theirs alone to share. This explains why neither was initially eager to have what both regarded as an easy prospective victory complicated by the participation of the Empire in a formally declared *Reichskrieg*—something which would have entitled the rest of the Empire to assist in determining the disposition of the spoils. Not until September was any formal request made to the Imperial Diet for assistance in the war, and even then it was asked for only in the form of a grant of the relatively large sum of one hundred Roman Months which was to be placed at the disposal of the two great powers, which would presumably continue to exercise their monopoly on military action. Hanover, however, immediately denounced such a grant as unconstitutional, and instead proposed the calling-up of a *Reichsarmee* in duplum, that is, 80,000 men. After long debate, the Diet actually authorized a triplum in November, but made it clear that this army was to serve only for the defense of the Empire against hostile attack. In February 1793, an Austrian proposal for a budget of one hundred Roman Months was refused in favor of a grant of only thirty, and that for the purpose of setting up an operations fund. By early spring of 1793, however, the success of French counterattacks on German soil had become a matter of some alarm, and on March 22 the Imperial Diet, without actually formally declaring war on France, simply declared the present war to be a *Reichskrieg*.

The slow and grudging response of the Diet to the requests for assistance in the war has to be seen partly in terms of a fear of war itself. This was most pronounced among the Rhenish states, both secular and ecclesiastical, which recoiled from the expenses of war not only from the standpoint of a fiscal parsimony which was shared by almost every territorial government, but also from the likelihood of direct war damage occasioned by campaigns fought on their soil and the economic losses which would result from possible enemy occupation. Not all rulers went as far as the Palatinate-Bavarian Elector and the Duke of Württemberg, who loudly proclaimed the neutrality of their territories immediately after the French declaration of war; but even some less immediately endangered north German states authorized the Hanoverian court to announce that there was no reason for them to become involved in the present war between France and *Hungary!*[2]

Even before the formal French declaration of war, there was a strong body of opinion in Germany which opposed military intervention in French affairs. Max Franz of Cologne, for example, in spite of a rapidly growing animosity toward the Revolution, had consistently recommended neutrality for the Empire and its members, a position he did not change until the fall of 1792.[3] And in January of 1792, as French relations with Austria and some of the emigré-laden ecclesiastical states were fast degenerating, an anonymous publicist argued with some urgency that the right of every territorial ruler, including the Emperor, to maintain his own armed forces did not confer a concomitant right to wage war with foreign powers. He justified this position on the ground that such a war must inevitably involve the entire Empire, that is, must necessarily become a *Reichskrieg*; as such, it and the considerations which might lead to it were properly subordinate to the imperial constitution, and a territorial ruler who engaged in such a war to the danger of the Empire or his fellow rulers must be returned to order by the Emperor or his princely colleagues or, on complaint of his own subjects, by the imperial courts.[4]

Just as important in accounting for the very dubious attitude with which the Estates approached the prospect of war was their widespread and profound suspicion of the motives of the two German great powers. Events of recent years had given rise to a distrust of both Vienna and Berlin throughout the rest of the Empire, and the cooperation of these two courts in almost any enterprise was regarded as a distinct signal of danger.[5] During the mobilization of the combined Austro-Prussian army which was soon to make the initial military thrust into France, Max Franz was full of the most severe reservations: "All of Germany is in an uproar," he wrote on June 26, 1792; "one fears the French less than these two powers, and one generally finds the cure worse than the malady."[6]

As the army began to move into position, and the visibility of its contingents became greater, other worried voices were raised. In August, one commentator, in spite of his strong feelings that his German fatherland ought to be defended, lamented the spectacle of the various Austrian and Prussian armies marching across the territories of other imperial princes without their permission. Even in the present just cause it set a nasty precedent for the future, when one day such a combined force might march in the Empire for not such a good reason, and under the orders of rulers not as high-minded as were Francis II and Frederick William II. At the same time, however, this writer indirectly foresaw the reasons why, in the end, the Empire as a whole would see itself obliged to support the Austro-Prussian war effort. It is deplorable, he wrote, when any kingdom is unable to help itself, and it is the harbinger of its destruction when powerful parties, whether foreign or domestic, "play the master and, without asking the shadow-empire (*Schatten-Reich*) itself, do entirely as they please."[7] The implication was clear: The Imperial Estates had better attempt to help themselves, and not permit Austria and Prussia alone by their actions to determine the fate of the Empire. Since war had already been declared, since France and her two German enemies would fight that war wherever it had to be fought, and since the results of the war would be determined more or less exclusively by those who participated in it, then it followed that those of the smaller states which refused to fight in it would surely be abandoned to the military and political convenience of the great powers. Participation, on the other hand, conferred at least the possibility that the course of the war and the nature of the peace could be shaped so as not to cause excessive harm to the lesser territories. This was the sense of the argument of Franz Joseph von Linden, an official in Electoral Mainz, whose plea for all German princes to assist in the defense of the integrity of the Empire in order to protect the European balance of power was only slightly stronger than his thinly veiled implication that

Austria and Prussia, left to themselves, cared nothing about the imperial association as such.[8]

There were good reasons for the suspicion directed against both Austria and Prussia by the other German states. Austria, for one thing, had never given up the idea of a Bavarian exchange, or even the possibility of an outright incorporation of all or part of Bavaria. Rumors that both Vienna and Berlin were entertaining notions of even more fundamental territorial reorganizations, some of them involving the secularization and absorption of ecclesiastical principalities, were rife and not all were groundless. Indeed, only the shifting fortunes of war in western Germany, as well as the preoccupation of both Austria and Prussia with the second and third partitions of Poland in 1793 and 1795 and the mutual jealousy and suspicion they occasioned, prevented the two German powers from attempting in some fashion to do what it ultimately fell to France to do. The second partition of Poland, in particular, arranged without Austria's participation by Prussia and Russia, created bitter hostility against Berlin in Vienna, and destroyed almost completely such degree of good feeling as had developed between the two courts in the years 1790–92. The rest of the Empire was aware from early 1793 on that the differences which separated the two formally allied German powers were nearly as great as those which separated both from France, and while earlier fears of a partition of the Empire by a common agreement of Austria and Prussia may have been eased in some quarters, it was replaced by a renewed sense that the Empire, under assault from without by French forces, was once again becoming the political battlefield for the old Austro-Prussian rivalry. Under such circumstances, it is understandable that a certain hopelessness, alternating with desperation, came to characterize the war effort of most of the principalities of the Empire.

By mid-1794, a general war-weariness was apparent throughout Germany. Based partly on the indecisiveness of the expensive campaigns of earlier years and the losses of early 1794, as well as on Prussia's increasingly apparent unwillingness to bear further costs of the war and her threats to withdraw her troops unless they were subsidized by other parties —England, Austria, and the western Imperial Circles, for example—the Empire was rapidly losing its will to fight. Still, the Diet voted a grant of 50 Roman Months for the war effort in June 1794, and in October approved not only another 100, but also a quintuplum of troop levies. This may well have been done in expectation that peace would soon be sought, and that these grants would assist in drawing France to the negotiating table; Max Franz of Cologne was not alone in believing that an honorable peace involving a restoration of all occupied German territory in return for recognition of the French Republic and a promise not to meddle in French affairs could be achieved best by arming strongly while

seeking peace.[9] That peace was in any case the primary concern of most
of the Empire was demonstrated in December when the Diet formally
requested that the Emperor, in cooperation with the King of Prussia, attempt to reach agreement with France.

The military efforts of the Empire had been beset by many difficulties. One of them, certainly, was the steadily improving war capability
of the French, whose military and political disarray of 1792 and early 1793
had been largely overcome by 1794; with an economy now more or less
fully geared to war, with military command problems solved, and with
the armed force of some 850,000 citizen-soldiers, which had been created
by the famous *levée en masse* by the spring of 1794, France had become
an enemy of awesome strength. Just as serious for the Germans, however, were the problems of their own military organization and command,
a major one of which was the lack of cooperation in the field between
Austrian and Prussian commanders stemming from the mutual hostility
of their respective governments.

Nor did the Austro-Prussian antagonism exhaust the political dissen-
sions which crippled the Empire's military efforts. Two writings of this
period show clearly that the Estates' jealous guardianship of their territorial prerogatives simply would not admit a national military emergency
as sufficient cause for an even momentary abdication of any of the rights
they ascribed to their *Landeshoheit*. The first of these two anonymously
published tracts was intended to refute arguments put forth in a recent
and also anonymous work suggesting that during a formally declared
Reichskrieg the entire Empire constituted but a single territory, in which
the Emperor or his supreme commander had the right to lead his army
into any territory and any fortress located within the Empire. Specifically, those arguments had set forth the following principles: (1) that
Germany was divided into parts with respect to the territorial rulers
among themselves, but not with respect to the Emperor; (2) that the
military rights of the Estates ceased during a *Reichskrieg*; (3) that the
exercise of such rights resumed only with the opening of a peace congress; (4) that the Emperor or his supreme commander had a right to
dispose over the whole territory of the Empire according to the requirements of their war plans; and (5) that in the absence of an Imperial Army
in the proper sense (i.e., the *Reichsarmee*), then the forces of the imperial
house itself, together with its auxiliaries, were to be regarded as the Imperial Army.[10]

Both offended and alarmed at the implication of the above propositions that all powers of *Landeshoheit* were terminated during a *Reichskrieg*, the author of the first refutation asserted that such a principle was
extremely dangerous for the freedom of the German Estates, and could
easily be abused in such a way as to lead to the overthrow of the entire

German constitution. He asserted that the right to build and occupy fortresses in the individual states was an exclusively territorial one. Neither the Emperor nor his commanders could have any such right, even during a *Reichskrieg,* as long as the territorial ruler was able adequately to occupy and provision such fortresses, and as long as his actions did not endanger the common security by obstructing offensive or defensive operations against the enemy. A ruler, to be sure, could make a voluntary convention for the acceptance of imperial troops, or could even be legally compelled to do so by a decision of the Diet, ratified by the Emperor; but in the latter case, provision would have to be made to provide compensation for any damages suffered. Any other grounds for imperial occupation of territorial fortresses were without legal force, and indeed constituted an unconstitutional presumption and arrogation of the rights of the territorial ruler.[11]

The strong provincialism of the above arguments was pushed to its uttermost in the second work, written as an apologia for the officials and army officers of the Palatinate-Bavarian Elector who had surrendered the fortifications of Mannheim to the French on September 21, 1795. This event, according to the author, had created no particular sensation at the time it occurred, but had begun to be denounced as treasonable in some quarters after imperial arms had begun to prevail against the French for a time early in the following month. Starting with a pronounced emphasis on *Landeshoheit* and the right it conferred on every imperial prince to make war or peace, as long as the war was not directed against the whole Empire and the peace was not made for the overthrow or alteration of the German constitution, he went on to assert that in a *Reichskrieg* no prince was required to do more than the imperial laws required of him, and that anyone who did more did so for selfish political reasons that could establish no obligation to him on the part of anyone else. If the entire military force of the Empire should prove inadequate to its task, this meant not that any individual prince should redouble his efforts, but that the whole Empire should do so; and if this were impossible because of deficiencies of the imperial constitution, then either they should be corrected or *Reichskriege* should simply be avoided. Once a prince had provided his legally required contingent to the *Reichsarmee,* he was free to use the remainder of his forces as he saw fit, as long as they were not combined with those of the enemy. If imperial fortresses were to be built, then the Empire itself should build them. All others were exclusively territorial, and their governors, commanders, and garrisons were under the sole command of the territorial prince. This being the case, the prince could at all times do what he wanted with his own fortresses, including demolishing them, without regard to the Empire as a whole. No accounting of the disposition of such fortresses was due anyone, unless they were intentionally misused against the Empire. From all this it followed that capitulation to an enemy of the Empire was not only permissible but, if done for the good of the prince's own land and subjects, was blameless in both a moral and a genuine political sense. The author concluded grandly that the Elector and all of his officials and officers were at the very least not to be censured for the surrender of Mannheim, with an implication that the capitulation was a positive good in a higher ethical sense.[12]

From documents such as these, and the conditions and attitudes to which they testify, it is not difficult to understand the considerations which had earlier moved Johann Jacob Moser to his much quoted judgment of the warmaking capacity of the Empire: "The deficiencies which are exposed in an Imperial War and in an Imperial Army are so great, [and] also so many and multifarious, that as long as the German Empire remains in its present constitution, it should forever be forbidden to wage an Imperial War insofar as it is at all possible."[13] The total absence of a spirit of self-sacrifice, the "minimalism" of princes whose only concern was to be certain that they did no more than anyone else or than the law, strictly interpreted, required (and that only grudgingly), and an egoism which virtually excluded the sense of being part of a collective body—all these would appear shocking to one who was not aware of the dangers and expenses of the war, especially in the territories of the western Imperial Circles, as well as of the widespread conviction that the purposes of the war were in the long run related less to the defense of the Empire than to the great power interests of Austria or Prussia, and that without their pressure an essentially inexpensive peace might otherwise be obtained. The fact that the princes were not altogether correct in this interpretation does not lessen the sincerity of their convictions; but those convictions clearly did reduce the willingness of many territorial rulers to make the sacrifices of men and money that were required by the seriousness of the French military challenge.

On the other hand, even if they had proved willing to vote and then, more important, actually to contribute the requisite funds and manpower within the framework of the traditional imperial military organization, as specified by the constitution, it is doubtful that it would have produced a much different result. There was probably no element of imperial organization more universally or severely condemned among publicists and commentators of every persuasion than the military constitution. Professor Danz in Stuttgart in 1792 might have been speaking for all of them in calling it simply the most imperfect of all imaginable ones, and an object of mockery to Germans as well as to foreigners. "Generally," in fact, "it is represented as a model of inappropriate institutions."[14] What all had primarily in mind, of course, was the *Reichsarmee*, the motley army raised by vote of the Imperial Diet in the Imperial Circles through levies imposed on the territories according to a fixed formula.[15] The effectiveness of this army as a fighting force in earlier times has been a matter of some dispute, but in its few appearances after the wars of Louis XIV it managed to do little but cover itself with shame. The most notorious demonstration of its ineptitude, from which its reputation never recovered, came at the battle of Rossbach in November 1757, when it, together with a combined Austro-French army, was completely routed in a short battle by a Prussian army of much inferior size commanded by Frederick the Great.[16] Its later appearances, whether as the smaller force of the Westphalian Circle called out to execute the judgment of the Imperial Cameral Tribunal against rebellious subjects of the Bishop of Liège in 1789–90,[17] or as the full triplum and later quintuplum of the wars of the French Revolution, was at best spotty, at worst disastrous, and in any case not at all comparable to the territorial armies of Hessen-Kassel, Saxony, or even Hanover, not to mention those of Austria and Prussia.[18] This is the major reason why in this war it was decided not to set up the *Reichsarmee* as an independent force, but to attach its contingents to the Austrian and Prussian armies which were already operative in the field.

The best description of the Imperial Army of this period was written by a certain Friedrich Christian Laukhard in 1795, and published in the following year. Laukhard was a highly original person, of fun-loving and independent character, who was in and out of scrapes of one kind or another for much of his life. The son of a Lutheran preacher from the Imperial County of Grehweiler in the Lower Palatinate, he attended several universities and returned home to try his hand at preaching. After being discharged and then rehired in this capacity, he left home for good. He took up a teaching position at the Prussian state orphanage in Halle in 1781, but exaggerated worry about some small debts he had incurred moved him to "emigrate" into the Prussian army in 1784. Captured by the French in the early 1790s, he was led off to France, and did not return to Germany until 1795. In that year, he joined up temporarily with a little army of French emigrés; finding their company intolerable, however, he soon deserted them and enlisted in a Swabian contingent of the Imperial Army. He sought and received formal release from his Prussian military obligations, also in 1795, whereupon he quit the *Reichsarmee* and returned to Halle, where he spent the remainder of his life first as a preacher—a position from which he was discharged—and finally as a private tutor.[19] Laukhard's description of the inadequacies of the Imperial Army is therefore based on solid military experience and personal observation and comparison stemming from service in both the Swabian corps and the Prussian army. As will become apparent, however, his book is more than a commentary on the *Reichsarmee*; it is also an analysis of many of the social and political conditions which crippled the whole Empire in its attempt to respond to the French challenge, and as such deserves lengthy consideration.

The problems of the Imperial Army, according to Laukhard, began at the very moment its call-up was announced, when "a panicky fear" arose in all the Circles, "and the wailing and lamentation [became] general." No youths wanted to serve as soldiers, and it became necessary for governments either to compel them to do so—at very small pay—either by grabbing them off the streets or by the employment of lotteries. If by chance a rich man's son were chosen by the latter method, then it was often possible for the father to bribe a poor man to go in his son's place for a payment that could reach as much as 200–300 Gulden. Foreigners, deserters, gypsies, or vagabonds would do as well; so, in fact, would anyone who could stand in a row and shoulder a musket. Some territories, however, solved two problems at once by sending their prison-sweepings to the army. Since all of this took time, however, the first contingents sent off to fulfill the territorial quotas of the smaller Estates frequently had to come from such military establishments as they already had; but these were little more than watchmen, whose training consisted of an occasional assembly in the prince's park, where they presented arms and fired off their muskets two or three times. These tiny "armies" of from six to twenty men, even if all showed up at the same time, often could not come to grips even with these simple exercises and fired ragged volleys, if indeed their guns discharged at all.[20]

With troops such as these to work with, the officers of the *Reichs-armee* obviously had their work cut out for them; but as Laukhard made abundantly clear, the majority of officers were neither inclined nor able to make a battle-ready force of the heterogeneous hordes under their command. The state of their military knowledge was shockingly low, because most officer positions within the territories were conferred not for merit, but for money or favor. While princes appointed only noblemen and Imperial Cities only members of the bourgeoisie to such positions, it was characteristic that neither would consider looking beyond their own territory for appointments even when no one there possessed proper qualifications. Furthermore, because even smaller units such as companies normally consisted of troops from more than one territory, their officers were also appointed by more than one territory; to cite Laukhard's example, drawn from a company consisting of troops from four Imperial Cities, Gmünd was entitled to choose the captain, Rottweil the first lieutenant, Rottenmünster the second lieutenant, and Gengenbach the cadet ensign. Since each of these cities had but one position to give, and at one specified rank only, there was no incentive among officers to distinguish themselves in the hope of promotion. The noncommissioned officers were, if anything, worse than their superiors: in Dinkelsbühl, a "depraved, drunken innkeeper" got the job of company sergeant, while a "miserable besotted student" from Halle in Swabia became quartermaster only because his father had once sat in the municipal senate; and the Cistercian monks of Salmansweiler nominated as quartermaster "a wretched man who had formerly been their gardener."[21]

The care and provisioning of troops also came in for their share of criticism from Laukhard. The most basic items of field equipment, such as cooking kettles, tents, axes, spades, straw for men to sleep on, packhorses, were often in short supply. Part of the problem was simple incompetence, but another part of it was the frequent and deliberate fraud perpetrated against individual territorial governments by the so-called *Provisor,* that is, the officer appointed by each territory to look after the supply of provisions and equipment for the troops of that territory, who in collusion with the supplier would make out false accounts and pocket the overcharge.

Laukhard's most bitter criticisms, however, were reserved for the medical care of the troops. Field surgeons were described as "bunglers, dabblers, and genuine beard-scrapers," while such hospitals as were available to the *Reichsarmee* were "murder-holes, where the pestilential air, the miserable nursing, the indescribable filth, the vermin and other deficiencies of the care of the sick only worsen diseases, and cause many people to bite the dust *(ins Gras beissen).*" So bad were these hospitals, indeed, that they were actively feared among the troops, "for it is thought that a man who is dragged into such a healing-hole, even with an otherwise insignificant disease, may well run the danger of never coming out again."

Although Laukhard condemned the attitudes that led to such neglect of the care of the soldiery, he also admitted that the character of many of the soldiers themselves was partly responsible for those attitudes: "whoever cannot amount to anything anywhere runs off to the soldiers, or is handed over to them for discipline—drunkards, sluggards, imbeciles, obstinate [and] undutiful sons, frivolous [and] restless deserters, rusticated students, disloyal servants, perjured business agents, the bankrupt and so on according to the proverb: Whoever is worthless must follow the calfskin, that is, the drum."[22]

Still, the original human material out of which soldiers were made was perhaps not that much different in the *Reichsarmee* from what it was in the crack territorial armies of Prussia, Austria, Hessen-Kassel, and so on. What was the real difference, then? Laukhard, in suggesting that the worst deficiency of the Imperial Army was simply that it was composed of too many sorts of people, put his finger on the central problem: Whereas Prussia or Austria took diversity and made it over into something resembling a uniform army, diversity was the very and inescapable nature of the *Reichsarmee*. The most obvious manifestation of this diversity was the multitude of different uniforms with which the various territories outfitted their contingents. While Laukhard saw nothing intrinsically disastrous in this, he also believed that in some Circles the variation in uniforms had gotten completely out of hand. Thus, he cited a colonel in the army of the Margrave of Baden who, upon first beholding a regiment of the Swabian Circle army as it had been reconstituted in the 1790s for the first time since the Seven Years' War, remarked disgustedly that the only thing lacking for a total caricature was "a few dozen jesters and chimney sweeps." Much more serious than the lack of uniformity in clothing, however, was the wide variation in the caliber and construction of armaments, which made common exercises all but impossible and, worse yet, meant that parts and ammunition were not interchangeable. Particularly noticeable in the artillery, this could have the most serious results: "When Mainz was challenged by [the French] General Custine in 1792, cannon and shells were available in Mainz, but according to the statement of the commandant the shells did not fit the cannon." The diversity of the various contingents also affected their provisioning, since the *Provisor* appointed by each territory was responsible only for the troops of that territory. That responsibility varied considerably for several reasons, resulting in an inequality in both the nature and quantity of provisions for different contingents which created envy and jealousy among them. Regimental officers themselves, being subjects of different rulers, respected the chain of command only grudgingly, and thus contributed to an atmosphere of jealousy and backbiting which badly undermined morale.[23]

Morale was as serious a problem for the common soldiers as it was for their officers. Indeed, the low spirits of the troops, their unwillingness to risk life and limb, was for Laukhard a better explanation for their lackluster performance in the field than the organizational and financial problems of the army. On several occasions, he contrasted the remarkable achievements of the French volunteer soldiery in recent years, as well as the high regard in which it was held in France, with the undistinguished accomplishments of the *Reichsarmee* and the general contempt which characterized public attitudes toward the military estate in Germany. The reason for that was simple: The Frenchman was fighting for his fatherland, his citizenship, his family, and his freedom, whereas the German could not. The German had no real fatherland, was incapable of fighting in defense of laws which oppressed him and which did not represent the will of the nation, had less reason to defend his fellow citizens against foreigners than against the depredations of the privileged classes at home, and, as a slave to those classes, was unable even to conceive of a national honor, much less to fight to redeem it.[24] In many respects, Laukhard suggested, these attitudes of the ordinary soldier were merely reflections of the indifference or hostility that characterized the relations between their princes. In particular, the smaller princes and other territorial authorities went about the business of raising their contingents with the greatest reluctance and sullenness, because they knew that, even though an unsuccessful war would force them to share the misfortunes of the larger states, they would receive none of the credit or spoils of victory. Consequently, they did only what they were required to do, without enthusiasm or any hint of genuine patriotism.[25]

In the end, of course, patriotism was the real issue for Laukhard—a patriotism which should arise from a national spirit and should confer a common spirit. Unfortunately, such a patriotism was not only momentarily lacking, but was altogether impossible under Germany's present constitution. Laukhard cited four general conditions which stifled the sentiment of patriotism: the fragmentation of Germany into "insignificant, powerless dynasties"; the excessive influence of "priestcraft" (*Pfafferey*) of various kinds, which diverted into religion the moral sentiments which could more profitably be applied to civic affairs; the tyranny of the nobility over other classes in most areas; and the lack of a genuinely powerful and influential Supreme Head.[26]

To these causes for the absence of a spirit of national self-sacrifice, Laukhard added the conviction that the present war against France, like so many other past wars in which the Empire had become involved, was not only in itself unjustified, but was the result of a plot of the two great German powers, which, as usual, were serving their own self-interest at the expense of the Empire. Austria's policies were judged with particular severity, with a suggestion that Prussia had been dragged into the war almost against her will; but Prussia was also implicated in the answer Laukhard gave to his own question as to why, given the weakness and multiple deficiencies of the *Reichsarmee,* it had ever been called up to begin with. Perhaps, said he, it was because the larger states desired a weakening of the Empire as a preliminary step toward the alteration of its constitution. If so, no better means could be found than the convocation of the Imperial Army, a measure which invariably exhausted Germany in men and money, plunged every territory into debt, spread inflation into all Circles, and set ruler against ruler in bitterness and jealousy: "Germany was perhaps never more enervated than it now is, and perhaps for that very reason, once the business with France is put to rest, the time is not far off when the imperial constitution will suffer a severe change."[27]

Early in his book, Laukhard had disavowed any intention of making recommendations for the improvement of the deplorable condition of the *Reichsarmee* because of his belief that the anarchic situation of the formless German Empire rendered any real improvement impossible. As his analysis unfolded, it became clear that the military deficiencies of the army were in fact rooted in a double political problem, the first of which was the obvious and frequently mentioned political division of Germany, but the second of which was the stark fact that the terms "Germany" and "the Empire" simply no longer included Austria and Prussia. Laukhard put it this way: "The great states of Austria and Prussia are incorrectly reckoned [as belonging] to Germany or to the Roman Empire. If they were genuine components of it: then both must have and pursue a single interest for the welfare of the fatherland. But—I think the present war against France has now shown clearly enough how far this common interest goes."[28] Badly crippled by its own fragmentation and the insuperable organizational problems which accompanied it, Laukhard's "Germany" was not permitted to have its own policy, including even the passive one of neutrality which could spare it the military challenges to which it was inadequate; it was simply too weak to declare and maintain such a policy. With imperial neutrality thus impossible in the event either Austria or Prussia might choose to go to war, Laukhard reduced the real choices of Germany to four: first, to keep a permanent standing army among the Circles, which could be as much as quadrupled in an emergency; second, to dissolve the imperial bond altogether, by common agreement of all Estates, to be followed by a choice of alliances with Austria, Prussia, or France; third, the formation of a new league of princes, excluding Austria and Prussia, with the possibility of a guarantee from France; or, finally and most comfortably, simply to let matters go on as at present until "the genius of the times" or some other power arrived at a new disposition of things.[29]

The first of Laukhard's four alternatives was frequently advocated by other students of the German military constitution who, like him, saw in the haphazard haste with which the *Reichsarmee* always had to be put together one of the chief reasons for its disorganization and inefficiency. If, they reasoned, a permanent and considerable force of well-trained and well-equipped imperial troops existed at all times within the Circles, then the ghastly problems of recruitment and supply which always attended the call-up could be avoided and, just as important, the basis would be laid for the introduction of a uniformity into the various Circle contingents which might produce something resembling a national army. The results which could be hoped for were illustrated in a proposal of 1794 by Friedrich von Bock, an Imperial Knight serving at the time as a captain in one of the regiments of the Westphalian Circle. Sensing that Germany was locked in a life-and-death struggle of a sort very different from earlier *Reichskriege,* Bock insisted that the Empire could no longer afford the luxury of doing without a permanent peacetime standing army, the size of which he set at 120,000 men—triple the simplum that was normally supposed to be needed in time of war. Raised within the Circles, the various regiments of this army would be required to conduct common maneuvers annually within each Circle, and every second year would exercise with corps from other Circles, each time in a different one. Each Circle would have its own artillery depot and general arsenal, as well as a military academy for the training of officers. The chain of higher military command would be re-formed so as to provide each Circle with a lieutenant general and, if necessary, three or four major generals, together with an adequate permanent general staff. Over every two Circles, an Imperial Lieutenant General would be appointed, and at the very top an Imperial Field Marshal over all Circles. All these appointments would be determined by merit alone. A War Council composed of military specialists would be set up at the central imperial level as well as within each Circle to advise on all matters pertaining to military operations and supply.

Like many others before and after him, Bock attributed much of the Empire's military weakness to the lack of national spirit and of the insight that the interests of one and of all, especially in wartime, were the same. Nowhere more than in the *Reichsarmee* were the results of this lack more obvious or debilitating, and Bock suggested several reforms that might help to remold the army into a truly national force. A single military code for the entire army, for example, which also included an oath to be taken to "all of the princes and Estates of the Empire, (and) thus to the whole nation," would not only make desertion a crime throughout the whole Empire, but would convey a sense of common purpose to all. Similar arms, exercises, and regulations, as well as standard uniforms, would also help to create a common spirit, a feeling of belonging to a national enterprise. Bock insisted, too, that in both peace and war, the contingents of the *Reichsarmee* be kept strictly separate from the "house troops," the territorial armies of the various princes: The princes must recognize that providing men for the Imperial Army was a duty they owed to the Empire, and that that army was under the sole command of Emperor and Empire. As the only German national army, furthermore, it should have the automatic right to occupy any fortress or position within the territory of the Empire during wartime, "For in wartime, especially, the Empire must be regarded as a whole, where all territorial differences cease." Thus, while Bock's proposals remained essentially within the structural framework established by the constitution, they did call for new laws based upon new attitudes, chief among which was a recognition that this war would be lost if it were fought as earlier *Reichskriege* had been fought, and that in Germany, as in other nations, "The fetters of tradition and custom" had to be broken in the name of "the law of necessity."[30]

As figures for a standing army of 120,000 men such as that proposed by Bock began to pale before the hundreds of thousands of French conscripts being rushed to arms by the *levée en masse,* it became increasingly apparent that no answer to Germany's military problems which did not provide for a massive utilization of manpower would be adequate. For a time after the failure of the campaigns of 1793, the idea of some sort of general conscription began to be talked about in many official circles in Germany, and it received formal Austrian support at the Imperial Diet in January 1794. In Württemberg and a few other western German and Rhenish territories, including Mainz, some steps were actually taken to implement this idea of *Volksbewaffnung,* but they were brought to a halt by Prussia's threat to withdraw her troops from the Rhine if such notions of popular participation in the war were not given up immediately.[31] Prussia's opposition to general conscription was based primarily on fear of the effects an armed people might have upon a strongly absolutist-authoritarian system; but while it probably required the disapproval of a state as strong as Prussia to guarantee the demise of the idea, many other rulers were not altogether unhappy to see it fail. Even the enlightened Carl August of Weimar, while prepared to accept popular mobilization in the Circles along the Rhine as a last resort, was extremely dubious about putting arms in the hands of peasants and creating "citizen officers." "I would rather pay my last crown (*écu*) to the Elector of Saxony to have a couple of his good regiments march than to arm five hundred of my peasants," he wrote early in 1794. Somewhat later he indicated disapproval and outright refusal of the Emperor's formal request to the Diet for a general popular conscription.[32] Even many middle-class persons were fearful of the long-term effects of popular participation in the war. Rudolph Z. Becker, an educator and editor who had strongly protective feelings toward the lower classes, and C. U. D. von Eggers, editor of the Hamburg *Deutsches Magazin,* observed with great uneasiness the spectacle of armed peasants in southern and southwestern Germany defending themselves against French marauders in 1795 and 1796. Sensing that what was at stake in the war was not merely territorial gain or loss, but the integrity of the entire traditional social system which could be endangered more by lower classes in arms with a feeling of their own power than by the French, they feared that mass mobilization as a cure might well be worse than the disease.[33]

The failure of the proposals for *Volksbewaffnung* in 1793–94 did not close the door to other possible schemes for raising the military manpower required by the war effort, but it did mean that any proposal with even the slightest chance for implementation would have to overcome the twin obstacles which had spelled the doom of general mobilization: the fear of social unrest and the widespread doubts among the professional military about the effectiveness of suddenly armed hordes of peasants and artisans who had never fired a gun in their lives and who had no experience of the discipline necessary for successful campaigning. A plan suggested

in 1794 by a certain Georg Franz von Blum would have gone some dis-
tance toward satisfying these criteria. Like Bock, Blum believed in the
need for a standing peacetime Imperial Army, to be composed of some
10 percent of all able-bodied males between the ages of eighteen and forty,
which would continue to be raised and administered through the Circles.
To this trained and ready field army, however, Blum would add a militia
(*Landmiliz*) to provide reserve manpower that could be called upon as
the need arose. The pool for the militia would be composed of able-bodied
males between eighteen and fifty who were not already in the standing
army, of whom about 20 percent, drawn mainly from single men in the
eighteen to thirty group, would actually serve in the militia. The other
80 percent would be divided by age groups into three classes which would
be called up in order as needed. Exemption from service would be given
to those in essential occupations, especially in agriculture, as well as to
only sons, students, and so on. The militia was to be divided into both
infantry and cavalry companies of 120–150 men, whose officers were to be
appointed by the territorial rulers, and into battalions of 2,000 men, led
by commissioned officers named by the Circle. The Circle would also be
responsible for providing the arms and munitions of the militia, which
were to be stored in guarded armories except during actual campaigns.
Blum felt it important that the regulations under which the militia operated should be the same as those of the army, and that the militia members be exercised frequently—for example, after mass on Sundays and
holidays.[34]

Blum's proposal would thus not only have provided a structure for
training and discipline that might have dispelled the nightmare of un-
controlled hordes of armed peasants running about the countryside, but
would also have solved the problem of numbers. Even after exemptions,
if all the Imperial Estates had put up the numbers of men required by this
proposal, the regular *Reichsarmee,* by Blum's estimate, would have totaled
386,000 men, with another 563,000 or so in the militia.[35] The fact that Blum
also worked out separate figures for the six western and most exposed
Circles is indicative not only of his realization of their more urgent need,
but also of his recognition that the rest of the Empire must do something
for itself regardless of the future policies of Austria and Prussia and of
the reluctance of the eastern or interior Circles to put much effort into a
war that did not affect their territories directly.

A much greater degree of cooperation among the Circles was also
seen as inescapable if good results were to be achieved from the above
plans. All of Blum's proposals in this regard aimed at greater uniformity
and centralization of administration and command. He suggested that
all troops be paid equally from funds contributed at least two months in
advance by all territories to a Circle War Commissioner, who would then

pay the troops directly; similarly, he recommended that the food provided for the troops be the same for all, and that this be done through the establishment of a single food depot or *Haupt-Magazin* funded by contributions from all the Estates of the Empire. Blum also urged uniformity in weaponry, as well as a reserve store of artillery pieces at some place in the Empire. On questions of military command, he wanted all officers and men of the *Reichsarmee* proper to be under the direct command of Emperor and Empire, that is, under the sole orders of the *Reichs-Generalität,* and believed that the Imperial Field Marshal should have the right to appoint new officers to fill vacancies created by death or injury, without having to consult the Circle or the individual ruler who had named the original officers.[36]

One particularly interesting feature of Blum's plan is that it included attention to the specific problems of financing these military innovations and reforms—an important aspect often wholly ignored by other writers. He recommended the abolition of the whole concept of the Roman Month as the basis of taxation, largely because it had fallen mostly to the lower classes to pay it and—since the amounts needed to fund his proposals were considerably larger than the fifty or one hundred Roman Months normally voted by the Diet—the peasantry, in particular, would be ruined by it. In its place, he suggested either a general head tax, with amounts ranging from 10,000 florins for a prince of the Empire down to one-half florin for day-laborers and artisans, or the reintroduction of the so-called "Common Penny" (*Gemeiner Pfennig*), a complicated tax based on income as well as property which had originally been voted by the Diet of Worms in 1495, but had been dropped a few years later. Either, according to Blum, would yield at least 15,000,000 Gulden, which was equivalent to the yield of 250 Roman Months. Even that, of course, would not be enough, since Blum was thinking in terms of an amount adequate to fund the entire payment and provisioning of troops from a central source; these had earlier been left to the responsibility of the individual territory, and were not part of the expenses for which Roman Months were voted by the Diet.[37] He therefore proposed that the Empire essentially borrow from itself by issuing some 100,000,000 florins' worth of securities—paper money, in effect—which would be backed by nothing less than the entire property of all the ecclesiastical and secular Estates of the Empire, but especially of the Circles most exposed to danger. Admitting that the absence of a real central government in Germany would make such money highly suspect, especially among merchants, and that a somewhat similar scheme—the assignats of the Revolutionary government in France—had not worked out very well, Blum yet believed that it could contribute to an economic boom in the Empire, that it was preferable to taking cash money out of everyone's hands, and that even merchants might accept the idea to prevent the collapse of the Empire which might otherwise result. Assuming that German arms were successful in the war with France, these securities, which were to be called "Imperial War Coupons" (*Reichs-Kriegs-Koupons*), could be redeemed after the war partly through lands taken from the enemy,[38] partly through revenues derived from a Common Penny which would be levied once every five years. If the war ended badly, Blum hinted, then the treasure of all mediate and immediate religious foundations, monasteries, and churches could be used for redemption instead.[39]

What the proposals of Bock, Blum, and Laukhard had in common, apart from their recognition of the need for a larger, better disciplined, and more uniform military force, was their assumption that this force had to belong to and be responsive to the direction of the Empire as a whole —that is, that it should not be merely an auxiliary force attached to the territorial armies of the two great German powers as it was in this war. Indeed, all the particular reforms suggested for the improvement of the *Reichsarmee* were ultimately designed to make of it a body capable of effective independent operation.

The fact that it had not been constituted as an autonomous force in this *Reichskrieg* was due not only to political pressures from the Austrian and Prussian courts, but also to the almost universal recognition that its multiple deficiencies simply rendered it incapable of successful action in the field, and that the only possibility of deriving any real utility from it lay in subordinating it to the command of the more experienced and disciplined Austrians and Prussians. But that, of course, meant almost total subjection to the policies of Austria and Prussia—the loss of any effective codeterminant role for the rest of the Empire in the great questions of war and peace. In view of the widespread and by now inveterate suspicion harbored by many Germans that Austrian and Prussian long-range plans included provision for some sort of partition of Germany, the inability of the medium-sized and smaller territories to protect themselves even by means of a common military force was terribly disturbing. By mid-1794, there was a mood of real desperation among many of the Estates. Austria had been forced to pull her army out of the Netherlands and into defensive positions to the east of the Rhine, while Prussia's Rhine army demonstrated an almost total inactivity which was rendered all the more alarming by hard rumors of Prussian negotiations with the French. With the very real possibility that one or the other, or both, of the German powers might attempt to cut their losses by a separate peace with France, and at the expense of the rest of the Empire if necessary, it is no wonder that interest in creating an independently viable *Reichsarmee* was high.[40]

It is also not surprising that those who were interested in evoking a fully imperial response to the dangers of the time should assume that their military proposals ought properly to be carried out within the traditional framework of the Imperial Circles. These were not only the legal and familiar agencies for the organization of the Empire's military efforts, whose acceptance bespoke the reformers' desire to remain within the terms of the imperial constitution, but were also the only way of ensuring that participation would be truly universal among all Estates large and small, and would not become the property of just a few. There were some, indeed, who regarded the Circles as the possible basis not just for a military self-strengthening, but for the eventual creation of a German national spirit and the renovation of the whole Empire. The views of the Oldenburg writer and poet Gerhard Anton von Halem provide a strong example of this. Halem's prescription for the military ills of the Empire was not much different from those of Bock or Blum: a peacetime standing army (in this instance 80,000 strong), organized by the Circles, with provision for common exercises not only of contingents within Circles, but with other Circles as well.[41] But with this kind of permanent cooperation of Estates firmly established as a beginning, Halem saw other benefits for the future: The improvement of highways within and between Circles, an increase in commerce, and possibly even a quickening and cheapening of imperial justice through a scheme whereby the Circles would establish their own court systems to take over most of the appellate jurisdiction of the two imperial courts, leaving them competence only in cases of quarrels involving territorial rulers either among themselves or with their subjects.[42]

As the Circles became increasingly active and trusted units for the achievement of a growing number of tangible benefits, furthermore, they could provide a supraterritorial identification for their members, a "Circle comradeship," which would be an incomparably valuable step toward the national common spirit whose absence was the cause of so many of Germany's present problems. Halem put it this way: "We do not want to stamp out all particularism immediately and to recognize only imperial citizens (*Reichsbürger*); that would be too hasty. But we do want to feel ourselves first as Circle members, Upper Saxons, Lower Saxons, and so on. That would be the first step towards the imperial citizen."[43] For Halem, then, a resolute strengthening and elaboration of the agencies of the Circles would serve an ultimately far more important goal than the immediate self-preservation of the individual territories; it would be a great leap toward the building of a true nation: "I repeat: the institution of the Circle, defective as it may be in many particulars, can save our constitution and raise us up to a self-sustaining nation. In the constitution itself lie the means for its improvement. The form is there: To give it spirit and life depends on us."[44]

By the time Halem penned these thoughts in 1797, the Circles might have appeared to be unlikely providers of an adequate imperial defense, much less a national regeneration, yet they were now the only refuge and hope for those who wanted to escape the dilemma of abject dependency on one or the other of the great German powers or the alternative of defeat and occupation by the French armies. The only other possibility for an imperial initiative independent of Austria and Prussia had been tried in 1794, and had failed. This was the proposal for a new kind of League of Princes whose purpose, through the establishment of a separate federative army, would be not only to defend the Empire but to insure a voice for it in the eventual peace negotiations with France. The plan was proposed originally by Karl Friedrich of Baden and his minister Edelsheim to Landgrave Wilhelm IX of Hessen-Kassel at the end of July 1794, was discussed tentatively with several other courts, including Hanover, Württemberg, Nassau, and Hessen-Darmstadt, and eventually led to a conference at Wilhelmsbad, near Hanau, in late September and early October. The participants were Wilhelm IX, Karl Friedrich, and F. L. von Botzheim, minister in Nassau, with a representative of the Imperial City of Frankfurt attending but not participating in the discussions. It was decided at this conference that a number of other specified territories would be invited to join in a league whose immediate purpose was that of establishing an independent army of some 40,000 men and contracting for loans of 24 million Gulden, of which one part would finance this army while the other would be placed at the disposal of the Emperor. Soon thereafter, both the Elector of Mainz and the Duke of Braunschweig announced their intention to accede to the league, but without the ability to contribute either troops or money. Three other important states, Palatinate-Bavaria, Mecklenburg-Schwerin, and Württemberg indicated that their accession would depend upon the position of the Emperor. Since all were confident that he would join, it appeared that the basis for a major new league had been firmly laid.

To the surprise and chagrin of all, however, the official Austrian position toward this association turned out to be not only cool but downright hostile. Baron Thugut, the Austrian foreign minister since 1793, and Prince Colloredo, Imperial Vice-Chancellor, had no wish to see an independent German army established within the Empire which might prove to be an embarrassment for Austria's plans to compensate herself at a future peace settlement. Both therefore represented the plan for the new league to Francis II as a dubious enterprise, and even insinuated that it might be a Prussian tool. In fact, nothing was further from the truth, since Berlin's reaction to the league was quite equivocal, and initial promises of Prussian support for it were not taken very seriously by anyone.

The temporizing Austrian policy of simply ignoring the league in the hope that the usual problems of negotiations among its prospective members would prevent its materialization had to be changed in late November when Catherine II of Russia expressed her full approval of it, thus giving the project a considerable diplomatic boost. In December, the Emperor made known his formal disapproval of the proposed league, and recommended instead the path of greater cooperation among the Circles—a recommendation commensurate with the Austrian view that it was the Empire's responsibility to provide men and money for the Emperor to use as he saw fit, but not to attempt to conduct war on its own initiative. By March of 1795, as the prospect of difficult spring campaigning loomed on the immediate horizon, Thugut had become convinced that a league of princes could in fact be supported by Austria as long as sufficient care was taken that Prussia not be permitted to use it for her own special advantage. By this time, however, it was too late. Many prospective members, discouraged by Vienna's opposition, had definitively turned away from the project and, unwilling to make any further extraordinary efforts, had begun to look toward peace as their only realistic alternative.[45]

Plans to shore up imperial defenses through a new league of princes such as the one discussed above had one important thing in common with the proposals for a strengthening and improved utilization of the Circles as proposed by Halem: a recognition of the need to escape the domination of Austria and Prussia and their self-interested definitions of the purposes of the war, as well as of the proper terms for the peace. But they differed in one equally important respect. Suggestions for a reform or renovation of the Circles implied a common participation and therefore also a certain equality of *all* the Estates of the Empire, since the Circles essentially embraced them all. A league of princes, however, insofar as it was not coextensive with the whole of the Empire itself, implied a common purpose and an equality only of its own members, whose views and goals might or might not be shared by nonmembers. In the case of the league proposed at the Wilhelmsbad Conference, the significance of this is illustrated by the equivocal attitudes of secular states toward the membership of ecclesiastical territories. Thus, an invitation to join the league was issued to the Prince-Bishop of Würzburg and Bamberg by Karl Friedrich of Baden, but with complete confidence that it would be refused. Its acceptance not only surprised both Baden and Hessen-Kassel, but embarrassed them, since it was one of the clear, if unspoken, purposes of the future league to buttress the claims of its members to territorial compensations from the reordering of Germany that all supposed would follow the war, and which were to come primarily from the secularization of ecclesiastical principalities. The irony of this situation was rendered complete in January 1795, when the 2,000 troops requested by Hessen-Kassel from Baden to defend the former against the approach of a French army were refused, while the Prince-Bishop of Würzburg, though unasked, sent 5,000![46]

In view of the hard political calculations which underlay the reasons for this new league of princes, it is not difficult to imagine the thoroughly mixed feelings with which at least the larger princes involved in its planning must have greeted the publication of a widely read appeal which, on the surface at least, seemed to call upon them to do more or less what they were already doing, but with conditions which to a large extent would have vitiated their ultimately selfish political purpose. Written by Hans Christoph von Gagern, an Imperial Knight and a minister in the government of Nassau, it appeared in August of 1794, as the planning for the Wilhelmsbad Conference was getting underway.[47] Starting from the proposition that Germany was in real danger at this moment, Gagern yet found the Empire by no means wholly exhausted, and asserted that what was urgently needed was good will, energy, and an intelligent application of the power, men, and money that were still available in fully adequate quantities. In searching for what he called "the *point de réunion*" which could organize these resources, he dismissed the larger courts—meaning chiefly Austria and Prussia—because of their selfishness, as well as the Imperial Diet and the Circle Diets because of their perpetual squabbling and ineffectiveness. In their place, he proposed a special league composed of the great and insightful men of Germany, characterized by harmony, honesty, and energy and dedicated to the goals of the welfare and salvation of the fatherland and an honorable peace. The men were to assemble in a kind of national convention of patriotic souls in Frankfurt, where they would confer on means of overcoming the disharmony and jealousy throughout the Empire which were the chief causes of Germany's misfortunes.

Proposals such as these were certainly bland enough to give no one much cause to take offense; but other features of Gagern's plan were sure to awaken a mixture of consternation and ridicule among the hardheaded princes. For example, he included among the great men of the nation who should assemble at Frankfurt not only princes of the Empire, but also such literary and philosophical luminaries as Goethe, Wieland, the historian Christoph Meiners and the enlightened Hanoverian official and publicist August Wilhelm Rehberg. The image Gagern evoked of princes and philosophers calmly discussing the salvation of Germany in an atmosphere of brotherhood and mutual respect was almost as fantastic as his recommendation that the fighting spirit of German troops be rekindled by promises to distribute land taken from France in a successful war or, that failing, to pay every soldier the sum of one hundred Thaler at the conclusion of hostilities. Again, no territorial rulers were likely to be very impressed with his suggestion that the clergy and rich nobility they governed be forced to shoulder a larger proportion of the costs of the war, while Gagern's firm stand against the secularization of imperial ecclesiastical territories on the grounds that it would be unconstitutional was not calculated to win him friends among the larger secular princes who had already enthusiastically committed themselves to the idea, if only secretly so.[48] Like the plans and hopes of so many other patriotic Germans of his day, those of Gagern and of the principals involved in the Wilhelmsbad Conference also shattered on the rocks of Austro-Prussian self-interest and the shortsightedness of the lesser Estates. And the war continued its dreary and unfavorable course.

CHAPTER TEN

Theoretical Responses
to War and Defeat

THE FAILURE OF THE proposals of Wilhelmsbad and of all other forms of closer association among the territories of the Empire merely reinforced the decline of German military fortunes from late 1794 into the spring of 1795. Although this decline had intensified the longing for peace which by now was almost universal within the Empire, many people were surprised by the sudden withdrawal of Prussia from the war in April 1795. The strain on Prussia's military and financial resources occasioned by her involvement in the war against France, and worsened by the costs and other complications of the second partition of Poland, had become so severe even by mid-1794 that the Prussian Field Marshal Möllendorf had been authorized at that time to engage in discussions with representatives of the French Republic designed to ease the military pressures on Prussia and to explore terms on which a more far reaching settlement might be possible. At this point—July 1794—Frederick William II was still thinking in terms of a general peace in which the integrity of the Empire could be preserved; but military events soon outran these negotiations. Prussia was forced to evacuate her lands west of the Rhine in October, and to sign an armistice with France in late November. Prussia's own needs now pushed all vestiges of imperial patriotism to one side, and at the urging of all his advisors, Frederick William authorized the separate Franco-Prussian Peace of Basel, which was signed on April 5, 1795.

By the public terms of this treaty, France would evacuate all Prussian territory east of the Rhine within fourteen days, but would continue to occupy those west of the Rhine until such time as this and other questions were regulated through a general peace settlement with the whole Empire. All imperial territories which acceded to this peace through Prus-

165

sian mediation within three months would share in its terms. In secret articles, Prussia promised to end hostile military action against French troops in Holland and elsewhere, and received a French promise that in case a later general peace resulted in the abdication of the entire west bank of the Rhine to France, Prussia would receive an unspecified amount of compensation for her lost territories, presumably through secularizations on the east bank. Those northern German states which acceded to the peace were promised neutrality and freedom of commerce within an area bounded by a line of demarcation which was agreed upon in May 1795, and which essentially included all of Germany north of the Main River. The eventuality of a Prussian military occupation of Hanover was also conceded by France.

The Peace of Basel came as a nasty shock to much, though not all, of Germany. Its promise of peace and neutrality was very appealing to most of the war-weary territories included within the line of demarcation or close enough to it to hope to be included within its protection by informal construction. Only one state—Hessen-Kassel—actually joined the peace (August 1795), but most of the others embraced by the line of demarcation observed unofficial neutrality. Saxony assured its neutrality by indirect means beginning in August of 1796. Official Prussian apologists represented the Peace of Basel as a first step toward the achievement of a general peace in which a neutral Prussia could employ her good offices as a belligerent could not, and this argument appears to have been accepted by those who were convinced that a continuation of war was simply not in the best interests of the Empire. A strong constitutionalist like Carl Friedrich Häberlin, editor of the *Staats-Archiv,* approved of Prussia's policy if only because it was an initiative that one way or another would move the Empire toward the peace it so desperately needed. Citing Johann Jacob Moser's judgment that "Germany is a state which is suited to nothing less than to the waging of war," he asserted that the Empire clearly no longer wanted war, and that it was fully entitled to reach a neutrality agreement with France with or without the approval of the Emperor, since the latter was not authorized to wage war in the name of the Empire when it did not wish to do so.[1]

The barely concealed implication of Häberlin's argument was that by now, at least, the Emperor was fighting the war not for the interests of the Empire but for those of the House of Austria and, as in the past, was merely using the resources of the Empire for his own dynastic ends. By thus casting the war in terms of the Franco-Austrian rivalry so familiar to Europe before 1756, it was possible to construe Prussia's separate peace not as an act of cowardice or treason toward the Empire, but as a laudable attempt to police a traditional balance of power which was the surest guarantee of the integrity of the Empire. It is certainly no accident

that an article published in 1795 after the Peace of Basel had been concluded, and which was mostly devoted to an analysis of Prussian foreign
policy from 1763 to 1790, argued that in view of the failure in recent decades of both France and Sweden to carry out their obligations as traditional guarantors of the Empire, and therefore also of the balance of power of Europe as a whole, Prussia had properly responded to the call of
necessity to assume this responsibility. Eminently suited to this role because of her medium size, which conferred enough power to oppose the
unjust designs of other states but not enough to encourage any policy of
conquest of her own, Prussia had thus unselfishly taken on the essential
duties of an impartial arbiter of that balance of power in central Europe
on which the entire continent's repose depended.[2]

These arguments could be fought in two ways. The first is probably
best illustrated in the several polemics published after the Peace of Basel
by Johannes von Müller, the one-time defender of the League of Princes,
who had taken a position in Austrian service in 1793. Just as Müller's
earlier defense of the League of Princes had arisen almost entirely from
his belief that Prussian power was needed as a counterweight to the danger of an Austrian hegemony in central Europe, so now he accused Prussia, in deserting her obligations to Emperor and Empire in the middle of
a war for survival, of desiring to see the overthrow of the imperial constitution and the establishment of her own indisputable predominance.
The Peace of Basel and the Prussian "neutrality system" were something
far different from the wholly constitutional "association for the preservation of the imperial constitution" that Müller had praised in the 1780s:
They represented not only a direct breach of faith with the Emperor, and
of the formal feudal oath to which every Estate was subject, but also an
encouragement to other Estates to do the same.[3] Müller was also disturbed
that France, through the support she appeared to be giving to Prussia's
striving for hegemony, was breaking with an important tradition of
French foreign policy, namely, support for the imperial constitution as an
instrument for the preservation of a divided but balanced central Europe
which in that condition could pose no severe threat to France.[4]

The second path of opposition to Prussia's actions is reminiscent of
one of the arguments employed by opponents of the League of Princes:
An insistence that the application of the balance of power principle to
the internal operations of the Empire was a distortion of the intent of the
constitution, whose results would merely assist the enemies of the Empire.
Thus, one author pleaded with his fellow Germans to reject the principle
of balance which had been so highly praised in Frederick II's history of
the House of Brandenburg, and added: "We want no division! We are
members of one state, Estates of one Empire, citizens of one Fatherland."
As such, and especially in this hour of danger, unity of head and mem-

bers was the only formula for salvation: "Our entire security will at all times lie in the observance of our general constitutional laws; and these will be the less misunderstood and challenged the less we ourselves give foreigners and Frenchmen the opportunity to interfere in our internal affairs."[5]

Finally, as might be expected, not everyone was convinced by the Prussian attempt to place an altruistic construction on Berlin's motives in concluding the Peace of Basel. One analyst, worried about the possibility that Germany might be on the verge of a great political revolution comparable to that of France, bitterly reproached the Prussians not so much for making peace, but for waiting to do so until the military situation had become so serious for Germany, and then doing it by and for herself rather than as part of a general peace initiative of the whole Empire. Regretting that this war, which had been declared a *Reichskrieg* without first reckoning with the question of how or even whether it could be waged successfully, had ever been engaged in to begin with, he nevertheless insisted that only the Empire as a whole—the Electors, princes, and other Estates together—could legally and properly end it. The occasion for Prussia's separate peace, he suggested, was given by the final partition of Poland in early 1795, after which friendship and cooperation between Prussia and Austria were no longer necessary. At that point, the failures of the Austrian and Imperial armies, as well as the chaotic political situation in general, presented Prussia with a splendid opportunity to become the first alliance partner and mediator of the powerful new French Republic, with the prospect of achieving many gains, including preponderance within the Empire. This example of naked self-interest on Prussia's part could serve not only to vitiate still more the already weak sense of common purpose among the territories of the Empire, but also to give the appearance of legality, by precedent, to the very idea of the separate peace; the ominous possibilities of the latter, the author averred, had already been realized in the actions of Hessen-Kassel, and could spread to other Estates as well.[6]

The resentment against Prussia's withdrawal from the war was understandably greatest in the territories of southern and southwestern Germany, for which the burden of war, already so severe, was now bound to become intolerable by virtue of the denial of men, money, and supplies not only by Prussia but also by most of northern Germany. The military prospects of the Empire, which had never looked terribly bright in any case, now began to take on the hues of real disaster. Austria was to some extent a beneficiary of the changing perception of the measures needed to ward off the suddenly far more serious French threat. In the same month the Peace of Basel was signed, Christian von Bentzel, an official in the government of Erfurt, aired his views of the reasons for Germany's troubles, with particular stress on the maddening slowness with which the Empire's affairs were conducted. While the enemy presses forward to victory, Bentzel complained, the Germans spend endless time in consultation and debate; that, in turn, had its roots in an exaggerated respect for forms, which Bentzel regarded as unpardonable when the forms themselves lacked spirit, and downright criminal in the kind of emergency the Empire now faced. While he recommended an extraordinary Imperial Deputation (*Reichsdeputation*) and a series of coordinated Circle Deputations as one remedy for this problem, he also left no doubt that the absence of an effective executive power was a major source of the Empire's woes. He exhorted all Germans to "give to the Emperor what belongs to the Emperor," and to trust and follow him: "In times of pressing need, a federative power has only the choice of committing itself to the executive power according to the legal forms, or of destruction."[7]

Views of precisely what such a commitment might mean varied, but a strong sense of impatience with the tangled legalities of the imperial constitution which made rapidity of decision and effective action so difficult can be met with in numerous publications of this period of military desperation. Friedrich von Bock, it may be recalled, had in effect urged the leadership of the Imperial Army to disregard the jealous provincialism of the territorial Estates with respect to marching and occupation rights in any part of the Empire; if a legal basis were needed, "the law of necessity" would provide it. At about the same time, another author recommended that the Emperor employ military force to coerce the reluctant and grumbling Estates into raising the contingents for the *Reichsarmee* required by the quintuplum which had been voted by the Diet in October 1794.[8] Even such partial measures seemed inadequate to some. A treatise written in 1796 by a certain Aulic Councillor Hofmann, then in the employ of Prince Taxis, the Imperial *Prinzipalkommissar* at the Diet, suggested nothing less than the full subjection of the territorial rulers to the unlimited command of the Emperor. No matter how powerful any prince of the Empire might think himself, Hofmann implied, his relationship to the Emperor was no different from that of an ordinary citizen and subject, who was bound to fulfill his duties.[9] By 1797, even the scrupulous Karl von Dalberg was prepared to advocate a virtual dictatorship for the House of Austria, to be exercised in this case throughout southern Germany by Archduke Charles, the talented commander of the Austrian army. In a crisis, wrote Dalberg, it is necessary to subordinate all energies to the will of a single man: "The constitutional form and the procedure which arises from it deserve all consideration; but they are calculated only for more peaceful times. In the danger of an immediately impending revolution, the approval of true German patriots and the silent consent of righteous men is sufficient to employ as lawful those measures which alone can salvage the common cause."[10]

In the event, however, the Austrians needed neither publicists nor even coadjutor bishops to convince them that with Prussia on the sidelines and with the military requirements of the war growing daily, it was both possible and necessary to take new and drastic steps. Whether or not to continue the war was no very real choice for Austria, since Prussia's agreement with France guaranteed Berlin certain advantages in the negotiations for a future peace which Vienna did not have. Continuation of the war was therefore the only possible way of forcing France to terms which might either negate the advantages promised to Prussia or secure equal or better provisions for Austria, or both. With two adversaries in mind, therefore, the Austrians determined to make a supreme effort to achieve control of the military situation and, through it, to regain the diplomatic initiative as well.[11] In late 1795 and early 1796, Austrian troops were able to expel the French from the east bank of the Rhine and to reoccupy virtually all of southern and southwestern Germany. This they did through the exercise of what virtually amounted to military dictatorship, treating the Empire almost as hostile territory and levying contributions in ways that were clearly contrary to imperial law.

French counterattacks in the summer of 1796, however, succeeded once again in breaching the Rhine and penetrating deep into southwestern Germany. By midsummer, Prussian observers were so certain of an Austrian defeat that Berlin hastened to assure at least some postwar gains by entering into a treaty with France on August 5, whereby the latter guaranteed the neutrality of northern Germany and promised Prussia territorial acquisitions, including the Bishopric of Münster, which were considerably greater than her losses on the Left Bank. Hessen-Kassel, too, was to be rewarded for its peace with France a year before, and was to receive both Electoral rank and new territory. In the south, the French successively forced Baden, Württemberg, the entire Swabian Circle and, finally, Bavaria to armistices, and completed their work by concluding separate peaces with the despairing rulers of the first two, also in August. It should be noted that while the principle of secularization as the basis for compensation for losses suffered on the Left Bank had merely been assumed in the Peace of Basel, it appeared explicitly for the first time in the Franco-Prussian treaty of August 5, and was confirmed in the treaties with Württemberg and Baden on August 7 and 22, respectively.[12]

While Prussia from mid-1796 on went about the business of organizing an "Army of Observation," a police force for the zone of neutrality composed mostly of Prussian and Hanoverian troops, but supported by contributions from many of the territories embraced by the neutral zone,

Archduke Charles in the south struck back against the French forces so successfully in the fall of 1796 that he was able to stabilize the front once again along the Rhine. Unfortunately for Austria, however, a new and even more serious threat had developed in the meantime in Italy, where the young Napoleon Bonaparte, commanding the French Army of Italy, had overrun most of the Italian peninsula in the course of 1796, and by April 1797, had broken into the southern Austrian provinces of Carinthia and Styria. He halted to regroup his forces near the city of Bruck, less than 100 miles from Vienna. In spite of his remarkable successes, Bonaparte knew that his position was not unassailable: He had long and tenuous supply lines, he was deep into enemy territory, and he knew that the prospects of uniting with the Rhine armies of his colleagues Moreau and Hoche were slim. He therefore proposed an armistice to Archduke Charles, who had taken command of Austria's southern army early in 1797; on April 7, Charles, well aware of the exhaustion of his troops and mistrustful of the war policy of the foreign minister Thugut, accepted Bonaparte's offer. Subsequent negotiations led to the preliminary Peace of Leoben of April 18. In the various public and secret articles of this treaty, Austria agreed to exchange Milan and the expectancy to the Duchy of Modena for the neutral Republic of Venice, which Bonaparte was to conquer and deliver over to Vienna. Austria also acquiesced in French possession of the fomer Austrian Netherlands, but refused to recognize the loss of the Left Bank (with the one exception of the Bishopric of Liège), in order to circumvent Prussian claims for compensation on the Right Bank promised to her in the Peace of Basel. A peace conference to conclude a definitive peace between France and the Empire was to be convoked in the Swiss city of Bern, and in the meantime a six months' armistice, valid for the whole Empire, was to obtain. The territorial integrity of the Empire, including the Left Bank, was specifically confirmed in the treaty.

Much of a war-weary Germany rejoiced at the news of the treaty—not only because it brought peace, but also because it appeared to offer terms which, from the Empire's standpoint, were unusually favorable given its somewhat dubious bargaining position. While some earnest souls appeared to believe that the Empire's problems were now essentially over,[13] others could not forget the troubles brought by five years of war, nor the serious inadequacies of the Empire's political and military response to this period of recurrent crisis. Among the critiques and suggestions for reform of the Empire that now appeared were some of the very few proposals for republicanization of the imperial government that are to be found in the public literature before the dissolution of 1806. One general and one specific cause can be cited for this momentary interest in the republican principle. In the first place, the remarkable achievements of French arms in

recent years, accomplished in spite of numerous and severe domestic problems, had invited a general reflection on the causes for French success.
With few exceptions, the reason was located in the patriotism of the citizen army; this derived from a common sense of participation in the
shaping of national destiny, which was in turn a result of the republican
constitution. F.C. Laukhard was one of many who called attention to the
self-sacrificing tenaciousness of the French soldier, and attributed the
Empire's military woes to the inability of the German soldier to perceive
any real self-interest or common interest in the war he was supposed to
fight.[14] In this sense, republicanism came to be thought of by some as a
solution to the profoundly and persistently troubling lack of patriotism
and *Gemeinsinn*—common spirit—in Germany.

In the second place, there was a deeply rooted conviction among many
Germans that war itself, an evil in all times and places, was an especially
severe danger to a state such as the Empire which, while incapable of
measuring up to the challenge of war, also seemed unable to avoid it. A
republican constitution as an answer to this problem was given a mighty
boost by the publication of Immanuel Kant's *Perpetual Peace* in 1795. In
this widely read treatise of the widely known and respected Königsberg
philosopher, Kant had argued that since under a republican constitution
the consent of subjects is required in all decisions affecting war and
peace, and since the subjects must carry all the burdens of war in both
blood and money, war would always be less impulsively entered into than
under nonrepublican constitutions, where the ruler, as the owner of the
state, really loses nothing by it and "can therefore decide on war for the
most trifling reasons, as if it were a kind of pleasure party."[15]

This philosophical point of view was no doubt reinforced here and
there by a tendency to take at face value the assurances of French propa-
gandists that the prospects for peace and the brotherhood of man would
be much enhanced if the tyranny of autocrats were ended everywhere in
Europe; or at least by a belief that France could be placated or set more
at ease by some gestures favoring the republican idea. Thus, the liberal
editor of the journal *Der Genius der Zeit,* August Hennings, who was
known as a "free thinker" and a somewhat controversial official in Danish
service,[16] suggested in 1795 that a possible road to peace might lie in the
secularization of the great Rhenish archbishoprics—Mainz, Trier, and
Cologne—and their conversion into independent republican states, dependent on neither Germany nor France. The following year, Hennings repeated this proposal, with the difference that he now presented these territories as a singe Rhenish free state, providing a strong defensive bulwark
against a conquest-oriented France. At once refreshing and tragic in its
naivete was Henning's explicit assumption that the French would be
willing to evacuate these territories for his purposes.[17]

The direct influence of Kant in the assertion of a need for the republicanization of Germany is nowhere clearer than in a work entitled *Sketch for a General German Republic,* published in 1797 and probably written by Wilhelm Traugott Krug, at that time professor of philosophy and theology at Wittenberg, but later chosen to be Kant's successor in Königsberg after the latter's death.[18] Foreseeing the imminent destruction of the imperial constitution and the impossibility of forestalling that eventuality through reform of existing laws and structures, Krug recommended a thoroughgoing reformation of the German state which would keep step with the progress of moral culture, including full recognition of the inborn rights of man. That, to him, meant the establishment of a republic. Convinced that this could be achieved without revolution through the recognition of the German princes that the time had come for them to confer freedom on their peoples voluntarily, Krug was also prepared to outline the steps necessary to the founding and constitutional elaboration of the republic. In view of his often repeated desire to dissociate himself from the idea of revolution, however, the first of these steps may have come as something of a surprise to his readers, for he proposed nothing less than a new geopolitical definition of Germany which would have excluded the hereditary lands of both Prussia and Austria from the territory on which he proposed to set up the new republic. Bohemia and Austria, as parts of the previous German Empire, should be given free and unencumbered to "The King of Hungary and Bohemia" in return for his abdication of the German imperial crown, while Prussia, in return for giving up Ansbach, Bayreuth, and her territories west of the Elbe, would be awarded both Upper and Lower Lusatia from Saxony. Thus, the new "German Republic" would essentially embrace all those territories of the former Empire which had been neither Austrian nor Prussian; and it would include the presently occupied territories of the Left Bank, for Krug, like Hennings, assumed that the French Republic would simply hand over these lands to a sister German republic.[19]

The government of Krug's German Republic would rest on a constitution to be drawn up by a national convention composed of delegates elected by the whole citizenry. The constitution would guarantee all basic human rights—freedom of speech, of the press, and so on—and would provide for a separation of executive and legislative powers, the latter of which would be exercised by an assembly elected directly by the people. This legislature would then choose all the members of the executive branch, the most important of whom would be a group of Directors, no one of whom was to serve for a period of more than four or five years.[20] Just as political power in the new state was derived from the people, so would the military force which Krug recognized as necessary to the defense of freedom and the constitution. Every able-bodied citizen was to be enrolled in militia regiments which could be called upon for active service as required to assist a permanent veteran army of 30,000–50,000 men which was to be apportioned to the various administrative districts (Circles) into which the republic would be divided. Krug construed the utilization of this army in exclusively defensive terms; indeed, the concern of the state in general, in respect to other sovereign states, was simply that of guaranteeing the security of the rights and property of its own citizens—which meant that wars of conquest would not be fought and the only just alliance would be a *Friedensbund,* a pact of friendship and nonaggression.[21] Like Kant, Krug believed that war itself would become less frequent because of the unwillingness of the citizens of a republic to subject themselves to its high costs for any but the most weighty of reasons. Furthermore, as war became less frequent, the "spirit of commerce" (*Handelsgeist*) would grow stronger in all states, and since that spirit was fundamentally incompatible with war, the incidence of armed hostilities between states would be reduced even further.[22]

Krug's work is interesting not only for its attempt to solve the problem of war by the adoption of a republican constitution, but also for its advocacy of the separation of Germany into three independent states: Austria, Prussia, and his new German Republic. This "trias" solution, it would appear, came not only from Krug's conviction that it was hopeless to think in terms of a republicanization of the already solidly established monarchies of the great powers Austria and Prussia, but also from the need to protect the "Third Germany" from the wholly self-interested rapaciousness of those two states and perhaps a few other of the more powerful territories. He justified his refusal to entertain the reform of the imperial constitution by his belief that the larger courts, far from desiring a meaningful renovation of the Empire, were themselves merely waiting for its collapse in order to grab whatever they could for themselves from its ruins.[23] The Empire, for Krug, was therefore already virtually dead, and not from a lack of means for its reform but from a total absence of the will to reform it on the part of the only states which had the resources to carry it out.

The republicanism he advocated takes on a special significance precisely because it was to be introduced only in the "Third Germany," that part of the Empire where the present constitution of territorial fragmentation and all the political, military, and economic problems it carried with it rendered absurd any idea of organizing it as an independent federation capable of maintaining an even minimal degree of internal cohesion or external defense. As a principle of political organization, however, republicanism could provide a unity and real strength for the area which hordes of squabbling territorial lords could not; it also had the additional attractions of satisfying the demands of "moral culture" so important to Krug, and perhaps of providing the means of converting republican France into a friend rather than an enemy, thus removing the scourge of war from the new state. Seen from the perspective of one whose concern was as much that of state-building as of carrying out the philosophical dictates of human freedom, republicanism was a not altogether unrealistic approach to a practical problem.

An even more self-consciously practical application of republicanism, but this time in an attempt to salvage the organic integrity of the Empire as a whole, was attempted by the author of what is almost certainly the most detailed and exhaustive critique and analysis of the problems and deficiencies of the Empire to have appeared in the eighteenth or any previous century. This remarkable work, which bears the simple general title *Critique of the German Imperial Constitution,* was published anonymously in three volumes between 1796 and 1798; astonishingly, its authorship remains unknown to this day. The first volume mercilessly listed the defects of all the organs of imperial government, both structural and operational, in very specific but by now essentially familiar terms. The author also faced squarely the issue of the governmental form of the Empire, flatly denying that it was a monarchy—even a limited one—in any sense of the term; it could not be that, said he, because in a monarchy the legislative power, as the source of all other rights of supreme power, belongs to a single person, whereas in the German Empire that power and the majesty which accompanies it belonged not just to the Emperor but also and to an even greater extent to the Imperial Estates as a body. The form of the Empire's government should therefore properly be defined as "a pantocracy of the representatives of the particular united German states under the lawful authority of the veto of a single person chosen from their own midst."[24]

The key to this author's critique lay in his use of the word "pantocracy," which carried the implication not only of an excessive and at the same time unequal diffusion of authority in the Empire, but also a confusion of legislative and executive powers. His entire work was designed to remedy this chaotic situation by reconstituting the Empire as a republic, which meant simply the clear and distinct separation of the legislative, executive, and judicial powers of the state.[25] Turning his attention first to the Imperial Diet, he made three recommendations which, taken together, would not only result in a greater rapidity of legislative business but would also convert the Diet into something resembling a true national legislature rather than the forum for the mutual "retaliation" of the Estates it had become. He suggested, first, that the Estates confer plenipotentiary voting power on their representatives, eliminating the frightful delays arising from consultation between delegates and principals; second, that principals choose their delegates from among the members of their

own legislative or consultative bodies (*Landstände*), a measure which
would tend to make the Diet representative of a broader constituency
than the single person of a ruling prince; and third, that the division of
the Diet into three colleges, with their subdivisions into benches, be abolished, thus creating a single body and mitigating the jealousies and
hostilities—including the debilitating religious ones—encouraged by the
present hierarchical division.[26] The first item of business of this reorganized Diet would be nothing less than the creation of an all-encompassing
and systematic code of laws which would embrace all branches of legislation, including the regulation of the relationships of the territorial rulers
to the Empire and to their own states and subjects as well. In this, the
author immediately signaled his intention to relocate much of the basic
legislative authority of the territories to a single national legislative body
whose legitimacy was founded on the broader base of representation his
earlier proposals would create. The Emperor, similarly, would be vested
by this code of laws with the powers of a true national executive, whose
only function in legislation would be that of granting or withholding approval to the laws proposed by the Diet—in other words, the right of veto
which he already possessed under the present constitution. In the new
constitution, however, the legitimacy of his position would also be based
on a broader constituency to be achieved by permitting the supreme executive authorities of *all* the territories of the Empire to participate in his
election.[27]

The author of this critique made increasingly clear throughout his
work that the worst violation of the fundamental principle of the separation of powers lay in territorial lordship—*Landeshoheit*—which, according to him, "consists of nothing less than the sovereignty of the Imperial
Estates in their particular states, or in the independence of the German
territorial rulers, as such, from Emperor and Empire."[28] All the basic
defects of the Empire in both domestic and foreign affairs were traceable
to the sharing by territorial authorities of both the legislative power that
ought to belong solely to the Imperial Diet and the executive power that
ought to rest exclusively with the Emperor. The absurd right of the territories to make separate alliances among themselves or with foreign states
stemmed from the principle of *Landeshoheit,* as did the lack of respect
for judgments of the imperial courts; in both cases, the fundamental integrity of the Empire was threatened by the very nature of its own constitution: "The German Empire is supposed to be a state, yet it gives and
leaves to the Estates thereof rights by whose exercise this unity of the state
is again dissolved, and every member again forms a particular and independent state for itself."[29] The most dangerous evil resulting from territorial lordship and its privileges, however, was the defective military
constitution of the Empire, which could not be improved until the whole

governmental form of the Empire were changed to provide clear lines of authority and subordination from a single highest power through the Circles and down to each particular territory, so that it would no longer be left to the choice of individual territorial authorities to decide whether and to what extent they would participate in military actions voted by the whole Empire.[30] The Imperial Army itself should be under the undivided command of the Emperor or his delegated appointee, and should consist largely of citizens rather than of professionals in order to prevent the growth of a separate *Kriegsstand,* or military caste, for which the waging of war all too often tended to be an end in itself.[31]

Not until the third and last volume, published in 1798, however, did the author draw up a complete sketch of what he believed a good republican or representative constitution for the Empire might look like. There were some basic changes from the earlier and piecemeal proposals of his first volume. One was a much stronger emphasis on the representative quality of the national legislative body, which he now referred to not as the Diet but as "a legislative Areopagus," whose members were to be chosen by election from within the various German peoples (*Völkerschaften*) rather than by appointment of the territorial executive authorities. At the instant this assembly was constituted, all legislative power in the territories would cease, and whatever bodies (e.g., territorial diets) had previously been vested with that power would now become mere commissions to report to the national group on legislative changes that might be necessary in their territories, as well as to collect the imperial taxes in them, retaining as much as was required for their needs and returning the rest to the national legislature, with an exact accounting. A second basic change was his proposal that the Emperor be chosen not by the princes, but from among the princes by the Areopagus. The heads of all the individual territories would be dependent upon the Emperor, who together with his ministers would constitute the supreme executive authority. A single supreme Imperial Court of Justice would also be created, to which all the highest courts of the individual territories would be subordinated—thus suggesting for the new court a considerably wider scope of judicial competence than that possessed by the two previous imperial supreme courts. Finally, an armed force dependent entirely on the command of the Emperor would have to exist to secure obedience for the laws of the Areopagus and the judgments of the supreme court.[32]

It is obvious that a fairly radical rethinking of the proposals contained in the first volume of 1796 had occurred by the time the second and third volumes were published in 1798. The representative character of the national legislative body had been greatly strengthened, as had that of the Emperor himself; both had now been given something approaching a popular base. The single supreme court was new, as was its vastly expanded appellate jurisdiction. So was the suggestion that the territorial rulers, now deprived of the legislative and executive attributes of *Landeshoheit,* would continue to function only as provincial governors under the delegated authority of the Emperor. The drift of all these proposals, in fact, was away from the earlier acceptance of the possibility of reforming the traditional imperial institutions, and toward a strongly unitary national state, in which all the territorial governments would essentially be converted into administrative agencies responsible to the legislative authority of the national Areopagus and the executive authority of the Emperor. The absence of any attention to the Circles as an intermediate level of government in the third volume contrasts sharply with the great importance assigned to them in the reform scheme of the first volume, and confirms the direction of this drift. So, for that matter, does the substantive concentration of the third volume on the political economy (*Staatswirthschaft*) of the Empire, which called for all expenses of government within the borders of the Empire to be paid from revenues derived exclusively from uniform national legislation. This measure, which among other things meant removing the ability of the imperial princes to tax their subjects on their own authority, was of fundamental importance to the creation of unity for the Empire, and was clearly recognized as such by the author: "For this unity can only be preserved [if] the legislation and government of all particular provinces of the Empire does not proceed from themselves, but from one and the same general legislation and executive power, and all individual rulers are dependent on the single common supreme head."[33]

If this dependence were to be real rather than theoretical, of course, then the supreme executive power would have to maintain a preponderance of actual physical power over all particular territories; that, in turn, meant not only that he had to be given the means to create and hold that preponderance, but that those means had to be accessible to him alone, and denied to all others who might use them to resist him. At the present time, the author pointed out, the Empire itself possessed neither separate domains nor any regalian rights, whereas the rulers of the individual territories had plenty of both. With respect to the control of immediate fiscal means, the parts were therefore more powerful than the whole. This situation could be corrected, he asserted, either by the complete abolition of all domains in the Empire, or by their assignment to the exclusive supervision, administration, and use of the supreme imperial executive. As far as regalian rights were concerned, they too should be turned over in toto to the imperial executive power. Regalia, assumed to be things not properly subject to private ownership, should be administered for the advantage of all who lived within the Empire: "In an Empire that is supposed to be one, all inhabitants thereof must by right be entitled to an equal enjoyment of all the rights and objects which cannot be the exclusive property of individuals." Apart from the fact that territorial regalia were all too often administered for the sole purpose of raising revenue for the private use of the princes rather than for the advantage of their subjects, there also existed vast differences between territories in the kind and amount of regalia (woodlands, navigable rivers, metal and salt mines, and so on), so that the enjoyment of their benefits by subjects was unequal. Since those territories better provided for by nature were usually unwilling to share their bounty with their less fortunate neighbors, the choice of whether or not to do so should be taken from them and placed in the hands of a national government for equal distribution to all imperial citizens.[34]

The concern shown here for improvement of the conditions of life of the Empire's people also underlay the author's lengthy commentary on the bad economic conditions to which the division of authority between Empire and territories led. Much of this involved the by now familiar condemnation of excessive taxation and regulation of both commerce and manufacturing, as well as restrictions on imports and exports from one territory to another. Although in recommending the abolition of barriers to free trade among all the German states he merely added another voice to an already existing chorus, he also broke new ground in calling for a much stronger interventionist role in the economy for national legislation than many other advocates of free trade would have been willing to permit. Perhaps the best example was his advocacy of the right of Emperor and Empire to force landlords whose lands were not being properly utilized for agricultural purposes to rent them out to others who would so employ them. Much more controversial (except to economic liberals, of course) was his proposal that imperial legislation abolish peasant serfdom in all its forms at one fell swoop—and with it the whole structure of feudal law from which it and most of the other social and political relationships in the Empire had heretofore derived! A common artisans' code for all of Germany to eliminate migration of artisans from territories in which restrictions were severe to those in which they were lax was another task for imperial legislation, as was the setting of limits to the size of territorial armies, which would be fixed according to the amount of public revenues in each; among other things, this would encourage the immigration of foreign artisans who now stayed away for fear of forcible impressment. The author also hinted that a strong imperial government could play an important role in the establishment of schools and academies for mechanical, industrial, and fine arts, and, finally, that it was the appropriate agency for securing the establishment of a kind of imperial merchant marine to enter into competition with the commercial navies of the existing maritime powers, and which would operate from the German coasts of the North, Baltic, and Adriatic seas.[35]

Several aspects of this extraordinary work require comment. First, while the author appears to have believed throughout that his fundamental critique as well as his proposals for reform and innovation related to the *form of government* of the Empire, it is clear that by the time of his complete (if also brief) sketch for a republican constitution in the third volume he had shifted his ground rather fundamentally. Kant, in his work on perpetual peace, had distinguished carefully between the terms "form of government" (*forma regiminis*) and "form of sovereignty" (*forma imperii*), the former referring to the alternatives of republicanism or despotism, the latter to the traditional Aristotelian categories of autocracy, aristocracy, and democracy.[36] The author of this work, in following Kant's characterization of republicanism as a form of government in which there was a clear separation of legislative and executive powers, seems initially to have aimed simply at overcoming the severe problems created by the sharing of legislative and executive functions by territorial and imperial levels of government by reversing the balance between them in favor of the latter. At the same time, by broadening the constituencies of both Diet and Emperor, he hoped to restore the cooperation between legislative and executive powers implied by the lofty formula *Kaiser und Reich,* the unfortunate reality of which in recent generations had more closely approximated *Kaiser versus Reich.* With the suggestions of the third volume, however, whereby the so-called Areopagus was to be elected by the peoples of the various territories and was in turn to select the Emperor, he had actually altered the locus of sovereignty itself, which now lay not with an elected Emperor and a combined group of elected and hereditary princes, but with the people. The formulation of this new basis of sovereignty was not sufficiently detailed to indicate how wide the electoral basis of the Areopagus might be, though one can be quite sure that it was not intended to approximate a universal franchise. It is important to recognize, however, that before the work was finished, the term "republicanism" had come to include a new principle of sovereignty as well as merely the separation of legislative from executive powers with which the author had started out.

The explanation for this probably lies in the author's increasing conviction that it was the principle of *Landeshoheit* more than any other single factor that made it impossible for the Empire to be a single state or to act like one. By the third volume, he was prepared to abolish it altogether, as he had not been in the first. But since the existing source of legislative authority in the Empire really lay with the territorial governments, both in their capacity to make law within their own states and in their right to appoint delegates to the Imperial Diet, and since that source of authority disappeared along with *Landeshoheit*, a new source had to be found. That was to be the people themselves, who would in effect subvert *Landeshoheit* by electing a single national legislative body which in turn would elect a single executive. The author, then, had obviously finally reached the conclusion that the severe and complicated problem of shared or diffused legislative and executive functions in the Empire was in fact ultimately a problem of divided sovereignty, and he proposed to solve both at once through his advocacy of an informally redefined republicanism. And while such a redefinition altered the meaning of republicanism in a very fundamental way, this probably created no problem for him. With his persistent linkage of republican principles to the idea of German unity, it is difficult to escape the impression that his interest in republicanism was less intrinsic than extrinsic—that is, that he believed in it less as an ideal in itself than as an instrument to achieve his primary objective of unity, and that he was quite prepared to be comfortable with whatever idiosyncratic definition of republicanism might accomplish this objective.

Notable by their absence from this critique were two things that had almost uniformly characterized most earlier general evaluations of the imperial constitution: the discussion of the balance of advantages and disadvantages of Germany's territorial fragmentation and the earnest exhortations to a moral self-conversion, especially among the princes, which would lead to the development of a common German spirit and patriotism, and thus of national unity. Not one word of this voluminous work was devoted to the advantages of fragmentation, whereas almost every page contained a direct or indirect condemnation of it. The unspoken assumption that all of the Empire's woes stemmed from its politically consecrated territorial incoherence ran so deep that the author did not bother to mention arguments for the supposed benefits of fragmentation even to refute them. Furthermore, since the only way to achieve German unity while retaining territorial division in its full traditional integrity was through moral suasion, that is, through the creation of the idea of unity as a compelling moral construct in the minds and hearts of the princes, and since this critic had already decided that the territories as independent units had to go, he spent little time on the problem of how to create unity while keeping them. Even in the first volume, where their continued existence was assumed, he indulged in no pious wishful thinking about the moral conversion of territorial authorities; instead, he went straight to the political changes he believed necessary to subvert and overcome the bad effects of their entirely self-serving autonomy which he regarded as a fixed, intractable datum.

By the third volume, he was able to express more clearly the insight that had been only obscurely present in the first, namely, that the creation of national unity for Germany was essentially a three-step process. It began with *reduction*—that is, with the removal of the political barriers which were responsible for creating and maintaining perceptible differences between the spiritual and material conditions of life of the various German peoples, and which prevented them from seeing themselves as a single people. This is what the excessive degree of legislative and executive autonomy of the territories had done. Once this was done away with, the second step—that of political *unification*—began, and this ended with the establishment of a centralized and republican government on the model sketched out by the author in the third volume. The final step, which would end in real unity, was the creation of a measure of *uniformity* with respect to at least the conditions of public life everywhere in the Empire: equal claims on public revenues, uniform laws with respect to civil liberty, economic opportunity, military obligation, and so on. The perception of these kinds of equality and uniformity throughout Germany would lead to the growth of a true common spirit as a common language and an increasingly meaningless imperial historical tradition had not.

It is true, of course, that the author of the *Critique* did not inform his readers of the means whereby the first and most essential of these steps could be accomplished, though it is possible, even probable, that the likelihood of the abolition of the ecclesiastical states established by the Peace of Campo Formio in 1797 not only gave him hope that a general process of reduction might now get underway, but may actually have been the cause for the basic shift in his thinking between 1796 and 1798. Still, if the work is seen not as a call to action as much as an invitation to analysis of fundamental political problems, even the deficiency of lack of attention to the means of implementing its proposals may not appear as serious. Its most basic insight, that the creation of a national state had to precede the creation of a political nation, and to prepare the way for it, represented a sharp break with previous commentators, most of whom wanted the latter but rejected the former—usually on philosophical and cultural grounds —and who persisted in the vaguely hopeful belief that good will and moral insight would create the *Gemeingeist* from which an adequate political nationhood would arise. It was this author's contribution to assert that in the present circumstances such abstract moralism must always shatter against the hard realities of territorial self-interest, and that *Gemeingeist,* far from being the starting point for political nationhood, was its final and highest product and the guarantor of the future integrity of the nation—that the state, in other words, must create the nation in which it subsequently takes root.

In spite of its novel approach, there is no evidence that this critique created much of a stir. The remedies it proposed were certainly visionary, given the political conditions of its time, and it went well beyond the desires even of convinced reformers, who for the most part really wanted to save the old imperial structure with as few basic modifications as possible. On the other hand, it may have had a certain appeal for some individuals who had become persuaded that a greater consolidation of political authority in Germany was necessary, that is, a reduction in the degree of political fragmentation, even if they did not go along with the idea of a single unitary state. For such individuals, the peace of Campo Formio of October 18, 1797, may well have appeared to provide at once the necessity and the opportunity for such consolidation. What they could not know, of course, was that it also set in motion the forces of a reconstitution of the Empire that would in less than nine years result not in a strengthening of the imperial union but in its dissolution.

Part IV

REORGANIZATION AND DISSOLUTION, 1797–1806

CHAPTER ELEVEN

Toward the Last
Constitutional Law of 1803

THE SURPRISINGLY FAVORABLE terms that Austria had received in the Peace of Leoben in April 1797 were largely due to a temporary over-extension of French military capabilities—the result of the unexpectedly deep and rapid penetration of Bonaparte's Italian armies into the Austrian heartland—as well as to the political situation in Paris, where the government of the Directory, divided against itself, was also for a time locked in a bitter quarrel with a domestic opposition composed of moderates and conservatives. These circumstances had inclined both military and civilian leaders in France to conclude a peace which would allow them to retrench and reorganize their resources. Leoben, of course, was a preliminary peace; and in the weeks and months of subsequent negotiations between French Austrian representatives which were intended to lead to a final peace, the Austrians found themselves facing a steadily stiffening series of French demands which paralleled the latters' success in restoring their fortunes. While the French Director Barras overcame the challenge to his leadership in Paris, Bonaparte had secured his Army of Italy by pulling back from Austrian territory, and had solidified his control of most of northern Italy by organizing the Ligurian and Cisalpine Republics as French satellites and by controlling the administration of Venice, whose Ionian Islands he subsequently seized and occupied. By late September and early October of 1797, the Austrian diplomat Cobenzl saw his government in too weak a position to resist the rapidly escalating demands and threats of Bonaparte, and on October 18 salvaged what he could from Vienna's unfortunate position by signing the Peace of Campo Formio.

By the terms of this treaty, Austria agreed to French possession of Milan, the Austrian Netherlands, and the Ionian Islands, and promised recognition of the Cisalpine Republic. Since that Republic also included the Duchy of Modena, which was to fall to the Habsburgs by inheritance after the death of the reigning Duke, Austria also promised to compensate him until his death with the Breisgau, Austria's small province in southwestern Germany. In return, Austria was to receive Venetian territory in Dalmatia, Istria, and mainland Italy as far west as the river Adige. In secret articles, Austria was also promised the Archbishopric of Salzburg and that part of Bavaria which lay east of the river Inn as compensation for the Breisgau. Peace between France and the Empire was to be negotiated at a conference in Rastatt, and Austria, in her capacity as an Estate of the Empire but not as head of it, promised to support French claims on the Left Bank, but with limited boundaries which would not result in French acquisition of the Archbishopric of Cologne nor of any of Prussia's Left Bank territories—thus excluding Prussia from any claim to the compensation on the Right Bank that the treaty promised to all other hereditary German states, including Austria, which lost territory to France as the result of the execution of this agreement.

Two aspects of the Peace of Campo Formio were significant, especially by contrast with the earlier terms of Leoben. First, Austria had consented to an at least partial abdication of imperial territory, whereas Austrian representatives had assured the Diet in April that peace with France would be concluded on the basis of the full integrity of the Empire. Second, by securing French agreement to the seizure of Salzburg as compensation for the loss of the Breisgau, Vienna had tacitly agreed to secularization as a basis for compensation, thus destroying an important part of Austria's claim to superiority over Prussia with respect to the protection of the Empire and its constitution.

The Rastatt Peace Congress provided for in the treaty of Campo Formio began its deliberations in November 1797 under the shadow of the suspicion that Austria, known already to have agreed to the violation of the territorial integrity of the Empire through her promises to France about the Left Bank, might have made even more extensive secret arrangements to the disadvantage of various Estates. The Austro-French agreement on the Habsburg seizure of Salzburg and part of Bavaria was still secret, but in view of the events and fears of recent years, little was required to stimulate the circulation of ominous rumors of all kinds. Even before the congress met, rumors that a general secularization might be part of its agenda had led the Elector of Mainz to propose a league of the four Rhenish Electors—Trier, Cologne, Bavaria, and himself—which would undertake to represent the interests of all at Rastatt. The proposal came to nothing, but it demonstrates the existence of a feeling that more would be at stake at Rastatt than was apparent from what was publicly known about the Austrian and French preconference positions. Besides France, the other participants at Rastatt were the members of the extraordinary deputation that had been appointed by the Imperial Diet in 1795 in anticipation of an eventual negotiation of peace with France. It included Mainz, as chairman, the Electorates of Saxony, Bavaria, and Hanover, the secular territories of Austria, Baden, and Hessen-Darmstadt, Würzburg for the ecclesiastical principalities, and Frankfurt for all of the Imperial Cities. Not surprisingly, the representatives of many other territories, including Prussia, were unofficially in attendance to protect their particular interests.

Austria's hopes of excluding Prussian influence from the congress and of keeping control of the German imperial delegation in order to preserve a united front in her own interests were dealt a shattering blow only a few weeks after the conference opened. The Peace of Campo Formio had provided that before Austria could take possession of Venice, she would have to agree to deliver over the fortress of Mainz to France. A formal agreement to this effect was signed by the Austrian representatives on December 1, 1797, who undertook to guarantee not only the surrender of Mainz but also the withdrawal of Austrian troops from the Empire to behind the river Inn—that is, onto Austrian territory proper—by December 30. This agreement, which was not even communicated to the representative of Mainz, Albini, until after the document had been signed, created an enormous uproar in the Empire, to which Austria's preparedness to sacrifice the German imperial cause to her own dynastic interests no longer seemed in doubt. For many, this represented a virtual abandonment of the Habsburgs' imperial responsibility, and under such circumstances it is understandable that many of the larger Estates, including even some of the ecclesiastical territories which had earlier been informed by Bonaparte himself that he intended their secularization, should turn to France as the sole apparent arbiter of the Empire's fate. Austria, meanwhile, having been made painfully aware of the extent of the confidence she had sacrificed, decided not to forfeit all of it, and postponed indefinitely her occupation of Salzburg and Bavaria east of the Inn.

The French delegates, who had always hoped to circumvent the provisions of Campo Formio and to acquire the entire Left Bank for France, now saw themselves free to orchestrate the deep divisions, suspicions, and fears among the Germans to their own advantage. When Prussia was successfully threatened into reaffirming the abdication of her Left Bank territories as originally promised in the Peace of Basel, all of Thugut's carefully laid plans to close the door to Prussian acquisition of compensatory territories on the Right Bank were exploded, and he too agreed to the sacrifice of the entire Left Bank. On March 9, 1798, the congress as a whole formally approved the loss. The issue of compensation was dealt with next. Austria, already compromised by the still secret promise of

Salzburg, had long been prepared to accept some degree of secularization, but was committed to oppose a general secularization for two reasons: First, it could lead to exaggerated gains for Prussia, and second, it would with one blow abolish altogether a group of territories from which the Emperor had generally received political and diplomatic support against the centrifugal force represented by the large secular states. Now that the loss of the entire Left Bank was a fact, however, the French position in favor of general secularization was accepted by Prussia; it also found eager adherents among the large secular states, which were attracted by the prospect of gains that could well exceed their Left Bank losses if they played their cards right. It was, at the time, small comfort to Austria when the deputies at Rastatt on April 4, 1798, approved a secularization of all ecclesiastical states except for the three ecclesiastical Electorates, which were to be reestablished or reconstituted on the Right Bank.

During the almost eighteen months the Congress of Rastatt was formally in session—a misleading figure, since real business was conducted only sporadically—a complicated series of negotiations between Austria, Prussia, and France took place, in which Austria sought desperately to prevent the realization of a total secularization which would almost certainly have resulted in a reformed imperial structure from which Habsburg influence would be all but excluded.[1] It was no love for the Empire as such, but rather the possibility that it might become a more formidable tool in the hands of the enemies of Austria, that led Thugut ultimately to reject all schemes that he could not control and gradually to conclude that a renewal of war against France offered the best hope of turning the situation to Vienna's advantage. There was, in fact, some reason to hope for success in a new war. Russia, which had withdrawn from the first coalition in 1796 following the death of Empress Catherine II, proved receptive to a new alliance, which was concluded with Austria on July 21, 1798, only days before the English destruction of the French fleet at Aboukir gave rise to hopes that Bonaparte, now off on his Egyptian adventure, might be stranded, defeated, and removed from the picture. A Russian alliance with England in late December tightened the bonds of France's enemies, and in late February of 1799 the Directory answered Austria's failure to respond to an earlier French ultimatum by ordering General Jourdan to breach the Rhine frontier, thus starting a new war with Austria and reopening hostilities with the Empire, which had not yet made peace in any case.

For many of the western and southern German Estates, though not all, this war was certainly more popular than the one which had ended at Leoben, because they now knew what war-weariness and their own convenience had led them to wish to deny earlier: That regardless of any self-interested motives Austria may have had in starting the war or in persisting in it so long, the Empire itself now truly had a stake in the war because the very existence of its constitution was at issue. The French demand for the entire Left Bank had surprised and horrified them, and the direction of the subsequent negotiations over the question of compensation could hardly be reassuring to many, including not only the ecclesiastical states whose future was the most obviously dubious, but also many of the smallest secular states, Imperial Cities, and Imperial Counts and Knights, who had good reason to wonder how much better their title to existence was than that of the prelates in a world where power, not justice, reigned supreme. For a time, much of the ill will Austria had brought upon herself through her manhandling of the lesser territories of southwestern Germany in the two years or so following the Peace of Basel disappeared, and it was even possible to find an occasional plea that in this crisis the Germans deliver themselves over entirely to the protection and unlimited command of the Emperor.[2] The initial successes of Austrian and Russian armies against the French in the spring and summer raised many hopes and even some occasional enthusiasm, and the Imperial Diet in September 1799 voted what was to be its last general military authorization in the form of one hundred Roman Months and the quintuplum. On the other hand, many Estates had not participated in the voting at all, while most of those within the northern zone of neutrality had voted negatively and refused to be held responsible for contributions of any kind. The result was that this last imperial military effort was also its most feeble both quantitatively and qualitatively.[3]

The startling victories of Austro-Russian armies, which wrested virtually all of Italy from French control by late summer of 1799, were wasted by political disagreements between the Russian and Austrian courts, as well as by a notable lack of cooperation between the armies themselves. Austrian failure to support Russian armies in Switzerland led to a severe defeat for the latter in late September and, much more serious, to the recall of these armies and the withdrawal of Russia from the coalition. This loss was only partly compensated by the conclusion of a formal alliance with England in the summer of 1800, which was signed only days after Bonaparte, who had returned from the Middle East to seize control of the French government the previous November, had inflicted a severe defeat on Austrian forces in Italy at the battle of Marengo. The Austrian evacuation of the entire Cisalpine Republic that followed proved to be only the first in a series of disasters for Vienna. The following month, July, the Austrian army in southern Germany was forced to an armistice by the French General Moreau. Four months of negotiations followed, in which Vienna, plagued by the indecisiveness of the Emperor, disarray among his foreign policy advisors, and the profound mistrust of other European courts, was unable to take advantage of the French desire for peace created by Bonaparte's wish to consolidate his newly won rule in France. When the armistice expired, toward the end of November, Austria had no choice but to take up arms once again. This time, however, there were to be no protracted campaigns; on December 3, 1800, the Austrian army under the command of the young and inexperienced Archduke John was handed a catastrophic defeat by Moreau at Hohenlinden, and only the recall of Archduke Charles, who had earlier been shoved aside because of his opposition to Thugut's war policy, enabled Vienna in late December to achieve an armistice against Moreau's advancing armies. A month and a half later, on February 9, 1801, terms of peace—a peace that led to the only major alteration of the imperial constitution between 1648 and its collapse in 1806—were agreed upon in Lunéville.

The provisions of the Peace of Lunéville were based largely on those of Campo Formio, but with a few changes and additions of which none was advantageous to Austria or to the Empire. As before, the Emperor agreed to recognize the Cisalpine and Ligurian Republics, which meant the cession of Milan as well as renunciation of the expectancy to Modena, whose duke was to be compensated with territory in Germany. This time, however, Austria was also forced to give up Tuscany, a secundogeniture of the Habsburgs since 1765, in order to permit Bonaparte to establish yet another satellite, the Kingdom of Etruria; the former Duke of Tuscany was also to be compensated in Germany. The loss of the Austrian Netherlands as well as of the entire Left Bank was reconfirmed, but now the Emperor also had to agree to the dismantling of a number of fortresses on the Right Bank. Furthermore, it was stated that compensation for the losses of secular princes on the Left Bank was to be accomplished according to the guidelines laid down at Rastatt—that is, by the secularization of ecclesiastical territories on the Right Bank, a process which France was now also given the right to supervise. As before, Austria received mainland Venetia (as far as the Adige), Dalmatia, and Istria, but was denied both Salzburg and the Bavarian lands promised at Campo Formio.

Because of the unsatisfactory experiences with the delays and multiple complications of the Congress of Rastatt, the Emperor chose to conclude the Peace of Lunéville not merely for the Habsburg dominions, but for the entire Empire as well—which of course meant that the treaty would have to be approved by the Imperial Diet. Acting with a rapidity which was nothing short of astounding for an assembly so notorious for its evasions and delays, the Diet in fact ratified the peace on March 7, and on April 3 even formally requested the Emperor, as plenipotentiary of the Empire, to execute its terms in detail in direct cooperation with France. Francis II, however, believing that acceptance of this request would place Austria in the unenviable position of bearing the full onus for the changes that were to occur, many or most of which were certain to be unpopular in various quarters, refused it. After months of renewed deliberation, the Diet in early October proposed the creation of an Imperial Deputation to be charged with the task of drawing up a specific plan of indemnification. This proposal was accepted by the Emperor in November, thus finally putting in place the formal German machinery for the transformation of the Empire.

The deputation consisted of the plenipotentiaries of five Electors— Mainz (as Archchancellor of the Empire), Saxony, Brandenburg, Bohemia, and Bavaria—and of three princes—Württemberg, Hessen-Kassel, and the Grand Master of the Teutonic Order (Archduke Charles of Austria, who in 1802 had succeeded his uncle Max Franz of Cologne in the Grand Mastership after the latter's death the previous year). Though negotiations and discussions among the members had occurred since their nomination, they did not meet as a group until late August of 1802. That was probably just as well, since some very basic parts of their work, had they met earlier, might have been undone by the decisions of other powers. France had advanced a compensation proposal as early as March of 1801, and in the face of the almost complete disorganization and confusion of the Austrian court and its advisors, a number of German princes decided to negotiate directly with Bonaparte. Between July 1801 and May 1802, Bavaria, Baden, Württemberg, Prussia, and even Mainz made separate treaties with France which not only guaranteed them substantial shares in the indemnification, but also removed many of the most important decisions from the as yet unconvoked deputation.[4] These treaties were arranged with the agreement of the new Russian Emperor, Alexander I, whose friendship was being courted by Bonaparte and who called upon Russia's rights as a coguarantor of the Empire not only to look after the interests of some of his southern German relatives, but also, in conjunction with France, to draw up a comprehensive plan of compensation in June of 1802. Immediately, while the eastern and western guarantors looked on benignly, some of the Estates, including Prussia, without bothering to wait for the Imperial Deputation even to meet, began to occupy the territories that had been promised them. Austria, not to be left behind, did the same. The Franco-Russian plan, submitted almost as an ultimatum to the deputation when it finally met in August, underwent a few modifications in the next few months—none of them basic—and was formally accepted on February 25, 1803. The Diet approved the decisions of the deputation on March 24, and with the ratification of the Emperor on April 27, the so-called Final Recess (*Reichsdeputationshauptschluss*) was given the force of law as a fundamental part of the imperial constitution it did so much to change.

The important provisions of the Final Recess can be summarized fairly briefly.[5] First, the ecclesiastical principalities—archbishoprics, bishoprics, and abbacies—were all dissolved, and the ecclesiastical princes

therefore also disappeared except for three: the Grand Master of the Teutonic Order, the Grand Prior of the Knights of St. John (the Maltese Order), and the Archchancellor of the Empire (Dalberg), whose archiepisco-
pal see was transferred from Mainz to Regensburg (which remained the
seat of the Diet) along with his electoral title and the additional designa-
tions of Metropolitan Archbishop and "Primate of Germany." He was also
provided with a small territory around Aschaffenburg (near Frankfurt),
and was awarded the former Imperial City of Wetzlar, where the Imperial Cameral Tribunal continued to sit. The Teutonic Order and the
Knights of St. John were also awarded or permitted to keep some territory; in the case of the former, this was done primarily to provide livings
for those of the some 700 members of the numerous Cathedral Chapters
who might prove unwilling or unable to support themselves in other ways
following the dissolution of the ecclesiastical states which had previously
provided their employment. Second, the Imperial Cities which remained
on German soil—four had already been lost to France with the Left Bank
—were abolished except for six: Lübeck, Bremen, Hamburg, Frankfurt,
Nürnberg and Augsburg. These survived for a combination of reasons.
One was Bonaparte's desire to keep back some prizes as a way of cajoling
cooperation from territorial princes who had hopes of absorbing some
of the cities at a later time. Another was Austria's concern to retain a
degree of influence in the Empire through the preservation of at least
some of the traditionally loyal Imperial Cities. A third was the jealousy
of the German princes themselves, who preferred the continued independence of some cities to the prospect of their absorption by competitors. And,
finally, in this as in so many other aspects of the diplomacy of the day,
the payment of large bribes—in this case mostly to the French—helped
the cities to achieve results which no amount of moral argumentation ever
could.[6] As part of the dispensation by which these six cities retained their
autonomy, they were required to remain perpetually neutral, even in time
of *Reichskrieg*—a provision which was greeted with undisguised joy by
their governments and citizens alike.

The Final Recess abolished no less than 112 Imperial Estates on the
Right Bank. In terms of wealth, population, and territory, by far the greatest change came with the secularization and absorption of the ecclesiastical territories, by which some 10,000 square kilometers and close to
3,250,000 people now fell under secular rule.[7] The complexion of the
Council of Electors had been drastically altered: Trier and Cologne had
disappeared, Mainz had been transformed into the Electorate of Aschaffenburg-Regensburg, and four new Electors—Salzburg (now secularized,
expanded, and awarded to Ferdinand, younger brother of Francis II, as
compensation for Tuscany), Württemberg, Baden, and Hessen-Kassel
—had taken their places in the Council alongside the five surviving ones,

namely, Bohemia, Brandenburg, Hanover, Saxony, and Bavaria.[8] For the first time, a majority of the Electors were Protestants (Brandenburg, Hanover, Saxony, Württemberg, Baden, and Hassen-Kassel), a circumstance against which Francis II protested vainly but vigorously, the more so because Protestants for the first time also outnumbered Catholics on the Council of Princes by a majority of 53–29, reversing the earlier Catholic majority of 55–45. The significance of the Council of Princes was greatly reduced by the Final Recess, however, since the creation of new Electorates meant that an absolute majority of the votes in the Council of Princes was now controlled by the Electors.[9]

The distribution of the territory of the secularized ecclesiastical states and of the mediatized Imperial Cities, as well as of a few very small secular princes, by no means removed the checkerboard appearance of the political map of the Empire altogether, but it did simplify it considerably. That simplification was largely the result of the abolition of well over one hundred territorial units and their absorption by others, but it was also assisted by a process of rounding off of existing territories (*Abründung*) designed to eliminate the troublesome enclaves of one political jurisdiction within another through appropriate exchanges. The states which had suffered losses on the Left Bank received compensation beyond their losses, sometimes considerably so; Prussia, for example, while losing some 220 square miles and 137,000 people, was awarded nearly 1,100 square miles with a population of 600,000 as indemnification, and some other states, while receiving less in absolute terms, got much more in relative ones— little Baden, with a total increase of more than 235 square miles and over 200,000 people, is the best example.[10]

With these compensations, Bonaparte realized one of the great goals of his German policy: the creation of a group of enlarged German client states on or near the French border, of sufficient size and internal cohesion as to diminish their sense of dependence on Austria, yet not so large as to be able to forget that their recent good fortune as well as their possible future expansion was due to the good will of France. Whether the Empire, for its part, in political disarray and preoccupied with the quarrels, ill will, and problems of territorial assimilation that had arisen from the decisions laid down in the Final Recess, could find a way to mold its reconstituted parts into a strengthened union was an open question. The answer to it would provide the key to Germany's future.

The decision to abdicate the Left Bank to France and to provide compensation for the Left Bank losses of hereditary secular princes set off one of the most vigorous publicistic controversies in the history of the Holy Roman Empire. Nor it is surprising that it did so, considering that the execution of the decision represented the most abrupt and serious change in the constitution of the Empire since the Peace of Westphalia, a change that all but eliminated two categories of Estates on which the formal structure of the Empire had rested: the ecclesiastical territories and the Imperial Cities. Three ecclesiastical princes (the Archchancellor and Elector of Aschaffenburg-Regensburg and the heads of the Teutonic Order and the Knights of St. John) and six Imperial Cities now constituted the forlorn remnants of two groups of Estates which had earlier numbered more than one hundred.

Yet while the chagrin and disappointment of many of the rulers, magistrates, and officials of the principalities and cities whose independence was abolished was profound and genuine, and was amply demonstrated in the flood of books, pamphlets, and articles in the years 1797 to 1802 which sought to ward off the impending decision against them, the provisions of the Final Recess cannot have come as a total surprise to them or anyone else. Why this is so in the case of the Imperial Cities will emerge later on. In the instance of the ecclesiastical states, two background factors must be kept in mind, which together give an appearance of virtual inevitability to their eventual secularization. First, of course, the fact of the secularization of ecclesiastical territories was nothing new, even if the scale of what was now being proposed was. One needs to look no further back than 1648 to find formal imperial ratification of the secularization of several ecclesiastical principalities and their absorption by secular states as part of the overall territorial settlement of the Peace of Westphalia. In the following century, while no actual secularization took place, there was a long history of half-baked plans and rumors about the possibility of it; beginning at least as early as 1742–43, when some proposals for ending the War of the Austrian Succession called for expanding the territory of the Wittelsbach Emperor Charles VII through his absorption of some imperial bishoprics, the issue was never entirely dead thereafter. It was actively discussed during the Seven Years' War, again during almost the whole period of Joseph II's scheming over the Bavarian inheritance, and yet again after the outbreak of war with revolutionary France, when both old and new plans and rumors began to become increasingly serious and more universal.[11] While secularization appears to have been discussed between Prussian and French diplomats as early as February 1793, it was not until after the Peace of Basel that much of Protestant Germany, at least, seems to have moved toward acceptance of the principle of secularization.[12] By 1797, when Austria in the Peace of Campo Formio in effect accepted the loss of the Left Bank and, by implication, the notion of an at least partial secularization by her participation in it through the promise of Salzburg, the die was cast. After that time, at the very latest, no person who was at all politically aware could doubt that secularization was, at last, an immediate and vivid alternative, if indeed not yet quite a wholly ineluctable one. The outpouring of opinions for and against secularization, beginning in 1797–98, shows clearly that few did in fact doubt it.

Part of the energy and enthusiasm with which the opponents of secularization went about the publicistic task of attempting to save the ecclesiastical territories probably stemmed from their own acute awareness of the second of the background factors which in the later eighteenth century conditioned public receptivity to the idea of abolishing the prelatic states: the generally bad reputation of the ecclesiastical governments and administrations, which (correctly or incorrectly) were commonly held to be so seriously deficient in relation to those of most secular states as to produce substandard conditions in every aspect of public life from education, morals, and general enlightenment to the economic well-being of the citizenry. While it is true that the growth of attitudes hostile to these governments was a slow one, stretching far back into the eighteenth century and to a considerable extent paralleling the diffusion of the Enlightenment in Germany, it is also true that in the last two decades of the Empire's existence such opinions became rather suddenly more widespread, and criticisms of the ecclesiastical states became more sharply focused and specific than ever before.

One chief reason for this is not far to seek. In 1786, the editor of the well-known periodical *Journal von und für Deutschland,* Philipp Anton von Bibra, published in his magazine a prize question for which he solicited a general response; the question, stripped to essentials, asked simply: What are the fundamental constitutional deficiencies of the ecclesiastical states, and how can they be remedied? The entries, of which there were eventually about twenty, were to be judged by the respected Osnabrück historian, publicist, and official Justus Möser and Karl von Dalberg, at this time still the delegated governor (*Statthalter*) of the Elector of Mainz in Erfurt; the winning essay was to be published in the journal.

It is indicative of the degree to which ecclesiastical princes and officials were conscious of the dubious repute in which their own governments stood that the man who proposed the prize question, P. A. von Bibra, was himself a member of the Cathedral Chapter of the Bishopric of Fulda and eventually occupied the post of *Regierungspräsident* for its Prince-Bishop (and his relative) Heinrich von Bibra.[13] Unfortunately, the essays which poured in—almost all of which were distressingly candid and specific in their recitation of the abuses of ecclesiastical government—gave clerical rulers and their servants very little cause to believe that their image was improving. A brief survey of the major points of criticism contained in the essays will demonstrate this.[14] First, the fact that the ecclesiastical principalities were elective states was quite generally regarded as a fundamental evil, and for several reasons. The elected prince, responsible for the quality of his government neither to his ancestors nor to his own posterity, was seen as too often indifferent to the condition of his territory, either during his reign or at the time of his death, and interested chiefly in exploiting his position to the advantage of himself and his family and friends during his lifetime. His subjects, seeing in him a nonnative (which was usually the case), raised and educated elsewhere and therefore not familiar with local conditions, showed a similar indifference to him, and felt little responsibility to help him in his endeavors. Since it was frequently true that older men, often well past their prime, were elected to these ecclesiastical principalities, even the best-intentioned of them had little time to implement their plans, a problem compounded by their coadjutors' (and probable successors') impatience and eagerness to try out their own ideas (and reap their own gains) while their superiors still lived. Since almost every election resulted in a competitive scramble between various German ruling houses, including the Habsburgs, to control the throne, whoever was elected was subject to the temptation to subordinate his territory to the interests of his family, from which involvement in wars and other political problems could arise.

The opinions of the prize essayists were rather more divided about two other characteristics of the ecclesiastical constitutions—the Electoral Capitulation and the Cathedral Chapter. Some asserted the value of both as restrictions on the ability of the prince to develop despotic and arbitrary government, while others saw them as limitations on the beneficence of well-intentioned and capable rulers. More unanimity existed in the criticism of the double role of the ecclesiastical ruler as cleric and as prince; with duties so very different, if not frequently downright incompatible, it was averred, the ruler would sooner or later be forced to neglect one of them—usually the clerical one—with a resulting decline in the spiritual and moral well-being of his subjects. Economic criticisms of the ecclesiastical states were legion and severe also; they ranged from the excessively luxurious lifestyle of princes, officials, and the overnumerous Chapter members which caused money to leave the country to pay for foreign luxury goods rather than to recirculate within the territory, to the general and baleful effect exercised on the economy by the hordes of clerics, especially monks and nuns, whose sheer numbers and claims on the resources of the territory seemed almost to suggest that the state and all its citizens existed solely for the benefit of the clergy. A rational and pragmatic impatience with the economically unproductive vocation of the clerical estate as such, as well as with the wasting of time and money by ordinary folk on pilgrimages, formulary prayer, and statuettes, pictures, and other religious bric-a-brac was characteristic of numerous writers on the prize questions.

What is, in a sense, most remarkable about the various essays submitted to Bibra's journal is that there was so little direct correspondence between the faults and defects of the ecclesiastical states pointed out by most of the writers, and the remedies they proposed for them. A real solution to the most basic problem, for example—the elective system— simply eluded most of them, who could come up with nothing better than suggestions such as the elimination of the rights of corulership of the Chapter or the composition of a new and permanent Electoral Capitulation under the supervision of the Emperor, and so on. The most radical remedy proposed for the economic ills of these territories was confiscation of clerical property by the state, a sort of internal secularization which would at least remove the "dead hand" of the church from a certain amount of wealth, but which did not really move very far toward the solution of fundamental problems of government. The refusal of almost all authors to draw the real consequences of their own critique—the complete secularization of the ecclesiastical states—was almost certainly deliberate; on the one hand, as philosophical meliorists and believers in the perfectability of administration, they really did not think it necessary to touch on basic constitutional questions, while, on the other hand, they realized full well that both the imperial constitution and the prize question itself set certain practical limits to what they might reasonably propose. In recognizing that the question was asking them to identify and suggest remedies for the deficiencies of actually existing governments and not to deny the very sense of the question by proposing the abolition of the governments it assumed, they were true to the pragmatic and sincere intentions of the ecclesiastical official who had posed it.[15]

Given these facts, it is not altogether astounding that the winner of the prize competition was a rather bland essay carrying the reassuring message that the flaws in the government of the ecclesiastical states were few and minor, and that all were susceptible to amelioration by what amounted to administrative tinkering. Written by Josef von Sartori, an expert on public law, an official of the Prince of Oettingen-Wallerstein, and later a librarian in Göttingen and Vienna, the piece was duly published in Bibra's journal in 1787 and as a separate book in Augsburg the same year.[16]

While there is no evidence to indicate that Sartori's essay aroused much interest or excitement in Germany, the same cannot be said of another of the entries which from several standpoints was certainly the single most significant analysis of the ecclesiastical states to appear before the period of the actual secularization itself. Written by Friedrich Carl von Moser, who by now had some claim to be regarded as the public conscience of the Empire, this lengthy treatise differed relatively little in its identification of the basic faults and abuses of the ecclesiastical governments from the other entries, except perhaps in its more detailed treatment of them. Like most others, Moser criticized the results of the elective system with its associated evils of political influence as they too often manifested themselves in superannuated princes or even "certified blockheads," as well as the cumbersome governmental apparatus with its confusion of legislative and executive powers between the prince and the Chapter. Although critical of the venality and the unpreparedness of far too many Chapter members for their responsibilities, he admitted that relatively few men reached the princely dignity who had not through various previous positions gained some experience for their new office, a circumstance he believed characteristically less true of the successors to heritable secular thrones. Moser also accepted as fact the economic stagnation of the ecclesiastical territories and the system of clerical privilege, which resulted not only in vast inequalities of wealth but a low standard of living for most citizens.[17]

While in these criticisms Moser was treading essentially the same path as that of his competitors in the prize question, he parted company with them in several important respects. In the first place, his emphasis on the supreme value of individual thought and conscience and his belief that the constitution of the ecclesiastical states not only protected these very little, but actually suppressed them, was much stronger than theirs. He attacked Catholic doctrine and clerical influence for limiting the human spirit, forbidding independent research and reflection, clapping human understanding into the chains of faith and obedience, keeping people in a state of permanent anxiety about their eternal fate, and, in short, perpetuating collective stupidity as a matter of principle. The Catholic notion that a man could pray, buy, or work off his sins without genuine inner improvement further helped to keep the people dumb and unfeeling, said Moser, and this situation was in no way improved by the lack of freedom of the press and of the book trade, as well as the deplorably bad educational system of the ecclesiastical territories, all of which he contrasted very unfavorably to those of most Protestant states—even down to the general level of enlightenment among the peasantry. He recognized—and praised—the efforts of a number of Catholic secular and ecclesiastical states to reform and improve education in recent decades, but added his hope that pedagogical amelioration would not be left solely in the hands of clerics, from whom, he implied, little of lasting value could be expected.[18]

The vehemence of Moser's critique of these kinds of abuses betrays more than the usual opposition to clerical "obscurantism" that was the property of so many enlightened thinkers of the period, not excluding Moser himself. In his case, however, an extraordinarily strong Pietist background equipped him with a special contempt for Catholicism as a religion which spoke only to the "outer man" through pictures, formulas, good works, and captivating rituals, but did not touch the "inner man" whose continuing conversion, for the Pietist, was the proper business of true religion.[19] This hostility had in no small measure the character of an emotionally based anti-Catholicism, which far outstripped Moser's political disapproval of the ecclesiastical states, toward whose governments and constitutions he showed a much greater degree of objectivity than to their official religion.[20]

In this instance, however, the political and religious aspects seem to have been related in a special way in Moser's mind. It was his conviction, along with many others of his time, that mild government was the best government, and that it was chiefly characterized by its relative invisibility and by as much nonintervention in either the material or spiritual lives of the citizenry as possible. But this conviction rested upon the assumption of a high degree of enlightenment among the citizens, which enabled them to set and pursue goals beneficial to them individually and collectively without the coercively guiding hand of government. An ignorant and unenlightened people, on the other hand, not only produced harsh and despotic government as the lamentable but inevitable solution to the problems caused by its incapacity to order its own affairs, but in producing such a government also guaranteed the perpetuation of its own ignorance, since the governors had no reason to wish to eliminate the very circumstance on which their power rested. Moser's plea that the first remedy for the ills of the ecclesiastical states must consist of returning basic understanding to their peoples, based on the freedom to think, research, question, worship, speak and write—a plea directed less at the prince than at what he regarded as the *real* government, namely, the ubiquitous clerical establishment—demonstrates that for him full freedom of thought and conscience was not only a basic human right, and therefore inherently desirable, but also the essential foundation of all good government.[21] In this attitude, Moser was also at least indirectly consistent with one prevailing argument for the excellence of the constitution of the Empire, which linked the supposedly widespread enlightenment of Germans to the mildness of their territorial governments.[22]

A second major difference between Moser and the other essayists who wrote on the prize question was his consistent refusal to regard the government of the ecclesiastical states as uniformly and drastically worse than that of the heritable secular states. The frequency with which he lashed out in both short and extended commentaries on the abuses of the latter almost gives the impression that he was uncomfortable with the limitations imposed by the prize question and that the heart of his desire was actually to write on the faults of the German territorial governments in general. His view that the preparation of the elective princes for their duties was probably better than that of the generality of successors to hereditary thrones has already been mentioned, but this was only one of numerous specific remarks suggesting that many secular rulers, in principle, had no reason to congratulate themselves on the excellence of their governments in comparison to those of the clerical princes. Indeed, he stated flatly that the old saying "Living is good under the crozier" (*Unterm Krummstab ist gut wohnen*) could be considered valid at least in comparison with the largest secular states. He gave the ecclesiastical princes higher marks than hereditary ones in the constancy of their concern for the stability of the "modern" imperial constitution against threats from Emperors, Popes, or foreign powers, though he also admitted that in times of general danger their zeal tended to manifest itself more in shrieking and trumpeting alarms than in material assistance.[23]

But what was most important, perhaps, was that the constitution of the ecclesiastical states, through the Electoral Capitulations and the Chapters, set limits to despotic tendencies of their princes, and therefore provided better institutional protection against governmental abuses for their peoples than was true of most secular states: "All the evil that twelve spiritual Electors and princes may have done does not equal what one Brühl brought to Saxony through his profligate political economy under the weak and apathetic Augustus III."[24] As such a statement indicates, Moser was far too alert to and concerned about the deficiencies of government in general to allow himself to be diverted into a one-sided attack on one group of states merely for the purpose of answering a prize question, though it is certainly arguable that the comprehensiveness of his approach may have helped to disqualify his essay for the prize in the minds of the judges.

There was, however, a better reason than this to award the prize to someone else: The solution that Moser proposed for the ills of ecclesiastical governments deviated radically from all other remedies suggested. Briefly, he recommended nothing less than the secularization of the ecclesiastical states, but the preservation of the elective method of choosing their rulers. This would involve drawing up a list of the so-called *stiftsfähige Familien*—those noble families inside or outside the territory which by tradition or statute formed an exclusive pool from which all members of the Cathedral Chapter were drawn—and entitling each to contribute one elector for the purpose of choosing the prince, who would rule for his lifetime but could not bequeath his throne to his heirs. The prince would preferably be chosen from among members of the *stiftsfähige Familien*, but Moser would not exclude election of an already reigning elective or hereditary prince from another territory even though that would result in the same "absentee rulership" that now existed in cases where an ecclesiastical prince governed more than one principality. The Cathedral Chapter, after reduction in the number of its members, would be converted into a permanent council comparable to the territorial diets; its original members would be chosen by the prince and his ministers, though subsequent vacancies would be filled by vote of the council itself, with the prince having only a veto on their choice. An Electoral Capitulation would remain, but would be carefully revised to insure that it served an intelligently conceived constitutional purpose.[25]

Since it was Moser's belief that many of the major faults of the government of the ecclesiastical states were rooted in the combination of political and religious powers and functions in the hands of a single person, his secularization was of course intended to separate the offices of prince and bishop (or other ecclesiastical position); and he made it clear that the new cleric, who was to be chosen by the prince, would not only be subordinate to him, but would henceforth possess no diocesan rights beyond the boundaries of his own territory, thus making the church in every principality a wholly territorial one. This would help to cut the pernicious ties to Rome, especially if, as Moser suggested, the prince was forbidden to choose a foreigner (and especially an Italian) for the episcopal post and was encouraged to nominate from among former members of the Cathedral Chapter. The duties of the new bishop would be restricted to spiritual ones: He would possess no secular jurisdiction of any kind nor any lordship over the persons and civil rights of subjects. He would have neither landed estates nor an episcopal court, and would live solely from a decent salary provided by the prince. Moser's secularization also extended to church property, including especially monasteries and nunneries, which were to be prohibited from accepting new arrivals and were to be closed up and confiscated by the state gradually, as existing monks and nuns died or were encouraged to leave them. Most of these former church properties were to be put to beneficial social uses such as schools, seminaries, hospitals, or even converted to productive industrial enterprise, but were not to be regarded by the prince as his private possessions.[26]

Viewed against the later secularization as it was actually executed according to the provisions of the Final Recess of 1803, Moser's essay is in some ways as interesting for what it did not propose as for what it did. Given the fact that in 1787 the secularization of the ecclesiastical governments was something of a fantasy in any case, since there was no reasonable expectation that it was going to be accomplished either by constitutional means or by force at that time,[27] Moser could as well have proposed that the ecclesiastical states be converted into hereditary rather than elective secular principalities, or that the several dozen of them be amalgamated into a few large ones, or even (as eventually happened) that they all simply be absorbed by existing secular states. That he did not do so is significant. It is suggestive in the first place of his continuing belief in small states as intrinsically less likely than large ones to cherish the political ambitions which had led the latter to develop bloated bureaucracies and military establishments, with a corresponding increase in taxes and government supervision of the lives of citizens, and a concomitant decrease in civil liberites and intellectual freedom. Secondly, just as he had learned to see largeness in states as predisposing to despotism, so he could not quite bring himself to approve the principle of hereditary government —in spite of his forceful critique of the evils attendant to elections—when it became necessary to choose between it and an elective system in which a moderately restrictive Electoral Capitulation and a semi-independent council would provide solid institutional safeguards against princely tyranny.

In particular, however, the scheme Moser proposed was deliberately calculated to preserve the character of the former ecclesiastical states as refuges for an independent nobility, which he saw as an indispensable mediator, "a middle estate which holds the balance" between prince and people. In far too many states, the nobility had been so thoroughly tamed or compromised by insatiable monarchs and violent princes as to be unable to fulfill this role, but the ecclesiastical states still had a strong and active nobility, for whose support, according to Moser, the religious foundations had been established in the first place. He referred to the "so-called Priests' Alley" of clerical states along the Rhine as a wonderful and invaluable "Pyrenees" which guaranteed that the wholesale emasculation of the nobility that had taken place in countries such as France and Spain would never occur in Germany; and, he concluded, "These Alps [sic] can remain even if the prince remains just prince and the bishop becomes again just bishop."[28]

That Moser's plan would also help to preserve a major source of employment for considerable numbers of his own class of Imperial Counts and Knights, who after all were heavily represented in the Cathedral Chapters and the governments of the ecclesiastical states, is certainly not without significance in the evaluation of his argument. It would be unfair, however, to ascribe this intention to guarantee the livelihood of the imperial nobility entirely to a narrow economic self-interest. Moser, it must be remembered, throughout his entire life labored with a single-minded and indeed desperate dedication toward the goal of restoring the integrity of the German imperial constitution as a strong and universally respected national framework within which the political and spiritual values he cherished could be asserted, nourished and protected. The imperial nobility was for him one of the pillars of that constitution, and he did not want to see it destroyed after the fashion of the territorial nobilities, which once upon a time had possessed a strong imperial consciousness, but now, after losing out in their struggle with the larger territorial rulers, had largely been converted into the meek servants of the proud, overmighty, and ambitious imperial princes whose policies were increasingly subverting both the theory and the reality of the imperial constitution.

It might seem paradoxical, in view of the fact that the ecclesiastical princes, on the whole, were also among the most loyal supporters of the imperial structure, that Moser would recommend their abolition. This apparent inconsistency is resolved, however, by the realization that Moser intended the destruction of the ecclesiastical character of these states, not the destruction of the states themselves. Moser knew that the dedication of the ecclesiastical rulers to the imperial constitution stemmed partly from the small size and the weakness of most of their states, which they had in common with the smaller secular territories, and partly from their elective nature which, all legalisms to the contrary notwithstanding, was not generally accepted as conferring quite the same entitlement to rulership as did hereditary succession.[29] Moser's scheme, in proposing retention of present territorial boundaries and of the elective system for the princely office, would therefore have preserved precisely those characteristics of the ecclesiastical states which had ensured their devotion to *Kaiser und Reich* in the past, and which would presumably continue to do so even after the secularization he recommended. This explanation serves not only to clarify some of the apparent contradictions of Moser's argument, but also to demonstrate that from an imperial constitutional standpoint, at least, his essay was not quite as much the radical or even revolutionary document it was held to be in some quarters.

CHAPTER TWELVE

The Ruin of the Ecclesiastical States and the Imperial Cities

R EGARDLESS OF ITS CONTRIBUTIONS in other respects, Moser's essay, like those of the other competitors in the prize question, was important in its time chiefly in helping to create or confirm a devastatingly one-sided picture of misgovernment and consequent popular misery in the ecclesiastical states. Understandably, these writings were appreciated for their barrage of criticisms of clerical government rather than for the very occasional favorable comments they contained. While brief references to these works of 1786–87 are sprinkled in some profusion throughout the polemics on both sides of the secularization issue in the years 1797–1802, it is significant that in general the proponents of secularization spent very little time exploring the characteristics of the government and constitution of the ecclesiastical states.[1] Their worthlessness, in both general and specific terms, was by this time simply taken for granted by most of them, and this attitude, though operating as a largely unstated assumption, was nevertheless invisibly present as a condition of argumentation throughout the entire debate over the future of these states. This became quickly apparent in the complex disputes over the whole issue of the compensation of hereditary princes for losses suffered on the Left Bank, a principle which had first been accepted at Campo Formio and later confirmed at Lunéville, and which, by the time of the Congress of Rastatt, also clearly spelled out a bleak future for the ecclesiastical states.

From the standpoint of the opponents of secularization, there were essentially five propositions around which to construct a defense for the continued existence of the ecclesiastical territories: First, that it was not necessary to accept the principle of compensation itself; second, that even if it were necessary, the ecclesiastical states should not bear the full burden of it alone; third, that these states did not intrinsically deserve to be dissolved; fourth, that is was illegal or unconstitutional to dissolve them; and, finally, that the results of their extinction would be disadvantageous not only for the Empire and its peoples, but for all of Europe, not excluding France itself.

The proposition that no compensation (and therefore, of course, also no secularization) was necessary was presented in two different kinds of approaches. The first, argued by Karl Moritz Fabritius, the author of one of the most extensive defenses of the ecclesiastical states and their governments to appear in this period, tried to argue that the Left Bank should not be abandoned to France at all, because it was too high a price to pay for a peace which the rapacious French Republic would not long respect in any case; the only course for Germany to follow was to continue the war until the French were defeated, at which point the whole issue of compensation would evaporate.[2] Much the same line was taken by a certain Baron O'Cahill, court chamberlain to the Princes of Wied-Neuwied, who saw in the impending Rhineland losses not only the prelude to the collapse of the imperial constitution and the conquest of the rest of Germany, but also the possible creation of numerous republics on the Right Bank. Yet while he implied that another war would not be too high a price to pay to avoid the abdication of the Left Bank, he also suggested that it might not be necessary; with astonishing naivete, he argued that republics in géneral cannot maintain themselves if they are too large, and that since the French Republic was already too large before occupying the Left Bank lands, it might well return them to Germany unasked—the more so because the Rhenish peoples were too unlike the French and too hostile to them to make their assimilation either possible or profitable.[3]

The other approach to preventing secularization as compensation was simply to deny that any legal or moral obligation existed on the part of the Empire or any of its princes to make up losses suffered by any member of the Empire in a legally declared *Reichskrieg*. Dalberg, for example, regarded the notion of compensation as contrary to the example of earlier peace treaties, such as Rastatt (1714) and Ryswick (1697), and suggested uncharitably that in the case at hand "Each bear his own fate" —a principle which, if adopted, would have shifted the burden of loss entirely to the Left Bank princes (and incidentally, have left his own expectancy to Mainz intact).[4] Others insisted that neither the nature of the imperial association, nor any principles of either private, international, or public law imposed an absolute obligation on some or all of the Estates of the Empire to make good the losses of others;[5] such an obligation could only be established by "treaties and voluntary agreement."

The answer of proponents of secularization to these two approaches was made easy by the course of events themselves. By 1801, they could

simply point to the final military defeat of the Empire and the Peace of
Lunéville to demonstrate, first, that the reconquest and retention of the
Left Bank had been tried in vain, and was no longer a real choice; and
second, that the terms of the peace, formally accepted by the Empire, had
now indeed established "by treaties and voluntary agreement" the very
obligation the earlier arguments had sought to deny. Both the authority
of the Empire to assume such an obligation and the wisdom of its decision
to do so as the lesser of two evils was defended by Christian Ernst Weisse
(certainly no enemy of the traditional constitution), who felt that the
Empire, in making this decision, was at least attempting to assert some
measure of elective control over its own fate rather than leaving everything entirely to accident.[6]

The second major proposition of the opponents of secularization was
that even if compensation had to be paid, the ecclesiastical states should
not be required to bear the full burden of it, and especially not to the
point of the extinction of an entire class of states. Broadly speaking, they
argued that the Empire as a whole was responsible for the loss of the Left
Bank, and that the Empire as a whole—that is, the sum of its Estates—was
therefore responsible for any compensation that was to be paid, ideally
on a strictly proportional basis.[7] Various means of payment were proposed: Baron O'Cahill suggested compensation entirely in the form of cash
from the *Reichskasse,* a view shared by Dalberg, who admitted, however,
that the scheme was probably impractical.[8] Others proposed complex plans
such as that of the Salzburg cleric and teacher Johann Baptist Graser, who
wrote that the amount of compensation should be determined only by the
actual income lost to the dispossessed princes, and not by the extent of
territory or size of population of their lost lands; their compensation
would then be awarded according to a formula by which 60 percent of
this lost wealth would be paid in territory, 20 percent in money, and 20
percent in *Arrondirung,* that is, in the administrative advantage to be
gained simply from border rectifications and the elimination of foreign
enclaves by means of territorial exchanges. Another author would have
reduced still further the amount of compensation by recommending not
only that dispossessed Imperial Counts ought not to be regarded as hereditary princes, and that their claims to compensation therefore not be
honored, but also that even those rulers who did have claims be paid
only for the loss of their domain lands, that is, the lands owned by the
ruling family itself.[9]

These different proposals had one thing in common: All wished to
limit either the *kind* or the *amount* of compensation to be paid for Left
Bank losses in such a way as to prevent the wholesale secularization of
the ecclesiastical states. In this sense, the most extreme position was taken
by those who proposed that compensation be paid exclusively in money,

and by all Estates of the Empire, for that would have meant the possibility of avoiding secularization entirely, or at least of restricting it to certain goods and property of mediate religious foundations rather than to the extinction of the very political existence of the prelatic territories. Such a position could no longer be taken seriously by anyone with political common sense after the Peace of Lunéville, where secularization had been called for in terms so specific as to be unmistakable.

At this point, the watchword came to be simply to salvage what one could. Most of the quarreling about which princes did or did not deserve compensation, how the balance of compensation in money, territory, or other things should be paid, and so on, belongs to this period. Dalberg, who like most others by this time knew that a fairly considerable secularization was inevitable, now tried to make a distinction between the destruction of ecclesiastical foundations and church property and their secularization, the latter of which was taken to connote partial abolition, the former total. Only that part of the clerical establishment which was actually expendable could be secularized, he averred, while the rest would have to be taken from the Empire as a whole. In this process, furthermore, no distinction should be made between Catholic and Protestant church property. Secularization, he admitted, was to be the *basis* of indemnification, but that implied that it should be associated with other means as well. J. B. Graser worked on the problem from much the same premise as Dalberg—that is, that the secularization should never go so far as to destroy an entire category of Estates—and asserted that the seizure of ecclesiastical foundations should start with the smallest—the monasteries, priories, abbacies, and so on—and proceed only as far as the compensation required.[10]

It is interesting that the advocates of secularization spilled very little ink to challenge the arguments of their opponents on the question of how much secularization should occur. Partly, no doubt, this is because many of them understood that the course of events was with them—that when the word "secularization" was pronounced in a formal treaty, it was to be interpreted as meaning the abolition of all the ecclesiastical states. A frequent argument for this interpretation was that the French interest clearly required and intended total secularization simply because the Catholic clergy in Germany at all levels were the most vehement and unforgiving enemies of the Republic, who had in fact provided the first cause of war between France and Germany through the hostile and provocative policies pursued by the ecclesiastical princes in permitting emigré French nobles and clergy to use their lands as the staging ground for counterrevolution in the early 1790s.[11]

Such allegations were hotly denied by the friends of the ecclesiastical states, who asserted not only that the German prince-prelates had no reason to hate the French Republic or its principles because, as Christians, they taught obedience to all authority, whether of kings or of peoples' senates, but also that far from instigating the war with France, these princes were merely doing their duty; if indeed they fought the French more tenaciously and surrendered to them less readily than many of the secular princes, it was because they took more seriously than these their obligations to the law and to the Empire, which demanded that they pursue the *Reichskrieg* with fortitude once hostilities had begun.[12] In general, however, it is likely that most proponents of secularization, convinced as they were that the existence of such states was simply not commensurate with the enlightened "spirit of the times," merely assumed that the political formula of compensation-with-secularization as it was accepted at Lunéville also carried within it a fundamental philosophical principle that did not allow of only partial application.[13]

The third proposition propounded by the enemies of secularization was that the governments of the ecclesiastical states, their bad reputation of recent years to the contrary notwithstanding, provided their citizens conditions of life that were as good as, and in some respects better than, those which characterized hereditary secular states.[14] This, of course, was designed to counter the argument—often unstated because taken for granted—that not the least of the reasons for secularization was the improvement it would bring to the benighted and impoverished peoples of the ecclesiastical territories. Since the critics of these territories had found in their elective system the best stick with which to beat them, it is not surprising that their defenders professed to find in that same system a chief cause of their superiority to the hereditary states. They pointed not only to the accidents of birth which in such states could bring physical or mental defectives to thrones, but also to the positive advantage of election in permitting prior scrutiny of candidates and their personal qualities and abilities, normally resulting in the selection of an individual with good family, education and experience, usually of middle age and therefore far from the intemperate passions of youth. Both the Electoral Capitulation and the Cathedral Chapter (the latter sometimes compared to the more effective territorial diets in Germany, the earlier *parlements* in France, or even the British Parliament) were cited in by now familiar ways as safeguards against some of the worst abuses of princely power—arbitrary taxation, whimsical and potentially dangerous foreign alliances, trafficking in soldiers, and so on. On the other hand, few restrictions were placed on the beneficence of the ecclesiastical prince, whose inability to leave heirs of his body, it was averred, led him to wish to be remembered for the good he might do in everything from roads and bridges to hospitals, schools, and orphanages.

Various other characteristics of the territories that possessed this elective system were compared favorably to those of hereditary states. Low levels of assessment and taxation, as well as the absence of burdensome fiscal responsibilities for the maintenance of princely widows, collateral lines, pensions, and so on, helped to preserve a moderate economy with few extremes of wealth or poverty, and consequently one in which the commercial and mercantile spirit with its tendency toward luxury and conspicuous consumption was kept within bounds. The very small military establishments of the ecclesiastical states also benefited the economy by removing fewer financial and human resources for unproductive activity; and if it be objected that these territories thereby rendered themselves weak, then that was more than compensated by the fact that governments too feeble to rule by force, as these were, had to rely on the power of justice and patriarchal love instead, as these did. Finally, the much criticized union of spiritual and temporal powers in the hands of a single man was not only defended but praised as a device which prevented the quarreling arising from the separation of church and state that had been a frequent source of violence and misfortune in many societies. Indeed, as Wende has pointed out, some of the proponents of ecclesiastical rulership, mindful of the insistence on the moralization of political life that was so characteristic of the late Enlightenment, claimed that the spiritual mission of the prince-prelates imbued their political behavior with an ethical quality that was absent in secular governments.[15] The equation of morality with religion that was implied here was unlikely to find much favor among devotees of the Enlightenment, but this argument in favor of ecclesiastical governments appears to have been greeted by their critics in the same way most of the other supposed advantages of these regimes were—by a silence which suggested that the case for the prosecution was proved and therefore closed.

The fourth proposition advanced against secularization was based on the legal and constitutional right of the ecclesiastical states to exist. This was asserted, flatly and without qualification, time and time again by their defenders, who found no differences between them and the hereditary secular states as coequal fiefs of the Empire, the sole distinguishing characteristic of the former being that their rulers arrived at their thrones through election rather than by hereditary succession. Both the general and the particular human rights which lay at the base of the imperial constitution, as one writer put it, guaranteed the ecclesiastical princes unshakable title to their lands and to all sanctioned regalian rights; their removal would constitute a direct violation and subversion of the imperial constitution.[16]

This argument, which relied on history and tradition and, more importantly, on the undeniable fact that the imperial constitution itself established no distinction between ecclesiastical and secular princes with respect to the degree of their legal entitlement to their lands, was nowhere directly contested by the proponents of secularization, most of whom, indeed, insofar as they chose to deal with legalities at all, admitted the validity of their opponents' constitutional stand; yet many of them betrayed attitudes suggesting that at base they did not in fact feel that title to rulership of secular and spiritual rulers was equal. Thus, the anonymous author of a letter to the editor of a prominent journal defended the constitutionality of the prelatic states, but also wrote that in the present situation it was preferable to take the territories of elective rulers rather than those of secular ones "who have received their dignity through the rights in inheritance."[17] Behind this statement was a conviction that the hereditary princes had a property in their states in a sense that the ecclesiastical princes did not—that the right of inheritance, with the entitlement it conferred by virtue of a single family's investment of time and energy in the stewardship of a given state over many generations, was superior to the right of election which gave rulership to an individual in an instant, without consideration for the historical nexus of time, territory, and blood. Another kind of statement of the differing nature of the property the two kinds of princes had in their states emerged in the work of another advocate of secularization, who justified it by pointing out that European rulers in the past had frequently appropriated church lands and income for the needs of their states when they were in great danger, and that this procedure had often been sanctioned by the church itself, not excluding the Pope.[18] The suggestion here, of course, was that, unlike secular princes, the ecclesiastical rulers held their territories in a kind of social trusteeship for the larger civil society—the Empire—of which they were indeed members, but members with a special responsibility for sacrifice in time of need.

The only major constitutional argument employed by the apologists of secularization was the assertion of the sovereignty of the Empire as a whole over the territories which composed it, with the concomitant derivation of its right to take whatever measures it deemed appropriate in a given situation, including the imposition of unequal sacrifices on its members. This was baldly stated by C. D. Voss, a professor in Halle, who applied it to the secularization question by citing the precedent of the Peace of Westphalia and by his assertion that any spiritual prince could remain in his office only as long as "the sovereign Empire" found it appropriate for him to do so. Christian Ernst Weisse agreed, saying that the legality of the secularizations in the present case was derived not from the *obligation* of the Empire to compensate hereditary princes for their lost lands, but from the *authority* of the Empire to choose among those persons whose rights should be sacrificed for the whole.[19] Some authors went so far as to suggest that not only the ecclesiastical princes, but indeed *all* the German princes actually had no private property in their states whatsoever, but only a kind of public property which belonged to the whole Empire. It then followed that the determination of the right of rulership in any and all territories belonged solely to the Empire.[20]

The fascinating answer to this kind of argument, employed by a handful of antisecularization writers, but best exemplified in the work of Johann M. Seuffert, was given in the form of a theory of popular sovereignty which denied to the Empire as a whole the right of disposition over its members. All the princes of Germany, Seuffert asserted, were but the delegated Supreme Commanders (*Oberbefehlshaber*) of the various peoples which were themselves sovereign; that the princes were said to be possessors (*Inhaber*) of sovereignty meant only that they represented the sovereignty inhering in their peoples. The Empire was a general association of these peoples, whose princes constituted an Imperial Council (*Reichsrath*) to represent them: "This imperial association . . . can only be a result of the sovereignty which the individual states of Germany possessed, and conferred upon their princes. It [the association] can therefore serve only for preservation of the sovereignty of the German peoples and their commanders, not for their destruction. It should protect, not dissolve." Since it was indisputable that the ecclesiastical princes were members of the Empire, Seuffert continued, the latter had no right either to deprive them of the sovereignty which they in no way lost by their entrance into the imperial constitution, or—which amounted to the same thing—to secularize the states they ruled.[21]

Two things should be noted about this unusual argument. First, by emphasizing the sovereignty of the peoples of the German states and the merely representative character of their princes, Seuffert was really attempting to efface or render irrelevant the distinction some of his opponents were trying to make between secular and ecclesiastical states and rulers in order to prove the lesser right of the latter to a continued political existence. His point was simply that the titles given to princes and the manner by which they attained them were of no significance, since all were equally expressions of the will of the sovereign people. Since all peoples were sovereign, and none more so than any other, and since their states and princes were all equally the constructions and instruments of their sovereign wills, no one group of states could establish a claim to existence superior to that of any other group.[22] Second, Seuffert's formulation equated the territorial lordship (*Landeshoheit*) of the member states of the Empire with full sovereignty, and in so doing denied the Empire the character of a true state in which a relationship of legal subordination of the parts to the whole existed. Seuffert's Empire was virtually a confederation of fully sovereign states rather than a single state or even a unitary federative system; to use the German, it was a *Staatenverein* or *Staatenbund,* not *Staat* or even *Bundesstaat.*

This argument not only flew in the face of all the formal teachings of public law at the time, but also went beyond even the most self-serving aristocratic interpretations of the nature of the Empire as preached on various occasions by the great secular princes in their steady expansion of the prerogatives of *Landeshoheit*.[23] It is deeply ironic that a defender of the ecclesiastical states should employ a principle so destructive of the theory of a vital and meaningful imperial government, for one of the most insistent claims of the antisecularization forces was that the extinction of the prelatic territories would remove from the scene precisely that group of states which had always done the most to preserve the unitary character of the Empire and give force to the decisions and decrees of its various organs of government—the Diet, the supreme courts, and the Emperor. It is only slightly less ironic that among the most zealous champions of imperial sovereignty in this controversy were some apologists for the large secular Estates who only a few years before had heatedly denied the right of the Empire to bind them to a war policy against France, or indeed to nearly any foreign or domestic policy of which they individually disapproved, but who now piously preached the obligation of the ecclesiastical states and the Imperial Cities to bow to the decision for their own destruction in the name of imperial sovereignty.

Yet for all these tortuous constitutional arguments and counterarguments, the legal justification for secularization on which its advocates chiefly relied was of a different kind; this was the law of necessity (*Notrecht*), a necessity so widely taken for granted among them that it was apparently often thought unnecessary to argue it in detail, or indeed even to mention it.[24] The most influential statement of this law of necessity, however, was made by Christian Ernst Weisse, who defended the constitutional authority of the Empire under any circumstances to accept the demand for compensation and to order secularization as the means of providing it. He also defended the actual decision to do so once the victorious French had finally and unequivocally demanded it: "In this case, the action of the Empire requires no further defense, because . . . the legality of secularization is immediately proved as soon as the supreme power proceeds under the conviction that peace is essential to the preservation of the state."[25] By this reasoning, then, the highest power of the state was not only permitted but obliged to sacrifice a part of the state if the preservation of the whole depended on it. Weisse held that this could apply to any part of the state by the ancient doctrines of *plenitudo potestatis* and *ius eminens,* but in citing such renowned legal scholars as Hugo Grotius, Thomas Hobbes, Hermann Conring, and Christian Thomasius on the specific right of the state to confiscate church property under some circumstances, he appeared to suggest the particular appropriateness of secularization in this instance. This was made even clearer in a subsequent passage in which he admitted that the ecclesiastical states recommended themselves as the means of compensation partly because their rulers, chosen mostly from the lower imperial nobility, did not have very powerful family connections. This meant that the possibility of successful resistance to the abolition of these states was less than that of the territories of better connected secular princes; that in turn meant that the requirements of the peace treaty (Campo Formio, in this case) were more likely to be executed, thus sparing the Empire the complete dissolution at the hands of France which might otherwise be the result of the failure to carry out the peace terms.[26]

There were three kinds of responses to this argument for secularization from a supposed necessity based on the obligation to preserve the Empire. One, which has been discussed already, was to deny that the necessity existed—to assert that with a little more common spirit and German will power, the Empire could successfully drive the French from the Left Bank and resist all further attempts on their part to reconquer it. As suggested earlier, this argument, along with an Austrian army, was blown to pieces on the battlefield of Hohenlinden in December of 1800, and was seldom heard after Lunéville.[27] Another, basing itself on a kind of social contract theory according to which individuals (or in this case individual states) bound themselves into a union for the specific purpose of ensuring their own preservation, maintained that since the whole (the Empire) existed only for the benefit of the parts (the particular territories), the sacrifice of any part for the whole was illogical and would make nonsense of the very reason for the formation and existence of the whole.[28] A third response was the assertion that secularization, far from preserving the Empire, would constitute the surest guarantee of its destruction. This would occur, according to one author, because of the severe weakening of the power and influence of the Emperor through the extinction of his heretofore most loyal allies, the prince-prelates, as well as because of the force of the example of the illegal action taken against the ecclesiastical states. It would result, first, in a "second partition" of Germany as larger secular princes pounced upon and absorbed the smaller, and later in popular revolutions produced by revulsion at the succession of injustices to which the by now wholly disintegrated lawful order of the Empire had given way.[29]

This argument leads to the fifth and final general proposition of the opponents of secularization: That the destruction of the ecclesiastical states and their absorption into large secular states would bring the most disastrous results of various kinds for Germany and for Europe. In the first place, as seen in one example, it was commonly supposed that a complete secularization would be such a blow to both the structure and the political operations of the Empire as to be tantamount to its dissolution. This would result not only from the disappearance of the prince-prelates from the Council of Electors and the Council of Princes and the loss of their loyal assistance to the Emperor, but also from the simultaneous growth in power of the secular states, whose historic drive to limit ever more the powers of the imperial office would be greatly strengthened.[30] While some authors hoped that Austria's self-interest would assure her successful opposition to general secularization, however, other more pragmatic heads recognized the likelihood or indeed the inevitability of the loss of some clerical territories, and began to concentrate their efforts on salvaging what they regarded as the constitutionally most essential of the ecclesiastical states: the three Electorates of Mainz, Trier, and Cologne, even if transplanted and with different names. Apart from the fact that their continuation would ensure the traditional Catholic majority in the Council of Electors, there also seems to have been a feeling among those who favored this plan that the diversity of Estates of which the Empire was composed was itself a fundamental principle of its constitution, and that the complete elimination of any class of states therefore had to be avoided.[31] These polemical efforts were not based altogether on naive and groundless hopes. There is some evidence that although in the end only one of these Electors was actually saved—the durable Archchancellor Dalberg—the extinction of the other two was not inevitable. But while Dalberg diligently went about the business of his own salvation, Vienna bungled whatever chance the others might have had by the appearance it gave of wishing to control them, thus sacrificing all possibility of French support against the German proponents of general secularization.[32] In this sense, one part of the formula for political disaster predicted by the opponents of secularization—the enfeeblement of the House of Austria—appeared to be realizing itself before their eyes, and before the secularization had even occurred!

The other part of the formula, of course, involved the dire consequences that would attend the sudden growth in strength of the medium-sized secular states stemming from their absorption of ecclesiastical territories. What was predicted was nothing less than a revival of the worst imaginable chaos of feudalism, in which each state, feeling the surge of pride in its own newly found power but at the same time unaccustomed to the responsible exercise of such power, would turn on its neighbors in hopes of further territorial gain. Where this might ultimately lead was sketched out in a fanciful but frightening scenario by Johann Baptist Graser. The feuding states of Germany, he supposed, being unable to resolve their conflicts satisfactorily by themselves, would turn as two groups to Austria and Prussia for alliances. No possibility of a legal solution to their hostilities would exist, since the Emperor would refuse to carry out the judgment of an imperial tribunal for fear of offending princes who might then fly off to Prussia for support. The Emperor's reputation would suffer so badly, and the internal situation of the Empire would degenerate so far, that finally Austria and Prussia, with their allies, would go to war. At first, Prussia would prevail, Graser surmised, but not in the long run, since all Catholic states would eventually gravitate toward Austria. At this point, the war having assumed the aspect of a confessional struggle, Austria would take the offensive, and all of Germany would become a battlefield. France and Russia would then intervene, and an arrangement would be worked out between these two powers and Austria, the victor of the German war: France would take western Germany, and probably organize it as a republic; Austria would incorporate all of southern Germany, and then strike off into southeastern Europe to plunder and absorb the whole rotten and crumbling Ottoman Empire; and Russia would extend her power over the whole of northern Europe, including not only Sweden and Denmark, but also all of Prussia. Graser then left his readers to ponder the final, awful result of secularization: the spectacle of swarthy Cossacks settling permanently into the sandy plains of Brandenburg.[33]

While most authors did not have Graser's flair for dramatic exaggeration, many of them certainly did share his conviction that the expansion of the medium-sized states would not lead to a stronger and politically more stable Germany, as the advocates of secularization constantly asserted, but to a weaker and less stable one that would endanger the peace and security not only of all the German states but of Europe as well. Their opponents contended, though it was as often implied as expressed, that the misfortunes of the Empire in recent years had resulted from a fragmentation of effort rooted in the multiplicity of its territories, and that the solution to this problem lay in a greater concentration of energies to be achieved through the absorption of smaller territories by larger.[34] Against this contention, the defenders of the ecclesiastical states asserted, first, that the problem lay not in the number of states in itself, but in the moral deficiencies of individuals and their lack of common spirit; and second, that larger territories were even less likely to devote their energies to the common cause than smaller ones. The Imperial Count Friedrich von Stadion, who was neither an enthusiast nor a fool, put it this way: "Of what use to Germany are strong medium-sized states, which are disunited among themselves, [and] must be disunited because each wants to gobble up the other, [and] if necessary even with the help of foreign powers. No, not the greater power of individuals, but greater unity and a firmer association of all is necessary, and that will more likely be at hand when states exist which by reason of their political structure must hold fast to the Empire, to the community."[35] The same thought was put even more bluntly by another author: "Love of fatherland is at home only in those states which for the sake of their self-preservation have an interest in the imperial union."[36]

This idea that small states honored their obligations to their confederation because they realized their own dependence on it, whereas larger states tended to forget that dependence, was shared by J. M. Seuffert, who also claimed to know something about the ability of cunning foreign neighbors to make use of the egoism of the larger states. He thus warned the rulers of medium-sized territories that their growth by enlargement would for the first time make it worthwhile for France to undertake a sustained campaign of influence for their allegiance—something which their own vain striving for greater autonomy and self-sufficiency would tend to encourage—thereby permitting France as both agitator and mediator a much more significant penetration of the German political scene than ever before.[37]

Warnings were also issued to the two German great powers, as well as to France, that they should rid themselves of any notions that secularization would mean a net gain for them. As has already been pointed out, the belief that Austrian power would be greatly lessened by the diminution of Habsburg influence in a secularized Empire was universal among the opponents of secularization; that they repeated such an argument again and again, however, may well betray their fear that Vienna might freely decide that potential Austrian territorial gains from secularization outweighed the advantages of the never altogether certain allegiance of the prince-prelates—a fear that was not wholly justifiable, but not completely groundless either.

Prussia, which was everywhere understood to be the most vigorous and powerful champion of secularization, was also informed of the pitfalls which awaited it in case compensation based on general secularization was realized. Graser, for example, whose tale of Cossack horror supposedly stemmed from his earnest concern to spare Berlin the dire consequences of its own ill-considered policies, also artfully attempted to convince his Prussian readers that their security could best be served by a renunciation of any compensation for Prussia's Left Bank losses; by thus avoiding common borders with France, and ensconced behind a buffer of smaller German states, Prussia would be less exposed to "collision" in the west.[38] It was elsewhere suggested that Prussian statesmen consider carefully the advantages their state derived from the general guarantees of the imperial constitution, as well as the perils which might arise from the growth of other powers in Germany after its destruction; there was no reason to believe that all the enlarged states would necessarily be natural allies of Prussia, this argument ran, but much reason to suppose that, resenting Prussia's dictatorial position, they might combine to destroy her.[39] Berlin was also warned that even if it were successful in establishing a political preponderance in Germany, the end result might not be worth the unsettling effect it would have on Germany and Europe and the uncertainties it could bring with it, including the likelihood of the active hostility of Austria and possibly that of Russia as well.[40]

France, finally, was admonished that secularization might prove destructive of her long-standing policy of ensuring that Germany never be unified under single leadership. If one of the two opposing "parties" in Germany—the Catholic states—were badly crippled by the elimination of the ecclesiastic princes, power would begin to gravitate into the hands of the Protestants, with the possibility of the establishment of a German hegemony, presumably in the hands of the King of Prussia. This, clearly, would not be in the best interests of France.[41]

There was also another aspect of the absorption of the ecclesiastical states that bothered the enemies of secularization: its effect on the quality of life of the peoples now to be transferred to secular rule. For many or most of them, in the first place, secularization had a spiritual as well as a political meaning; it was an attack on religion as such, and with their already noted propensity to associate morality with religion, they saw it as tending infallibly towards the destruction of good morals, which some of them supposed to be especially characteristic of the peoples of the clerical states.[42] J. B. Graser asserted that Catholic peoples which fell to Protestant princes who believed that Catholicism was nonsense, or worse, could expect at the very best an indifference toward their religion on the part of the state; the enthusiasm of their spiritual teachers would then slowly wane, while the "half-learned" would no longer be restrained from criticizing the faith. The result would be an increasing erosion of belief and spiritual discipline with all of its unfortunate consequences for human behavior. Things would be little better under a Catholic secular prince, Graser gloomily predicted, since even the best-intentioned temporal rulers of both religions were disinclined to provide support for religion (or indeed for all "science and culture in the proper sense"—philosophy, pedagogy, history, etc.), and were interested only in those "practical" disciplines such as law, medicine, physics, and chemistry, which contributed in observable ways to fill their treasuries. The rapid decline of religious and philosophical studies together with the increased emphasis on the material arts, would lead to a growth of material well-being and luxury—materialism, in short—which would further distract the people from their spiritual obligations.[43]

In spite of its focus on religion, however, this argument was merely a special case of a more general objection to the incorporation of the clerical territories by larger states: the disappearance of the benefits supposed by many, and not only the opponents of secularization, to attach to small states. In one sense, indeed, the slogan "One lives well under the crozier" was a kind of code-phrase well understood by those who employed it to include the various advantages attributed to *Kleinstaaterei*. Since listing those supposed advantages would merely repeat much of the detailed examination of defenses of the imperial constitution in Chapter 8, a few lines will suffice to illustrate this aspect of opposition to secularization. Very simply, it was asserted that the absorption of small territories would rob their inhabitants of the blessings of governments which, being close-by, could service their peoples better than more impersonal larger govern-ments, and, being small and not very powerful, were more obedient to those imperial institutions such as the supreme courts which protected the legitimate rights of individual subjects. The moderate level of well-being of the peoples of small states, furthermore, would be transformed into extremes of wealth and poverty in larger states, where the expenses of the court, the capital city, a bloated civil bureaucracy, and a large mili-tary establishment resulted in high levels of taxation, and where too much money left the country to satisfy the luxury requirements of an overre-fined and prideful governing class. Awareness of their own profligacy and of the discontent it caused among the people, especially those arbitrarily transferred from other and happier jurisdictions to their own, would eventually lead governments to employ violent measures of repression against their peoples, beginning with the extinction of freedom of the press, the palladium of the liberty of all Germans. At this point, the vaunt-ed efficiency of larger governments would have revealed itself for what it really was: the efficiency of the army barracks.[44]

Again here, as in earlier debates about the German constitution, a single assumption about the purpose of government itself tended to shape the judgment of those who defended small states; the goodness of a con-stitution, and of a government, they said, rested on the sole criterion of the sum of the well-being they brought to their citizens. Not the achieve-ment of power, but the striving for the happiness of the largest number of people legitimized government, and not even the most colossal world power that had established its greatness through conquest could claim to have fulfilled its civil mandate, since war and conquest had nothing to do with the basic purpose of civic union, but were only a sad means for its preservation.[45] In this view, the larger a state became, the more suscep-tible its ruler was to the seductions of power, and the greater its efforts and expenditures for the military and other similarly unproductive means necessary to acquire and sustain power. The ruler of the small state, on the other hand, forbidden by his own weakness to harbor even the illu-sions of power, was forced to seek the glory denied him on the battlefield in his own little community through notable achievements in improving the welfare and happiness of his subjects. Having arrived at this con-clusion, it then became possible to assert, as several authors did, that the greater level of popular contentment in the beneficently governed small states made them less susceptible to revolutionary fevers and distempers than large ones, and even to praise Germany's political fragmentation as the chief reason for its continued existence as a state: "Mocking politicians may thus always laugh about the Holy Roman Empire that is neither holy nor Roman nor an Empire; they may call it a many-headed Hydra. So much the better if it is. So much the more difficult it becomes for the French Hercules to conquer it." And again: "one can almost confidently assert that we owe our salvation to [that very] fragmentation which weakened our resistance. The Roman Empire would now otherwise be a Germanic Republic. . . ."[46]

The fury of the debate over the secularization of the ecclesiastical states could almost lead one to forget that since the Peace of Lunéville another whole class of territories also stood on the brink of extinction. These, of course, were the Imperial Cities, nine-tenths of which were ultimately thrown together with the clerical principalities to form the territorial mass from which compensation for the Left Bank losses was to be drawn. It should be noted immediately that the prospective abolition of these "states" did not stimulate a public controversy which even approached in intensity that which surrounded the secularization issue. There are at least two major reasons for this. First, with the exclusion of the handful of the largest and wealthiest of them (whose continued independence was virtually guaranteed from an early date in any case), the sum total of the resources of the Imperial Cities in territory, wealth, and population did not compare with that of the ecclesiastical states. Neither did their political weight in the Empire, whose constitution, to be sure, gave them their own curia at the Diet, but whose operation virtually excluded them from the exercise of any real influence.[47] From the standpoint of the overall effect the extinction of the imperial immediacy of the cities, or their absorption by other states, would have on the political configuration of the Empire, it was simply not easy for most people to get excited about their future.

Second, in the late eighteenth century the cities as a group had, if possible, an even worse press than the ecclesiastical territories. If indeed the latter suffered from a degree of clerical obscurantism, government by whim, and other deficiencies both economic and social, most of them were at least large and significant enough to possess a certain mitigating diversity of conditions which even their critics did not entirely overlook. The cities, on the other hand, with many of the same faults, and others that were worse, were too small to hide their generally deteriorating situation from even the casual visitor. As victims of fundamental changes in the geography of trade and commerce from the sixteenth century onward, a fair number of once prosperous and populous cities had shrunk to the size of villages, in which the desperate attempt to maintain the proud traditions of a time long past now impressed outsiders as a ludicrous and unwarranted vanity. Subjected to periodic economic and politi-

cal harassment by the annoyed rulers of the larger territories which surrounded them, and who coveted such little wealth and territory as they
had, the governments of many cities, once at least semidemocratic in nature, had degenerated into rigid patrician oligarchies whose exclusive hold
on the reins of government became even tighter as economic distress and
popular discontent created increasingly serious challenges to their misrule.
Unequal tax burdens, mismanagement of municipal property and funds,
and large and growing public debts were characteristic features of far too
many Imperial Cities, and were widely known and reported.[48]

These two factors, then—the practical insignificance of the cities as
Estates of the Empire and their extraordinarily bad public reputation—
help to account for the lack of interest in the issue of their absorption,
which is obvious in the scant attention shown to it in the public press.
The profound sense of both the inevitability and the appropriateness of
the abolition of the ecclesiastical states which had characterized the proponents of secularization, and which had led so many of them to treat
the whole question so brusquely, seems in this case to have affected not
only the advocates of absorption, but even those whose privileged positions in the cities were at stake in the destruction of their independence;
most appear to have accepted this probable consequence with a kind of
dumb resignation that is not the stuff of which lively public controversy
is made.

Still, the Imperial Cities had a few active defenders, some of whose
arguments are again illustrative of basic convictions about the nature of
the Empire and the values it represented. First, some tentative and rather
lame attempts were made to defend the governments and constitutions
of the cities against their critics, either by denying that abuses were in fact
as widespread as they were said to be, or by pleading special causes for
the admittedly less than flourishing condition of the cities that had nothing to do with their government as such. Thus, the publicity given to the
frequency of complaints and criticisms made by the citizens of Imperial
Cities against their own governments, it was frequently asserted, was
merely evidence of the freedom to criticize, which was greater in the cities
than in princely states, where much more numerous and serious abuses
were hidden under an iron cloak of silence imposed on suffering subjects
by their arbitrary rulers. Furthermore, no small part of the economic
misery which gave rise to so much complaint about the cities was due not
to misgovernment but to the disproportionately oppressive contributions
the cities had made to easing the general burdens of the Empire, especially in the imperial wars of the eighteenth century and of the French
Revolution, which, according to one author, would have inflicted virtually
unhealable wounds on the cities "even if they had received their constitutions from Heaven."[49]

Apart from a few farfetched arguments designed to prove that the Imperial Cities, because they were so widely scattered, were not appropriate for purposes of compensation, or that because they were mostly small and poor no prince who absorbed them could expect to gain very much and therefore might as well leave them alone,[50] the spokesmen for the cities rested their case pretty largely on their historical and legal right to exist, as well as on the special value they claimed these territories had for Germany and the Empire. J. G. Påhl not only stoutly defended the constitutionally sanctioned and inviolable independence of the cities, but even suggested that whereas the rights of territorial possession of many princes were rooted in nothing more than simple inveteracy, or even in the "injustices of the times" (*injuria temporum*), those of the Imperial Cities could often be proved by the existence of formal contracts. He also warned that trade always flourished best in places where merchants had a voice in government—better in republics than in monarchies, for example—thus suggesting that German commerce as a whole would suffer from the incorporation of the cities into princely territories. Finally, like all those who spoke out in favor of the cities, Pahl referred to their great loyalty to the Emperor and the Empire, their unswerving devotion to the constitution, and their extraordinary sacrifices in the recent war.[51]

To the extent that an argument such as this was designed to call forth to the cities' defense all those souls from whom danger to the integrity of the traditional structure of the Empire, including especially the supreme headship of the Emperor, could be expected to evoke a strong response, it was little different from one of the appeals consistently made by the opponents of the secularization of the ecclesiastical states. In the case of the cities, however, there was a very deep and special feeling for the unique historical role played by these islands of imperial immediacy. One author, possibly Pahl again, in pleading for the reform and improvement of the cities as the alternative to their political destruction, tried to convey this almost touching concern when he referred to them as "the first-born of German freedom."[52] Another writer developed the thought more fully, recalling to his readers the wild, warlike, and barbarous medieval Germany from which these Imperial Cities sprang as the special protégés of the Emperors, the illumination they had brought to a dark age by their hospitality to the arts and sciences, and their incomparably great contribution to the material well-being and civilization of the German nation by the security they offered to industry, commerce, and to the civic-minded and progressive elements of German society. In this last respect, in particular, the cities still had a valuable role to play, especially "for the private German citizen of independent means": "He loves them as peaceful and pleasant sanctuaries (*Freystätte*) . . . . He sees in them so many meeting places for impartial common interest, for independent spiritual culture, for scholarly development." Or again: "Where are otherwise the neutralized places, so to speak, where each may relax from the role [assigned him by] his own special territorial circumstances? where he almost needs to be nothing but a calm, dispassionate person, [and] finds undisturbed enjoyment and release from every restraint, [but] without illegality? where, without [being thought] forward, he may speak freely about anything and everything, and may give voice to thoughts which, while not forbidden, might yet be found inappropriate elsewhere?"[53]

The author of this paean to the Imperial Cities, who made a point of identifying himself as a person of high birth and an official of an electoral court in order to prove that his opinions did not stem from the bias of citizenship in one of the cities, was not prepared to abandon his "pleasant sanctuaries" without a fight. He called on the cities to begin planning immediately for a close and general association, not only as a means of self-preservation but also as a duty they owed to Emperor and Empire. As a first step, a diet of the Swabian Imperial Cities could be convoked, followed at the appropriate time by a general diet to which all the cities would send representatives. These deputies should be guided by a short but pointed set of instructions, for which he suggested two cardinal points: the principle that all the cities without exception should be preserved, and the principle of maintaining an especially close connection with the Imperial Circles and their agencies and organs. Praising the German constitution which so greatly facilitated the foundation of internal alliances against foreign dangers, this writer saw the means for the salvation of the cities in their utmost utilization of the institutional structures provided by the imperial constitution. On the other hand, he also admonished the cities to improve their own internal situations, especially with respect to their sinking economies; reducing the excessive number of municipal jobs, introduction of a well-organized and strictly controlled accounting system, and the reduction of taxes on industry, the trades, and commerce were the most important of the suggestions he made, though he also emphasized the need to reestablish civic harmony in this time of peril, and specifically urged that religious quarreling in the "mixed" cities whose constitutions provided for equal numbers of Catholics and Protestants in official positions be put aside.[54]

The above proposal is notable, among other reasons, because it is almost unique in the considerable literature produced by the crisis that eventuated in the disappearance of the ecclesiastical states and all but a handful of the Imperial Cities in suggesting active self-help for the threatened Estates as a means of preserving their independence. Among the many defenders of the ecclesiastical states and of the cities, almost none seemed prepared to admit that unless they tried to do something for themselves by means of leagues or other kinds of associations they were almost certainly lost. The fact that such measures would probably not have affected the outcome of their case is largely irrelevant; what is important is that they were not tried, nor even very much explored as ideas.

It is arguable, of course, that the absence of such proposals among polemicists stemmed at least partly from a sense of sheer helplessness in the face of overwhelming events, further bolstered by the knowledge that resistance might only hasten the fate they feared. But one can also sense in many works an almost indefinable conviction that the only correct and appropriate path to follow was that of reliance on the justice and the righteousness of Emperor and Empire. Firmly persuaded as the opponents of secularization and absorption were that the Empire, by all traditional understanding of its structure, its constitution, but above all of its *meaning* and its *purpose* as a state, would cease to exist with the extinction of the clerical territories and the cities, there was a feeling among them that an imperial decision against them would be evidence that the values that underlay *their* Empire had already collapsed—that the Empire which would reject them was at the same time one which neither they nor any other morally upright German could fully accept in any case. This was surely the sense of the statement of Max Franz of Cologne, made in response to a plan submitted in the summer of 1798 by one of his officials for the creation of a new secular Electorate for him in case of general secularization; rejecting this proposal, Maria Theresia's youngest son proudly wrote: "I became a spiritual prince and Elector by election; my right to land and people is based purely and solely on this election, on this [investiture of] dignity and office." He realized that in taking this position he was sacrificing his political future: "In case of general secularization, my role is played out."[55]

The illegitimacy that Max Franz clearly felt would attach to an Electorate created by means of the destruction of the old ecclesiastical states reflects the sentiment of many Germans that the legitimacy of the entire Empire itself was at stake in the deliberations about the future of the prelatic territories and the Imperial Cities. Over and over again in the pleas for the preservation of the traditional form and structure of the Empire there appears a most profound conviction that the realization of the contemplated extinction of these two imperial Estates, while perhaps preserving the empty name of Empire, would rob it of its soul. More than on any other single thing, its claim to greatness, to a very special place among all historic states, lay in its commitment to law and to scrupulously observed legal procedure as the very reason of its existence. Having long since eschewed conquest or power as one of its purposes, it had consecrated itself as a perfect *Rechtsordnung;* in that *Rechtsordnung,* there was no place for the kind of arbitrary assault on the well-established rights of some members by others that was now in prospect. If that assault was sanctioned, and if it was successful, the Empire would at that moment have divested itself utterly of the one characteristic which above all others lent it its superior moral dignity among the states of Europe.

The other most precious achievement of this Empire, as seen by the opponents of basic change, would also be compromised severely, and perhaps fatally: Its preservation of diversity within unity, wherein the unity was seen as the servant and the guardian of diversity. As has been shown, an overwhelming proportion of the specific advantages advanced as proof of the goodness of the Empire and its constitution had to do with the political multiformity of Germany and the host of local and regional variations in economic, social, and cultural conditions to which it gave rise. Unity, praised almost always as an instrumental value rather than a primal one, was seen as proceeding from diversity for the purpose of protecting it, but was on the other hand itself strengthened by diversity, since the relative weakness of the numerous Estates of the Empire regarded as individuals gave all of them a powerful collective interest in maintaining the common bond which protected them. The proposed secularization and absorption, as their opponents saw it, would represent a blow to each component of the formula "diversity in unity": By reducing the number of states, and dramatically so, it would lessen diversity, while at the same time, in making individual states more powerful through enlargement, it lessened in them that sense of dependence on the whole on which the will to preserve unity depended. In this important respect, too, then, the Empire would cease to be an Empire; it would simply dissolve into the larger states, and the Holy Roman Empire would become little more than a geographical expression, a place where neither diversity nor unity would find a genuine home.

The extensive debate over the secularization of the ecclesiastical territories, the abolition of the immediacy of the Imperial Cities, and the enlargement of some states by absorptions was therefore more than merely a self-interested struggle to avoid loss, on the one side, and achieve gain, on the other. It was a clash between two different and rapidly diverging visions of what the Empire was and ought to be. But to the victor belong the spoils. If, as is often averred, the abdication of Emperor Francis in 1806 and the dissolution of the Empire produced comparatively little in the way of public expressions of sadness or regret, it is certainly due partly to the preoccupation of the victors with digesting the gains to which the Final Recess had formally entitled them. But among those who had waged such a desperate struggle to save the clerical states and the Imperial Cities, it is just as certainly due in large part to the fact that they had already cried, and dried, their tears: The Empire they understood and had fought so hard to preserve had, after all, died three years before.

CHAPTER THIRTEEN

The Death Struggle
of the Imperial Knights

IN ADDITION TO THE ecclesiastical states and the Imperial Cities, there was
another group of imperial territories whose fate was uncertain throughout most of this period, and whose final disappearance in 1806 removed
one of the last components of the territorial composition that had helped
to define the old Empire. These, of course, were the tiny lands of the
hundreds of Imperial Knights who, though never Estates of the Empire,
had provided a significant and constant source of political support for
both the Emperor and the imperial constitution. Many knightly families
had a proud history of generations of service to the Habsburg Emperors in
military, diplomatic, and civil service positions in Vienna, Regensburg,
and elsewhere, and the loyalty of the *Ritterschaft* to the imperial idea was
at least as strong and consistent as that of the ecclesiastical princes or the
Imperial Cities. That loyalty, of course, stemmed largely from a sharp
awareness among the Knights that they, more than any other immediate
subjects of the Emperor, were dependent on the maintenance of the imperial constitution and its protective mechanisms to shield them against
the ambitions of the princes of nearly all degrees of power within whose
territories their own lands lay as pockets of wholly independent governance and jurisdiction. Whether *Landeshoheit* in the proper sense belonged
to the Knights was much debated in the formal constitutional literature
of the time; but in practice, this problem reduced only to the question of
whether they had the right to pronounce sentences of death in criminal
justice, while in all other things their full territorial lordship was admitted.

That was precisely the source of their precariousness, especially (and
increasingly) in the century and a half following the Peace of Westphalia,
a period during which more modern and efficient governmental practice

in the medium-sized and larger territories made rulers and officials of the latter look with growing annoyance on the sovereign enclaves of the Knights. They stood as disturbing reminders that neither political and economic unity nor a coherent civil and military administration could ever be achieved in the princely territories as long as the Knights' lands had to be treated as essentially sovereign states. After 1648, quite a number of princes' leagues against the Knights were established; most of the earlier ones were secret, but by the beginning of the eighteenth century, they were very openly concluded and discussed—as at the Imperial Diet, for example. In the middle of the century, from 1749–53, the mutual complaints and recriminations of princes and Knights erupted into a series of full-scale debates at the Diet and in the public press, from which came no fewer than forty-six polemics on both sides. While no action was taken by either Emperor or Diet in this quarrel, it illustrates the continual irritation that characterized the relations between princes and Knights, and which, if anything, tended to increase over time.[1] One thing, in any case, was certain: If either internal or external forces should ever create the prospect of fundamental territorial or constitutional changes in the Empire, the Knights would find little support for their continued independence among the secular princes.

In the ten years between the outbreak of war with revolutionary France and the Final Recess, there were three series of events in particular that both weakened the Knights' position and pointed the way towards their ultimate fate. The first of these occurred in the wake of the Prussian absorption by inheritance of the Franconian principalities of Ansbach and Bayreuth in 1791.[2] The Prussian government, which had never had anything to do with the Knights before, simply because none of their jurisdictions existed in other Prussian territories, now found itself confronted with new lands in which fully one-third of the inhabitants lived in independent enclaves, most of them belonging to Knights. This was intolerable to Karl von Hardenberg, at this time the directing minister in charge of the Ansbach-Bayreuth inheritance, who, though an Imperial Knight himself, was contemptuous of the imperial constitution and who had been attracted to Prussian service precisely because of the unitary characteristics of the Hohenzollern state. Regarding the imperial immediacy of the Knights as wholly incompatible with a modern governmental and administrative system, Hardenberg in 1792 began a campaign to assert full Prussian sovereignty over the Knights of Ansbach-Bayreuth, which involved not only requiring civil and military payments and services directly to the Prussian government by the subjects of the Knights, but also the prohibition of payment of direct contributions to the imperial government through the *Charitativ-Subsidien*. Protests from the Knights and finally from Austria itself—still at this time a formal ally of Berlin—slowed the Prussian drive somewhat, but after the alliance was effectively ended by the Peace of Basel in 1795, it was resumed with even greater vigor. Further diplomatic protests, including a legal injunction (*Inhibitorium*) from the Aulic Council, were ignored or rejected by Prussian authorities, and the process of subjection of the Knights was essentially complete by 1797. For Knights elsewhere in the Empire, dismay at the success of Prussian strong-arm measures and at the failure of Vienna to stop them was increased by the disheartening readiness of many of the Franconian Knights, after only token resistance, to accept Prussian sovereignty because of the host of special considerations and privileges promised them by the Berlin government.

The relative rapidity of the Prussian success was itself partly due to a second major cause of the increasing troubles of the Knights: their financial and territorial losses through the war itself. This was not only a matter of the permanent loss of both lordship and land by Knights of the Left Bank, but of damage from temporary occupations and the ravages of campaigns throughout the German south and southwest, as well as the drain on financial resources occasioned by the Knights' self-imposed contributions to the imperial war effort. Needless to say, the ability of the Emperor to carry out his responsibility to protect the Knights against either foreign depredations or domestic violations of their rights—as in Ansbach-Bayreuth—was greatly weakened by Austria's military misfortunes during most of the 1790s.

Finally, of course, the long process of the territorial reorganization of the Empire, beginning at Campo Formio and ending with the Final Recess, brought little cheer to the Knights and their friends. It is true that the Final Recess itself specifically called for the preservation of the Knights and their imperial immediacy—a provision that was partly due to the influence of the Emperor himself. It was due even more, however, to bribes paid to the French and to the preoccupation of the larger secular states with their huge gains from the secularizations, which temporarily eclipsed their interest in the Knights' territories.[3]

Many Knights congratulated themselves on their victory, certain that the renewed confirmation of the Final Recess, as but the latest in a long series of constitutional guarantees, would assure their continued independence, and the more so since the larger secular princes had a stake in strict observance of the terms of the Final Recess which, after all, had awarded them their recent gains. Such optimistic souls were reminded, however, and almost prophetically, that if a really revolutionary change such as that which had destroyed the politically much more significant ecclesiastical princes could be carried out, there was no reason to suppose that another and much more minor adjustment could not be made in future; that the history and present maxims of the secular princes who now governed virtually all of Germany gave no grounds for rejoicing about the likelihood of their observance of imperial law; and that even if they did observe the strict letter of the law, the princes could find so many licit ways of harrassing the Knights and their subjects by raising transit tolls, import and export duties, and so on, that the Knights might soon find themselves cordially hating both their immediacy and the independence it brought with it.[4] In fact, of course, regardless of what else the future might bring, even the terms of the Final Recess themselves could not have been greeted by the Knights with unrelieved joy, since they had provided no compensation for their dispossessed colleagues from the Left Bank, and had abolished more than 700 seats in Cathedral Chapters, which would thus be unavailable for occupancy by needy Knights' sons in the future.

The princes, as it turned out, believed in striking while the iron of annexation was still hot. Even before the formal ratification of the Final Recess, Bavaria, followed shortly thereafter by Hessen-Kassel and Württemberg, began assaults on the independence of Knights' lands lying within their new territories. Castles were taken by force, and there were occasional pitched battles which led to injuries and some deaths. Elector Frederick of Württemberg is said to have urged his commissioners of occupation on to their work with the assurance that "Whoever among you attracts the most complaints is the most gratifying to me."[5] In some places—Bavaria is the best example—a "carrot and stick" approach was used on the Knights, who in return for submission to the territorial sovereignty of the ruling prince were to be given numerous preferments and advantages which extended well beyond those of the ordinary territorial nobility; refusal to submit, however, would result in military occupation. Close to half of the Knights in Bavaria to whom this option was offered chose to accept it.[6]

Just as it appeared that the hard-pressed Knights were about to lose their battle everywhere, however, the tide turned miraculously in their favor. The Emperor, encouraged by quarreling between France and Russia as well as by the renewed hostilities between France and Britain, and supported by a great wave of public indignation against those princes who were disturbing the peace of the Empire by their actions against the Knights, chose to intervene in the desperate situation of the latter.[7] On January 23, 1804, the Aulic Council in Vienna issued a decree, called a *Konservatorium,* chiefly directed at Bavaria, which ordered the restoration of the Knights to the position they had enjoyed on December 1, 1802. Execution of this decree, which would occur by force and at Bavarian expense if necessary, was entrusted to the Archchancellor Dalberg, the Electors of Saxony and Baden, and the Archduke of Austria. All agreed to accept the charge, and while they prepared to set up a commission in Regensburg to hold conversations on the matter, Austria moved troops to the Bavarian border. With his benefactor in France occupied with more serious problems, and his friends in Prussia unwilling to act in the face of German public opinion and Russian support for Austria's action, Elector Max Joseph of Bavaria now gave at least the appearance of capitulation, and in February 1804 notified the Emperor, the Diet, and the princes named to execute the `Konservatorium` that he would comply with its demands. The other offending states were forced to follow suit.

While the Knights sang the praises of their Austrian savior, Vienna itself was not altogether happy about the course of events. There is evidence that the heart of Austria's intention in this matter was not only (and perhaps not even) to save the Knights but also to use the dispute as an excuse to march troops into Bavaria and acquire part of its territory at a moment regarded as favorable in international terms. Bavaria's early surrender, as well as unmistakably threatening hints from France that it would be displeased to have the *Konservatorium* enforced too strictly, compelled the Austrians to abandon permanently this part of their plan.[8] Encouraged by Austria's frustration, Max Joseph, who had momentarily been coerced into abandoning his actions but not his intentions against the Knights, began to renege on his promises of full restitution and even compensatory damages to them, and instituted a triple policy of evasion, procrastination, and harrassment of their territories. After appealing in vain against these actions to the commission which had been established to execute and monitor the observance of the *Konservatorium,* the Knights went directly to the Aulic Council, which in March 1805 issued a special decree known as an *Exzitatorium,* commanding full observance of its original order within two months. It is sufficient commentary on who was running German affairs at this moment to note that a single letter to the commission from Napoleon's hand in July 1805 was enough to destroy the effect of the *Exzitatorium* and virtually to end the activity of the commission itself. Throughout most of 1805, therefore, several princes resumed the slow but effective process of whittling away at the independence of the Knights.

The Knights themselves, of course, were active in their own cause throughout this period not only in Vienna, Regensburg, Paris, and elsewhere, but also in the public press. Those of them who were at all politically aware—the majority, certainly—had regarded themselves for years as an endangered species, and especially so in the tense later decades of the eighteenth century, when the territorial expansion and governmental consolidation and rationalization of the great secular princes presented the growing threat of a "Sultanism," as one Knight put it, that could overwhelm the freedom of all who lacked adequate power to resist.[9] All Knights, of course, justified their continued independence by calling on the imperial constitution and the specific provisions of the Final Recess, which conferred on them rights as firmly grounded in law as were those of any Estate of the Empire. In the years after Lunéville they frequently asserted as well that they had a special significance, now that the ecclesiastical states and most of the Imperial Cities were disappearing, as the only organized group that still kept an awareness of the Emperor and indeed of the whole imperial bond alive among the princes of Germany.[10]

Two other arguments appeared with sufficient frequency to deserve mention even though they echo themes that had become familiar to the reading public during the debate over the future of the ecclesiastical states and the Imperial Cities. The first tried to make a virtue out of what was commonly regarded as the source of most of the evils of the Knights' territories. It praised the diminutive size of these "states," claiming not only that it permitted a closer contact of ruler with subjects than was true of any other territories, but also that the tiny revenues of the Knights, while admittedly making large expenditures for social welfare projects impossible, freed them from the political ambitions and the lust for conquest that were the curse of large states. The result, according to one author, was that the Knights' lands provided rest for the politically weary, refuge for free opinions, and a fertile soil for progress in all the arts and sciences except those of high politics and the military.[11] The second argument called attention to the benefits for both Germany and Europe of that sacred *Kleinstaaterei* of which the Knights' territories were by all odds the best example. "The multitude of sovereigns in the German Empire is . . . the firmest pillar of its constitution," one writer declared, and he went on to demonstrate that the freedom of all, but especially of the weak, was better protected in proportion as the number of separate states in Germany increased, resulting in more and more irritation, collisions of interest, and mutual jealousies.[12] The true cosmopolitan would also not fail to appreciate "that thoughtful spirit which . . . has created a dead mass in the middle of Europe in order to separate the great powers of the north and south, to remove the points of contact, and at least to milden the storms which otherwise . . . would ceaselessly lacerate and in the end devastate Europe." The much-mocked constitution of Germany, with its multitude of states and rulers, was in fact the protective spirit of all the European peoples: It had set up an insurmountable dam against "the swindle of revolution," and had saved them from the horrors of anarchy and "the despotism of demagogues."[13]

Such arguments were simply not taken very seriously by educated public opinion, and this was particularly true after Lunéville had virtually sealed the fate of the clerical territories and the Imperial Cities. That change, which was clearly in the direction of less rather than more political fragmentation, made the hundreds of miniscule Knights' territories into even more of an anomaly than they had been before; for many people, furthermore, the whole question of their future simply paled beside the enormity of the secularization decision.

To some, the persistent demand of the Knights that their lands be regarded and treated as states, on an equal footing with all others in Germany in spite of their size, became intolerable. Karl Ernst Adolf von Hoff, an official in the Duchy of Gotha and a well-known geographer and geologist of the time, published a refutation of some of the Knights' claims in a work tinged with genuine and unmistakable impatience. Disclaiming any dislike of small states—his own, after all, was hardly a giant—Hoff simply denied the quality of statehood to the Knights' lands. They were lordships (*Oberherrlichkeiten*), not states, Hoff insisted, and they were ruled by feudal law (*Herren Recht*), not public law (*Staats-Recht*). For that reason, and because of their size, they had none of the legal and institutional structures such as constitutions, territorial diets, Cathedral Chapters, or even bureaucratic administration, that operated as safeguards against the tyranny of a single ruler in larger states. In the Knights' territories, all government was in the hands of a single person, aided by a few officials, so that the spirit of government and the treatment of subjects could change from mild and beneficent to harsh and despotic, and back again—or vice versa—within two or three generations. It was irrelevant to argue, as many Knights did, that the number of their colleagues who governed badly was small; what was important was that their governments, by their very nature, could not provide safeguards against tyranny, so that the rights and freedoms of subjects were always precarious, depending as they did entirely on the accidents of inheritance and personality.

Having thus disposed of the argument that the small size of the Knights' lands guaranteed better rather than worse government, Hoff turned to the issue of the importance of the Knights to the constitution and the preservation of the imperial nexus. Against those who maintained that the Knights as a group now constituted virtually the pedestal on which the German constitution rested, Hoff could only laugh; entitled to membership in neither the Imperial Diet nor the Circle diets, the Knights had no voice in deliberations on imperial affairs, and also contributed nothing to the ongoing costs of imperial government. They were therefore to be regarded as appendices or outgrowths of the constitution, said Hoff, but in no way a basic buttress thereof.[14]

Hoff's recommendation to the Knights in their present situation was one shared by an increasing number of publicists, including even many who were essentially sympathetic to the Knights: That they voluntarily abandon the imperial immediacy which was the basis of their political independence, but also a costly vanity, and submit to the territorial sov-

ereignty of adjacent princes. In Hoff's scheme, they were to receive the
guarantee that their lands would remain their private property and that
they would enjoy all the rights and privileges of the territorial nobility
whose ranks they would join.[15] This solution, however, was actually one
of the less favorable to the Knights, since it would have permitted them
only the prerogatives of local nobles which, moreover, varied considerably
from one state to another.

More seductive and efficacious were plans that promised the Knights
advantages well beyond those enjoyed by the *Landadel,* of which the
proposals of an anonymous writing of 1802 were fairly typical. Its author,
believing that his plan represented the only realistic possibility for a happy
future for the Knights, recommended their subjection to territorial *Landeshoheit,* together with acceptance of a permanent but fixed tax in place
of certain feudal obligations arising from the nexus of subjection, and
continued payment of the *Charitativ-Subsidien* in time of war, but now
to the territorial ruler rather than to the Emperor. In return, the Knights
would receive not only the confirmation of most rights of jurisdiction
over their subjects which they had previously exercised, but also various
administrative preferments in their new state, freedom from tolls and customs duties on duly attested household needs, as well as from military
conscription, quartering of troops, and requisitions on them or their families. They would also not be subject to ordinary taxes on either their
persons, their movable or immovable property, or any of the lands they
possessed at the time of their subjection. As appealing as these concessions, given the intangible but powerful sense of pride of the Knights,
was the proposal that they be permitted to preserve their corporate identity through retention of the existing organization and administration of
common affairs, with a managing Directory, consultants, chancellery, and
so on. New members could be accepted into the corporation of Knights,
and the Directory would have extensive powers not only to regulate property and juridical relationships among the Knights, but also to negotiate the terms of the relationship between the Knights and their new
territorial ruler—as, for example, in the determination of the amount of
taxes to be paid by the subjects of the Knights to the Directory for transferral to the state treasury.[16]

Both the date and the probable place of publication of this work suggest that it appeared late in 1802, and may very well have been commissioned by the Bavarian government itself, which in November had
anticipated the determinations of the Final Recess by occupying not only
the ecclesiastical states Max Joseph knew would be awarded to him, but
the Knights' territories which lay within them as well. This massive and
naked aggression against the Knights, the first of any consequence since
the Prussian actions in Ansbach-Bayreuth in the 1790s, created an enor-

mous stir among the Knights, and at least a few of them—as noted earlier —made a quick decision to give up their immediacy in return for special considerations. The above plan, which in many particulars approached the conditions actually offered to submissive Knights by Max Joseph and his able official Friedrich von Thürheim from late 1802 until the following year, may thus have been designed to give publicity to the kinds of concessions the Knights might expect if they acted soon.

Since the Bavarian terms required that the Knights withdraw from the old district and cantonal arrangement and be reorganized as a new and strictly territorial corporation, however, the majority who had determined not to give in to the Bavarian pressures or to similar ones in other states denounced this offer as a scheme to break their solid front and tried to demonstrate the hidden pitfalls that lurked within the proposals. Chief among the latter was the strong possibility that promises to permit the Knights at least the same participation in territorial government and legislation as was already possessed by the territorial nobility were nothing but a verbal trick, since that participation had been steadily declining in most states for years, and might even be abolished altogether in the future, thus leaving precious little in the way of guarantees for other promises. The only answer lay in stubborn and resolute refusal to abandon imperial immediacy: "Duty to Emperor, Empire, Knighthood and family demands unremittingly of each member of the Knighthood that in the closest association with the fellowship he apply all means to the general goal of preservation, loyally fulfill all assumed obligations, and not withdraw from the society as long as he lives."[17]

As many Knights themselves had long recognized, part of their political problem lay in a weakness stemming from the extreme fragmentation of their small territories, scattered in such profusion throughout the whole of the German south and southwest, which prevented them from acting as a single group with a united will. This was a source of enfeeblement with respect not only to the pursuit of a common political purpose in the Empire, but also to the achievement of a great measure of governmental efficiency within their own little states—something that was clearly necessary if they were to reverse the reputation of their lands as absolutely the worst administered in the Empire. The Knights liked to think of themselves as a single political body, or even as "a kind of state in the Holy Roman Empire," as an article in one of their own journals put it;[18] their problem, however, like that of the Empire itself, was that they could not act like a state. There were enormous variations in the relative prosperity of Knights' territories, as well as in the conscientiousness and efficiency with which they were governed; and while it was no doubt true, as many Knights maintained, that the most careless, irresponsible, or even vicious of their number attracted the most publicity and diverted attention from the rest, it was an undeniable fact that educated public opinion regarded most aspects of administration in these lands—especially in matters of police (*Polizey*) and justice—as abominable, and impossible to justify by "modern" standards.[19]

In the last years of the Knights' existence, a number of them devoted considerable thought to the question of how to strengthen and consolidate their scattered forces in order to act with maximum efficacy on their political environment. To the extent that the weakness of the Knights' corporation was traceable to the weakness of its individual members, the problem was commonly seen in terms of the financial woes which reduced many Knights to virtual poverty and left them without the resources to govern much more than their own households. As early as 1788, a detailed and anonymously published work proposed a number of means to improve the economic fortunes of the Knights and, in doing so, offers the modern reader some fascinating and almost poignant glimpses into the big problems of the little world of the *Reichsritter*. The author, obviously a Knight himself, first suggested that the general collapse of the credit of the Knights, which forced them into borrowing money in times of need at rates of interest so high as to endanger the integrity of their estates, had to be stopped. The real problem here was the confidence of creditors, who would demand high interest as long as they were dubious about their chances of being repaid on schedule. If, however, each Knight's canton maintained a fund, raised from its membership either by borrowing or taxation, to guarantee the timely repayment of loans contracted by individual Knights, interest rates would drop. If the borrower defaulted to his creditor, the cantonal fund would pay the latter, and deal with the debtor in equitable ways which would exclude outsiders and above all prevent alienation of Knights' property to them.

Equally serious was the problem of the scattering of individual resources by the necessity of providing incomes for families that increased in size from generation to generation while the resources with which to support them did not. Here, the author recommended that Knights' sons whenever possible be preferred over outsiders for employment in the various clerical, administrative, and juridical positions at cantonal and district levels. He suggested that, ultimately, a system of strict primogeniture be introduced among the Knights, so that, as in England, only the eldest son would retain the aristocratic title, while the others would be forced to take up the trades, merchandizing, manufacturing, or one of the liberal professions: "Is it wiser," he asked, "to acquire for oneself through commerce the means for enjoyment, for the comforts and joys of life, or in the shadow of a family tree to drag out a troubled and woeful existence until the grave?" Daughters presented an even worse problem: While a growing distaste for rural life and other factors reduced the number of their suitors, and the church could absorb only a few as nuns, they were also excluded from gainful employment in society. This added up to a terrible financial burden for the Knights who had to support them, and the author proposed several means for easing the strain. Of these, two were especially significant: the encouragement of Knights' sons to marry others' daughters by requiring proof of four male *and* female knightly ancestors from any Knight who wished to enter the cantonal Directory, and the establishment by all three Knights' Districts of a common trust fund from which unmarried daughters would receive a small benefice beginning at age fifteen, and which would be increased considerably at age thirty, when they were presumed to be no longer marriageable. Finally, the disastrously crippling financial effect of fires, which could not only wipe out much of a smaller Knight's inheritance in a matter of minutes but also create a lifelong problem with his creditors, could be solved by the foundation of a fire insurance association which would be funded by annual premiums paid by all Knights.[20]

While the immediate intention of all these suggestions was that of providing assistance to the family economies of individual Knights, every one of them obviously spoke to the strengthening of the entire body of Knights through the promise of greater solvency and security for its parts. This author was also concerned to remind the Knights that their individual welfare and even survival depended on the collective strength of their corporation, and he made several suggestions designed to increase the sense of community among them. Some of these were minor—the adoption of a common Knight's uniform in all three Districts and the establishment of a special order of merit to reward outstanding achievement, for example—while others were of much greater significance. First in importance, probably, was halting the alienation of Knights' property, a process which according to the author had halved the strength and influence of the corporation over the preceding two centuries, and which could be stopped if the Knighthood as a whole would automatically buy up all properties that would otherwise be sold outside its membership, raising the funds for this purpose by a combination of taxing and borrowing from within its own ranks.

Nearly as important, however, was the consolidation of the collective government and administration of the whole Knighthood; he proposed the establishment of a new and permanent General Directory or Knights' Council (*Ritterrath*) for all three Districts, made up of three men, each elected from a different District, who would devote all their time to the affairs of the Knights. It would be advisable for as much common business as possible to be dealt with at this central level rather than in the separate Districts or cantons, the writer urged, simply in order to concentrate and unify decisions as much as possible to create a single Knights' policy in all important matters. This was especially true of all political quarrels with neighboring jurisdictions, which preferably should not be dealt with by the Districts or cantons, much less by individual Knights themselves, but by the supreme Knights' Council alone. Such a reform would, of course, presume an expansion of the number of chancellery personnel, probably at all levels; and the author not only recommended this expansion, but asked that all subordinate positions be paid well. He also suggested establishing a special professorship at an institution of higher learning in some larger princely territory whose ruler had no collision of interest with any Knights for the specific purpose of teaching the public and private law of the Knighthood. Such an innovation would help to give a better and more uniform training to the consultants and councillors who made up the administrative and juridical bureaucracies of the Knights.[21]

This author had admonished his readers at the beginning of his work that it was a time of struggle between freedom and "Sultanism," and that it was therefore high time for the Knights to reinvigorate their common constitution and revive their corporate strength. If this was true of 1788, it was doubly so of the years following the Peace of Lunéville, and the principles this author had so ardently advocated were not forgotten by his fellows a decade and a half later. In the urgent appeals for reform that emerged in this period, there was a strong emphasis on the need for improvement in virtually all matters which pertained to the Knights' role as rulers and administrators, including taxation, police, public welfare, and especially justice. This emphasis did not necessarily amount to an admission that all or even most Knights' territories were so badly run in all these respects as to be a public disgrace; it did, however, imply an awareness that the present corporate structure of the Knights did not provide sufficient guarantees that an adequate level of public administration existed in all their territories. The most commonly proposed solution to this problem was the creation of uniform standards through adoption of new codes for the entire Knighthood which would regulate almost all relationships and procedures that fell into the category of public law and administration. But since the mere establishment of new standards did not automatically ensure their execution in practice, most knightly reformers were prepared to remove a considerable amount of governmental authority from individual Knights and to confer it instead on either the District Directories or a much strengthened General Directory.[22]

The intended effect of such proposals, of course, was partly to improve the situation of individual Knights as well as the quality of the government they afforded their subjects. But laudable enough as these purposes were in themselves, they also served a politically more important and immediate goal: the reconstitution of the Knighthood as a true state. The establishment of modern government and administration would remove two of the reasons commonly advanced to justify absorption of the Knights' territories by larger states: the desire to improve the welfare of the supposedly misgoverned subjects of the Knights, and the need of surrounding princes to protect their own peoples against the inconveniences (tolls, bad roads, and bridges, and so on) or the depredations (from criminals and other social undesirables who found refuge in the Knights' lands) arising from the existence of these essentially sovereign enclaves within the borders of their own larger states.

The consolidation of political functions in the hands of a single General Directory would permit a single voice to speak loudly and clearly in defense of the interests of the entire Knighthood, replacing the cacophony of peepings and squeakings from the hundreds of voices of isolated individual Knights. One major problem remained, however: Whatever internal reorganization might occur, there was still no constitutional channel of their own through which the Knights might attempt to shore up their political position in Germany; and there were those who, like the influential Knight Karl von Gemmingen, believed that unless the Knights achieved a formal voice in the Empire's affairs, they were doomed to political nullity. This was the intention of some proposals which held out the possibility of exchanging the numerous scattered Knights' lands for an equivalent single territory of sufficient size and population as to apply for Estate status, with seat and vote in the Imperial Diet.[23] Less visionary, but still impractical in view of existing political realities, was the suggestion that the Directors of the three Knights' Districts be admitted to membership in the Diet on the basis of the Knights' acceptance of the right and duty to establish a military force in each District and to help shoulder the financial burdens of the Empire and of the Imperial Circles.[24]

None of this helped, of course. It is true that a few of the larger and better connected Knights' families applied for and were received into the ranks of the Imperial Counts, which raised their status and conferred on them the right to participate in the deliberations of the Diet through the Counts' curial votes.[25] But the Diet was virtually moribund after 1803, while the Empire itself was to be at an end in the immediate future, and was to sweep even the Counts with it into the abyss. What all the suggestions and proposals for knightly reform assumed was that by making themselves more visible and more acceptable to enlightened public opinion, the Knights would attract the appreciation of powerful protectors. A more naive piece of self-deception can hardly be imagined. Any greater visibility or evidence of cohesion among the Knights would only have made them more odious than ever to the ambitious secular princes, who after Lunéville and in spite of the assurances of the Final Recess had made their decision to absorb the Knights' territories as soon as circum-

stances permitted it. The only powerful state with an interest in protecting them was Austria; but that interest had never been a really vital one,
and could exist at all only while Vienna could still find other and stronger
allies in the Empire with which to group the Knights.

Any possibilities for that which existed after 1803—and they were
weak ones—were utterly destroyed by the Peace of Pressburg imposed on
Austria in December 1805, as the result of her unsuccessful participation
in the War of the Third Coalition against France.[26] Since Napoleon had
succeeded in bribing or browbeating Württemberg, Baden, and Bavaria
into joining the war against Austria, their rulers did not hesitate to seize
immediately the territories of the Knights whose position they had been
eroding piecemeal for some time. The well-intentioned but wholly unrealistic admonition (*Dehortatorium*) to stop this activity issued during
the short war by the ever-faithful Archchancellor Karl von Dalberg to the
Elector of Württemberg—probably because he was known as a relatively
loyal friend of the Empire—served only to fortify Dalberg's reputation
for political naivete, and earned him a nasty verbal slap from Napoleon
himself.[27] The *Dehortatorium* remained without effect, of course. The
ex post facto justification for these illegal usurpations came with the peace
treaty, which forced Austria to recognize the full and formal sovereignty
of the three states, thus effectively removing even the shadow of imperial
legal protection for the Knights of these territories.

The Knights, to be sure, made one last effort to avoid their fate. Many
of them had long since convinced themselves that Napoleon, primarily
because of his military interests and background, had a special soft spot
for the Knights, whose traditions were themselves full of martial exploits,
whether factual or legendary; indeed, some were sure that his recently
created Legion of Honor had been deliberately modeled on their own
knighthood.[28] In spite of reminders of the absurdity of such notions, which
had been contradicted by recent experience in both principle and practice,
they persisted even after the Peace of Pressburg.[29] In January 1806, a
delegation of Knights decided to call upon their supposed French admirer
while he was in Munich, and to lay their case before him. The meeting
quickly dispelled all their illusions whatsoever, and was notable chiefly
for its almost instantaneous effect on many previously stubbornly independent Knights, who now hastened to acknowledge the secular princes
as their new masters. The remainder were absorbed either as the result
of the Act of Confederation of June 1806, which established a separate
union for sixteen of Napoleon's German satellites and which specifically
asserted the sovereignty of the members over the Knights' territories that
lay within their borders, or in consequence of the abdication of Francis II
and the final dissolution of the Empire in August of the same year.[30]

A typical example of the reaction to the disappearance of the Imperial Knights as independent lords came from Johann Gottfried Pahl, writing not many months before the imperial abdication. The Peace of Pressburg, he said, had to bring with it the collapse of the Knighthood, simply because sovereignty cannot tolerate within itself a state power different from its own; but, he suggested, the Knights were no real loss, since they had never constituted a formal Estate of the Empire in any case, and therefore could be absorbed by other states without actually touching the structure of the Empire itself. It was true that another chapter of German public law had now been extinguished, he concluded, but admonished his readers not to judge Bonaparte's work before it was concluded.[31] It was probably fortunate for Pahl's state of mind at this time, and for that of others as well, that they could not know either how short a time or what directions that conclusion would take.

CHAPTER FOURTEEN

Theories vs. Realities:
Last Proposals for Reform

Iᴛ sʜᴏᴜʟᴅ ʙᴇ obvious from the arguments on both sides of the question of the preservation or extinction of the ecclesiastical states, the Imperial Cities and the Knights, that regardless of the intrinsic value these territories were or were not supposed to have for their own inhabitants, the real importance of their fate lay in the issues it raised about the future of the Empire itself. From one standpoint, indeed, the whole controversy about secularizations and absorptions can be seen as merely a part—though a very important part—of what was probably the most serious national problem that faced both statesmen and publicists in Germany in the last decade of the Empire's existence: the fundamental political organization of Germany or, in other words, the shape of the imperial constitution. With the partial exception of the two war years of 1799 and 1800—when, in a sense, everyone was holding his breath and all bets were off—every year since the call for the imperial Peace Congress at Rastatt following the Peace of Campo Formio in late 1797 witnessed the publication of numerous analyses and commentaries on the imperial constitution and proposals for its reform.[1] The vast majority of these tracts belong to the period 1801–6, after the Peace of Lunéville had established as fact (e.g., the loss of the Left Bank) or as extreme probability (e.g., the secularization of the ecclesiastical states) certain things that could only be guessed at earlier. But the political disarray and military misfortunes which had steadily mounted during almost the entire period of the Empire's war with France had made it increasingly obvious that functional and perhaps even structural changes in the Empire would be required to stop the descent into collapse that was so apparent to even the warmest friends of its traditional constitution.

242

In the period before the Final Recess of 1803, it was still possible for some stubborn souls to insist that the old constitution as it had been passed down since the Peace of Westphalia, with a territorial composition which included ecclesiastical states and Imperial Cities, could and ought to be preserved as it stood. Nearly all opponents of secularization, whether they actually said so or not, took this position, because it was the only one that fully justified the retention of the clerical territories. This did not mean that they saw the present situation of the Empire as a strong and healthy one, or that they were not ready to propose reforms for it; it does mean, however, that their ideas for reform were few and that they almost necessarily did not stray far from known ground. One author might have been speaking for all of them when he wrote in April of 1798 that while a rethinking of the constitution was clearly in order, now that the Congress of Rastatt was deliberating the terms of a future peace with France, an amelioration of the old structure was better than the uncertainties which would attend the construction of an entirely new one, and that the best plan would likely be the one that varied least from the existing constitution.

He was typical of many who took this viewpoint in that nearly all of his suggestions for changes in the constitution were designed simply to increase the defensive military capability of the Empire. He would have increased the total available resources of both money and manpower not only by requiring Austria and Prussia to constitute Venetia and Silesia, respectively, as new Circles of the Empire, and therefore subject to the same war contributions as all other Estates,[2] but also by drawing up a new *Reichsmatrikel* by whose provisions Germany would have a standing army of 200,000 in peacetime and 300,000 in wartime, together with a greatly strengthened military treasury. The nature of the army itself would be changed to overcome the multiple deficiencies resulting from its previous composition from so many separate contingents: All Estates would henceforth be classified as "military" or "nonmilitary," the latter of which—the smaller territories—would contribute no troops, but instead would pay sums of money to the central war treasury for the support of the larger "military" Estates, and would permit the latter to recruit in their lands. In this way, the author was convinced, the number of contingents could be reduced to about twenty, or less than one-tenth the present figure. The result would be a greater uniformity in equipment and training and a stronger tendency of the army as a whole to regard itself as serving the German Empire collectively rather than the separate princes individually.[3]

Almost as common as this argument, which located the only serious problem of the Empire in its inefficient military constitution, and which therefore proposed to strengthen it, was another which at first glance seems in almost perfect contradiction to the first. Far from wishing to improve the Empire's ability to wage war, one group of writers simply wanted Germany to stay out of wars altogether, thus recalling the exhortations of the elder Moser and other earlier analysts to that effect. Bemoaning the mistakes that had led the Empire into war with France in the first place, one writer whose views were representative of this group went so far as to suggest that Germany ought not to have a military constitution at all; instead, "Let us take up the policy of the Quakers," he wrote. A double reliance on righteousness and on the jealousy of foreign neighbors—that is, on the European balance of power, essentially—would produce results less damaging to the Empire than would the creation of the largest imaginable defensive army. He insisted, however, that no conclusions unfavorable to the existing constitution could be drawn from the unfortunate outcome of recent wars, which proved "only that it was impolitic to undertake what was unsuited to [the constitution]. It proves that our situation forbids us to participate in the wars of our neighbors, on pain of seeing Germany laid waste and torn apart by the armies of the struggling powers." Similarly, he asserted, the constitution itself could hardly be faulted for the failure of men to avail themselves of the means of salvation it permitted—such as, for example, the appointment of a temporary dictator to direct the resources of the whole Empire in cases of immediate and serious danger where, presumably, war was literally being forced upon it.[4]

What unites this approach with that of those who, as in the previous argument, wanted a stronger (and permanent) military force for the Empire, in spite of the quite opposite remedies they proposed, was their common assumption about the basic cause of the hapless condition in which the Empire now found itself: its involvement in foreign war. What this suggested, of course, was that the only real threat to the integrity of the Empire was an *external* one. Left to itself, Germany had no problems that were in any sense fundamental or basic ones; its constitution suited its character perfectly, and certain reforms that could be carried out entirely within the framework of that constitution could guarantee either that wiser decisions about questions of war and peace would be made in the future, or at least that the Empire would be capable of successful resistance to armed violations of its territory as it now was not.

Still, it remained for the advocates of this point of view to explain how any of the reforms they proposed were actually to be implemented. On this, they were characteristically silent, though their explanations of the recent misfortunes of the Empire yield some clues: "We are only weak because we want to be, because a mutual mistrust cripples our powers, because a misbegotten policy sustains the neighboring hatred of the Bavarian (or) of the Brandenburger against the Austrian, and widens the breach between dissenting religious parties;" or as more succinctly expressed elsewhere, "We do not see ourselves as one state—the German Empire—but as three hundred different states."[5] This, in short, repeats the already venerable refrain that the essential problem of the Empire was one of erroneous perception and inadequate will on the part of its members, resulting in a lack of "common spirit" and "patriotism"—or in other words, in a fragmentation of purpose that coincided more or less exactly with the territorial multiplicity of the Empire.

But for the very conservative defenders of the old constitution, this diagnosis, regardless of its accuracy, proved almost useless as a positive first step toward a cure. One important reason for this is illustrated in a book of 1798 which proposed several measures for heightening German national awareness, including not only making the use of the German language universal at the princely courts and within the learned and scholarly community, but also a "national education" (*Nationalerziehung*) to inculcate knowledge of the special strengths and virtues of the German nation as a whole. At the same time, however, the author of this work specifically advised the retention of the "original" and "natural" division of the German nation into many distinct peoples (*Völkerschaften*); this, he averred, would always facilitate the construction of whatever constitution the Germans might deem appropriate for themselves, and which could be used for much that was good. The alternative, he suggested—a politically united Germany—would result only in eternal bitterness, discord, and even civil war.[6]

What this author and others like him, all of whom accepted political fragmentation as a fixed and desirable datum, seemed unable or unwilling to recognize was that the numerous princes and princelings of Germany had no real reason to inaugurate a national education or any other institutions of an overarching national scope as long as a compelling political motivation was lacking, and that as long as it remained their perception that territorial independence—not the integrity of the Empire as such—was the chief object to be attained or preserved, there was little likelihood that they would show much interest in creating a German national awareness that was of no utility to them in the assertion of their autonomy and which might even compromise it. For the writers of this persuasion, who could not get beyond the often unperceived dilemma posed by the practical contradiction presented by their desire to create a saving national will while at the same time preserving the political division which worked so strongly against that possibility, there was no alternative but to lapse back into the tired and shopworn moral exhortations to imperial unity that had been the property of so many sincere but equally hapless reformers before them, or else—as this particular author did—to admit the contradiction as a serious problem, and in effect to dismiss it by simply urging others to think carefully about it.[7]

The nature of the reforms proposed in the works discussed above, together with their authors' desperate pleas to maintain the old constitution in both root and branch, provides evidence of reliance on the by now familiar theme that all the major problems of the Empire stemmed from inadequate or mistaken administration (*Verwaltung*), not from any basic errors or weaknesses in the constitution itself. Not surprisingly, perhaps, many of the advocates of secularization both before and after the Final Recess, with an obvious stake in proving that the territorial changes they proposed would not shatter the constitution, were not inclined to disagree with their foes on this question: "The constitution is excellent," as one of them put it, "but unfortunately its application is often lacking."[8] The continuation of the major elements of the old constitution, if not always expressly stated in their works, was at least assumed, and they even accepted much of the analysis of their opponents concerning the specific reasons for the misfortunes of the Empire. They claimed, however, that the policy of territorial enlargements would provide better remedies for its weakness than would theirs: The problem of the excessively variegated territorial composition of the Imperial Army, for example, would be largely corrected by the absorption of small states by larger ones, while the economic base of military strength would be improved by the great expansion of commerce produced by the abolition of the numerous tolls and other hindrances to trade which characterized the states to be eliminated.[9]

The enlargements even gave some of their defenders reason to believe that lack of a common spirit as a cause of German disunity could be overcome. Since the compensations would now provide a number of Estates with votes in the Council of Princes commensurate with the actual importance of their possessions, this argument ran, one might hope that for the first time in many years the Imperial Diet would be able to act like a true legislative assembly and to get on with the work of revising the body of imperial law to provide a stronger and more efficient government.[10] There is at least the hint in some writings, furthermore, that insofar as bad government and the numerous public ills to which it gave rise was responsible for smothering the sentiment of public spirit at its very source—that is, in the breast of the individual citizen or subject—the avowedly more efficient administration of larger states would contribute to creating the cherished *Gemeinsinn*, the common spirit, of the German patriot.[11]

In spite of hopeful predictions such as these, however, the early advocates of enlargements were in fact beginning a process of redefinition of the imperial constitution that reflected the rapidly decreasing political cohesion of the Empire. This redefinition emerges most clearly in their analysis of the problem of how Germany might be spared the scourge of war, which nearly all accepted as the main and immediate danger to the integrity of the Empire. The weight of this analysis rested upon the old distinction between those Estates of the Empire with exclusively German possessions and interests, and those which had important nonimperial or foreign interests as well. The most important of the latter was Austria. Very simply, it was asserted that as long as the German imperial crown and the Austrian hereditary crown rested on the same head, there existed the possibility that the Habsburgs would define their imperial responsibilities only in ways calculated to serve their dynastic interests. Indeed, it was said, this had happened all too frequently in the past, with the result that the Empire as a whole had been drawn into long, bloody, and expensive wars whose purposes had little or nothing to do with the welfare of Germany, but much to do with protecting or expanding the territories or other interests of the House of Austria. This was as true of the recent war with France as of many others in the past, and the losses suffered by the Empire must therefore be regarded as stemming from its inability to separate and assert its true interest from and against that of Austria.[12]

But how could the Empire be helped to make that separation and to assert it successfully? The French, the victors of the moment, had fortunately provided the answer. Not wanting the Empire to fall completely to pieces, lest it be partitioned to the advantage of their present or potential enemies, yet desirous of ending the Emperor's domination of that part of Germany—the west and southwest—whose territorial fragmentation had led to its permanent dependence on Vienna, the French had ordered the small states absorbed into larger ones. The latter would be drawn away from their Austrian ties not only by their gratitude to France but because they now possessed sufficient size and resources to stand on their own without Austrian help, as did the larger states of northern and eastern Germany (Hanover, Prussia, and Saxony, for example), which had successfully resisted being drawn into dangerous wars for some time. Clearly, as one author put it, in pursuing this policy of strengthening the German states through enlargement enough to allow them to have "a will of their own" in the future, the French were following their own self-interest; yet because it would not permit the selfish interests of Austria to drag the rest of Germany into fruitless but devastating wars, he concluded, "The interest of the French Republic is at one in this point with the wishes of the German patriot."[13]

The key phrase in the above analysis is "a will of their own," which the enlarged states of western Germany were supposed to develop as the result of the completed compensation. Apart from the fact that this au-

thor, like many others, failed to see a contradiction between the increased
dependence of these states on their French benefactor and the greater
independence they were supposed to attain by virtue of their expansion,
almost no argument was advanced to explain how the cohesion of the
German imperial body was to be enhanced or even maintained by now
conferring on several new states much the same power to flaunt the constitution that several more powerful older states had had for some time,
and which had frequently been lamented as a chief cause of the Empire's
troubles. To be sure, there was much talk about the need or desirability
of increasing cooperation between Estates by reforming the constitution
of the Imperial Circles and establishing close and ongoing correspondence
between them. But even in this no reason whatsoever was given to suppose that the enlarged states would be any more receptive to such cooperation than they had been when they were smaller, while, on the contrary,
solid historical evidence suggested that the exact opposite would more
likely be the case. In fact, much of what political cohesion the Empire as
a whole still possessed was clearly being sacrificed to the immediate necessity of peace with France, but with the further assumption that the
long-term stability of all of Germany would be assured as long as it was
not permitted to become a tool in the hands of any great power; the long-
established rules of the European balance of power, it was supposed,
would see to that.[14] While an Austrian still sat on the Emperor's throne,
however, it would be necessary to strengthen the centrifugal forces within
the Empire simply to guarantee that Vienna could no longer bind other
imperial Estates to its own adventurism and thereby keep Germany from
an unvarying pursuit of that "prudent neutrality," as one writer put it,
which was the sole means of its security.[15]

   While it may seem obvious to the historian that the advocacy of enlargement of the medium-sized states—in being at the same time an
advocacy of greater independence for their rulers—was a step toward the
dissolution of the imperial bond, it was not so obvious to most of those
who took this position. For them, the worst threat to the Empire was
war, and if war could be avoided by this means, they were prepared to
accept the consequences. But it is important to understand also that they
did not believe the consequences would necessarily mean a radical departure from past constitutional practice. Nearly all assumed the continuation
of the organs and agencies of imperial government—the Emperor, the
Diet, the supreme courts, the Circles, and so on—and interpreted the
changes embodied in the Final Recess entirely in the light of the long
historical evolution of the imperial constitution. What was important was
that the essence of the constitution remained the same. That essence was
defined by one author simply as the unification of many states under a
common supreme head, whose spirit lay in the reciprocal relations of head

and members to each other; and while he admitted that recent events had redounded to the benefit of the Estates in their struggle toward independence from the Emperor, he saw that as merely the continuation of a process long since consecrated by history and tradition to the point where the process itself—that is, the possibility for alteration in the relationship between head and members—had become virtually a part of the constitution. As long as the Estates did not attain full sovereignty and independence, therefore, the constitution continued to exist.[16]

Furthermore, unity itself did not have to fall victim to the increased independence of the Estates if the recommendations embodied in one group of constitutional proposals of the period were followed. The authors of these plans, seeking a formula that would preserve the imperial bond and permit a greater concentration of national energies while at the same time avoiding the disasters of unnecessary war, in effect suggested organizational schemes that would have separated the Empire into three distinct blocs insofar as decisions on war (or, more broadly, foreign policy in general) were concerned, while maintaining traditional imperial relationships with respect to purely domestic affairs.

Perhaps the most interesting idea was presented by Johann Gottfried Pahl as part of a widely read appeal he directed to the peace conferees at Lunéville in 1801. According to this plan, which assumed the unconditional absorption of the ecclesiastical states, Germany would consist of a total of fourteen so-called "Imperial Princes,"[17] ruling territories into which all the secular Estates of the Empire had been *conditionally* absorbed. These fourteen Princes alone would be "active citizens" of the Empire, forming its legislative body and electing its Emperor, each disposing of a number of votes to be determined by the size of his territory. The princes whose territories had been absorbed by these fourteen states, and who were now to be known as "Imperial Associates" (*Reichsgenossen*), would retain *Landeshoheit* over their lands, whose traditional constitutions would also be kept in force, though appeals against their authority could be carried to the government of the Imperial Prince into whose territory they had been absorbed. Differences between Imperial Princes, or between them and Imperial Associates, would be decided by an imperial supreme court, presumably modeled on the old Cameral Tribunal. The Associates would be required to pay a military contribution to their Princes, and during *Reichskrieg* the latter would also have the right to draw as much in the way of troops and extra money from the lands of the former as they deemed necessary. In addition to the general imperial ties that linked them, twelve of the Princes would be allied in an especially close and permanent union which neither Austria nor Prussia would be permitted to join except under extraordinary circumstances, and then only temporarily.[18]

This ingenious plan is remarkable in at least two respects. First and
most obviously, it did provide for a concentration of energies in two important imperial concerns: legislation and defense. The making of imperial laws would now be the prerogative of only fourteen Princes instead
of the hordes of Estates which had paralyzed deliberations of the old
Diet, while the imperial army would not only be funded in a simpler and
more direct way, but would approach a degree of uniformity impossible
to achieve under the old system. All of this was accomplished, furthermore, in a way calculated to create as little opposition as possible on the
part of princes or peoples by leaving most of the governmental powers
of the absorbed Imperial Associates intact and by guaranteeing their peoples against alterations of their traditional constitutions. Second, this
scheme afforded most of the Empire what amounted to a diplomatic
protection against the possibility of involvement in the great-power adventurism and wars of Prussia and Austria, but particularly of the latter.
The union of the twelve Imperial Princes, as a not inconsiderable power
in itself, would be more likely to attract protection from all the European
powers than would the disunited array of small and insignificant states
it replaced, simply because no great power would wish to see it dominated by another. Its neutrality, therefore, would probably not only be
respected but insisted upon by the rest of Europe. If necessary, however,
the union could ask for formal protection from one or more foreign powers, of which Pahl regarded Russia as the most appropriate.

A somewhat more conservative plan, but with the same basic goals
as that of Pahl, was put forward by Karl von Soden not long after the
Peace of Lunéville had been concluded. Like Pahl, Soden assumed the
secularization and absorption of the ecclesiastical states, but unlike him
he wanted to rely on a reorganization of the traditional Imperial Circles
as the basis for greater unity and strength. He would have established a
total of seven Circles—Austrian, Bavarian, Swabian, Rhenish, Westphalian, Brandenburg, and Saxon—all of which would be better consolidated
geographically than the old Circles. Where possible, a single Circle would
include the territories of but one ruling house; this meant primarily the
Austrian and Brandenburg Circles, which now, however, would be expanded to include Bohemia and Silesia, respectively, lands which lay
within the borders of the Empire but which had not previously been parts
of any Circle. Each of the other five "mixed" Circles was to maintain
a standing army of between 8,000 and 10,000 men, which could be increased by at least half under emergency conditions. No territory which
could not contribute at least one battalion of 1,000 men would participate
directly in the military establishment, but, like all others, would help
to pay for the maintenance of the army. To guarantee that the troops
were at all times battle-ready, a Circle Colonel (*Kreis-Obrist*) would be

appointed from one of the territories which did *not* contribute troops as a sort of inspector-general for all the separate contingents. Soden made it clear that these Circle troops were to be kept entirely separate from the *Haustruppen* of the individual courts, so that their allegiance would be directed toward the Circle as a whole and not just to their own territory or ruler. The Circles, in this way, would be restored to the military effectiveness they had so long lacked.

The political features of Soden's plan were the most innovative and interesting, however. First, he assumed a close alliance of the five "mixed" Circles (which, significantly, he referred to as "Germany"), the basic purpose of which was to maintain a permanent armed neutrality; foreign alliances to this end, as well as to resist aggression, were entirely appropriate, and Soden saw Switzerland as a good candidate for the honor. Second, he wanted a single German city—he suggested Erfurt—to be designated as a meeting place for the united Circles to consult on common affairs; importantly, however, he wanted plenary sessions in which all the Estates of all five Circles would be represented limited to only the most extraordinary occasions, while in all other times the power to make decisions affecting the allied Circles would be vested in the five Directors of the individual Circles. Finally, Soden specified that all the arrangements so far discussed would merely be set down within the context of the existing imperial constitution; Emperor, courts, and Diet would not only remain, but would become a stronger bond for the Empire through increased activity. How that would occur was left unanswered by the author, whose suggestions for improving the actual operations of imperial institutions reduced to the single proposal that the supreme courts not be limited, as in the past, to calling upon the Circle Directors as the executors of their judgments, but that they be empowered to ask any member of the Empire to act in this capacity, according to their own judgment.

At first glance, it would appear that Soden's plan, in preserving the full traditional "German liberty" of each and every imperial Estate within the Circles would not result in as great a consolidation of energies as would Pahl's; yet there is at least a hint of an expectation in the former that the five Circle Directors would possess powers of decision that went considerably beyond those of their earlier counterparts, thus reducing the effective centers of power in Germany to five rather than the twelve proposed by Pahl (assuming the exclusion of Prussia and Austria in both cases). What is most important in both, however, is that a very substantial concentration of political power for military purposes is provided for as the essential underpinning of the independence of the "third Germany" from Austria and Prussia in all matters of foreign policy.[19]

A final proposal, written by the Gera bookdealer Heinrich Gottlob Heinse, and published after all the territorial changes and absorptions of

1803 had been carried out, called again for a separate league of all the German states, excluding Austria and Prussia, superimposed on the old imperial structure. Typically, its only detailed recommendations for common institutions pertained to the army, which was supposed to number no less than 200,000 men even in peacetime. The various contingents would be grouped around four Electors (Bavaria, Saxony, Hanover or Hessen, Württemberg or Baden) as Supreme Commanders (*Oberbefehlshaber*), who would give leadership to a General War Council of the whole league. This Council would not only appoint a single man as the field commander of the united army, but would also provide the administrative supervision necessary to guarantee that the training discipline, pay, equipment, rules for promotion, and field exercises of the army would be absolutely uniform. None but inhabitants of the territories of the league would be allowed to serve in the army, but their terms of active service would be twelve years, followed by another six on reserve status. The author also insisted that while the various territories should retain their traditional independence, the league should conduct its diplomatic relations with other states through a single common plenipotentiary, thus emphasizing again the overriding importance assigned to maintaining a united front in foreign affairs. He had high hopes for the union he proposed, and predicted that it could not only assert its own independence successfully, but that it might even become an arbiter between France and Prussia or Austria, salvage the European balance, and perhaps regain Germany's lost provinces from France. Like Pahl and Soden before him, Heinse stated that no changes in the structure or functioning of the Empire were to be made. The imperial tie should continue to bind all states, including Austria and Prussia, to observance of the judgments of the supreme courts, and the Diet should continue its deliberations. Questions of war and peace, however, would not be debated by members of the league at Regensburg, for fear of collision with Austria and Prussia, but would be separately decided within the league itself, after which that decision would be binding on all its members.[20]

How the Emperor, supposedly retaining his lordship over the Empire, fit into this arrangement—indeed, how all the various imperial agencies were intended to continue their functions—was not explained in Heinse's proposal any better than it had been in the other two. This apparent oversight seems peculiar until one realizes what the probable intention of the authors in calling for the retention of the imperial nexus really was: to provide a continuing constitutional protection for the smaller secular princes and the remaining Imperial Cities, and especially for those smallest lords— the Imperial Counts and Knights—whose existence had become extremely precarious once serious debate about territorial absorptions and consolidation had gotten underway after Lunéville. The association or leaguing of the territories of the "third Germany" was intended to take care of the dangers of war and possible partition for that part of the Empire that was neither Austrian nor Prussian, but it would not necessarily protect smaller states of that alliance from being gobbled up by the larger princes within it, whose appetite for expansion, as was well known, had by no means been satiated even by the considerable gains of the Final Recess. The special care taken by all three authors to emphasize the continuing jurisdiction of the Imperial Cameral Tribunal and the Aulic Council—the courts before which violations of the *Landeshoheit* of one Estate by another would be brought—would seem to speak for this interpretation.

For the rest of it, there is no reason to suppose that Pahl, Soden (an Imperial Count himself), or Heinse really believed either that the whole Empire would act as more of a unit in the future than it had in the past, or that it was even necessary for it to do so, now that the security of the Germany they had most worried about—the "third Germany"—was guaranteed in their own proposals. It was therefore unimportant (and perhaps impossible as well) to talk much about the details of the Empire's operation, but it was very necessary to posit the continued existence of its constitution and its Emperor, since it was only the former which conferred legitimacy on the small territories as Estates of the Empire, and only the latter who might have both the interest and power to defend their existence if they were attacked by their larger German neighbors. Finally, as the title of Heinse's work clearly suggests, all these proposals were in one sense little more than the attempt to create a new and more powerful and united model of the old League of Princes under a very different set of circumstances. To the extent that such associations of imperial princes among themselves had a long history already, and were generally regarded as constitutionally permissible, the authors of these plans may very well have felt that their plans, precisely because they were consistent with the preservation of the existing constitution, were capable of realization, while the ones which posited the destruction of the constitution and the formal breaking of ties with Austria and Prussia were not.

Although all the constitutional proposals so far discussed left at least the shell of the Empire intact, and thus still included Austria and Prussia within it—if indeed to purposes that had little to do with real unity—there were a few publicists who actually wanted the "third Germany" to constitute an altogether separate political entity. Starting, as did the others, from the premise that the disasters which had befallen Germany both recently and in the distant past had their origin in the dual character of a number of German princes as Estates of the Empire, on the one hand, and rulers of foreign kingdoms, on the other, they proposed to reconstitute Germany in such a way as to exclude the influence of foreign interests on its political decision-making process altogether. One scheme put forth dur-

ing the Congress of Rastatt in 1798, and which called for secularizations
and absorptions that approximated to a remarkable degree the final determinations of 1803, proposed the abdication of the Emperor, the dissolution of the existing constitution, and the formation of a new league of
states (*Staatenbund*) under the name "German Empire" (*Deutsches
Reich*). Austria, Prussia, Denmark, Sweden, and Russia would lose all
territorial connection with this new Empire, while Hanover, in order to
remain a part of it, would either become a permanent secundogeniture of
the British ruling house or would pass to the rulership of the collateral
line of Braunschweig-Wolfenbüttel. The three remaining Electors (Bavaria, Hanover, and Saxony) would lay down their titles and assume those
of Grand Dukes of Bavaria, Lower Saxony, and Upper Saxony instead.
Greatly strengthened by territorial absorptions, these three Grand Dukes
would become the pillars of power in the new league: The title of Vicar
(*Verweser*) or Regent of the Empire would alternate between them, and
they would head the three new Circles into which the Empire was to be
divided, and which would embrace all the other secular states. Not surprisingly, the military aspects of this plan were worked out in some detail.
Each Grand Duke would be obliged to keep a trained army of at least
50,000 men which, together with the contributions of the other territories
in his Circle, would result in a Circle army of some 60,000 to 70,000. The
usual care was to be taken to assure military uniformity, ideally in the
whole imperial force, but at a minimum within each Circle. Army leadership, at least in wartime, was to be entrusted to a general staff named by
the three Grand Dukes together.

Very sensitive to the centrifugal forces inherent in any league of
states, this author took several steps to put mortar between the bricks of
this now altogether independent "third Germany." Thus, while the Aulic
Council would be abolished, the Imperial Cameral Tribunal would merely
be moved to Regensburg; the Imperial Diet would also continue to meet,
though voting would be changed to reflect the real power and influence
of the members. All organizational accommodations based on religious
differences would cease. The ability of individual members of the Empire
to conduct their own foreign policy would stop, and all were to be bound
absolutely to the decisions of the Empire—which meant, among other
things, that unilateral declarations of neutrality and separate peaces during a *Reichskrieg* would be forbidden. Economically, too, efforts would be
made to increase the internal cohesion of the federation by standardizing
the coinage, abolishing all tolls on river traffic, mandating the upkeep of
roads, and prohibiting the imposition of import and export restrictions
between the member states. These measures were designed, as much as
anything else, to give the new Empire a strength and self-reliance that
would obviate the necessity for guarantees from any foreign power, toward

which the author showed an almost perfect distrust. While he was ready to invite Switzerland to join the league, and was convinced that France would welcome the establishment of a *Mittelstaat* between it and the two German great powers, he rejected a security based on the protection of any foreign powers: "This would provide the opportunity [for them] to mix into domestic affairs, to create factions and to split unity and interest. Internal power, undivided interest, national spirit and mutual jealousy of the foreign powers will be the best guarantees."[21]

Not much different in basic intent was the plan of the Mainz professor Niklas Vogt who, like the previous author, wanted the influence of "the Kings of Hungary, Prussia, England, Sweden, and Denmark" removed from Germany; with fine contempt for legal forms, he was prepared to allow them to remain Estates of the Empire if they wished, but without seat or vote in the Imperial Diet. The real Germany, however, would unite into two great federations or vicariates (*Vikariate*), one of which would be presided over by the Elector of Bavaria, the other by the Elector of Saxony. As in other plans, the territorial intermixture of Austrian and Prussian lands within the area of the proposed vicariates would be eliminated by offering compensations in the east to both in return for their abdication of these lands. Each vicariate was to have an armed force of at least 100,000 men, commanded by Bavaria and Saxony, respectively. The two federations would be united not only by the retention of a single diet, but by a German or Roman kingship which would no longer be elective but would alternate automatically between the two vicariates. Vogt proposed that Switzerland and Holland be linked to his new German Empire in an alliance system that would provide a bulwark against the power of France.[22]

The visionary character of all these proposals for a "third Germany," whether conceived within the context of the existing Empire or as a political body entirely separate from Austria and Prussia, is nowhere more clearly apparent than in Vogt's absurd supposition that France would permit her two satellite republics—the Helvetian and Batavian—to ally with this truncated German Empire to form a defensive ring around herself. Indeed, while some authors busied themselves with detailed analyses of the international situation designed to prove that the interests of all the great powers could not possibly be opposed to the establishment of a reasonably strong *Mittelmacht* in Germany, neither Austria nor Prussia nor France had at this point any intention of permitting a cohesive and militarily significant state of any kind to grow up in their midst, a state which at best might be powerful enough to assert an independent foreign policy, or at worst become a satellite of one of their enemies.

Nor, for that matter, did any but the faintest sparks of interest in this sort of reorganization come from the Estates of the Empire, most of whom were too cautious and, for the moment at least, too busy figuring out the details of absorptions, border rectifications, and so on, to entertain any grandiose plans for imperial reform. This does not mean that they were not worried about the problem of their security in the power vacuum created by their relative political insignificance,[23] a problem solved at least temporarily by their collective acceptance of the Napoleonic protectorate in the form of the Confederation of the Rhine in 1806; but it does mean that they still accepted the fact of their own weakness, and were completely unwilling to entertain the notion of a self-generated collective security outside the relationship of clientage to one or another of the great powers, which they knew to be their probable fate for a long time to come.

Unrealistic though the schemes for the "third Germany" may have been as answers to a problem, the outlines of the problem itself had been perceived very accurately indeed by these authors and an increasing number of others: The Empire as a unit, as presently organized, was incapable of providing the most basic single service that citizens expect of the state, and which indeed formed the original raison d'être of the state as such— protection against external aggression. Why was this so? The simplest and most direct answer was probably given by the young Georg Wilhelm Friedrich Hegel, who in an unpublished critique of the imperial constitution written in the years 1799–1802 was already working out some of the ideas on state and power which were to help to propel him to philosophical fame in later years. "Germany," Hegel began his manuscript, "is no longer a state." A state must have state power (*Staatsmacht*), he reasoned, and Germany had shown in the recent conflicts with France that it had none. Over the centuries of the Empire's existence, this power had migrated from the center, or the whole, to the parts, and in unequal measure, as the result of that long drive for freedom which explained why the Germans as a people had never been subordinated to a common political authority as all other European peoples long since had been. At the present moment, therefore, "The German state structure (*Staatsgebäude*) is nothing other than the sum of the rights which the individual parts have removed from the whole, and this claim of justice (*Gerechtigkeit*) which carefully watches to be sure that no power remains to the state is the essence of the constitution."[24]

The problem, then, was to return to the state such power as it required to be a state, that is, by Hegel's definition of what a state was: "A group of people can . . . call itself a state if it is associated for the common defense of the totality of its property."[25] This extremely broad and unrestrictive definition of "state," by which Hegel deliberately intended to indicate that it could embrace an enormous variety of forms of government, administrative systems, differences in morals, education, language, religion, and so on, provides the key to the remarkably few and simple reforms he believed necessary to reconstitute Germany as a state.[26] What was wrong with the Empire, he wrote, was not that it lacked a single authoritative government or legislation or administration for its whole area, but that it lacked the power to execute the purpose of a state—"the common defense of the totality of its property." The actual instrument for carrying out this purpose—military force, essentially—did not have to be in existence at all times, but the means of acquiring it in sufficient quantity when needed did have to be available to the state at all times. That was what state power really meant. To realize it, Hegel recommended the consolidation of all military forces in Germany into a single army under the supreme command of the Emperor, though each larger prince might reserve some small portion of it as his own bodyguard or garrison. The funding of this army would continue to be borne by the individual states, but would not, as in the past, be channeled through the individual princes; instead, it would be voted directly to Emperor and Empire on an annual basis by the peoples of the territories through delegates elected according to population from subdivisions which were to be created within the Circles and which were to have no relationship to any existing jurisdictions of any kind. For the purpose of this voting only, these delegates were to join the Council of Cities at the Diet. Hegel further wondered if it might not be a good idea for the cantons of the Imperial Knights to send delegates into either the Council of Princes or the Council of Cities for the formal voting of their *Charitativ-Subsidien,* and for the Electors and princes to attend the Diet in person or at least to be represented by members of their own family or by their most important vassals.[27]

These few reforms, so Hegel thought, would accomplish the two things he believed essential to the existence of the Empire as a state: the organization of a state power, and the reconnection of the German people with Emperor and Empire.[28] These were indissolubly linked in Hegel's thinking, for while the former would be accomplished in the creation of a single imperial army under the sole and direct command of the Emperor, that could only happen by eliminating what was in practice the almost complete discretionary power of the individual princes in matters of military recruitment and funding as well as in the question of whether and how long they would participate in a legally declared *Reichskrieg.* That would be done either by forcing the princes to share decision-making authority on the imperial military budget with the representatives of the German people, or by bypassing them altogether (Hegel is not clear on whether the elected representatives and the Council of Cities which they joined would have complete control of military funding or whether they would share this control with the other two Councils of the Diet). Proposing that the Imperial Knights as well as these representatives of the people have some participation in the Diet, and asking that princes and Electors either attend its meetings in person or send truly illustrious personages to represent them were measures designed not only to enhance the solemnity of the meetings of the Diet and to educate the princes and the people about their obligations to the whole of which they were parts, but also to create a more broadly based and in some sense truly national legislative body in place of the forum for mutual aristocratic recrimination which the old Diet had far too often resembled. Still, it was the immediate result that most interested the practical young Hegel. The whole change, he said, would simply be that the territories would now give directly to Emperor and Empire the money they had previously granted directly to the princes and only indirectly to the former. With this change, "The Emperor would once again be placed at the head of the German Empire."[29]

The reforms Hegel preached, then, were designed to place a real and effective power of state in the hands of the Emperor. Insofar as many other publicists who had concentrated their attention on the military crisis had called for much the same thing, that is, a temporary imperial dictatorship, there was nothing startlingly novel about Hegel's idea—until one reads the remarkable final paragraphs of this critique, which represent about as bitter and powerful an assault on German particularism as will be found in the contemporary literature, and which may provide a further insight into his ultimate purpose. Here is Hegel on "German liberty": "When the gregarious nature of man has once been disordered and forced to throw itself into peculiarities, there arises in it a perversity so profound that it now applies its power to this separation from others and goes on in the assertion of its isolation to the point of insanity; for insanity is nothing other than the perfected isolation of the individual from his kind, and even if the German nation is not capable of raising its stubborn attachment to the particular to [the level of] the insanity of the Jewish nation, . . . even if it cannot arrive at [the] madness of isolation, to murder and be murdered until the state is demolished, the particular and privilege and preferment is nevertheless something so deeply personal that the concept and insight of necessity is far too weak to affect action itself; the concept and the insight brings with it something so mistrustful of itself that it must be justified by force, [and] then man will subject himself to it." For Hegel, the necessity of German unity was obvious; but even the unequivocal recognition of necessity in places where the habit of political unsociability was as deeply ingrained as it was in the German territories carried with it no force adequate to effect changes in policy. Even if all parties clearly stood to gain through making Germany a state, such an occurrence could never be brought about by deliberation, but only by an act of force, said Hegel: "The common multitude of the German people, together with their territorial estates, who know of absolutely nothing but the separation of the German peoples, and to whom their unification is something utterly strange, would have to be gathered into one mass by the power of a conqueror; they would have to be forced to regard themselves as belonging to Germany."[30]

Coming as they did at the very end of his manuscript, and just after the reform proposals had been laid out, these comments seem to hint that the Emperor ought to employ the state power that would be conferred upon him by those proposals to consolidate and unify all of Germany, by armed force if necessary, to create the permanent foundation for a modern state—a *Machtstaat*—by eliminating once and for all that distorted version of freedom that went by the name of *Deutsche Libertät,* which, in denying the state access to power—the means necessary to guarantee the security of the whole—profoundly endangered the real liberties of all.[31] Yet while the ultimate implications of his reform suggestions may thus have been tantamount to an imperial coup d'état—an idea that was almost unique in the political publicists of the time—Hegel was by no means original in his characterization of Germany as a political body that had ceased to be a state. Even those who in some confusion persisted in calling it a state, but then criticized it for not acting like one,[32] were saying something not much different from what he was, and Hegel himself explained the confusion. The riddle of how it was possible for Germany to be a state and yet not to be a state, he wrote, was easily solved by the explanation "That it is a state in thought and not a state in reality, that formality and reality part company, [that] the empty formality appertains to the state, but the reality to the nonexistence of the state."[33]

While Hegel and others were concentrating their attention on what the Empire was not, or on what it should be, or both, the execution of the vast changes contained in the Final Recess of 1803 created for some scholars and writers a need to reexamine thes basic nature of the imperial structure and constitution and, as so often in the past, to attempt to classify them according to known categories. For some, this attempt eventuated in the reassuring conclusion that the Final Recess had brought no basic change to the form of the Empire's government. The Oldenburg professor Adam Christian Gaspari, for example, who composed one of the better-known explanations and analyses of the Final Recess, appears to have been worried about growing speculation that the recent territorial changes had altered the constitution in the direction of a confederate union. Specifically denying that the Empire was a states-system, a federal state made up of individual states leagued together merely for purposes of common defense, Gaspari insisted that it was a single state, a monarchy restricted by the participation of the Estates. The latter had no right of corulership, but only of advice and judgment. The highest authority lay in the totality of the Empire and in the monarch—in *Kaiser und Reich*—from which every other authority originally derived. The territorial lords (*Landesherren*) were *not* lords of the territories (*Herren des Landes*) Gaspari emphasized, but "deputies and representatives of the monarch, as it were," who in that capacity were not sovereigns; nor were their territories states in the strict sense, because they possessed neither unlimited right of armament (*Waffenrecht*) nor of legislation, and were entitled to such armament as they had only in the name and for the protection of the Empire.[34]

A somewhat similar formulation of the subordinate relationship of the territories to *Kaiser und Reich* appeared in the works of Nikolaus Thaddäus Gönner, a professor of law at the Bavarian University of Landshut. In his view, Germany was indeed a state, a limited elective monarchy, but one that was divided into a number of particular states for purposes of administrative convenience. The Empire had chosen by its fundamental laws to rule itself by means of the transferral of governmental authority to the territories; and while this authority was permanently attached to the territories, and could not be recalled, both its origin and its continuing legal efficacy were rooted in the sovereignty of the Empire. Like Gaspari, Gönner was therefore able to deny that the Empire was but a confederation of otherwise altogether independent states.[35]

These interpretations, which flatly refused to recognize that the disappearance of some territories and the expansion of others altered the character of the Empire as the single state it had always been, were essential to those who still clung to the idea that only the superior sovereignty of Emperor and Empire guaranteed the various German peoples against possible violation of their freedoms by despotically inclined territorial authorities. Gaspari, much more the polemicist than was Gönner, argued in this sense that the power of the Emperor to veto proposed imperial laws operated to prevent the princes from doing collectively what all could freely do individually if a confederate definition of the Empire, implying full internal sovereignty for the princes, were to assert itself successfully: "Only through the Emperor are we free; without him we are Germans no more, except perhaps in the sense in which South Prussians or Galicians are still Poles. Because who is German liberty for? For the twenty million Germans living in Germany, or for the seventy to eighty ruling families in Germany? . . . Take the veto away from the Emperor, and Germany ceases to be an Empire, and we are slaves."[36] Yet while Gaspari strongly believed that the *reputation* of the Emperor (as well as of the imperial courts) ought to be strengthened, he did not believe that his *power* should be increased, and went on to praise the various components of the German balance of power, including the Austro-Prussian dualism, that gave the constitution its unique and admirable form.[37]

   In spite of the almost desperate attempts of scholars like Gaspari and
Gönner to rescue the character of the Empire as a true, if unusual, state
by emphasizing the unitary features of its constitution and by the denial
of absolute sovereignty to its territories, an increasing number of political
commentators even before 1803 had begun to shift their focus away from
the old laws and traditions upon which so many attempts at classifying
the constitutional type of the Empire had been based, and to turn instead
to the functional political relationships of the German states with each
other as the key to the character of the imperial association. For one group
of such writers, of whom the brilliant and perceptive Wittenberg law professor Karl S. Zachariae may serve as a good example, the Final Recess
merely made clear through its purification of the political map of Germany a fact that had previously been somewhat obscured by the multiplicity and vast inequality of its states: that Germany now was, and for
some time had been in all but name, a league of independent states
(*Völker-* or *Staatenbund*) rather than a single federated state (*Völker-* or
Bundesstaat). For Zachariae, the disappearance of the ecclesiastical states
and virtually all the Imperial Cities did not cause the transformation from
state to league, but was a result of it. The nature of a league, he said, demands that each of its members have the means to be truly independent;
lacking these, they are in no position to contribute what is required of all
to achieve the basic purposes of the league. The clerical states and the
cities had in fact lacked such means for a long time, but their special relationship with the Emperor had hidden this from view until external
pressure from the French forced the Germans to do some serious thinking
about their political association. At that point, their relative uselessness as
members of a league became obvious, and all were abolished and absorbed
by other states except, essentially, for those six Imperial Cities whose
successful "finance system" conferred upon them an independence the
others lacked, and which therefore saved them from the others' fate. At
the same time, Zachariae maintained, it was recognized as desirable to
give a greater inner consistency to the German *Staatenbund* than it had
previously possessed; politically, this meant putting the more powerful
German princes into a closer association with each other and giving them
a more decisive influence on the conduct of public affairs, and the constitutional means chosen to do this was by the elevation of all the mightier
princes to the College of Electors, whereby claims of actual political power
were transformed into legal ones as well. The changes wrought by the
Final Recess, therefore, while not creating anything radically new in terms
of the real character of the German union, had helped both to destroy the
myth of the Empire as a single state and to enhance the efficiency of its
operation as a league.[38]

Zachariae faced head-on the constitutional arguments of the traditionalists on the supposed overlordship of Emperor and Empire by simply
asserting that the member states were outfitted with all the characteristics
of sovereignty, thus implying that the theory of imperial sovereignty was
of no importance against the reality of full territorial independence. The
fact that the member states did not exercise certain rights which the Emperor did, furthermore, did not prove that they were not legally permitted
to do so, but only that they did not choose to do so for any of several reasons, including the entirely practical one of conferring certain rights on
the head of the league for administrative convenience. What about the
supraterritorial institutions of the Empire, as well as its laws? None of
these was incommensurate with the nature of a league of independent
states, wrote Zachariae. The first and political purpose of this league is the
external and internal security of the German states, for which certain
military and judicial organs, respectively, had been established; and the
second and cosmopolitan purpose, to facilitate the intercourse of Germans
among themselves and with foreign nations, accounted for the legislative
enactments pertaining to postal affairs, coinage, tolls, and so on. The
various smaller unions of states inside the Empire, including even the Imperial Circles, that had been a regular feature of its history, carried within
themselves no principle inimical to the idea of a league, and were in fact
as much as anything else evidences of the evolution of Germany toward
a *Staatenbund* since the time of the Reformation.[39]

Zachariae's analysis is important because it broke rather sharply with
the tendency of most legal scholars of his day to attempt to force the events
of recent years, including the determinations of the Final Recess, into a
preconceived constitutional mold. Gaspari and Gönner, for example, starting from the absolute principle that sovereignty resided in *Kaiser und
Reich,* were forced to interpret the ongoing changes in the relationship of
the territories to the Empire in terms of mere quantitative shifts in the
political balance between the Emperor and the princes—a process with a
long history already—rather than in terms of basic constitutional change.

Zachariae, on the other hand, starting from the facts of the existing
relationship of territories to the whole of which they were indeed in some
sense parts, found that this relationship was the result of a long evolutionary process whose steadily mounting quantitative political effects had finally brought about a qualitative constitutional change through the migration of the reality of sovereignty to the territories. He would certainly have
agreed with Hegel's assertion that Germany was a single state in thought
but not in reality, and he would have explained the disjunction between
the two in the works of traditionalists as an understandable result of the
"uncertainty and reaction" that attended the transition from a *Staatsver-*

fassung to a *Bundesverfassung*.[40] Unlike Hegel, however, whose analysis was intended to make a state out of an essentially formless political mass, Zachariae asserted that the Empire had a form—that of a league—but he was not very sure of the implications of this conclusion for the future. On the one hand, he seems to have believed that if the Empire were everywhere consciously accepted for what it had in fact become, it would then be possible to proceed with an imperial reform appropriate to a league of independent states, and which could result in an effective constitution for that form of association. On the other hand, however, he saw in recent events—the establishment of the Prussian zone of neutrality and the strengthening of a number of territorial princes in the south and southwest in particular—some reason to fear that the single league into which he had redefined the Empire might sooner or later dissolve into several.[41]

Here, of course, was the ominous reality that underlay Zachariae's analysis. A true imperial state (*Reichsstaat*) such as the Empire was held to be by traditional constitutional lawyers might hope to keep its unity, however precariously, as long as its members acknowledged that they were to at least some extent legally bound to the whole by a superior or sovereign authority. A true league, on the other hand, was by definition composed of wholly sovereign and independent states to which the right of association or dissociation was at all times reserved. As one author described it, with the understanding of his time, this kind of union had nothing to do with internal affairs, and its common decisions, which were only advisory opinions, not laws, bound its members only if they chose individually to be bound by them, exclusion from the league being the only penalty for noncompliance.[42] To call the Empire simply a league of states, therefore, was not only to abandon the idea of superior sovereignty of Emperor and Empire, but also to concede that the existence of any union of the German states at all was really dependent on the whim of individual rulers. No one could maintain, of course, that the increasing currency of this interpretation of the character of the imperial association was more than a reflection of the growing independence of the larger territories and of the actual political disarray of the Empire whenever, as in war and diplomacy, it had to try to show a unified face to the world. But in the years from 1803 to 1806, when the politically influential classes of the middle-sized states of Germany, in particular, were groping for formulas that would rescue their territories from the perils associated with imperial sovereignty, but at the same time safeguard their continued existence as states, this interpretation had much to recommend it as a rationale for declaring independence of those with whom they wanted no ties, while continuing an association with others that was their only protection in the no-man's-land between the great powers. Thus, while a Zachariae may have seen his *Staatenbund* as a means of salvaging the unity of the old Empire by putting it on a new conceptual footing, the world into which he helped to introduce it had lost its ability to employ it for that purpose. When the full-fledged league finally did appear, in August of 1806, it bore not the stamp of German construction, but of French.

CHAPTER FIFTEEN

The Final Years

IN SPITE OF THE optimistic tone of at least some of the proposals for constitutional reorganization, and especially of those which regarded
the Final Recess as creating the conditions for a reinvigorated imperial
structure, virtually not a single event after the formal ratification of the
territorial and other changes of 1803 gave even the most ardent imperial patriots anything to be sanguine about. In the first place, the enlarged
middle-sized states whose ambitions had temporarily been satisfied showed
no interest in sitting down to plan out a new basis for imperial cooperation, though many of the publicists who had approved their enlargement had certainly counted on this. In particular, all the reforms associated with a restructuring of the Imperial Circles, which had been seen
as urgently necessary if the Empire's defenses were to be strengthened,
evaporated in the atmosphere of political self-interest and internal consolidation of the months and years following the Final Recess; indeed,
only the Swabian Circle held a diet at all after 1803, and any promise it
may have had was dissipated in the quarreling between Austria, Württemberg, and Baden, whose differences had become too great for any kind of
real programmatic cooperation.[1] The Imperial Diet, from which it would
have been visionary to expect much in the way of truly helpful initiatives
in any case, was for a considerable time almost paralyzed by Austria's
tortuous attempts to equalize the number of Protestant and Catholic votes
in the Council of Electors, the Council of Princes, or both. Even the imperial court at Vienna, the only other possible source of reform, was in almost full retreat from what was left of its belief that it was either useful
or possible, under present circumstances, to keep up more than the mere
appearance of an imperial headship, and instead began to busy itself in

the pursuit of policies of dynastic self-interest which looked ahead to the day when another and perhaps final territorial reorganization of Germany would occur.[2]

The increasingly heavy and more intrusive hand of Bonaparte was another factor which certainly could give little comfort to the German patriot. The occupation of Hanover by French troops in July 1803, after the resumption of war between France and England only two months before, could perhaps be justified or explained away on the grounds of the accursed connection of some German states with foreign princes—George III of England, in this case—but it was still a violation of the integrity of the Empire, and one that was hardly challenged even in word. Less important in practical terms, but also greatly less justifiable, and therefore unmistakably indicative of the contempt Bonaparte felt for the Empire as well as of his sentiments about its reconstruction, was the affair of the Duke d'Enghien in March 1804. This young French nobleman, living at the time in Baden, was incorrectly implicated by Bonaparte's secret police in a partly manufactured royalist plot against the First Consul. Bonaparte, determined to make an example of d'Enghien as a warning to all his domestic political enemies, including unrepentant republicans, ordered troops to invade Baden and to seize the Bourbon prince, who was hastened to the castle of Vincennes. On March 20, the day of his arrival, he was subjected to a hasty military trial, condemned, and shot the same night. This brutal and summary act created a great stir all over Europe, but again was met mostly with public silence in Germany, and especially in the southwest, where the rulers of Baden and Württemberg had earlier imposed a press censorship against the publication of any opinions which might cause offense to be taken by a foreign power.[3]

In France, however, Bonaparte cleverly utilized the wave of public sympathy that had grown up after the revelation of the royalist conspiracy against him to persuade an entirely compliant Senate that the only way for the French people to be assured of the uninterrupted benefits of his regime was to guarantee the hereditary succession of the Bonapartist line. Bonaparte himself directed the drafting of a new constitution, known as the Constitution of the Year XII, which declared him "Emperor of the French" and provided for the hereditary succession to this title of his direct or adoptive heirs. Accepted by the Senate in May, this new arrangement was subsequently ratified by popular plebiscite, and Bonaparte crowned himself as Napoleon I in a famous ceremony in the cathedral of Nôtre Dame on December 2, 1804.

The adoption of an imperial constitution in France came as unpleasant news to an Austrian court which for some time had been contemplating the dubious future of the German imperial crown with unrelieved gloom. Since 1648, the real importance even of the Emperor's formal constitutional prerogatives had shrunk to a mere shadow of what they had once been, of course, but quite recent events had also dealt a new and shattering blow to the informal but significant political influence the Emperor could exercise throughout Germany. Much of the north was virtually closed to Austrian authority through its domination by Prussia since 1795, while the Final Recess had both eliminated those very territories where support for the Emperor had been most consistent, and at the same time had strengthened the ability of the remainder to resist pressure from Vienna. Finally, Napoleon's diplomatic representatives were more active, numerous, and successful in the courts of the "third Germany" than were those of Francis II, and the reorientation of those states toward Paris as a source of protection and further benefit was unmistakable. In the face of these depressing realities, there was a real question of whether the elective German imperial title could keep an even approximate parity with the hereditary one that Bonaparte was about to assume, especially since almost no one any longer supposed that the territorial and political conditions of 1803 were fixed for all time; they could easily undergo another transformation to the further disadvantage of the imperial reputation. It was this, even more than the severe constitutional problems involved, that led Vienna to reject the idea proposed in some quarters of making the German imperial crown hereditary in the House of Habsburg.[4]

There was another possibility, however: the assumption of a second and hereditary imperial title for all the dynastic lands presently ruled by the Habsburg family. This had the double advantage of creating a title which was at once the equal of Bonaparte's but also separable from whatever fate might await the German Empire and its crown, and of providing another element of institutional and psychological unity within the diverse and sprawling territories of the Habsburg dynastic inheritance. The fact that such an action would also constitute a violation of the German imperial constitution, whose traditions called for only one emperor within its boundaries, was regarded as manageable, especially if Bonaparte's prior consent could be obtained. This was procured as part of a bargain of reciprocal recognition of the two new imperial dignities, and the proclamation that Francis II, German Emperor, was now also Francis I, Emperor of Austria, was made on August 10, 1804. In spite of opposition in some quarters, delays on the part of some states, and a certain amount of grumbling in the Imperial Diet, Francis was able to secure general recognition for his new title without much difficulty.[5] And while this act appears to have created little visible excitement in the censored German press, it must surely have been received and understood very largely for what it was: the most significant formal evidence yet of Austria's forced retreat from the burdens and dangers of her German imperial responsibilities.

Pessimistic Germans who looked at all these events as ominous portents of evils yet to come did not have long to wait for the realization of their fears. Bonaparte's actions in many parts of Europe following the resumption of war between France and England in 1803, including his occupation of Hanover and his illegal seizure of the Duke d'Enghien, had chilled relations between him and the Russian Czar, Alexander I, who after all was a guarantor of the imperial constitution and a coauthor of the plan which had eventuated in the Final Recess. As early as November 1804, Alexander had persuaded a hesitant Francis II to conclude a defensive alliance which bound the two countries to resist further French aggression in Italy or Germany. As Alexander's suspicions of French intentions mounted, furthermore, he had drawn closer to England, and in April of 1805, England and Russia concluded an alliance (ratified in July) dedicated essentially to forcing French evacuation of the Batavian and Helvetian Republics, as well as of Hanover, and to the eventual restructuring of Europe in ways designed to guarantee the security of its various states and peoples. This agreement, which went well beyond what the uncertain Austrians would have been willing to join when it was first concluded, suddenly became more appealing to Vienna after May 1805, in consequence of Napoleon's assumption of the title of King of Italy and his annexation of Parma, Piacenza, and the Ligurian Republic to the French Empire. While continuing negotiations with France, Austria speeded up her military preparations, worked out a plan for collaboration with Russia, and, in August, finally joined the Anglo-Russian pact.

Less than a full month later, on September 3, Francis formally declared war on Napoleon. The latter, who had already given orders for troops from northern France and Belgium to mass along the Rhine frontier, and had concluded offensive and defensive alliances with Baden, Württemberg, and Bavaria, struck into southwestern Germany with lightning speed, attacking the Austrians (who had expected the main assault to come in northern Italy) at a weak point. One Austrian army was surrounded and forced to capitulate at Ulm on October 17, and in spite of the arrival of Russian auxiliaries, Napoleon was able to reach and occupy Vienna in mid-November. The combined Austro-Russian forces under General Kutuzov fell back to the northern bank of the Danube; had they waited there for Austrian reinforcements from Italy and the possible intervention of Prussia, they might well have overwhelmed Napoleon's army, whose long supply lines and depletion in numbers from occupation duty rendered it vulnerable. Unfortunately, the young and overanxious Alexander I decided to join combat with the French Emperor immediately, enabling the latter to inflict a devastating defeat on the allied army at Austerlitz on December 2.

In a meeting with Francis II on December 4, Napoleon gave assurances that if Czar Alexander were prepared to make peace with France and to close Russia to English commerce, Austria might escape her recent defeat with no territorial losses. Alexander refused these terms, however, as he also did an Austrian proposal to continue the war in spite of the disaster of Austerlitz, and withdrew his troops to Russia. Napoleon, rejecting a plan suggested by his Foreign Minister Talleyrand that would have pushed Austria out of southern Germany and Italy, but would also have compensated her with Balkan lands in such a way as to create friction between her and Russia, decided on harsher terms designed both to isolate and to weaken the Habsburg monarchy. In the final Peace of Pressburg of December 26, 1805, Austria was forced to agree not only to pay a war indemnity to Napoleon, but to abdicate territories amounting to some 5,000 square miles, with 2,500,000 inhabitants. These included Venetia, Istria, and Dalmatia which went to France; the Vorarlberg, the Tyrol (including Trent and Brixen), and the Burgau to Bavaria; and the remainder of the Swabian possessions, including the Breisgau, to Baden and Württemberg. While Austria was permitted to annex Salzburg and Berchtesgaden, Bavaria was awarded the principalities of Passau and Eichstätt in return for giving up Würzburg to the former ruler of all these territories, the Habsburg Ferdinand of Tuscany, and, finally, was allowed to absorb the Imperial City of Augsburg. France's policy of building up the southern German states as allies and satellites was thus continued in the Peace of Pressburg, and was indeed intensified by the grant of full sovereignty to the rulers of Bavaria, Württemberg, and Baden, and by the corresponding elevation of all to new titles—the first two as kings, the last as grand duke.

Prussia's policy during this period, meanwhile, provides an instructive commentary on the problems of attempting to profit by friendship with a great power without becoming exposed to any of the risks of such a friendship. Settled into a comfortably peaceful position since 1795 as a political and territorial beneficiary of France's consistently pursued policy of keeping a friendly northern Germany as a counterweight against Austria, the Prussians wanted no involvement in war to complicate their quiet enjoyment of gains achieved at almost no cost to themselves. While Frederick William III resisted all early attempts to drag him into war with Napoleon, he also refused Napoleon's offer of Hanover as the price for joining him. Only when French troops in October were marched through Ansbach without his permission did Frederick William rouse himself to respond to this insult by concluding an alliance with Austria and Russia in early November, in which he promised to join the war against France on December 15, 1805, if by that date Napoleon had not accepted a Prussian ultimatum for a peace on the basis of Lunéville.

The Prussian envoy, Count Haugwitz, arrived at French headquarters not long before the battle of Austerlitz, and proved sufficiently susceptible to Napoleon's evasions as to be put off until after the Austro-Russian alliance had been shattered on the battlefield. Under these circumstances,

Haugwitz chose not only to ignore the now worthless and indeed down-right dangerous ultimatum he had brought, but in a remarkable and sub-sequently much condemned about-face also entered into negotiations with the French Emperor that eventuated in a defensive and offensive Franco-Prussian alliance signed at Schönbrunn on December 15—the very date set by the ultimatum for Prussia's entry into the war against France. By the terms of this treaty, Prussia recognized all French conquests, agreed to the elevation of Bavaria to a kingdom and to its enlargement at Aus-trian expense, and abdicated several territories: Ansbach to Bavaria, the principality of Neuchâtel to France, and the Duchy of Cleves to a Ger-man prince yet to be named by Napoleon. In return, Prussia was to re-ceive Hanover.

Frederick William III, who was desperately hoping to avoid war with anyone, and who realized that the assumption of sovereignty over Han-over as a gift of France would result in war with England, tried to avoid this trap by refusing to ratify the treaty.[6] Instead, he sent Haugwitz to Paris to renegotiate its terms, hoping to get Napoleon to settle for im-mediate Prussian occupation but not incorporation of Hanover, reserving the latter action until conclusion of an Anglo-French peace. Napoleon, however, whose precise intention was to create as much trouble as possible between Prussia and England and Russia, and to force the latter two to the peace table, refused to accept the Prussian initiative, and instead bullied Berlin not only into assuming immediate sovereignty over Hanover, but into closing Prussia's North Sea ports to England and guaranteeing the territorial integrity of the Turkish Empire as well—a step certain to pro-duce a hostile reaction in Russia. The almost reluctant Prussian annexa-tion of Hanover which followed a few months after this Treaty of Paris of February 15, 1806, produced the expected result in the form of an im-mediate English declaration of war on Prussia.

The seizure of Hanover put another nail in the coffin of the Empire, not only because it was in itself an altogether unconstitutional act, but also because no German state of comparable size and dignity—it was, after all, an Electorate—had been abolished so brusquely and with so little concern for even the appearance of legality. Still, by the time this occurred, in mid-1806, so many other almost equally distressing events had transpired that it created little sensation anywhere. Many of those events were di-rectly or indirectly traceable to the Peace of Pressburg, and especially to the sovereignty its Article XIV had granted to the rulers of Bavaria, Württemberg, and Baden. There was some dispute about just what this new sovereignty meant in terms of the relationship of these states to the Empire as a whole. Interestingly enough, while almost everyone agreed that it had to mean full independence and freedom of action with respect to internal affairs, almost no one came forward to assert that it meant absolute independence in external affairs.[7] Thus, several commentators took pains to point out that the relationship of these rulers to Emperor and Empire had not changed with their new titles; referring to Article VII of the Peace of Pressburg, which had specifically recognized the new kingdoms as belonging to the *Confédération Germanique*—that is, to a single body—such authors concluded that all remained subject to imperial law as well as to the jurisdiction of the Imperial Cameral Tribunal at least in its capacity as judge in quarrels between the various Estates of the Empire.[8]

Here and there, one could even find patriotic diehards who believed it still possible to reform and strengthen the Empire through timely changes. One enthusiastic soul, obviously representing the point of view of the smaller Estates which justifiably feared absorption by the new sovereigns of southern Germany, proposed territorial exchanges which would set the smaller princes away from the neighborhood of the larger and lump them together, after which they could form a new league among themselves. This author believed that the Elector and Archchancellor Dalberg would make an ideal director for this league, whose security would be guaranteed not only by a common, unified military force, but also by a protectorship to be exercised by one of the more powerful (and sympathetic) German princes. An Emperor for all of Germany would continue to exist, but both his power to execute legal judgments and his financial resources would be increased; that, in turn, would enable a prince from a lesser ruling house to be elected Emperor, and would make possible the beneficial stipulation that no two successive Emperors from the same house could be elected. The supreme courts were to remain essentially the same in this plan, except that their jurisdiction would be expanded by a limitation or abolition of the *privilegium de non appellando,* and their impartiality better guaranteed through fixed and adequate funding and through regular visitations by the Archchancellor. The financing of this imperial renovation was partly predicated on the conviction that England would eventually choose to give up Hanover, which could then be partitioned in such a way that a goodly part of it would be reserved to produce income for imperial purposes exclusively. In addition, every imperial Estate would grant 3 percent of its yearly income to the Empire.[9]

The author of this plan did not possess even the voice of the present, much less that of the future; his apparent belief that the forces of unity had sufficient strength, even after Pressburg, not only to recreate the Empire of yesteryear, but even to make it stronger than it had been before, was nothing short of utopian. By this time, such exhortations to imperial unity were truly cries in the wilderness, and the initiative for new proposals had passed almost completely into the hands of individuals prepared to accept as fact the dissolution of the Empire in its old form. One such individual was a certain Georg Heinrich Kayser, to whom authorship of one of the last controversial public proposals for the political reordering of Germany before the demise of the Empire has been ascribed. Published as articles in Häberlin's *Staats-Archiv* as well as in book form, Kayser's work was composed after the Peace of Pressburg as an unabashedly pro-Bavarian polemic which sought to bring southern Germany under much the same kind of directorship by Munich that Prussia then exercised in the north. Starting from the principle that the imperial nexus had dissolved itself de facto if not de jure, and that any attempt to reestablish it would be vain, Kayser advocated the mediatization of all the German territories, except the three cities of Hamburg, Bremen, and Lübeck, into seven relatively large states: Austria, Bavaria, Württemberg, Baden, Hessen-Kassel, Brandenburg (Prussia), and Saxony. Full incorporation of the territories to be absorbed would be delayed until the deaths of their presently ruling princes in order to reduce the shock of change, though control of military establishments and foreign policy, as well as supervision of fiscal affairs, would pass to the incorporating states immediately. Kayser found it appropriate for two centers of "political energy" to be established, one in northern and one in southern Germany; the former would be Berlin, the latter Munich, and each would exercise the functions of a "central cabinet" in military and foreign policy matters for itself and two other states to be assigned to it—Hessen-Kassel and Saxony in the case of Berlin, Baden and Württemberg in that of Munich.[10]

These proposals, aimed though they were at excluding Austrian influence from southern Germany and transferring it to Bavaria instead, did not preclude the continued existence of either an Empire or an Emperor. But that Empire would now have to be a confederative one based on treaties between the members rather than a unitary one based on a constitution, and the Emperor would be but a representative of the members of the confederation, exercising only such powers as were explicitly assigned to him. With no reserved or prerogative rights, he would be only "first among equals," and his Electoral Capitulation would be valid only for his own reign, while a new one would be drawn up for each successor. Kayser also believed it a good idea for the imperial dignity to rotate among all members of the confederation in order to preclude its employment as a means of strengthening any single ruling house. The old Imperial Diet would be converted into a permanent congress of diplomats, who would negotiate with each other as envoys of sovereign states. In addition to the seven previously mentioned states, Holstein and the three Hanseatic cities would be permitted to send delegates. Since all these states were indeed sovereign, no provision was to be made for common institutions in military or juridical matters: The previous supreme courts and the Circles were therefore to be abolished. But the full meaning of the sovereignty Kayser wished to ascribe to the rulers of the handful of states of which Germany was now to be composed is best illustrated by his recommendation that all representative institutions of whatsoever kind within these states be eliminated, on the grounds of the greater efficiency of unlimited monarchical government and the failure of previous representative systems to give any voice to middle- and lower-class interests in any case. Freedom of thought, protected by the abolition of all press censorship, would in his opinion operate as a sufficient guarantee for the liberty and welfare of subjects.[11]

Kayser's work produced a minor flurry of responses, which attest to the interest it aroused. One powerful reason for that interest was that Kayser had given voice in a clear and unequivocal fashion to ideas about the future of Germany that had existed as silent fears in the minds of many Germans since the Peace of Pressburg. One commentary on the first section of his work remarked that it seemed more an official writing (*Staatsschrift*) than a private one, since it so well summarized the principles and attitudes of Napoleon and must also have been composed with the prior knowledge of some of the most powerful princes of Germany. Speculating that the author had probably written on commission, this reviewer noted that it had long since become standard practice for pamphlets to appear just before some great political action was to take place, in order to prepare public opinion for it, and he supposed it not improbable that the basic proposals it contained would in fact be implemented before long.[12]

In the criticisms of Kayser, two points bulked especially large. One, not surprisingly, was that the mediatization of virtually all the smaller Estates of the Empire was neither necessary nor desirable and that it would constitute a grave injustice as well as an outright invasion of property rights. The other, advanced with equal conviction, was that the reduction of the number of separate states to just a few, far from laying a basis for greater unity, would strengthen the political egoism and therefore the autonomous tendencies of all, resulting in the dissolution of a single German nation into several small nations. Looking back to the traditional constitution, one author wrote: "Even if the Hessian was very much a stranger to the Bavarian, he yet saw him as a German, a man from the same nation; the idea of the German nation as one and the same nation was not strange to even the least individual, because he knew well that even the territorial rulers still recognized a common supreme head over them." In the arrangement preached by Kayser, however, "The Bavarian will become as strange to the Lower Saxon as the Spaniard, since no bond, no idea of any sort of constitution, holds them together any longer."[13] Closely connected to this concern about the loss of a common German national identity through the disappearance of the various imperial organs and agencies the old constitution had provided was the fear that the sovereignty granted at Pressburg would collapse a system of justice which had protected the subjects of the territorial rulers precisely because it had provided the very sort of appeal beyond territorial boundaries that Kayser's proposal specifically rejected.[14]

One of the most significant characteristics of many of the discussions of Kayser's work, however, as indeed of most of the decreasing number of political commentaries on German public life after Pressburg, was their acceptance of the transformation of the Empire into a simple league or federation of independent states—an acceptance gaining ground so rapidly that almost no authors appear to have found it necessary to argue the point in detail with the handful of imperial loyalists who persisted in emphasizing the unitary features of the Empire as a single state. Regardless of their opinions as to whether the long-term effects of a federative system would be good or bad for Germany in political, economic, or cultural respects, the fact that it had become such a system was beyond dispute. When a *Reichspatriot* like Johann Gottfried Pahl could soberly assess the intent of Article XIV of the Peace of Pressburg as that of granting full and true sovereignty, not just unlimited *Landeshoheit,* to the states concerned, and could sadly admit that French official documents which had heretofore wrongly referred to "the Germanic body" or "the Germanic federation" were now correct, a major milestone in the abandonment of the imperial-monarchical idea had clearly been reached.[15]

Other later articles in Pahl's journal expressed diametrically opposed views about the future of the German federation. One took the optimistic line that all Pressburg had really done was to grant a formal sovereignty to states which had possessed it in all but name for some time, and that this sovereignty could exist without destroying the union which in time of need would continue to bind all to mutual assistance. Germany, to be sure, would no longer be a state, but would be a powerful and unconquerable federation, like the ancient Greeks or the Swiss Confederation. Another author, however, after reading this article as well as Kayser's proposals, doubted that a firm and permanent union of sovereign German states could ever be created. The geographical unity and homogeneity of interests of the Swiss had no counterpart in the infinite diversity of Germany, and while it might be possible to create a new document called "the constitution of the German Empire," he wrote, it would be a dead letter from its very inception.[16]

While such fruitless speculations as these were occupying the troubled minds of German political commentators, Napoleon himself was adding to their confusion by his own silence on the great question of the future of the Empire, which it appeared only he could answer. Some German voices were raised to ask him to bring peace by simply putting an end to the imperial bond which had subjected Germany to so many miseries and had perpetuated its disunity to the point that there no longer existed either a nation or a German national interest—with the implication that the various German states henceforth be permitted to work out their individual destinies without external interference of any kind.[17] Napoleon, however, was not done with Germany, as he made clear, in March 1806, in naming his brother-in-law Joachim Murat as Duke of Cleves and Berg, lower Rhenish territories delivered over to French disposition by Prussia and Bavaria respectively as part of their various bargains with France.

There was one important individual in Germany to whom this act appears to have signaled Napoleon's intention to prevent the collapse of the Empire, perhaps by himself assuming the crown now worn by Francis II. This was the Archchancellor Karl von Dalberg, who for some time had been an outspoken admirer of the French Emperor. He had attended Napoleon's coronation in Paris in late 1804, and had made an excellent impression on him, probably because Napoleon not only saw in him a member of one of the most ancient and well-known German noble families, but also because the Archchancellor had a reputation as a true German patriot—qualities a parvenu like Napoleon could appreciate.[18] The highly impressionable Dalberg, for his part, was immensely flattered by the attention the French Emperor lavished upon him, and returned to Germany erroneously convinced that he and Napoleon had achieved a meeting of the minds on the need to support the tottering structure of the Empire. By this time, he had also come to see himself as perhaps the chief German defender of the imperial constitution; his confidence in Francis II had been shaken not only by Austria's military and political defeats of recent years, but by Vienna's refusal to support his half-baked scheme for a national concordat which would have converted the German Catholic church into a national one, similar to that of France, under his leadership. This plan, which stemmed from the desire to salvage what was left of the old *Reichskirche* as a prop for the constitution, was consistent with Dalberg's sincere but politically unwise and ultimately unsuccessful campaign to save the Imperial Knights, the *Reichsadel,* as another historic buttress of the imperial idea.

Although Dalberg observed a more than merely correct relationship with Vienna in the last few years of the Empire's existence, he had begun to cast about for an alternative imperial political leadership as far back as the Peace of Lunéville, and in early 1803 had even spoken of "an Empire of the Carolingians under Bonaparte"—a largely playful thought, perhaps, but one which recurred to him at the time of Napoleon's coronation and which was never entirely absent from his mind thereafter.[19] When the War of the Third Coalition broke out, Dalberg proclaimed his neutrality, and it was entirely in keeping with his image of himself as the custodian of the imperial constitution that he undertook, in November 1805, to issue a declaration to the Imperial Diet, calling attention to the dangers that existed for the constitution and exhorting all and sundry to unite in observing the laws of the Empire and in attaining an honorable and lasting peace. Issued to Bavaria, Württemberg, and Baden, all allies of France, and at a moment when Napoleon's armies were pressing toward Vienna virtually without resistance, the declaration was the very epitome of futility. Designated by one of Dalberg's biographers as "a miserable document," it earned the Archchancellor only amused scorn at Regensburg, as well as the annoyance of the French Emperor.[20] Following Austria's defeat at Austerlitz, Dalberg, whose desperate concern was to preserve as much of both the idea and the reality of empire as possible, was forced to conclude that Austria could no longer provide the moral and material power necessary to hold the traditional Empire together, and that only France could now do it. Before 1805 was over, he called upon Francis II to abdicate in favor of Napoleon, and in April of the following year, faced with the prospect of a host of mediatizations of smaller territories which would remove the last supports of the imperial constitution, he turned directly to Napoleon himself as a last hope.

In a famous letter of April 19, 1806, directed to the French ambassador Hédouville, the Archchancellor spoke of the necessity for a renascence of the constitution of the German nation, saying that the majority of its laws contained only "meaningless words" because of the inability of the courts, the Circles, and the Diet to protect the property or personal security of individuals. This anarchy could be overcome by but one means: "The German constitution can only be regenerated by a Supreme Imperial Head of splendid character, who returns force to the laws through concentrating the executive power in his hands." Francis of Austria had many excellent personal qualities, Dalberg's letter continued, but through his violations of his Electoral Capitulation—the occupation of Bavaria, calling in the Russians, and giving away parts of the Empire to pay for mistakes committed in the service of an exclusively dynastic interest—he had turned the majority of the Diet against him and had in effect let the scepter of Germany fall from his hand. What a happy circumstance it would be, Dalberg opined, if only Francis would confine himself to the role of an eastern Emperor, withstanding the dangerous expansionist desires of the Russians and allowing the western empire to arise again in the person of Napoleon, "as it was under Charlemagne, composed of Italy, France, and Germany."[21]

This remarkable letter was accompanied by specific suggestions designed to provide the French Emperor with personal reasons for a continuing interest in the survival of the imperial constitution, regardless of whether he chose to assume the German crown or not. Thus, in addition to pledging support for the elevation of the newly installed Murat to the rank of Elector, Dalberg held out the prospect of a favor that he could unquestionably deliver: the selection of Napoleon's uncle, the Corsican Cardinal Fesch, as his coadjutor, with the right to succeed him as Archchancellor, Primate of Germany, and Elector. With Napoleon's approval, Dalberg hastened to give evidence of his good faith, and on May 27 announced to a surprised Diet that he had chosen Fesch as his successor.[22] There is little doubt that Dalberg, along with most other Germans, was expecting Napoleon almost momentarily to give a signal indicating his intention to assume the German crown. It is equally clear that Napoleon did indeed entertain the idea seriously, but as an option whose realization would have to depend on the course of events. He appears, for one thing, not to have wanted to place the crown on his own head by arbitrarily removing it from that of Francis, but instead to accept it by German acclamation—whether real or manufactured—after the Habsburg could be persuaded to abdicate it. In this as in so many other things in this period of desperation, however, Vienna could not make up its mind on the abdication question which had been a subject of intense debate since early in 1806, and an impatient Napoleon therefore found himself forced to resolve the German problem in a way that surprised most Germans. On July 12, 1806, following a series of private negotiations with the representatives of a number of princes of western Germany, the French Foreign Minister Talleyrand presented to all of them a collective treaty for a new union which they were to join. With their signatures—a matter about which they had no choice—the Confederation of the Rhine (*Rheinbund*) was born.

The original members, sixteen in number, included the rulers of Bavaria, Württemberg, Baden, Berg, Hessen-Darmstadt, and ten lesser dukes and princes. It also included Karl von Dalberg, who received the new title of "Prince-Primate" (*Fürstprimas*), the presidency of the Confederation, and the city of Frankfurt, with surrounding territories, as his own principality. Napoleon proclaimed himself protector of the new Confederation, which was to be utterly separated from the German Empire, and whose members entered into a permanent military alliance with France by which they were pledged to maintain a collective force of 63,000 men and to join in any war in which any single member became involved. The internal workings of the Confederation were to be left to the later deliberations of the members; the Act of Confederation itself mentioned only the establishment of two colleges—one for the kings, the other for the remaining princes. It was made clear at the time that the accession of other German states was not only permissible but expected. Article XXV of the Act of Confederation removed all doubt about the status of the territories of Imperial Knights by specifically asserting the sovereignty of the members over them; indeed, the formation of the Confederation also signaled the demise of the remaining Imperial Cities (Nürnberg and Frankfurt) as well as most of the Imperial Counts and a majority of the very small princes. As a result of these mediatizations and of subsequent accessions, the Confederation by 1808 came to consist of thirty-nine states, excluding only Austria, Prussia, Holstein (Denmark), and Western Pomerania (Sweden).[23]

In spite of the clarification of the immediate political future of western Germany brought about by the Act of Confederation, which undoubtedly gave relief to some who had almost begun to believe that any solution might be better than the uncertainty in which they had lived for so long, there were many highly placed individuals within its membership who did not greet the establishment of the Confederation with any joy, and who entered it only with profound reluctance. One of them was its new Prince-Primate Dalberg, who was initially deeply disappointed by a solution which posited not only secession from the Empire, but a secession for which no real constitutional precedent existed. Seriously considering immediate retirement from public life, he was dissuaded from this course only by the suggestion that he might have a major influence on the future constitution and operations of the Confederation.[24]

Like Dalberg, for whom the survival of the historic Empire was of supreme importance, the Nassau minister Hans Christoph von Gagern had been prepared if necessary to accept a Napoleonic emperorship to preserve the imperial union. When Talleyrand revealed to him Napoleon's plan for the Confederation, he told the Foreign Minister that since Nassau lay fully in the French Emperor's hands, he could obviously raise no objection to the scheme; "But," as Gagern later wrote, "as a private individual and German I deeply felt and regretted what was about to happen. My general fatherland, divided and disunited indeed—yet in a certain sense still one, was to be fragmented and forever dissolved. My nation—a great, noble, cultured nation, was in effect to cease to be such. I had for a long time observed [Napoleon's] aspirations to the power of Charlemagne. If he had attained the imperial crown by whatever means, I would have accommodated myself to this fate, because I would have expected great things from it—but this league would not vouchsafe that."[25]

King Frederick of Württemberg and the able minister Montgelas of Bavaria, though for different reasons, also entered the Confederation with many misgivings—the former because he retained a stubborn dynastic loyalty to the old Empire (he had assisted Napoleon against Austria in the fall of 1805 without enthusiasm), the latter because he saw any union not under Bavarian leadership as an obstacle to the autonomous development of his own state.[26] With little more choice in the matter than that of the smaller principalities, Württemberg and Bavaria signed up, but with an undiminished jealousy of their own independence which largely accounts for the subsequent failure of the Confederation to develop any but the most rudimentary constitutional organs.

Elsewhere in Germany, the formation of the Confederation created a renewed sense of crisis. The smaller states of central and northern Germany, desperately confused about their future in a truncated Empire now divided between the virtually meaningless headship of a remote and isolated Austria in the south and an unofficial Prussian guardianship in the north, had no alternative for the moment but to await the reactions of the mighty. In Prussia, where in spite of formal agreements suggesting the contrary a combination of disenchantment with and apprehension of Napoleon's policies had been growing steadily since late in 1805, the news of the formation of the *Rheinbund* produced an almost immediate response in the form of a determined effort on the part of Frederick William III and his ministers to strengthen Prussia through a formalization of the heretofore loose cooperation between Berlin and other major northern German courts, especially those of Saxony and Electoral Hessen. While Napoleon, anxious at this moment above all to secure Prussian recognition of the newly formed Confederation, had made it clear that he was prepared to assist Berlin in uniting northern Germany under Hohenzollern leadership into a league or even a new empire, the Prussians themselves were no longer thinking in terms of what would please the French Emperor. Awakened at last—and too late, as events would prove—to the dangers Napoleon's France posed to their own state, they were now prepared to erect a league not only without him, but against him. By a letter of July 25, 1806, to the Elector of Saxony, Frederick William III took the first step toward the formation of a north German union. Stating specifically the need for another federative system to oppose the new Confederation, he proposed that discussions for a closer association of Prussia, Saxony, and Hessen begin immediately in Berlin. The negotiations dragged on for some two months, finally foundering on the jealous sovereignty of the latter two courts, as well as on their well-grounded fears of the consequences of committing themselves to a Prussian policy that seemed increasingly likely to lead to a direct confrontation with Napoleon. Indeed, it was to be so. Only three days after a Saxon note which politely but definitively ended the discussions was received in Berlin, Prussia issued the ultimatum to the French Emperor which was to result in war and in the stunning double defeat of the Prussian armies at Jena and Auerstädt on October 14, with all its disastrous consequences.[27]

Meanwhile, the states of the Confederation, following the stipulations of Article III of the Act of Confederation, issued a formal *Dictatum* at Regensburg on August 1, 1806, officially informing the Imperial Diet of their separation from the Empire; the statement justified this action on the grounds that the bond of empire had already been dissolved by events in all but name, and that Germany could no longer be found in the German Empire. At the same time and place, the French chargé d'affaires Bacher delivered a declaration which ended with the statement that the French Emperor no longer recognized the existence of a German constitution.[28] By this time, Karl von Dalberg, with a heavy heart, had abdicated his imperial titles (July 31), and a French note amounting to an ultimatum calling for the abdication of Francis II as German Emperor by August 10 had been received in Vienna.

In view of the cascade of bad news of recent weeks, the note occasioned no real surprise to Francis and his advisors; it came, in fact, almost as a relief in the sense that it reduced Francis' options with respect to the German crown to the single one that Napoleon was demanding. Those options had been debated at considerable length since the Peace of Pressburg by two men whose advice in imperial matters was prized and trusted in Vienna: Johann Alois von Hügel, Imperial *Konkommissar,* and Friedrich Lothar Stadion, the Bohemian delegate to the Diet and brother of the Austrian Foreign Minister, Johann Philipp Stadion. Both men approached the question of the Empire's future almost exclusively from the standpoint of the dynastic interest of the House of Habsburg, and both believed that renunciation of the crown was indicated by all circumstances. In May—well before the Confederation of the Rhine was formed—both submitted memoranda to the Foreign Minister in which they called attention to the disadvantages of retaining an imperial crown whose functions could be performed only by Napoleon's permission—in which case the German Emperor would sink to the level of a French vassal—or by forcing the issue against his wishes, thus risking the war that Austria at this time had at all costs to avoid. The timing of the abdication was of utmost importance, however; in particular, there existed the dangerous possibility that if the crown was renounced before the imperial bond itself was dissolved, then Napoleon or one of his satraps might assume the throne and use it, perhaps with enhanced powers, against an Austria which would now enjoy nothing more than electoral status in the Empire. Both Stadion and Hügel therefore believed it necessary to negotiate with Napoleon, while there was still time, for such immunities, privileges, and exemptions as might be required to prevent this eventuality, and perhaps to gain other concessions or advantages as well. What is remarkable, in view of the general acceptance of this position at the Austrian court, is that no initiatives were taken by Vienna to realize such objectives before the formation of the Confederation rendered them irrelevant.[29]

Once Napoleon's intentions with respect to most of the "third Germany" had been clarified, along with his will regarding the disposition of the German crown, Francis was advised to proceed with an immediate abdication, but under circumstances which would practically guarantee the simultaneous dissolution of the imperial nexus and therefore of the Empire itself. In a carefully worded statement of August 6, 1806, the last head of the Holy Roman Empire renounced the Roman-German crown and expressly freed all Estates and imperial officials whatsoever from any and all constitutional responsibilities they bore to him as Emperor, while at the same time declaring the complete and formal withdrawal of his hereditary lands from imperial jurisdiction. A last glimmer of the long fading Habsburg sense of imperial obligation was provided in a separate document which generously promised to continue the payment of salaries of imperial functionaries—the members of the supreme courts, for example—from the Austrian treasury for the lifetime of those concerned. While it is true that Vienna recognized at least the possibility of the survival of the Empire beyond Francis' abdication and deliberately sought to guarantee itself against any possible compromise of its interests in that case by explicitly announcing the secession of its dynastic territories from the Empire, there is little doubt that Francis and his advisors both intended and expected the Empire to collapse with his abdication.

The legality of Francis' abdication is beyond question, but nearly all scholars are agreed that his release of Estates and officials from their imperial obligations was illegal not only because it broke his coronation vows, but because he did not consult the Diet in Regensburg.[30] This view was shared by more than a few contemporaries, who saw in the renunciation of the crown nothing more than an illegal result of Napoleon's brutal coercion, and who refused to recognize the legal extinction of the Empire. Though it was hardly known in Germany because of the censorship, George III of Great Britain, Elector of Hanover, asserted that he would never recognize the abolition of the imperial constitution as valid, and would regard the Empire and its head as continuing. Much the same position was taken by Alexander I of Russia and by the King of Sweden in his capacity as Duke of Western Pomerania and a guarantor of the imperial constitution since 1648, and there were many lesser "patriotic" individuals who shared their sentiments.[31]

For all such stubborn loyalties, the Empire was in fact dead, and was not to be resurrected. The conventional wisdom—though not altogether unchallenged—has generally held that the events leading to the final dissolution of the Empire, as well as the imperial abdication itself, created little stir in German public opinion, and that the prevailing mood was one of indifference. Perhaps the most commonly cited evidence of this political apathy was the entry Goethe made in his diary on August 7, 1806, in which he noted that a quarrel among servants in the coach in which he was returning home from Karlsbad generated more interest among the

passengers than the news they had just received of the secession of the
states of the Confederation of the Rhine.[32] Christian Daniel Voss, writing
only a few weeks later, pronounced himself neither surprised nor disturbed at the Empire's collapse; the only wonder in this otherwise essentially uninteresting event, he declared, was that it had not occurred as
much as two or three centuries earlier.[33] And the Hamburg bookdealer
Friedrich Perthes wrote that few people in that former Imperial City wept
at the disappearance of the imperial bond; on the contrary, they celebrated
the end of the expenses Vienna and Regensburg had occasioned them,
and reassured themselves with the conviction that Hamburg would remain Hamburg in any case.[34] Indeed, even in Vienna, in the midst of an
atmosphere of general depression after Francis laid down his crown, there
was a somewhat redeeming feeling of relief that Austria could consider
herself fortunate to have gotten rid of the "theatrical decoration" or the
"crown of thorns" of the old universal Empire.[35]

Yet this picture of public relief, indifference, or outright pleasure at
the demise of the Empire has to be modified by several important considerations. In the first place, the traditional eighteenth-century imperial
structure was not ended by a single blow, but by a rapid succession of
blows over a period of nearly ten years, beginning in a formal sense with
the Peace of Campo Formio. The sheer pace of change eventually produced in some people almost a numbness to what was going on around
them, combined with a sense of confusion and desperation at their own
helplessness in the face of events; as one historian has written, "The men
of this time often said that changes were following one upon another so
fast that it was difficult to keep pace with them." The result was a kind of
battered insensitivity.[36] Furthermore, as the loss of the Left Bank was
succeeded by the secularization of the ecclesiastical states and the mediatization of the Imperial Cities, Knights, and Counts, and the smaller
princes, the special stake that all these groups and their dependents as
separate Estates or lords of the Empire had in preserving the integrity of
the imperial nexus was greatly weakened. For most of them, as stated
earlier, *their* Empire had ended before August of 1806, and they could not
maintain the same level of interest in the political fate of their new masters
that they had had in their own. In their view, the territorial consolidations
which proceeded so rapidly after the turn of the century had so reinforced
the autonomous tendencies of the remaining states—their "state-egoism,"
as it was frequently put—as virtually to destroy the wholeness of the Empire itself; in doing so, it also eroded the realities of mutual dependency
from which the sentiment of *Reichspatriotismus* had derived its force and
had vaporized the latter into nothing more than an idle idea.[37]

As the foregoing suggests, there was a period of psychological preparation for the final end of the Empire which, in spite of the sheer bewilder-

ment of some people and the cautious optimism of others, appears as a very strong undercurrent of pessimism in the public literature of the last years. As early as 1798, one author, while enjoining all Germans to remain loyal to their constitution, frankly admitted that under present circumstances he could not see how the constitution could last much longer.[38] Thereafter, the mood of many publicists became steadily gloomier. An article in Häberlin's *Staats-Archiv* of 1803, posing the question "What will become of Germany?", answered it by confidently predicting the imminent demise of the old imperial constitution, while Häberlin himself, in a footnote, asserted that Germany would become the same congeries of French vassal states that Italy then was.[39] The following year, a writer for the same journal referred to the Empire as an "interim partition between Russians and Franks in Europe," which would last only until both decided how to carve it up.[40] By early 1806, even Pahl's *National-Chronik* had given the Empire up for lost, and various articles pictured the imperial structure as a thoroughly rotten building ready to fall at the first puff of wind, or revived Häberlin's earlier prediction that Italy's fate would momentarily befall Germany as well.[41] The direst of all futures, "to see the name and the nation of the Germans sink into the ranks of the antiquities," with the added chance that after a number of generations even the German language itself, like Latin, might die out, was projected by one writer, also in 1806, who saw such horrors as an at least possible consequence of the destruction of the Empire.[42]

For such people as these, the imperial abdication elicited few expressions of sorrow, if only because their tears had already been shed in anticipation of a collapse they had come to see as inevitable. But there were others who had consoled themselves in advance of the event by the argument that what was truly and ultimately important and significant about Germany and the Germans had little to do with politics in any case, and would therefore survive even so momentous an eventuality as the destruction of the only national political framework they possessed. In this view, of which examples are legion, the moral and cultural qualities of the German nation lent it a dignity that was unassailable precisely because it was wholly spiritual and not of this world, a world defined by political power, military resources, and boundary lines drawn on maps.

Probably the strongest and most unequivocal statement of this attitude appears in a prose sketch for an unfinished poem written by Friedrich Schiller after the Peace of Lunéville in 1801. Posing the rhetorical question of whether the German was entitled to have any pride in himself even after an unsuccessful war whose results were disastrous in a political sense, Schiller answered: "Yes, he may! He comes defeated from the battle, but he has not lost what constitutes his worth. The German Empire and the German nation are two different things. The majesty of the German never rested on the head of his prince. The German has founded his own value apart from politics, and even if the Empire perished, German dignity would remain uncontested. This dignity is a moral greatness. It resides in the culture and in the character of the nation that are both independent of her political vicissitudes. . . . While the political Empire has tottered, the spiritual realm has become all the firmer and richer."[43] Uncannily similar to this statement was that of a writer for the *National-Chronik* early in 1802, who found no real reason for sadness in the fact of Germany's political powerlessness: "The rule of wisdom is the triumph of the Germans," said he. "Our political greatness may sink away; all the more gloriously will be raised up the intellectual and moral Empire which the German spirit plants and spreads, and whose limits are without end in space and time."[44]

The spiritual mission of the German nation to the world, then, did not depend on the power of the sword, but on the force of ideas and of moral example. As a universal mission, it could not and even should not be tied to or contained within a limiting political structure; this was the thought expressed by Friedrich Perthes in a letter to Johannes von Müller in 1807: "We Germans are a chosen people, which represented humanity and made everything into a matter of universal concern. We were never merely national."[45] This was also the meaning of Schiller's remark that "Every people has its day in history, but the German's day is the harvest of all times," as well as of the poet Novalis' two statements: "The instinctive policy and tendency of the Romans towards universalism also lies in the German people;" and "No nation can compete with us in vigorous universalism."[46]

This cultural cosmopolitanism, seen in the already familiar terms of a singularly German ability to absorb the creative products of all other times and peoples, to reinterpret and synthesize them in the light of a higher morality, and to reissue them to the world as the unique gift of the German spirit, did not require a political framework to guarantee the ongoing fulfillment of its mission. When Christoph Martin Wieland, attempting to give some comfort to his fellow Germans after the losses of Campo Formio, wrote that "Only the true cosmopolitan can be a good citizen—regardless of under what [governmental] form and constitution,"[47] he was simply giving expression to the conviction so common among the members of the German republic of letters of the later eighteenth century that the virtues of good citizenship were constant, absolute, and universal. They had to do with moral obligations to human values that were apolitical in nature, and hence could and should be cherished by the individual irrespective of the form of his government. That these sorts of attitudes were a genuine consolation to many intellectuals and men of letters in the last dreary years of the Empire and at its final moment is nowhere more clearly revealed than in a statement of Goethe of 1806: "Our Germanness (*Deutschheit*) lies deeper than in the dilapidated forms of our gothic and chaotic constitution, which [continued to exist] in such bad shape simply because it was still there, and for whose demolition only a single heroic arm was required. If I were not as sincerely certain of that as of my own being, I would grieve at the collapse of the German Empire; but Germany and what is more, German spirit, German culture and language will not collapse."[48]

Since opinions such as these came from very much the same groups which only a few years before had praised the imperial constitution because of the diversity it protected, a diversity they believed to be in some measure responsible for the spiritual greatness of the nation, they should not be seen as indicative of an indifference to the demise of the Empire. Instead, they were attempts of concerned individuals to make the best of a situation that could not be changed, to put as optimistic a construction as possible on the consequences of events over which, as impotent onlookers, they had no control.[49] Their views, very simply, amounted to a hopeful affirmation that the distinctive cultural characteristics of the Germans would continue to provide the basis for a national unity even in the absence of a common political bond.

An article in the *National-Chronik,* which appeared shortly after the abdication of Emperor Francis, provides a fascinating commentary on attitudes toward the relationship between state and nationality as seen by one contemporary—probably the editor of the journal, Pahl. The name "Germany," the author wrote, had indeed now disappeared as a political concept, and had no more meaning than that of Italy or Poland. But, he insisted, there are relationships among men besides those which relate to civic affairs, one of which lies in the common descent, language, customs, and culture of a people, which together produce a common character that preserves unity; and while it might now well be that the *citizen* will cease to be German, the *man* will not: "The positive laws of the state will separate German from German; but the unchangeable laws of nature will again unite the one and the other." Yet there was also a hint of pessimism in the warning the author issued about the long-term effects of political separation between the peoples that make up a single nation. National individuality, said he, can be vitiated by the appropriation of foreign features to the point where, after several centuries, it may scarcely be visible except in coarsest outline. Consequently, the loss of statehood by a nation was not to be taken lightly with respect to the preservation of nationality even in only its cultural or cosmopolitan definition, "For man becomes nearly everything he is through the state."[50]

It was, no doubt, a perception such as this that led some Germans to look toward the Confederation of the Rhine as a political substitute for the Empire, one which might provide a continuing framework for the development of a German national life. The Oldenburg poet G.A. von Halem, who for several years after 1802 was an outspoken admirer of Napoleon and his works, found his favorable judgment of the French Emperor confirmed in the formation of the Confederation. In 1806, he wrote a short but emotional poem entitled *"Der Rheinbund,"* in which he praised the new union as a true German construction that would be the salvation of the German people for generations to come; there was no reason to be concerned about the future, since a new diet as evidence of a continuing German unity was about to be formed, and since, after all, a Dalberg was still at hand.[51] The new Prince-Primate himself, meanwhile, was doing his best to realize the great expectations of the Confederation cherished by hopefuls like Halem. As early as August 1806, he had composed and rushed off to Paris a project for a constitution for the Confederation. This and subsequent proposals designed to provide some measure of institutional unity among the members got nowhere, partly because of strong opposition from the kings of Bavaria and Württemberg, especially, who feared any compromise of their complete sovereignty and independence, and partly because Napoleon did not want to offend the two kings and was in any case wholly indifferent to the ardent desires of the former Archchancellor for a reconstituted German fatherland.[52]

But neither Dalberg nor anyone else, in the first months of the new league, could know that the Confederation would never develop a cohesive governmental structure of any kind during its short life, and many people had the highest hopes for it. Even a man like Nicolas Thaddäus von Gönner, perhaps "the last public lawyer of the Empire,"[53] to whom the end of the Empire came as an especially heavy blow because of his field of academic specialization, regarded the Confederation as something which had given his German fatherland "a better form, without which it would perhaps have become only a province of foreign states," and asserted that only those who "cleave slavishly and without examination to the old" could doubt that the recent constitutional changes would contribute a great deal to the happiness of the German nation.[54] Nor was Gönner the only last-ditch defender of the old imperial constitution to make his peace with the new Confederation, and even to see in it the first glow of a brighter dawn. After Prussia's defeats at the hands of Napoleon in late 1806 and 1807, and the addition of a number of new members to the Confederation, J. G. Pahl was visibly cheered to note that the Confederation could now, "as we always hoped and wished," properly be termed "The German Confederation"; by April of 1807, indeed, he was prepared to assert that the patriotic German could now set his hopes for a common fatherland on the new association, and that the division of the whole of Germany into several parts did not bother him as long as some sort of tie continued to exist to bind those parts together.[55]

As might perhaps be expected, the readiness of many important figures in German public life to switch their allegiance and loyalties from their old Empire and Emperor to a new and foreign-dominated political union created a considerable indignation among some later and very nationalistic German historians. To cite but one twentieth-century example, a history of the Confederation which appeared in 1936 purported to find in it a baleful spirit that had helped to propagate German disunity far into the nineteenth century: "The spirit of the Confederation of the Rhine is the readiness of Germans to conspire with foreigners against their own land and people, whether that may be demonstrated in its final literal form as in the years 1806–13 or in some other way."[56] Such a judgment, of course, not only fails to take into account that most Germans had little choice in the matter—a point apparently better appreciated by contemporaries, from whom far more sympathy than criticism was forthcoming—but also neglects the real fear and desperation with which the rulers, officials, and intellectuals of the smaller states of Swabia and Franconia, especially, had viewed the rapid collapse of the imperial structure as the indispensable context of their own political existence. Too small and powerless even after the Final Recess to shape their own destiny, such states had found their only protection against predators both foreign and domestic in an association whose integrity was now disappearing before their very eyes. Almost literally unable to posit a raison d'être for themselves as distinct entities except as parts of a larger whole, it is not difficult to understand why many of them would see the formation of and their inclusion in the Confederation as a positive good, especially when compared against the almost certain fate of dissolution and absorption that would otherwise have befallen them.[57]

All of the foregoing, then, provides some explanation for the relative equanimity with which the imperial abdication of August 1806 appears to have been received by German public opinion. Two further things must be said, however. First, since the official policy of the states of the Confederation was by that time formally allied with Napoleonic France, and since censorship in those states tended to follow the French lead, opinions hinting at unhappiness or dissatisfaction with the present state of affairs— including lamentations about the fall of the Empire—could not be very freely expressed even where they existed. This is merely to suggest the obvious: that here, as in all cases in which censorship of the press exists and is enforced with respect to controversial questions, the press is usually a poor guide to the true character of public opinion. Second, a variety of sources indicates that private grief over the passing of the Empire was both widespread and genuine. Goethe's mother, in an often cited letter of August 19, 1806, wrote her famous son of the mood of depression and sadness that gripped the city of Frankfurt at the news of Francis' abdication. There were, she said, "Illuminations, fireworks, and the like, but no sign of joy. They are like funerals—that's how our joys appear!"[58] And while many of the delegates to the Imperial Diet at Regensburg, according to the testimony of no less reliable a witness than the Prussian ambassador, Count Görtz, were expressing undeniably sincere feelings of pain and regret at the imperial collapse,[59] a village schoolmaster in the Prussian province of East Frisia was instructing his charges that the disappearance of the Holy Roman Empire was a great calamity for all of them.[60] King Frederick of Württemberg and Duchess Luise of Weimar were only two of a number of important public figures who privately gave vent to feelings of both sorrow and indignation at the tragic end of the German constitution.[61]

Nor did such feelings fade with the passage of time. The years between 1806 and 1813 are full of evidences of a continuing belief in the possible revivification of the Empire—or, differently put, of a refusal to believe that it could ever be finally and truly dead.[62] For understandable reasons, this persistent devotion was perhaps most often expressed in private conversations and correspondence, and surfaced in the public press only in rather circumspect and oblique references; but it burst forth in full ardor once again during the campaigns against Napoleon in 1813–14, when the question of the political reconstitution of Germany was hotly debated as the single most important national issue. The solution finally arrived at in 1815, of course, came in the form of the Germanic Confederation rather than a renewed Empire; but this fact should not be allowed to obscure either the vigor with which the imperial ideal was urged throughout Germany in these years, the seriousness with which it was entertained in high places before its final rejection, nor the strength and durability of the ideal, together with the host of spiritual connotations it carried, after 1815 and far into the nineteenth century.

It is ironic that in dying the Empire may have given rise to a greatly more purified and deeply rooted *Gemeinsinn* than it was capable of creating or sustaining while it still lived. As an idea, it was able after its demise to escape the harsh political realities and frustrations that had not only vitiated the ideal of German unity, but had even obscured the moral postulates which were regarded as the indispensable underpinning of that unity and which the Empire above all represented. The north German poet and writer Ernst Moritz Arndt, later one of the most ardent champions of German nationalism, paid an almost reverential tribute to this imperial ideal and mission, as well as to its meaning in the history of the Germans, in a work composed shortly after the collapse of the Empire: "In all states and peoples," he wrote, "there is something obscure and secret, that is equivalent to its innermost life, and by which the whole is maintained as with invisible bonds; the ultimate religion, the most fervent feeling of necessity, which inexplicably attracts and holds. Such a vestal flame has been sanctified by the primal faith (*Aberglaube*) of all nations and times. In Germany, this ultimate common religion bore the name *Kaiser und Reich.*"[63]

Conclusion

A s ERNST MORITZ ARNDT with his powers of poetic imagination had perceived, the Empire in its last phases did indeed in certain ways more
closely approximate a religion than a state for many of those who lived
within it. As a faith, it embraced a community of believers many of whose
assumptions about important political aspects of public life were shaped
by the ancient bonds of an imperial nexus which were nonetheless important for being increasingly imperceptible. If in fact in its final years
the Empire had come to resemble "the invisible Christian church," to quote
Friedrich Carl von Moser, this phrase should serve not just to call attention to the political fecklessness of the Empire regarded as a single body,
but also to emphasize the long transformation process of the Empire in
German thought from a state to a political, social, and cultural values-
system which was not only unlike that of other major bodies politic in
Europe, but was also inimical in some respects to their fundamental
theoretical foundations. Neither the history nor the meaning of the Empire in this period can properly be appreciated without understanding that
the imperial structure stood as one of the last grand institutional rebukes
to the theory of raison d'état as it had developed elsewhere in Europe in
the early modern period. By that theory, the state possessed its own internal logic, developed according to its own intrinsic laws and morality,
and was directed toward the acquisition of power and its utilization for
its own aggrandizement. The Empire, however, stood not for the acquisition and centralization of power, but for its limitation and dispersal. The
law and morality that operated in other places as the servants of the state
were to be the master of the state in the Empire, and its raison d'être was

290

to be fulfilled not in aggrandizement but in its continual perfecting of itself in its role as a servitor and protector of higher values.

What were these values? Learned and enlightened Germans spoke to this point with virtually a single voice. In the deepest sense, they were not political, but cultural, and revolved around the ultimate purpose ascribed by them to individual man: the fulfillment of his moral and spiritual potential, and under circumstances which imposed as little in the way of obstacles to that goal as possible. The obligation of the state, in this formulation, was limited to the preservation and protection of external conditions under which this individual self-perfection could take place. It was to have only a very circumscribed role in positively assisting this process, since any attempt by it to impart higher values to its own citizens would necessarily impose uniformity on an achievement that, on the contrary, had to be as fully diverse as the number of distinct individuals who made up society. Above all, however, political authority was to protect the freedom necessary to this individual self-development or, putting it negatively, was to be kept from infringing upon an already existing freedom. In this respect, the Empire was perceived as possessing a supreme advantage over other states in the more or less exact balance that existed between imperial and territorial levels of government, in which a mutual watchfulness permitted to neither level actions which could tend toward the systematic limitation of the freedom of subjects. At the same time, that balance permitted the growth of diverse social, economic, political, and cultural conditions within the various territories of the Empire, thus presenting the German a broad range of choice with respect to the kinds of environment in which his own growth as an individual might best be nurtured.

That this balance between imperial and territorial governments also unfitted the Empire for foreign conquests was a truth everywhere known, admitted, and accepted. It was in fact praised as one of the great superiorities of the Empire that a political union so large, so populous, and so well outfitted with soldiery—well over half a million in all its territories—did not and indeed could not, like other states, employ its resources for conquest, but instead used them for the perpetual consecration of an intricate constitutional system designed to promote the highest moral calling of mankind. A Voltaire might mock the Empire's ancient claim to universal dominion by calling it neither holy, nor Roman, nor even an Empire; but many Germans would have rejected that famous aphorism as the product of a mind which, consciously or unconsciously, had come to accept a definition of the state exclusively as the embodiment of power and which did not understand that dominion did not have to be physical, that it could be exercised by example and precept rather than by power, and that the state could have a mission which was both universal and unselfish. Against such misconceptions, it was asserted, the highest mission of the Empire was to provide the framework of peace, order, and liberty within which the spiritual greatness of the German nation, free from the politicized national pride which served the ambitions of monarchs in other states by its exclusive loyalty—that is, by blinding their peoples to the goodness and utility of cultures other than their own—could reach out to embrace universal human experience and make it a living and comprehensible reality for the entire human race. Freedom, it was said again and again, was and had always been the national will of the Germans, and their great contribution to saving mankind from the tyranny of monolithic systems, whether political, religious, or cultural. The Empire embodied that freedom for Germans in a diversity which encouraged intellectual and spiritual investigation and speculation and thereby attained truths which could become the property of all men everywhere. The universalism of the Empire, therefore, while no longer a geographical or political one, or even a religious one in the old Christian sense, existed still as a spiritual one.

As a model for or teacher to other peoples, rather than their scourge, according to its defenders, the Empire also embodied the triumph of law over will, and in this capacity could serve to illustrate the successful claims of justice over sheer power. This justice was even a part of the concept of the "golden mean" preached by Christoph Martin Wieland, and accepted by many others, because that phrase was intended to represent a norm by whose observance not only all extremes—for example, excessive wealth or poverty—were greatly mitigated, but narrow one-sidedness in all human activities, including spiritual culture, was avoided, thus doing justice to the differences between men as well as to the multiple capabilities of each individual. Single dimensional men were characteristic of societies where power, triumphing over justice, had forced individuals into slots according to their ability to contribute to the needs and requirements of power, not of humanity. To regard the imperial association as an intricate *Rechtsordnung* was absolutely fundamental to the definition of the Empire accepted by most Germans, especially those outside of Austria and Prussia, and in the face of rapidly increasing odds they stoutly resisted attempts to redefine the Empire in the categories of *Realpolitik,* that is in ways conformable to shifting constellations of political power within Germany. In the late eighteenth century, their resistance first became obvious in several reactions to the formation and development of the League of Princes. One of these reactions took the form of a denial that the integrity of the imperial union either did or ought to rest on a balance of power, as such, and especially on a balance between Austria and Prussia regarded as great powers. In this view, the balance of the German constitution rested on the mixed form of government which was fixed in its laws, not simply on the inability of one or another of the mixed elements to overturn the balance to its own particular advantage. Thus it was law, not power, that both defined and preserved the Empire. This extremely conservative and in many ways very unrealistic position already represented the voice of a dying age, though it was shared at least in their public utterances by most disputants on either side of the League debate, who, regardless of their individually differing views, professed the most profound concern for the preservation of the existing constitution. This was true even when they accepted as both a philosophical and historical fact the necessity to guard the constitutional status quo, and if necessary by the threat or actual employment of physical power against encroachments from whatever quarter.

Certainly it was not hatred of Joseph II or of Austria, much less of the imperial office itself, that led such men as Carl August of Weimar and Karl von Dalberg to join the Prussian-led League. Joseph had given much cause for alarm in his policies toward the Empire, and these undoubted imperial patriots, with others, in spite of strong reservations about Prussia's secret intentions, believed that a show of determination on the part of the Empire was necessary to bring the Emperor back to the observance of the law. Just as important as their membership in the League, however, was their desire to make of it a reforming agent to restore what they regarded as the lost reality of imperial cooperation. This desire was squarely rooted in the recognition that the imperial association, all arguments of dissenting constitutional lawyers notwithstanding, had in recent generations increasingly come to resemble a multiple political balance based in fact on power rather than on law—a balance in which the smaller territories had steadily lost influence in the Empire's affairs and would continue to do so unless the primacy of law over power could once again be asserted. That, for them, was what reform was intended to do. Although Dalberg's proposal that a reforming League ultimately include even the Emperor himself was politically unthinkable, given the circumstances that had developed in the Empire since 1648, it was the only plan that might conceivably reestablish the full integrity of the prescription *Kaiser und Reich*. Carl August and most other smaller princes, however, rejected the idea of the Emperor's inclusion in the League not only because they regarded it as absurd in the actual political situation of the 1780s, but also because they had come to accept as a permanent datum the by now historic dualism between Emperor and Empire—a formula that in fact closely approximated *Kaiser versus Reich*. Their reform plans were therefore intended less to restore cooperation between head and members than to recall members, that is, the *Reich* alone, to a more perfect observance of the law as a means of counteracting the undeniable drive of the larger territories toward independence from both the Emperor and the restrictions and obligations of the imperial constitution itself—a drive which could threaten the very existence of smaller territories whose only guarantee, other than the risky vagaries of power balances, lay in appeal to the law.

The failure of plans to employ the League as a vehicle for imperial reform was due not only to the opposition of Prussia, whose sole interest in the League was its utility as the instrument of an anti-Austrian policy, but to the fear of many territories both large and small of offending an Austria whose good will could on occasion be as advantageous for them as its ill will could be harmful. But while the insistence of larger territories such as Hanover and Saxony, in particular, that the League not step out of its publicly asserted role and purpose of maintaining the constitutional status quo was in part due to their anxiety that a reforming League might be interpreted in Vienna as an assault on the legitimate powers of the Emperor, there was another and equally important reason for the more powerful princes to abjure reform. From their standpoint, the reforming princes were not trying to preserve the constitution as it then existed, but to roll it back to an earlier time, a time when the prerogatives of *Landeshoheit* had been far fewer and their obligations to the Empire much greater—a time when, in short, their political independence as lords in their own territories was greatly curtailed in comparison with the present. They had come to see the constitution as a framework within which a more or less steady progress toward internal autonomy was possible, and they were not prepared to see the status quo of the moment locked in place for all time, much less dissolved in favor of a return to the constraints of yesteryear.

This divergence of interest between larger and smaller princes also accounts for the unwillingness of many of the latter to support imperial reform under the auspices of the League. Aware that the association was dominated by the larger courts, they could not bring themselves to believe that any reform would not bear the stamp of the exclusive self-interest of those courts; a reformed Empire might then be one in which the greater territories had merely secured for themselves a license to deal with the smaller in the same arbitrary way they had professed to believe that the Emperor was attempting to deal with them, and to prevent which they had supposedly formed the League in the first place. Under such circumstances, many smaller courts—not for the first or last time—chose inaction over a course whose risks seemed greater than the uncertain promise of unspecified advantages. Indeed, by 1790 the fear of an Electoral domination of the Empire in a period of momentary but serious setbacks in Austrian policy led to an unmistakable reaction in many quarters in favor of Vienna; the deep suspicions of an overmighty Emperor of the mid-1780s had given way to an equally profound mistrust of overmighty Electors, especially Prussia. The vigorous publicistic protests against any further reduction of the Emperor's powers in the election of 1790 provide evidence of an acute awareness that the Empire had indeed become a miniature balance of power system within a larger European balance, and that the preservation of the constitution rested upon the keeping of that balance.

But this was not the simple traditional balance as the lawyers had chiefly understood and explained it in their treatments of the history of the constitution since the time of the Reformation, that is, the balance between the aristocratic and monarchical principles of government, wherein the princes of the Empire, striving to defend or assert their "German liberty" were pitted against an Emperor striving for universal autocratic dominion within the boundaries of the Empire. The new balance was a more complicated and dangerous one, because one territory—Prussia—had now clearly revealed herself as a state with power and interests which transcended those of a mere Imperial Estate, and which were directed toward competition with Austria in Germany. This meant that if the other territories were to maintain their traditional positions, they now had not only to keep up their watchfulness against encroachments by the Emperor, but in doing so also prevent falling into a Prussian clientage whose results could be as menacing to their independence as attempts at domination by Austria. Thus arose the concept of a "third Germany" as the guardian of the true, historic Empire and its constitution against the political egoism of two German great powers whose raison d'état inclined their governments towards policies in which the Empire was increasingly irrelevant except as an object of their own rivalry. This guardianship, which of course served the self-interest of the lesser states, would be a difficult one to maintain, but could be managed as long as the Austro-Prussian balance remained relatively even, and as long as it remained in the traditional interest of the other European great powers, and especially of France and Russia as guarantors of the imperial constitution, to see to it that no single great power controlled that majority of German resources in land, wealth, and population which lay within the Germany that was neither Habsburg nor Hohenzollern.

Just how much Germans of the real Empire—as this "third Germany" was to be increasingly regarded by its inhabitants, in order to distinguish it from Austria and Prussia—had come to rely on the Austro-Prussian standoff as the chief guarantee of a constitutional arrangement by which they kept their fragmented independence, but which they were largely powerless to defend except with words, may be seen in the consternation created throughout the Empire by the news of the Austro-Prussian rapprochment of 1790. Since Austria's long-standing designs on Bavaria were well known, since further designs by both Vienna and Berlin were rumored, and since France had to some extent momentarily withdrawn from great power politics because of the ongoing revolution at home, many political observers feared that the stage was being set for some sort of partition of Germany by prior agreement between Austria and Prussia. The outbreak of war between these two powers and France, far from calming such fears, heightened them; the movement of Austro-Prussian military forces to and fro across Germany was seen as a nasty precedent at best, and at worst as a mild form of disguised military occupation preliminary to partition. Even after the Empire itself voted to join the war—a decision about which it had practically no choice—there was a strong and persistent suspicion that the two great powers would not hesitate to wage the war and make the peace in terms exclusively conformable to their own interests. In the early years, this suspicion was evident in writings which expressed the extreme touchiness of the territories about the extent of their obligations to the war effort itself, as well as about any suggestions that a *Reichskrieg* in any way altered or reduced the prerogatives of their territorial lordship, or *Landeshoheit*. In particular, the notion that the Emperor or his immediate military staff might be entitled to assume special and essentially political powers during a legally declared imperial war was rejected with considerable asperity, reflecting in another aspect the fear expressed as late as 1795 by Friedrich Christian Laukhard that the war could serve the interests of Austria and Prussia, especially the former, by weakening the Empire and its territorial rulers as a step preliminary to a major alteration of the constitution.

The "third Germany"—the Empire—persisted throughout the war years to 1797 in its feeling that the dangers to its integrity from within were as great or greater than those posed by the militant French Republic from without. It is true that as the military situation became really desperate, especially after Prussia's withdrawal from the war in 1795, some isolated voices were raised to pronounce that now, at least, all of nonneutral Germany really did have an important stake in the war, that Austria was the true (and, incidentally, the only militarily powerful) champion of the Empire, and that a temporary Austrian dictatorship would not be too high a price to pay for a successful conclusion to the war. Others—a larger number—saw in Austria's grim determination to pursue the struggle merely a selfish and obstinate refusal to admit that the gains she had hoped to acquire from France or from the Empire itself by means of this war were now impossible.

What is noteworthy, however, is that even among those who believed that reform was needed to strengthen the military arm of the Empire, either because they thought that the Empire as a whole was indeed locked in a mortal and righteous combat which it ought to win, or merely because they felt that only greater strength could convince the French to grant a peace that would not be disastrous for Germany—even among these, most of the military reforms proposed not only remained carefully within the traditional framework of the constitution, but were specifically designed to give the "third Germany" a military force of sufficient size and quality as to enable it to play a coequal role with Austria and Prussia in all questions of peace and war. There is no doubt that the stubborn adherence of the small and medium-sized territories to the old and horribly deficient forms of imperial military organization stemmed largely from the sheer inveteracy of the latter, as well as from the sense of justice impacted into the careful (if by now also outdated) distribution of burdens they imposed. But in the present war, where the various territorial troops of the *Reichsarmee* were simply combined with the Austro-Prussian (later only the Austrian) armies, there was also a positive advantage in the tragicomic inefficiency of these ill-trained, ill-commanded, and ill-equipped contingents: They could not be turned into a massive Austrian- or Prussian-led strike force against the other territories of the Empire.

The problem, stripped to essentials, was that the German princes were not prepared to contribute significant military forces even to an admittedly important cause as long as there existed a distinct possibility that those forces could be made responsive to the command of those—Austrians or Prussians—whose policies were not their own. Many of the proposals for military reform in the mid-1790s or so, therefore, were designed not only to increase the number and quality of troops at the Empire's disposal, but to do so in ways that could not give either of the great powers the possibility of undue advantage from that increase. The pronounced preference in many writings for the Circles as the organizational framework for reform is politically more significant than the individual reforms themselves, because it assured the Third Germany collectively of control over a combined standing army which by most estimates (and by no accident) was not very far off the strength of the separate Austrian and Prussian armies. The particular reforms were important too, however, because they would have given to the diverse Circle contingents a uniformity in training, equipment, and command that would enable them to act in the field like a single army—something the present *Reichsarmee* could never manage. Had such reform ideas been implemented, the Circles, representing the Empire, could not only claim their rightful share of decision-making power with respect to the course Germany ought to take in the present war, but could become a codeterminant of the German and European balance of power rather than a precarious beneficiary (and possibly someday also a victim) of it. Unfortunately, however, such reforms were predicated upon the assumption that the territories which made up the Circles were capable of a measure of institutional agreement that went considerably beyond their common fear of Austria and Prussia. This assumption was faulty, and had already been demonstrated to be so in the failure of the Wilhelmsbad Conference of 1794, where the fruitful possibilities of a new kind of league of princes were terminated by the inability of the participants from the Empire to assert an independent interest in the face of Austrian hostility to the establishment of a major new armed force not under the supervision of Vienna.

When Prussia left the war in April of 1795, taking much of northern Germany into neutrality, and as the course of the war for Austria and her remaining imperial allies thereafter tended slowly but steadily toward its unfavorable outcome at Campo Formio, there arose for the first time among some Germans a conviction that the prescription for imperial unity that had heretofore been virtually universal among analysts and commentators on the constitution was wholly inadequate, and that fundamental constitutional changes were needed if the cooperation required to meet the challenges of the times were ever to be achieved. A brief review of the earlier standard prescription for cooperation will help to explain this conviction. As long ago as the 1760s, Friedrich Carl von Moser had based his hopes for a renewed harmony between all members of the imperial union on a revivification of a German "national spirit." He was never very successful in defining that spirit, or in isolating and asserting the truly all-German interest or interests it represented—as his critics were quick to point out. But it is important to note, in this context, that Moser's whole argument for the possibility of greater imperial cooperation rested squarely on the belief that a change in attitudes—a sort of political moral conversion—among the princes was all that was necessary to reestablish the reality of unity between head and members as well as between the latter among themselves. His assertion that the disunity and quarreling which enervated the Empire were the result of the moral deficiencies of individuals and of failures of human will was or became a standard explanation for the inability of the Empire to act as the single body it was held to be in theory. Typical of this view was the often repeated assertion that the problems of the Empire derived from *Verwaltung* (administration), not *Verfassung* (constitution), that the laws and the structure of the Empire were adequate and appropriate, and that if they were only permitted to function as the constitution intended they should, the Empire would become in reality the model system of polity it was supposed to be. That they did not function as they should was due to the shortsightedness of human beings who, however, were presumably susceptible to instruction in the advantages of imperial cooperation in such a way as to return them to the high ideal of German concord. The salvation of the Empire, then, lay in a conversion to be worked in the hearts and minds of its princes and their officials and advisors.

Whatever this answer to the Empire's problems may have had to recommend it, it was deliberately chosen by those who employed it because it appeared to them not only as the only possible solution, but also as an alternative preferable to the path of legal or structural reform. Moser himself, even when pressed by his critics, managed to produce only the vaguest and blandest proposals for concrete reform, and the same was true of most others who followed his lead. The fact is that they, like so many of the lesser princes who opposed the notion that the League of Princes should become an agent for reform of the Empire, did not want much in the way of visible reform. Structural reform, in particular, was a tricky and unpredictable business in a constitution as complex and delicately balanced as was that of the Empire, and could as easily lead to results worse than what was presently available as to better. To be sure, Moser, along with many others, believed that the powers or at least the functions of the Emperor had been too much restricted by the princes, and that the former should be permitted to fulfill the role legally assigned him by the constitution without the numerous obstructions both formal and informal which the princes had learned so well to use for what they supposed was their own advantage. But Moser was also no caesarist, which is confirmed by his frequent and sincere praise of "German liberty." He could probably as easily have concentrated his attention on the Imperial Diet or even the supreme courts of the Empire—as indeed he did to some extent—as on the Emperor, but chose the latter because of his greater symbolic significance to the imperial system.

What he was really trying to do was to call attention to the very thin line that separated German freedom from pure anarchy—a line too often overlooked by too many of the princes—and to remind the latter that their cherished liberty depended ultimately on the integrity of the system of which they were parts. Just as too great an imbalance in favor of the Emperor within that system could lead to a monarchical despotism, so could too much of an imbalance in favor of the princes lead to a universal license—a sort of Hobbesian rapaciousness in which no state would be safe from the possible depredations of others, including foreign ones. Moser was genuinely convinced that an awareness of these truths—which probably can be seen as approximating his understanding of "national spirit" about as closely as his own obscurity on the point permits—lay buried in the consciences of the princes, waiting to be brought to full consciousness. If this could be done, as he hoped it could, then all would be well; if it could not, it was vain to suppose that more concrete reforms, even if possible, would do any good for the ideal of greater unity, and might even further endanger it. In that case, it might be just as well to leave matters in their present state of disarray, which while admittedly imperfect was not yet fatal.

By shortly after the mid-1790s, however, the seriousness of the French challenge had convinced some that imperial disunity could indeed be fatal, and perhaps in the immediate future. From this deep concern arose two new and very different kinds of political solutions to Germany's ills. One of these, which will be discussed later, was based on a constitutional formalization of the "third Germany" concept, and called for an explicit division of the Empire which would essentially exclude the influence of both Prussia and Austria from the rest of Germany. The other, which retained the national framework of a single imperial structure, located the essential reason for the Empire's weakness in the division of the real power of the state among a multitude of princes with divergent interests, and sought constitutional changes which would subvert their authority. Thus, the republican ideas of the anonymous author of the *Critique of the German Imperial Constitution* of 1796–98 were designed to create a single national government which would no longer share legislative and executive authority with the territories, and would ultimately have reduced the territorial princes to nothing more than administrative agents of the national government. Georg Wilhelm Friedrich Hegel, unwilling to give up either the forms or the realities of the traditional constitution altogether, was nonetheless prepared to remove permanently from the princes all authority with respect to the one most important ingredient of true power—military force, including its recruitment, funding, and command —and to give its exercise over to the exclusive control of the Emperor.

What is interesting about these proposals is not only that they implicitly abandoned the belief of Moser and others of his kind in the ability of moral suasion to create the common will among the princes necessary to bring about imperial harmony, but also that they rejected the princes as the basis for the definition of the Empire itself. Both authors, if in different ways, went directly to a broader constituency beneath the princes as the foundation for the national effort they found urgently necessary, thus recalling the belief of many of Moser's critics of the 1760s—for example, Möser, Creutz and Bülau—that if a "national spirit" that could be tapped for the benefit of the entire Empire existed at all, it would have to be found not at the courts of the princes but in the common interests of their subjects. In an obscure way, these critics were telling Moser that a nation divided more or less arbitrarily into parts whose interests were permitted to be defined entirely by the selfish dynastic requirements of their princes could never develop a common or national spirit. In their works and those of many others, the almost universal criticism of the baleful effects of political division on the growth of material prosperity, especially among the middle classes, was one sharp reminder that the Empire as presently constituted did not provide a majority of Germans with benefits that were at once real and visible, thus explaining why the German people as a whole—as Günther Heinrich von Berg perceived in 1795—were not so much actively dissatisfied with the imperial constitution as simply indifferent to it.

For the unknown author of the *Critique,* as to a lesser degree for Hegel as well, what all of this implied was a need to create a single national state as the prerequisite for the emergence of an active national spirit. If, as Hegel put it, Germany was no longer a state, then it had to be remade into a state; and, as his hints about an imperial dictatorship indicated, this would more likely have to come as an act of force from a single source than as the result of a spontaneous national movement, for the latter would require a common national will, or spirit, that was not yet in existence. The author of the *Critique,* in calling for a single elected national legislative body, for the election of the Emperor by that body, and finally for laws that would create not only better but also more uniform cultural and material conditions for the Germans, believed that the separate peoples of Germany needed first to create a common state by an act of faith and will, after which its legislature would go about the business of creating the commonly shared conditions on which alone the growth of a common and national spirit was possible. Implicit in these proposals was a denial of any and all purely educational or hortatory approaches to developing a national spirit, such as the various schemes for a national education suggested by Herder and others, not to mention the early work of Moser himself. Prepared to accept the existence of a German nationality as a fact, Hegel and his republican colleague denied that it could be politically active as a self-conscious spirit without a common political goal, which did not exist in the fragmented Empire of their day.

Against such unitary ideas, which were clearly outside the mainstream if only because they were now regarded as impossible to realize, other political publicists began toying with formal redefinitions of the Empire which would have restricted the effective boundaries of "Germany" to those territories which were neither Prussian nor Austrian. Operating from the assumption that all the German states except Austria and Prussia (whose possessions outside the Empire made them in some sense also "foreign" states) had a common interest not shared by the great powers—lack of political power or ambition and a desire for the quiet enjoyment of peace and order being the most frequently mentioned—a number of theorists broke with all past practice to recommend what amounted to the dissolution of the Empire in its previous extent and form and its contraction to the "third Germany." The basic motivation behind such recommendations was to escape the all too obvious dangers of involvement in the wars of the great powers to which the lesser territories were essentially committed by virtue of their entrapment in a political union that also embraced Austria and Prussia. This is demonstrated not only by those proposals which called for formal separation of the "third Germany" from Austria and Prussia and its organization as a distinct confederate

union, but also by those which, while maintaining the constitutional integrity of the Empire, drew a sharp line between domestic and foreign
affairs, specifically reserving all decisions on the latter that affected the
Empire to the "third Germany" organized as a sort of new league of
princes. In both formulations, the traditional reliance on the European
balance of power to protect the basic integrity of the whole Empire gave
way to a recognition that only if the Empire was politically redefined in
such a way as to set it outside the exclusive sphere of influence of any one
or two great powers could there be any hope that that balance could continue to operate as a guarantee for a group of states too feeble to protect
themselves.

The hope of some writers that this "third Germany" might achieve a
degree of strength and cooperation within itself sufficient to share actively
in the protection of the German and European balance was probably unrealistic, but it was in any case made irrelevant by the increasingly absolute preponderance of France. When, in 1806, Napoleon finally commanded the political formalization of a "third Germany," the resultant
union was perhaps in many details not what either princes or publicists
would have created for themselves if they had had a choice. But they did
not have a choice, and the Confederation of the Rhine did after all accomplish, for the moment at least, one thing which all desired: the
guarantee of a structure which secured their states against dissolution and
absorption by others.

Of course, most of the proposals for a politically or constitutionally
distinct "third Germany" were predicated on either the expectation or the
actual realization of the determinations of the Final Recess of 1803. This
is so partly because it was supposed that the enlargement and eventual internal consolidation of secular states through their absorption of the
ecclesiastical territories and the Imperial Cities would confer on them,
collectively, a considerably greater political weight and military power
than had characterized the much more fragmented area they now en-
compassed. At the same time it would eliminate the pro-Austrian tendencies of the weak ecclesiastical states which had kept that area from developing an independent foreign policy based on the common self-interest of
preservation through some sort of armed neutrality.

It should also be emphasized, however, that the willingness to entertain any radically new constitutional ideas, including that of a separate
"third Germany," also rested on the conviction, increasingly widespread
after Lunéville, that the old Empire had been or was about to be so fatally
compromised as to render new constitutional arrangements not only desirable but necessary. In other words, quite apart from the immediate advantages that might be derived from new constitutional schemes, a drastic
rethinking of forms of political association for Germany was imperative

simply because the imperial structure could not survive the changes in prospect. Even some of the most dedicated supporters of the imperial idea felt that the enlargements would confer on a number of secular princes a measure of independence that was no longer compatible with even the loosest possible construction of the traditional imperial constitution. Probably the most striking effect of this conviction on formal constitutional thought in the few years before the dissolution in 1806 came in the attempt to redefine the Empire as a simple confederation—a *Staatenbund*—in which the relationship between head an members, as well as between the members themselves, was explicitly predicated on the full sovereignty of each and all. As proposed by someone like Karl Zachariae, this formula, though radically different from those of all older theorists (including Hegel and the author of *Critique of the German Imperial Constitution,* who in spite of their own unusual ideas persisted in seeing the Empire as a single state, albeit an extremely deficient and degenerated one), was nonetheless intended to preserve a German unity by emphasizing the continued cooperation between the German states that might be possible if only the basis of their association were brought into a realistic perspective. Still, this beneficent intent could not obscure the basic message of Zachariae's work: That the old Empire was now structurally and politically dead.

For many other people, the Final Recess also pronounced the demise of the Empire in another and even more profound sense. To those for whom the Empire had stood as a shining example of the embodiment of morality in law on a grand scale, the ruthless elimination of scores of the ancient territories and jurisdictions within the Empire represented more than just the coerced results of an unsuccessful war; it represented the destruction of the very ideals the imperial state was supposed to typify and serve. For them, the Empire in the name of sheer political expediency had killed its own soul, a spirit of justice and freedom that had ennobled the peoples of Germany above others and which had served their continual spiritual self-perfection. Beneath all the voluminous verbiage and the obviously self-serving character of much of the debate over the extinction of the ecclesiastical states, the Imperial Cities, and the knightly territories, there is a strong and unmistakable current of righteous indignation at the arbitrary removal of rights long since sanctioned by both law and common observance, and a genuine feeling that in an ethical sense the Empire had flawed itself fatally in the Final Recess—that the moral basis of its claim to existence, the only basis on which it could hope to survive in a world where its power no longer counted, was now gone. The Empire, for many who lived within it, was not just a political organization, but also—and perhaps chiefly—a moral construct. Max Franz of Cologne was speaking for others besides the smaller princes when he wrote in 1790 that only morality could save them. It was almost the last vestiges of that morality which were driven from the moribund body of the Empire in 1803.

The Goethes, Schillers, and others like them were of course correct in their assertions that the German nation, its cultural achievements of the past unblemished by its recent misfortunes, would survive the political collapse of the Empire to carry on its spiritual mission in the future. A German nationality, after all, continued to exist even after its only common political raiment had been stripped from it. But the ethical content of German national political life, which the Empire, in spite of its practical deficiencies, had kept alive in theory virtually to the last moment of its existence, might not be as easy to revive in the future as would be the mere constitutional forms of unity. German national unity in this period was never seen as a goal in itself, but at most as an instrument for the defense and propagation of higher values which were universally human in character. But it was power that had in the end defeated that unity, and—as the growing concentration of publicists on practical political questions in the last decade or so of the Empire's existence suggested—power was henceforth likely to play a much larger role in defining both the possibilities for and the purposes of any future German national state. In the struggles of the last years of the Empire which for many Germans had taken on the increasingly clarified sense of a confrontation between *Macht* and *Recht*, *Macht* had, for the moment, won.

The lesson was not entirely lost on the Germans. To be sure, *Recht* was not dead in the Germany which survived the imperial collapse. Far from it; its territories were filled with people in whose minds the long traditions and the ethical ideals of the imperial legal order had taken root. It must not be forgotten that the imperial *Rechtsordnung* was also an *Advokatenordnung*; thousands upon thousands of people acting as ministers, officials, bureaucrats, professors, and in private occupations all over Germany had been trained in the discipline of imperial public law which set a very high value on the concept of a freedom defined by law. The influence of this idea, especially in the "third Germany," was to make itself felt quite powerfully in the growing liberalism of the first half of the nineteenth century. But deprived as it was of a national base, the concept of *Recht* had largely retreated to the territories. Neither the national nor the imperial ideal in Germany, for their part, would ever again be quite as free of the corruptive aspects of the concept of power as was the vision of the Empire cherished by the Mosers, the Wielands, and even the Dalbergs and Carl Augusts, not to mention the vast majority of the teachers of German public law.

At the moment of Francis II's abdication in 1806, Johann Gottfried Pahl had sounded a warning about some of the potential dangers awaiting the nation that lost its identity as a state. While he insisted that man becomes nearly everything he is through the state, even Pahl, perhaps, did not adequately appreciate the contributions the Empire as a state had made to the shaping of fundamental political attitudes among the Germans, nor the effects its extinction could have in removing the most important national institutional buttresses of the high ethical ideals with which those attitudes were invested. The German national spirit, deprived of the last realities of the formula *Kaiser und Reich,* was now forced to seek another motto. The one it eventually found and embraced—*Deutschland über Alles* —was a fatal choice; it had not only a different sound, but a different moral content as well, with the most fateful results for Germany as a state and as a nation. The imperial patriots of the last years of the Empire would not have liked nor even understood this phrase, with which the German national anthem until after World War II began. Undoubtedly more just and appropriate to their way of thinking are the words with which the third and presently official verse of that anthem begins: "Unity and justice and freedom for the German fatherland." But it was the tragedy of the Holy Roman Empire that the definitions of the justice and freedom it stood for forbade even its most ardent admirers from so much as desiring the kind and degree of unity without which the structure itself could no longer be maintained against its foreign and domestic enemies. The dilemma was simply that the very benefits conferred by the imperial nexus—its raison d'être—were incompatible with the means required to save it. Recognized here and there as a dilemma, it was never resolved.

Finally, however, one obvious but important fact should be emphasized. The Empire was not ended by Germans. They had weakened its ability to act as a single state, they had rendered its constitutional organs increasingly ineffective, they had deliberately acted contrary to their own understanding of the law and the imperial constitution, and they had even gone outside the Empire itself to seek help in their illicit acts. But the Empire was brought to an end by a Frenchman from whose dictates there was simply no escape in a militarily prostrate Germany. The formation of the Confederation of the Rhine, as well as the secession of its members from the Empire, resulted from his express command, as did the abdication of the imperial crown by Francis II. There were many reasons for the German princes and others to want the Empire continuously redefined in the various different ways that would be conformable to their individual interests, and, in particular, in ways that avoided confusing the Habsburg dynasty with the Empire. But there were few who wanted it dead, and even they wanted it so only after it had become fully comatose. For most, the Empire not only represented the larger framework that gave them their place in space and defined them politically through its web of complex interactions, but it was also their point of reference for locating themselves in time and history. They could hardly conceive or speak of themselves, even to defy the Empire, except in terms of the Empire. This consciousness of an irrevocable and indefeasible participation in something larger than themselves remained with the Germans who survived the collapse of the imperial structure. In this sense, the Holy Roman Empire had fulfilled a German national need and a German national mission to the very end.

Notes

INTRODUCTION

1. The final part of the title, however, as it came into existence in the fifteenth century, was intended neither to embrace all those who spoke German, nor to limit the Empire to German-speaking peoples alone, but simply to stake the formal claim of the German kings to the imperial title, and thus to anchor German leadership of the entire *imperium*. Ernst Rudolf Huber, *Deutsche Verfassungsgeschichte seit 1789. Band I: Reform und Restauration 1789 bis 1830* (Stuttgart, 1957), pp. 3-4.

2. Hanns Gross, *Empire and Sovereignty: A History of the Public Law Literature in the Holy Roman Empire, 1599-1804* (Chicago, 1973).

3. G. P. Gooch, *Germany and the French Revolution* (London, 1920; reprinted, New York, 1966), p. 516.

4. Klaus Epstein, *The Genesis of German Conservatism* (Princeton, 1966), p. 596.

CHAPTER ONE

1. Treatments of the imperial constitution in the eighteenth century are numerous, but the modern reader is perhaps best referred to Conrad Bornhak, *Deutsche Verfassungsgeschichte vom Westfälischen Frieden an* (Stuttgart, 1934), esp. pp. 46-134; Karl Otmar Freiherr von Aretin, *Heiliges Römisches Reich, 1776-1806: Reichsverfassung und Staatssouveränität*, 2 vols. (Wiesbaden, 1967), I, 7-109; and to relevant sections of Hellmuth Rössler and Günther Franz, *Sachwörterbuch zur deutschen Geschichte*, 2 vols. (Munich, 1958), esp. vol. II, where detailed summaries of the nature and history of the institutions of the Empire can be found under headings beginning with the prefix *Reichs-* (e.g., *Reichskrieg, Reichsstädte, Reichstag*). Among a variety of older works, Johann Stephan Pütter, *Historische Entwickelung der heutigen Staatsverfassung des Teutschen Reichs*, 3 vols. (Göttingen, 1786-87) is still useful.

2. As suggested above, the same was not so true of the ecclesiastical states, where the unique combination of episcopal and princely power in the person of the ruler lent special weight to religious considerations. The specter of secularization, in particular, made the balance of Protestant versus Catholic states in the Empire of great concern to the ecclesiastical princes.

3. The number of territories formally listed as independent for purposes of certain imperial financial and military obligations sank from 405 in 1521 to 314 in 1780. Aretin, *Heiliges Römisches Reich*, I, 69.

4. See below, pp. 26–32, for a more detailed discussion of the Aulic Council.

5. See below, pp. 32–35, for a more detailed discussion of the Circles.

6. One of the largest employers was Prussia under Frederick II. In Franconia, there was not a single family of the imperial nobility that did not have some members in Prussian military service at the outbreak of the Seven Years' War in 1756. Heinrich Müller, *Der letzte Kampf der Reichsritterschaft um ihre Selbstständigkeit (1790–1815)* (Berlin, 1910), p. 33.

7. Employment by a secular prince was recognized as essentially incompatible with the immediate status of the imperial nobility, and led to the establishment of a rule that cantonal Directors and Councillors could not accept such employment. An impossible rule to observe in practice, it proved unable to prevent continued conflicts of interest. Ibid.

CHAPTER TWO

1. Bornhak, *Deutsche Verfassungsgeschichte*, pp. 46–54.

2. The exception was the election of the Bavarian Wittelsbach Charles VII, who reigned from 1742 to 1745. His successor, Francis I (1745–65), though not a Habsburg, was the husband of Maria Theresia, who governed the Habsburg hereditary lands, but who as a woman was ineligible for the imperial office. At Francis' death, their son Joseph assumed the emperorship and was admitted to coregency of the Habsburg lands by his mother, thus reestablishing the formal connection between the Habsburg family and the imperial crown.

3. Bornhak, *Deutsche Verfassungsgeschichte*, p. 68.

4. Unlike his predecessors, Emperor Joseph II was as little sensitive to this political fact of life as he was to many others, and helped to defeat his own imperial policies by resurrecting certain of these practices which long disuse had effectively deprived of legal validity.

5. Here, as elsewhere, the peculiar history of the Empire had produced some illogical arrangements. Thus, both Austria and Burgundy, though secular principalities, had seats on the spiritual, not the temporal bench.

6. Aretin, *Heiliges Römisches Reich*, I, 66–67.

7. As suggested below on pp. 21–22, this was a problem that afflicted the entire Diet. It stemmed partly from a lack of interest and partly from parsimony. The Electors, for reasons having to do with their own position in the Empire, normally saw to it that they were permanently represented, usually by men of considerable ability who possessed a detailed and sophisticated knowledge of the imperial constitution. The same thing was true of some of the other larger secular and ecclesiastical princes. Aretin has remarked that the deliberations of the Diet required such a degree of juristic knowledge that inexperienced or unknowledgeable representatives would simply not have been able to handle them: "If an important member of the Empire had sent an insignificant representative to Regensburg, he would not only have lost his influence at the Diet, but largely in the Empire as well." Ibid., p. 55. While crisis situations could result in a sudden and considerable increase in the number of delegates at any of the councils, the number seems to have hovered around twenty for the one-hundred-vote Council of Princes, while it was quite usual for fewer than half of the Imperial Cities to be represented in any way in their council. It was a common practice not only for the Cities but also for smaller principalities to commission some citizen of the city of Regensburg, usually a lawyer, to represent their interests at the Diet for a small fee. It was equally common for one individual to represent several such clients. Ibid., pp. 54–55, 66, 68.

8. Another of the irrationalities of the imperial constitution becomes apparent

in the fact that a ruler's conversion to the other faith not only did not have to result in his expulsion from the *corpus* to which his territory had earlier belonged, but usually did not. At one time or another, and for varying periods, several important Protestant princes converted to Catholicism, but in only one case did this result in a departure from the *corpus evangelicorum* (the Elector Palatine after 1685). One major conversion was that of the Elector of Saxony in 1697. His ancestors had traditionally headed the Directory of the Protestant *corpus*, and indeed had been the leaders of the whole Protestant party in the Empire since the days of the Reformation. For reasons of prestige, and to the chagrin of some other Protestant Estates, the Saxon ruler refused to give up the directorship of the Protestant body even after his conversion. His own Privy Council, however, forced him to abdicate to it the conduct of policy relative to the Empire, so that the government of Saxony, as distinct from its ruler, remained bound to the Protestants. Much the same kind of compromise was arranged within the governments of other rulers who converted to Catholicism. The de facto leadership of the *corpus evangelicorum* in the eighteenth century rested with Brandenburg, at least until the second half of the reign of Frederick II, when he found political advantage in a certain degree of neutrality and thus increasingly tended to abdicate this leadership to the Saxon delegates once again.

9. Epstein, *Genesis*, p. 241.

10. A list of the territories which enjoyed the *privilegium de non appellando* can be found in Bornhak, *Deutsche Verfassungsgeschichte*, pp. 116–117, and Rössler and Franz, *Sachwörterbuch*, I, 32.

11. Aretin, *Heiliges Römisches Reich*, I, 100–101. Figures cited by Aretin would indicate that the number of cases appealed from verdicts of the supreme courts to the Diet between 1663 and 1788 was 144, divided in origin almost equally between the Cameral Tribunal and the Aulic Council. Ibid., p. 101, n. 452. While this number may not seem excessive, being just over one case a year on the average, in contrast to the 200–300 cases initiated each year at the Cameral Tribunal and the 2,000–3,000 annually at the Aulic Council, it must be remembered that the slowest judicial proceedings in the whole Empire were those of the Diet sitting as a court. Subject as it was to the myriad immediate political and religious crosscurrents of its complex membership, the Diet sometimes abandoned its ordinary business for months on end in this often trivial litigation.

12. This result was particularly noticeable among larger princes who through multiple rulership had membership in more than one Circle, and therefore had a divided interest. Ibid., p. 75.

13. There were really two distinct legal bases for the declaration of an imperial war (*Reichskrieg*). One was in execution of the judgment of the Imperial Cameral Tribunal or the Aulic Council against an internal breach of the peace by some member or members of the Empire when the coercive power of the Circle to which this execution would otherwise be entrusted was inadequate to the task. The other was the more familiar response to violation of the rights or boundaries of the Empire by another state. After 1648, the conduct of either kind of war by the Emperor on behalf of the Empire required the agreement of the Diet.

14. A distinction, awkward to make in translation from the German, must always be made between the *Reichsarmee* (the army of the Empire) and the *kaiserliche Armee* or *kaiserliches Heer* (the army of the Emperor, with both imperial and dynastic attributes). The temptation to translate both as "imperial army" must be avoided, because the difference is a crucial one. In the eighteenth century, Germans often referred to the former as the *Kreisarmee* or the *Kreistruppen* (Circle army or Circle troops) to carry the distinction.

15. Max Jähns, "Zur Geschichte der Kriegsverfassung des Deutschen Reiches," *Preussische Jahrbücher*, 39 (1877), 467–468.

16. Rössler and Franz, *Sachwörterbuch*, II, 1002.

17. Jähns, "Zur Geschichte," p. 463.

CHAPTER THREE

1. Severinus de Monzambano [Samuel Pufendorf], *Ueber die Verfassung des deutschen Reiches*, trans. Harry Bresslau (Berlin, 1922), p. 94.

2. See Gross, *Empire and Sovereignty*, pp. 315–326; Ulrich Schlie, *Johann Stephan Pütters Reichsbegriff* (Göttingen, 1961), p. 42.

3. This is what Aretin means when he speaks of Pufendorf as cleaving to the unchangeability of the imperial constitution in his critique of the Empire, seeing "as the real task of the Empire not so much the cultivation of power as the organization of the protection of rights (*die Organisation des Rechtsschutzes*)." *Heiliges Römisches Reich*, I, 10.

4. Johann Jacob Moser, *Von Teutschland und dessen Staats-Verfassung überhaupt* (Stuttgart, 1766), pp. 546, 550.

5. Ibid., p. 549.

6. Reinhard Rürup, *Johann Jacob Moser: Pietismus und Reform* (Weisbaden, 1965), p. 145.

7. Gross, *Empire and Sovereignty*, esp. pp. 405–409.

8. Rürup, *Johann Jacob Moser*, pp. 146–149.

9. Unlike Moser, Pütter seems to have lacked a real interest in politics; one author has even suggested that he lacked not only the ability but also the courage to so much as consider political reform of the Empire. Arnold Berney, "Reichstradition and Nationalstaatsgedanke (1789–1815)," *Historische Zeitschrift*, 140 (1929), 69.

10. See, for example, Pütter's anonymously published *Patriotische Abbildung des heutigen Zustandes beyder höchsten Reichsgerichte*, etc. (Frankfurt and Leipzig, 1751).

11. Schlie, *Pütters Reichsbegriff*, pp. 5, 8. See also Gross, *Empire and Sovereignty*, esp. pp. 442–455.

12. Aretin, *Heiliges Römisches Reich*, I, 11.

13. Aretin again contributes the word. Ibid., p. 9.

CHAPTER FOUR

1. Perhaps symbolic of this relatively rapid shift towards dynastic self-interest and away from the old German (and world) imperial mission was one notable difference in the decoration which was planned by Charles VI (1711–40) for his expansion of the palace of Klosterneuburg, which was never carried out, and that actually executed by Maria Theresia in the construction of her palace of Schönbrunn. Charles had planned to affix a representation of the crown of the Empire on the central cupola of Klosterneuburg, and to flank it—in second place, as it were—with Habsburg dynastic crowns, including that of Spain. Schönbrunn, however, was adorned by the Austrian crown alone. Heinrich Ritter von Srbik, *Deutsche Einheit: Idee und Wirklichkeit vom Heiligen Reich bis Königgrätz*, 4 vols. (Munich, 1940–42), I, 111.

2. Aretin, *Heiliges Römisches Reich*, I, 13. For more detail on Beck's teachings, see Hermann Conrad, ed., *Recht und Verfassung des Reiches in der Zeit Maria Theresias: die Vorträge zum Unterricht des Erzherzogs Joseph in Natur- und Völkerrecht sowie im deutschen Staats- und Lehnrecht* (Cologne and Opladen, 1964).

3. Aretin, *Heiliges Römisches Reich*, I, 5.

4. Hans-Heinrich Kaufmann, *Friedrich Carl von Moser als Politiker und Publizist (vornehmlich in den Jahren 1750–1770)* (Darmstadt, 1931), p. 101.

5. Bruno Renner, *Die nationalen Einigungsbestrebungen Friedrich Carl von Mosers (1765–1767)* (Dissertation, Königsberg, 1919), pp. 12–13.

6. Ibid., pp. 14–17.

7. Kaufmann, *Friedrich Carl von Moser*, pp. 109–113.

8. Ibid., pp. 117–119; Renner, *Einigungsbestrebungen*, pp. 28–30. Moser reprinted this pamphlet in his own journal in 1792; see below, pp. 139–140.

9. Kaufmann, *Friedrich Carl von Moser*, p. 125.

10. [Friedrich Carl von Moser], *Von dem Deutschen national-Geist* (n.p., 1765), pp. 5–6, 10–12, 19–25, 29–32.

11. Ibid., pp. 33–34, 49, 54–60.

12. Ibid., pp. 77–78, 99–103.

13. Ibid., p. 73.

14. Justus Möser, review of F. C. von Moser's *Von dem Deutschen national-Geist*, in *Justus Mösers sämmtliche Werke*, new edition, ed. B. R. Abeken, 10 vols. in 7 (Berlin, 1842–43), IX, 240–243. The review was first published in the *Allgemeine Deutsche Bibliothek* in 1766.

15. See Wolfgang Zorn, "Reichs- und Freiheitsgedanken in der deutschen Publizistik des ausgehenden achtzehnten Jahrhunderts," *Darstellungen und Quellen zur Geschichte der deutschen Einheitsbewegung im neunzehnten und zwanzigsten Jahrhundert*, ed. Paul Wentzcke, II (Heidelberg, 1959), p. 27. See also Renner, *Einigungsbestrebungen*, pp. 47–49.

16. [Johann Jakob Bülau], *Noch etwas zum Deutschen Nationalgeist* (Lindau am Bodensee, 1766), p. 214. See also Renner, *Einigungsbestrebungen*, pp. 51–52; and Zorn, "Reichs- und Freiheitsgedanken," p. 30.

17. Renner, *Einigungsbestrebungen*, p. 61.

18. [Bülau], *Noch etwas*, p. 198.

19. Zorn, "Reichs- und Freiheitsgedanken," pp. 28–29; Renner, *Einigungsbestrebungen*, p. 50. While it is true, as Zorn points out, that Creutz in the end agreed with Moser on the need to preserve the unity of the imperial system under a single supreme head, he took this position as the representative of a small state who believed that the security of the lesser Estates depended on an imperial power strong enough to safeguard the status quo against the ambitions of the larger territories, but not so strong as to be able to challenge existing conditions. Hence his opposition to what appeared to be Moser's advocacy of something approaching an imperial unitary state.

20. This was the tone of a rather favorable review that appeared in the *Göttinger gelehrte Anzeigen* in 1765, cited by Renner, *Einigungsbestrebungen*, p. 59. It should be noted that the University of Göttingen was the most prestigious and widely known exponent of *Reichsrecht* among all the institutions of higher learning in Germany, and was so recognized by Moser himself; see his *Von dem Deutschen national-Geist*, pp. 23–24.

21. Renner, *Einigungsbestrebungen*, p. 70.

22. [Friedrich Carl von Moser], *Was ist: gut Kayserlich, und: nicht gut Kayserlich?* Second improved edition (Vaterland, 1766), pp. 31–35, 74–86.

23. Ibid., pp. 178–188, 213–214.

24. Ibid., pp. 220–223.

25. Ibid., pp. 287–297.

26. Such was the argument of the anonymously published book of Johann Heinrich Eberhard, *Freie Gedanken über einige der neuesten Staats-Streitigkeiten* ([Frankfurt], 1767). Eberhard was at the time a young professor of law and moral philosophy in Zerbst.

27. Eberhard's reviews of 1769 are summarized in Zorn, "Reichs- und Freiheitsgedanken," pp. 32–33, and in Renner, *Einigungsbestrebungen*, p. 71.

28. [Friedrich Carl von Moser], *Patriotische Briefe* (n.p., 1767), pp. 24–35.

29. Moser did not deny that the government of the Empire was cumbersome and extremely slow in comparison with that of other states, but he regarded this as a necessary and therefore acceptable result of the praiseworthy attempt to protect liberty, the "mainspring" of the constitution. "To be sure," he wrote, "we have but a single spring in the clock of our constitution, but so many wheels have to be wound up first, [and] so many weights attached before it can start, that it naturally runs slower by half a day than all others in Europe." Ibid., p. 56.

30. Ibid., pp. 257–258.

31. Ibid., p. 231.
32. Ibid., pp. 263, 272, 386–387.
33. Ibid., pp. 62–65.
34. Ibid., p. 416.
35. Renner, *Einigungsbestrebungen*, p. 93.
36. Creutz, for example, was downright nasty in a few of his comments, and seems to have carried his personal animosity toward Johann Jacob Moser over to his son. Ibid., pp. 89–90, 95.
37. Kaufmann, *Friedrich Carl von Moser*, pp. 140–144.
38. Ibid., pp. 144–146.
39. Renner, *Einigungsbestrebungen*, pp. 93–94. The quotation is from 1790.

CHAPTER FIVE

1. For this largely narrative chapter on the background, formation, and history of the League of Princes, I have relied chiefly on Aretin, *Heiliges Römisches Reich*, I; Paul P. Bernard, *Joseph II and Bavaria: Two Eighteenth-Century Attempts at German Unification* (The Hague, 1965); Herta Mittelberger, *Johann Christian Freiherr von Hofenfels, 1744-1787* (Munich, 1934); Leopold von Ranke, *Die deutschen Mächte und der Fürstenbund. Deutsche Geschichte von 1780 bis 1790* (Leipzig, 1875); and two works by Wilhelm Adolf Schmidt, *Preussens deutsche Politik*, second edition (Berlin, 1850), and *Geschichte der preussisch-deutschen Unionsbestrebungen seit der Zeit Friedrich's des Grossen*, 1 vol. in 2 (Berlin, 1851).
2. Bernard, *Joseph II and Bavaria*, pp. 11, 15.
3. Ibid., p. 21.
4. Aretin, *Heiliges Römisches Reich*, I, 114.

CHAPTER SIX

1. *Allgemeine deutsche Biographie*, herausgegeben durch die Historische Commission bei der königlichen Akademie der Wissenschaften, 56 vols. (Leipzig, 1875–1912), V, 297–299.
2. At the time of the publication of his attack on the League (1785), Otto von Gemmingen (1755–1836) was a political agent of the Margrave of Baden in Vienna. A strong believer in the Empire, he always favored Austria against Prussia in his evaluation of their intentions with respect to the Empire, and from 1799–1805 he served as Baden's ambassador to Austria. Associated with freemasonry in Vienna, he became rather well known as a devotee of the Enlightenment, a dramatist, and a commentator on social problems. *Neue deutsche Biographie*, herausgegeben von der Historischen Kommission bei der Bayerischen Akademie der Wissenschaften, 9 vols. and continuing (Berlin, 1953–), VI, 179–180. His critical commentary on the League, *Ueber die königl. Preussische Assoziazion zu Erhaltung des Reichssystems* (Deutschland, 1785), though supposedly published in "Germany," was actually printed in Vienna. See Schmidt, *Preussens deutsche Politik*, pp. 55–56.
3. Christian Wilhelm Dohm, *Ueber den deutschen Fürstenbund*, second edition (?) (Berlin, [December] 1785), pp. 135, n., 34, 37.
4. Anon., "Ueber den deutschen Fürstenbund," etc., *Ephemeriden der Menschheit*, Drittes Stück (March, 1786), 300.
5. C. G. Rössig, *Ueber deutsches Staatsinteresse, Ländertausch, und das Schuzbündnis deutscher Fürsten. Zur Widerlegung der Schrift des Freyherrn von Gemmingen* (Leipzig, 1786), pp. 73–74.
6. Anon., "Gedanken eines Cosmopoliten über den deutschen Fürstenbund," *Litteratur und Völkerkunde*, Jahrgang 4, Band 7 (1786), p. 1028.
7. Müller (1752–1809), though Swiss, studied and spent most of his life in Germany, and always showed a lively interest in the political situation of Germany

and Europe. This defense of the League of Princes immediately won him a position with the government of Electoral Mainz. He later served in both Austrian and Prussian civil services at different times.

8. Johannes von Müller, *Darstellung des Fürstenbundes*, in *Sämmtliche Werke*, ed. Johann Georg Müller, 27 vols. (Stuttgart and Tübingen, 1810–19), XXIV, 89–92, 226–228.

9. Pütter ventured about as far into the arena of practical politics as he ever did in a brief comment in a work of 1787, where he expressed his approval of the League, whose purpose was only "the preservation of the hitherto existing constitution." Pütter, *Historische Entwickelung*, III, 212.

10. Dohm, *Fürstenbund*, pp. 15–16, 16–27. Johann Jacob Moser expressed the same general idea very simply: "Strength cannot rest." [Johann Jacob Moser], *Betrachtungen über das Gleichgewicht von Europa und Teutschland in Rücksicht auf den Umtausch von Baiern* (Frankfurt and Leipzig, 1785), p. 3.

11. Dohm, *Fürstenbund*, pp. 28–29.

12. [J. J. Moser], *Betrachtungen*, pp. 10–11.

13. Dohm, *Fürstenbund*, pp. 40–42.

14. See, for example, the absurdly low value placed on the Austrian Netherlands by the anonymous pro-League author of *Freymüthige Anmerkungen zur Schrift des Freyherrn Otto von Gemmingen über die Königl. Preussische Association zu Erhaltung des Reichssystems* (Teutschland, 1785), p. 32, n., who estimated their population at 1,200,000 and their annual tax yield at between two and three million florins, with corresponding figures for the Bavarian lands of 1,300,000 people and seven million florins. Pro-Austrian publicists denied such figures, as in J.R.R.v.P. [Johann von Pacassi], *Betrachtung über die Berliner Beantwortung der Königlich Preussischen Association: Darin die Stärke von Preussen gezeigt, und die eigentlichen Absichten des Berliner Kabinets unter dem Scheine der grosmütigen Beschüzung der Rechte Deutschlands aufgesucht werden* (Munich, 1786), p. 5. The Austrian view that Karl Theodor would be getting a good bargain, at least from a statistical point of view, seems to have been an honest one; certainly their in-house information on the current economic value of Bavaria, based on careful estimates of their representatives in Munich, was anything but encouraging. See Aretin, *Heiliges Römisches Reich*, I, 115. The Austrian case is strengthened by the recent estimates of Hellmuth Rössler, which put the population of Bavaria at 1,400,000 and its tax yield (after subtraction of debts) at 3,400,000 florins, against the Netherlands' 1,800,000 people and 7,600,000 florins of governmental income. Rössler and Franz, *Sachwörterbuch*, I, 307.

15. This appears to be the somewhat tortuous line taken by the anonymous author of *Bemerkungen bey Gelegenheit des neuesten Fürstenbundes im Deutschen Reiche* (Berlin and Leipzig, 1786), pp. 16–17.

16. [J. J. Moser], *Betrachtungen*, pp. 10–12.

17. Dohm, *Fürstenbund*, pp. 30–33. The fact that France and Austria were formally allied at this time was considered by most writers as of too little importance even to mention. The alliance seems to have been regarded as unnatural, and unlikely to withstand any real pressure, since the permanent interests of France as a European great power and as a guarantor of the Peace of Westphalia were clearly more hostile than friendly to Austria. French reservations about the exchange project were known, and seemed to prove the point.

18. [J. J. Moser], *Betrachtungen*, pp. 3–4, 8.

19. Dohm, *Fürstenbund*, p. 2.

20. Paul Stauffer, *Die Idee des europäischen Gleichgewichts im politischen Denken Johannes von Müllers* (Basel and Stuttgart, 1960), pp. 38–39.

21. J. von Müller, *Darstellung*, pp. 83–86.

22. Stauffer, *Die Idee*, p. 42.

23. J. von Müller, *Darstellung*, pp. 64, 188–189. See also Stauffer, *Die Idee*, p. 42.

24. Johannes von Müller, "Zweierlei Freiheit," *Sämmtliche Werke*, XXIV, 1–7. This piece first appeared in the *Deutsches Museum* in July 1786.

25. J. von Müller, *Darstellung*, pp. 28–29, 82.

26. Müller's paranoia about Austrian designs on Switzerland, on the other hand, led him at one point to suggest inclusion of the Swiss cantons in the League, a proposal that was actually discussed by Carl August of Weimar and Frederick William II in August of 1787, but rejected. Ulrich Crämer, *Carl August von Weimar und der Deutsche Fürstenbund, 1783–1790* (Wiesbaden, 1961), p. 73.

27. Stauffer, *Die Idee*, p. 43.

28. In this argument, Müller deviated slightly from some other opponents of the Bavarian exchange who believed that the weakness of the new kingdom, by inviting French attack, would make war more likely. See, for example, Anon., *Freymüthige Anmerkungen*, p. 39, note m. Agreeing on the point of its weakness, Müller nevertheless believed that Burgundy could protect itself by diplomatic means alone.

29. J. von Müller, *Darstellung*, pp. 196–201.

30. J.R.R.v.P. [J. von Pacassi], *Betrachtung*, pp. 9, 12–13.

31. Fairly typical was the charge that if the Emperors had long ago given up their ambitions in Italy, and had not built so many "expansionist castles in the air" (*Luftschlösser zur Vergrösserung*), they would not have been led into so many unjustified and harmful wars, and would have been able to devote more of their efforts to the improvement and enlightenment of Germany. J. E*** zu M***, *Sendschreiben des Hofammerkanzlei-Dieners J. E*** zu M*** an Herrn Otto von Gemmingen Reichsfreiherrn, als eine einfältige Antwort auf desselben Gedanken über die Königliche Preussische Assoziation zu Erhaltung des Reichssystems* (n.p., 1786), p. 17.

32. Gemmingen, *Ueber die . . . Assoziazion*, pp. 6–8.

33. Christoph Ludwig Pfeiffer, *Was ist teutsche Volksfreiheit, teutsche Reichsfreiheit, und teutscher Fürstenbund? Eine teutschpatriotisch-staatsrechtliche Betrachtung* (n.p. [Heilbronn?], 1786), pp. 58–60. See also Zorn, "Reichs- und Freiheitsgedanken," p. 56.

34. Just as Dohm had earlier recognized the advantage of presenting Prussia as only a medium-sized power, so did Prussia's opponents see the benefit of insisting that she was as much a great power as Austria. Johann von Pacassi went even further, suggesting that whereas Austrian power had once stood in a ratio of 3:2 to that of Prussia, the latter's Polish acquisitions of 1772 had altered the ratio to 6:5 in her favor. *Betrachtung*, pp. 19–20, 22.

35. See Max Braubach, *Maria Theresias jüngster Sohn Max Franz, letzter Kurfürst von Köln und Fürstbischof von Münster* (Vienna and Munich, 1961), pp. 212–217.

36. See reports of C. W. Dohm to Frederick and to Hertzberg, both of July 20, 1785, in Willy Andreas, ed., *Politischer Briefwechsel des Herzogs und Grossherzogs Carl August von Weimar*, 2 vols. (Stuttgart, 1954–58), I, 152–155.

37. Pfeiffer, *Was ist teutsche Volksfreiheit*, pp. 53–54.

38. Gemmingen, *Ueber die . . . Assoziazion*, p. 5.

39. See Aretin, *Heiliges Römisches Reich*, I, 121–122, where it is also pointed out that the delicacy of the term first became obvious during the War of the Bavarian Succession. Freiherr von Borié, Austria's chief representative at the Imperial Diet, found himself compelled to protest to Kaunitz the latter's reliance on this principle in attempting to explain Austria's position to her own ambassadors in the Empire. Borié felt that it derogated from the position of the Emperor and conceded to Prussia something that did not in fact belong to her. When at about the same time Prussia began to emphasize the same term as justification for her position, she was immediately reproached by her staunchest allies, Hanover and Hessen-Kassel, who wanted to avoid the suggestion of polarity and consequent implication of their dependence on Berlin contained in the principle. A few years later,

in 1783, the Austrian statesman Count Trauttmansdorf penned his sentiments on the term: "The word balance in the Empire, as one immediately thinks back to its constitution . . . , is a monstrous expression, since indeed head and members must work for the attainment of the common good with united forces, yet with full sub-ordination of the latter to the former, between which no balance can exist." Ibid., II, 88.

40. Gemmingen, *Ueber die . . . Assoziazion*, pp. 17–18.

41. [Friedrich Wernhard Grimm], *Umfang und Gränzen des Reichsständischen Bündnissrechts nach dem wahren Sinn der Reichsgeseze* (Berlin, 1786), esp. pp. 59–62.

42. Anon., *Politische Betrachtungen und Nachrichten*, 2 vols. (n.p., 1785), I, 24–41.

43. Gemmingen, *Ueber die . . . Assoziazion*, p. 11.

44. J. E*** zu M***, *Sendschreiben*, p. 26. Pfeiffer's views, from his Der *teutsche Fürstenbund: Noli me tangere!* of 1786, are summarized in Zorn, "Reichs-und Freiheitsgedanken," pp. 56–57.

45. Schmidt, *Preussens deutsche Politik*, p. 60. Schmidt suggests that the League became all but moribund at the moment of Frederick's death, because his less than able successor simply did not know what to do with it. He also argues that the original agreement of the three Electors of July 23, 1785, aimed at controlling imperial elections in the future, and even that the three were prepared to accept an extinction of the imperial office if it could not be continued in the interest of the League. For Schmidt, one active purpose of the League was therefore nothing less than that of supplanting the Empire—of reconstituting the German system under Prussian guidance. Ibid., p. 50. The evidence cited by Schmidt for such a far-reaching conclusion is flimsy, however, and is not supported by any discussions of the Electors subsequent to the formation of the League.

46. See his letter of February 10, 1779, to Duke Ernst of Sachsen-Gotha in W. Andreas, ed., *Politischer Briefwechsel*, I, 63–64.

47. See especially Carl August's long and candid letter of complaint of February 20, 1786, to Count Görtz, his friend and former tutor, who was at this time Bran-denburg's representative at the Imperial Diet. Ibid., pp. 222–225.

48. Ibid., p. 383.

49. Ranke, *Die deutschen Mächte*, pp. 275–276.

50. These exchanges can be traced in W. Andreas, ed., *Politischer Briefwechsel*, I, 293–302.

51. Precisely this position was expressed by the Electoral Saxon minister Loeben in a letter to Carl August of April 12, 1788. Loeben suggested that the individual territories of the Empire were the proper arena for improvement of laws. Here, every prince could ameliorate the lot of his subjects as he saw fit, without having to go through the wearisome process of a majority vote at the Imperial Diet, the ratifi-cation of the Emperor, and so on. The real object of the League, he insisted, was the preservation, not the improvement, of the imperial constitution, and any attempt to do the latter could lead to something worse than what now existed. Ibid., p. 480.

52. This was certainly not the intention of the reform-minded princes, whose correspondence makes it clear that the purpose of such a conference was simply that of reaching prior agreement on reform proposals in order to guarantee that they would be given serious attention when brought before the Diet. A memorandum of Karl von Dalberg of August 30, 1787, for example, contained a long shopping list of important reforms, all of which, however, were to be placed before deputa-tions of the Diet for study and action. This would in itself constitute a most impor-tant reform, according to Dalberg, simply because the Diet would thereby be raised to a new level of activity, through which the representatives would begin to acquire a better knowledge of the things that were of real importance to the nation. Indeed, all Germans, seeing that their Diet was finally busying itself with matters having to do with their welfare, would conceive a greater devotion to the entire constitution.

See Karl Freiherr von Beaulieu-Marconnay, *Karl von Dalberg und seine Zeit. Zur Biographie und Charakteristik des Fürsten Primas*, 2 vols. (Weimar, 1879), I, 353–363.

53. Ranke, *Die deutschen Mächte*, p. 281.

54. Letter to Carl August, December 27, 1788, in W. Andreas, ed., *Politischer Briefwechsel*, I, 507.

55. See the memorandum of the *Geheimes Kabinettsministerium* of January 31, 1788, and Frederick William II's instruction to Friedrich vom Stein of February 2, 1788. Ibid., pp. 422–423, 424–425.

56. See the letter of the Saxon minister Freiherr von Gutschmid to the Prussian Count Görtz of April 12, 1788. Ibid., pp. 479–480. The Saxon position was among the most timid and conservative of all the members, as indicated by Gutschmid's statement in this letter that not only improvement of the Empire but even defense of the existing constitution were matters that properly belonged before the Imperial Diet, and that only the presence of an immediate danger of the employment of unlawful force should justify a closer association of the allied courts. This came very close to an assertion that the League was, and ought to be, moribund.

57. J. von Müller, *Darstellung*, pp. 254–257.

58. Johannes von Müller, *Teutschlands Erwartungen vom Fürstenbunde*, in *Sämmtliche Werke*, ed. Johann Georg Müller, 27 vols. (Stuttgart and Tübingen, 1810–19), XXIV, 263–264.

59. Ibid., pp. 265, 276.

60. Ibid., pp. 274, 283.

61. Anon., *Etwas vom Patriotismus im deutschen Reiche. Von einem Deutschen mit deutscher Freiheit* (n.p., 1788), esp. pp. 10–11, 16–20, 146–147.

62. Anon., "Teutschland erwartet was recht ist. 1789," *Staatswissenschaftliche Zeitung*, 1 (1789), no. 6, pp. 41–48; no. 8, pp. 61–64; no. 9, pp. 65–72; no. 10, pp. 73–80. It is certainly no accident that criticism of the Electors and of the League appeared so closely linked in this article, since Electoral domination of the League was a commonly recognized fact.

63. Anon., *Betrachtungen über den deutschen Reichstag* (n.p., 1789), pp. 7–9, 14–16.

64. Christoph Ludwig Pfeiffer, *Die teutsche Reichsverwirrung im Grundrisse. Oder: die Staatsgebrechen des heiligen Römischen Reichs teutscher Nation* (Mannheim, 1787), pp. 30–31, 37–38.

CHAPTER SEVEN

1. Aretin points to the significance of Prussia's "return" to the Empire in consequence of the decision in 1785 to take on the role of an "anti-Emperor" which had been available to her since the Peace of Teschen. This new role meant, among other things, an observance of the political laws of the Empire that was a bit strange and uncomfortable for a state whose rise to greatness had been accomplished independently of the Empire. *Heiliges Römisches Reich*, I, 238.

2. Zorn, "Reichs- und Freiheitsgedanken," p. 58, while unable to supply an author for it, suggests from internal evidence that it was probably composed by someone with juristic training in the Duchy of Braunschweig. In the bibliography of his more recent work, on the other hand, Aretin ascribes it to Christoph Ludwig Pfeiffer. *Heiliges Römisches Reich*, II, 397. This appears improbable, however, unless one assumes that it was written almost wholly tongue-in-cheek, since its approach radically contradicts that taken by Pfeiffer in earlier writings.

3. Anon., *Warum soll Deutschland einen Kayser haben?* (n.p., 1787), pp. 6–31, 62–63.

4. Ibid., pp. 41–107 passim.

5. [Julius von Soden], *Teutschland muss einen Kaiser haben* (n.p., 1788), pp. 4–5.

6. Ibid., pp. 10, 14–19, 29.

7. Ibid., pp. 24–25, 28, 38.

8. Ibid., pp. 18, 32–33.

9. Ibid., p. 14.

10. The political machinations of the German courts in this and other events of the interregnum of 1790 is covered briefly but lucidly by Aretin, *Heiliges Römisches Reich*, I, 229–238.

11. A secret article of the original treaty of the League of Princes had provided for a cooperative attempt of the members to replace the Habsburgs with the House of Zweibrücken after the death of Karl Theodor raised that house to possession of the Palatinate-Bavarian inheritance. In 1790, of course, Karl Theodor was still very much alive, and some of the original signatories, especially Saxony, had come to have grave reservations about this provision in any case.

12. Anon., *Uber die Lage und Bedürfnisse des deutschen Reichs. Oder braucht Deutschland einen mächtigen Kaiser?* (n.p., 1790), pp. 12–13.

13. Ibid., pp. 13–16.

14. Ibid., pp. 15–16, 47.

15. Ibid., pp. 24–35.

16. Ibid., pp. 37–38.

17. Johann Traugott Plant, *Schon wieder ein Kaiser aus dem Oesterreichischem Hause? . . . oder freimüthige Aufklärung über die Kaiserwahl Leopolds II.* (n.p., 1790), pp. 21–22, 34, 59–73, 83–92.

18. Ibid., pp. 98–119.

19. Anon., *Uber die Lage*, p. 50.

20. F. D., *Ist die teutsche Kaiserkrone für das Haus Oesterreich wichtig? . . . freymüthig beantwortet von einem Patrioten* (Vaterland, 1790), pp. 9–13.

21. Plant, *Schon wieder*, pp. 120–174 passim.

22. [Johann Michael Schweighofer], *Unpartheyische Betrachtungen über die Vorrechte und Vortheile der Kaiserkrone* (n.p., 1790), pp. 8–9, 34–36, 47–48.

23. Judgments such as these can be found in [Karl Friedrich Freiherr von Kruse], *Freimüthige Betrachtungen über die Gesezgebung der Teutschen bey Gelegenheit der Wahl eines römischen Kaisers* (n.p. [Wiesbaden], 1790), pp. 24–41; F. D., *Ist die teutsche Kaiserkrone*, p. 8, n. 1; and Anon., *Ist es rathsam, den deutschen Kayser in der neuen Wahl-Capitulation noch mehr einzuschränken, als er es jetzt schon ist?* (Frankfurt and Leipzig, 1790), esp. pp. 4–8. Schweighofer's examination of the real as against the imagined benefits of the imperial crown was also stimulated, according to him, by noises from some quarters, going back to 1785, that the powers of the Emperor should be reduced at the next election. *Unpartheyische Betrachtungen*, p. 3.

24. Anon., *Ist es rathsam*, p. 8.

25. Kruse's life and career are treated in detail in the *Allgemeine deutsche Biographie*, XVII, 265–268.

26. [Kruse], *Freimüthige Betrachtungen*, pp. 40–41.

27. Ibid., pp. 42, 45–49.

28. Ibid., pp. 42–45.

29. Anon., *Betrachtungen über die Freiheit und Wolfarth des deutschen Reichs, und über die Mittel zu deren Erhaltung von einem Patrioten* (n.p., 1789), pp. 15–18.

30. Ibid., pp. 12–14, 29–31.

31. See above, esp. pp. 87–88.

32. Such fears were well founded. Before their solid front broke, the Electoral members of the League had contributed no less than one hundred of the total of 128 propositions originally put forward for addition to the Capitulation of 1790! Aretin, *Heiliges Römisches Reich*, I, 236–237.

33. [Kruse], *Freimüthige Betrachtungen*, pp. 5–8.

34. Summarized from *Die Verbindung des Reichsszepters mit dem Krummstab, eine politische Phantasie* (Regensburg, 1790) by Braubach, *Maria Theresias jüngster Sohn*, p. 211.

35. Quoted from an undated letter of Max Franz to Baron Schall, ibid., pp. 207–208.

CHAPTER EIGHT

1. Kaunitz' position that a reconciliation of the two powers had to mean Austria's recognition of full Prussian equality in the Empire, which was only a step away from the division of Germany into two spheres of influence or even two states, was widely shared as a fear by lesser princes. As other evidences of Austro-Prussian agreement became known, this concern mounted, and was well expressed by Franz Ludwig von Erthal, the Prince-Bishop of Würzburg, whose blunt comment in late 1791 was reported to Vienna by one of the Emperor's ambassadors in the Empire: "When Austria and Prussia are united, the end of the Empire has come." Aretin, *Heiliges Römisches Reich*, I, 241, 250, and 250, n. 36.

It was possible to put an optimistic construction on the Austro-Prussian agreement, of course, by emphasizing the great power this could confer on Germany with respect to external relations with other states. Wilhelm Ludwig Wekhrlin and Christian Daniel Friedrich Schubart, both editors of well-known journals, supposed in their comments on the Austro-Prussian rapprochement that the Empire could become the arbiter of Europe if it were ever truly united in purpose. Both, however, while unhappy about Germany's traditional role as a battlefield for other powers, also had reservations about the possible results of German preponderance in Europe. Schubart, in particular, was also worried about the domestic results. After pointing out the potential benefits of the alliance of the two courts as seen through the rose-colored glasses of "good souls," he wrote: "Other more profound and more cautious souls, however, also see in the future doleful results for the freedom of Germans: when the lion and the eagle are friends, then forest and heavens may tremble." Quoted in Zorn, "Reichs- und Freiheitsgedanken," p. 38. For more on Schubart and Wekhrlin, see Frederick Hertz, *The Development of the German Public Mind: A Social History of German Political Sentiments, Aspirations, and Ideas. Vol. II: The Age of Enlightenment* (London, 1962), pp. 404–408.

2. Among the more interesting of these writings was an article of 1780 by Christoph Martin Wieland, "Patriotischer Beytrag zu Deutschlands höchstem Flor, veranlasst durch einen im Jahr 1780 gedruckten Vorschlag dieses Nahmens," which appeared on pp. 90–102 of the April issue of his journal *Der teutsche Merkur*. Examining the effects of the principle of disunity which characterized the German constitution, he found a more or less exact balance between good and bad, and concluded with philosophical equanimity that while the German patriot ought to support the present constitution and contribute to its perfection according to his abilities, the destruction of this constitution would be compensated by the loss of its disadvantages and the acquisition of advantages from a new one, so that everything would work out evenly in the end.

3. The best general surveys of German public opinion and the Revolution are Jacques Droz, *L'Allemagne et la Révolution Française* (Paris, 1949) and Fritz Valjavec, *Die Entstehung der politischen Strömungen in Deutschland, 1770–1815* (Munich, 1951). See also the older but still useful G. P. Gooch, *Germany and the French Revolution*, and Adalbert Wahl, *Über die Nachwirkungen der französischen Revolution vornehmlich in Deutschland* (Stuttgart, 1939). Epstein, *Genesis*, also contributes valuable insights and information.

4. Christian Ernst Weisse, *Von den Vortheilen der teutschen Reichsverbindung. Nebst einem kleinen Beytrage zum Staatsrecht des Mittelalters, nach Anleitung der schwäbischen Dichter* (Leipzig, 1790), pp. vii–viii, 1.

5. Ibid., pp. 22–33, 41–43.

6. Ibid., pp. 64–67, 78, 106, 111, 131, 149–152, 171, 188–189.

7. Weisse, *Von den Vortheilen*, pp. 162, 199–200.

8. Carl Friedrich Häberlin, "Ueber die Güte der deutschen Staatsverfassung," *Deutsche Monatsschrift*, 1 (January-April, 1793), 8–9. This is a reprint of the original article which appeared in the *Braunschweigisches Magazin* in October 1792.

9. Ibid., pp. 11–23, 25–27.

10. Wilhelm von Humboldt, "Ideen zu einem Versuch, die Gränzen der Wirksamkeit des Staats zu bestimmen" (1792), in *Gesammelte Schriften*, ed. Albert Leitzmann, 17 vols. (Berlin, 1903–36), I, 134.

11. Ibid., p. 236.

12. Friedrich Meinecke, *Cosmopolitanism and the National State*, trans. Robert B. Kimber (Princeton, 1970), p. 36.

13. Kriegsrat Randel, "Summarische Uebersicht von Deutschland," *Deutsche Monatsschrift*, 1 (January-April, 1792), 289–291.

14. Christoph Martin Wieland, "Vorrede" to Schiller's *Historischer Kalender für Damen* (1792), in *C. M. Wielands sämmtliche Werke*, ed. J. G. Gruber, 53 vols. (Leipzig, 1818–28), XLII, 455–456.

15. Karl von Dalberg, *Von Erhaltung der Staatsverfassungen* (Erfurt, 1795), p. 21. Dalberg's genuine devotion to the imperial constitution, and his attempts to awaken such devotion in others, had also found expression in 1792 in his establishment of a prize for the best answer to the question: "What are the means for making the value and advantages of the imperial constitution palpable to the German citizen, and for making him still more attached to it?" The prize was offered through the Academy of Electoral Mainz at Erfurt, of which Dalberg, as coadjutor, was the governor (*Statthalter*). A fairly considerable response was forthcoming; in fact, the essay of Häberlin discussed above was one of the entries.

16. Günther Heinrich von Berg, *Ueber Teutschlands Verfassung und die Erhaltung der öffentlichen Ruhe in Teutschland* (Göttingen, 1795), pp. 56–62.

17. Wilhelm August Friedrich Danz, "Deutschland, wie es war, wie es ist, und wie es vielleicht werden wird," *Neues Patriotisches Archiv für Deutschland*, 2 (1794), 139–144. The lecture printed here was originally delivered in Stuttgart in February, 1792.

18. Dalberg, *Von Erhaltung*, pp. 21–22.

19. Berg, *Ueber Teutschlands Verfassung*, pp. 63–64.

20. This statement admits of only one major exception: the Imperial Army (*Reichsarmee*), whose glaring weaknesses were the object of severe and almost universal condemnation. See below, pp. 148–153.

21. Berg, *Ueber Teutschlands Verfassung*, p. 97; W. A. F. Danz, "Deutschland," etc., *Neues Patriotisches Archiv für Deutschland*, 2 (1794), 150.

22. On the subject of the advantages of small states in the political thought of the eighteenth century, see Eduard Sieber, *Die Idee des Kleinstaats bei den Denkern des 18. Jahrhunderts in Frankreich und Deutschland* (Basel, 1920).

23. Ibid., p. 74. See also Joist Grolle, *Landesgeschichte in der Zeit der deutschen Spätaufklärung: Ludwig Timotheus Spittler (1752–1810)* (Göttingen, 1963), pp. 80–81.

24. Karl Leonhard Reinhold, "Ueber die Teutschen Beurtheilungen der französischen Revoluzion," *Der teutsche Merkur*, 1793 (April), 398–399.

25. These and similar arguments were advanced by Randel, "Summarische Uebersicht," etc., *Deutsche Monatsschrift*, 1 (January-April, 1792), 290; Häberlin, "Ueber die Güte," etc., ibid., 1 (January-April, 1793), 32–33; W. A. F. Danz, "Deutschland," etc., *Neues Patriotisches Archiv für Deutschland*, 2 (1794), 151–157.

26. Anon., "Ueber die wirksamsten Mittel gewaltsamen Revolutionen in Deutschland vorzubeugen," *Deutsches Magazin*, 8 (July-December, 1794), 405–408.

27. Berg, *Ueber Teutschlands Verfassung*, p. 127.

28. Wieland, "Vorrede," pp. 453–455. These observations were repeated and expanded in Wieland's "Betrachtungen über die gegenwärtige Lage des Vaterlandes" (1793) in *C. M. Wielands sämmtliche Werke*, XLI, 283–333. The views expressed in this article, which first appeared in *Der teutsche Merkur* in January 1793, differ little from those he had aired as early as 1780. See above p. 318, n. 2.

29. Karl Leonhard Reinhold, "Ueber den Geist unsres Zeitalters in Teutschland," *Der teutsche Merkur*, 1790 (March), 232.

30. The background and development of this German sense of mission is treated at length by Aira Kemiläinen, *Auffassungen über die Sendung des deutschen Volkes um die Wende des 18. und 19. Jahrhunderts* (Helsinki, 1956). Kemiläinen asserts on pp. 269–270 that the concept of mission was almost wholly spiritual in nature, as were the means proposed for its accomplishment. While this statement is certainly correct, it is interesting to note that one of the last services solicited from the League of Princes by one writer involved nothing less than the liberation of much of southern Europe—specifically France and Spain—from the double yoke of bad government and bad ideas. This request was justified on the grounds of the putative right of a people such as the Germans to give laws of reason to other, weaker peoples in order to improve their condition. Enjoining the princes of the League to be "rational cosmopolitans," he urged them to see "that the higher culture of a people gives it claims to transplant its abilities into a better climate, where they can be displayed in better blossoms and bring forth more voluptuous fruit." Anon., "Meine Träume vom Fürstenbunde," *Der neue deutsche Zuschauer*, 3, Heft 7 (1790), 67.

31. Reinhold, "Ueber die Teutschen Beurtheilungen," etc., *Der teutsche Merkur*, 1793 (April), 398–399.

32. Gerhard Anton von Halem, "Hat der Deutsche Ursache, auf seine Nation stolz zu seyn?" (1790), *Schriften*, 7 vols. (Münster, 1803–10), IV, 288, 299.

33. Anon., *Sendschreiben an die Kurmaynzische Akademie zu Erfurt über die von derselben ausgesetzte Preisfrage: Welches sind die Mittel dem teutschen Bürger den Werth und die Vortheile der Reichs-Konstitution recht fühlbar und ihn derselben noch anhänglicher zu machen?* (n.p., [August] 1792), esp. pp. 9–13, 21–23.

34. Even this supposed efficacy of the Empire in the single area of the maintenance of peaceful relations between the territories was not accepted by everyone, however. Many people who were otherwise quite supportive of the imperial constitution—L. T. Spittler, for example—saw this much more as the result of the balance of power that had gradually been established between the larger territories than of the legal machinery of the Empire itself. See Grolle, *Landesgeschichte*, p. 80.

35. [Franz Joseas von Hendrich], *Freymüthige Gedanken über die allerwichtigste Angelegenheit Deutschlands*, third edition, 3 vols. (Germanien [Zürich], 1795–96), I, 125–244 passim, but esp. 198–199.

36. The true position of the unprivileged classes relative to that of the princes and nobility was earlier summarized by the French lawyer, writer, and editor S. N. H. Linguet, who found almost nothing praiseworthy in the entire German constitution. Writing in Ludwig Wekhrlin's journal *Die Chronologen*, he had commented that "Germany appears to me not otherwise than a great park, where everything that wears a hunting uniform can pretty much have a good time: but whatever has fur or feathers has to creep off into a corner if it does not want to be trodden underfoot." And: "In order to enjoy a proper existence in Germany, one must be at least an imperial noble (*Reichs-Elder*) or the citizen of a free Imperial City." "Deutschland. Eine politische Lektion. Fortsetzung," *Die Chronologen*, 7 (1780), 115, 119.

37. See above, p. 127.

38. K., "Betrachtungen über den Einfluss der deutschen Staatsverfassung auf das Nazionalglück der Deutschen," *Berlinische Monatsschrift*, 19 (January-June, 1792), esp. 275–277, 278–280, 292.

39. Weisse, *Von den Vortheilen*, pp. 52–55, 60.

40. Such views are contained in two articles in a Hamburg journal published by Christian Ulrich Detlev von Eggers, an economic expert who held a professorship at the University of Copenhagen and who eventually attained very high official positions in royal Danish service. He himself probably composed the first article, "Ueber gemeinschaftliches Handelsinteresse der Deutschen nicht zu Oestreich und Preussen gehörigen Reichsländer," *Deutsches Magazin*, 1 (January-June, 1791), 337–357. The second article, "Ist die deutsche Verfassung dem inländischen Handel und der Aufnahme der Manufacturen schädlich oder nüzlich?" ibid., 5 (January-June, 1793), 717–753, was the work of W. J. C. von Florencourt, a French immigrant in the service of the Duke of Braunschweig.

41. Ibid., pp. 720–721.

42. K., "Betrachtungen," etc., *Berlinische Monatsschrift*, 19 (January-June, 1792), 280–285.

43. See Zorn, "Reichs- und Freiheitsgedanken," pp. 61–63.

44. [C. U. D. von Eggers?], "Ueber gemeinschaftliches Handelsinteresse," etc., *Deutsches Magazin*, 1 (January-June, 1791), 340–341.

45. Ibid., pp. 337–357.

46. Hanover was the only western German state regarded as marginally capable of self-sufficiency in trade by this writer, who also pointed out, however, that even her trade would be greater through union with her neighbors. Ibid., p. 341.

47. Christoph Martin Wieland, "Ueber deutschen Patriotismus. Betrachtungen, Fragen and Zweifel" (1793), in *C. M. Wielands sämmtliche Werke*, ed. J. G. Gruber, XLI, esp. pp. 336–337, 344–345, 350–351.

48. Randel, "Summarische Uebersicht," etc., *Deutsche Monatsschrift*, 1 (January-April, 1792), 292.

49. See Berg, *Ueber Teutschlands Verfassung*, pp. 89–91, and Anon., *Sendschreiben*, p. 17.

50. Justus Möser, "Ueber die deutsche Sprache und Litteratur" (1781), in *Justus Möser's sämmtliche Werke*, new edition, ed. B. R. Abeken, 10 vols. in 7 (Berlin, 1842–43), IX, 139.

51. See Kemiläinen, *Auffassungen*, pp. 23–28.

52. Johann Gottfried Herder, "Idee zum ersten patriotischen Institut für den Allgemeingeist Deutschlands" (1787), in *Sämtliche Werke*, ed. Bernhard Suphan, 33 vols. (Berlin, 1877–1913), XVI, 606–616.

53. Johann Gottfried Herder, "Warum wir noch keine Geschichte der Deutschen haben?" (1795), ibid., XVIII, 380–384.

54. Zorn, "Reichs- und Freiheitsgedanken," p. 43.

55. K., "Betrachtungen," etc., *Berlinische Monatsschrift*, 19 (January-June, 1792), 297.

56. Kemiläinen, *Auffassungen*, p. 235. Kemiläinen emphasizes the importance of the views of Herder and Wilhelm von Humboldt in particular. For Humboldt, see also Meinecke, *Cosmopolitanism and the National State*, p. 45.

57. See, for example, C. F. Sangerhausen, "Anrede an die deutsche Nation, die Stimmung des Zeitalters angemessen," *Deutsche Monatsschrift*, 1 (January-April, 1794), 319–320.

58. Berg, *Ueber Teutschlands Verfassung*, pp. 65–66.

59. Anon., *Sendschreiben*, pp. 17, 24.

60. F. C. von Moser, "(Ein aufgewärmer alter) Neujahrs-Wunsch an den Reichs-Tag zu Regensburg Vom Jahr 1765," *Neues Patriotisches Archiv für Deutschland*, 1 (1792), 295–296.

61. Zorn, "Reichs- und Freiheitsgedanken," pp. 63–65.

CHAPTER NINE

1. This applies more to the revolutionaries' threats to the French crown and the royal family than to the issue of the violation of the rights of a handful of German ecclesiastical prelates and other landlords, whose income from estates in the French province of Alsace was reduced by the abolition of the feudal nexus and of non-French ecclesiastical jurisdictions declared by the French National Assembly in 1789 and 1790. Their protests, as well as those of emigré French nobles who for a time, at least, found a hospitable refuge in some of the ecclesiastical principalities of the Rhineland, were all but ignored by both Leopold II and Frederick William II.

2. Huber, *Deutsche Verfassungsgeschichte*, I, 26.

3. Braubach, *Maria Theresias jüngster Sohn*, p. 261.

4. Anon., *Unpartheiische Gedanken über die Unabhängigkeit einzelner deutscher Reichsstände in Beziehung auf auswärtige Mächte, und über ihr Recht mit denselben Krieg zu führen* (Frankfurt and Leipzig, 1792), pp. 29–34, 60–61.

5. See above, p. 118 and n. 1.

6. Letter to Count Metternich, cited in Braubach, *Maria Theresias jüngster Sohn*, p. 278.

7. Anon., *Sendschreiben*, pp. 19–20.

8. Franz Joseph von Linden, *Sind die Stände des deutschen Reichs verbunden an dem gegenwärtigen Kriege Frankreichs gegen den König von Ungarn und Böhmen Theil zu nehmen?* (Mainz, 1792), pp. 100–103.

9. Braubach, *Maria Theresias jüngster Sohn*, pp. 319–323. See also Klaus Oldenhage, *Kurfürst Erzherzog Maximilian Franz als Hoch- und Deutschmeister (1780–1801)* (Bad Godesberg, 1969), p. 280.

10. Anon., *Reichsgesetzmässige Erörterung der Reichsständischen Verhältnisse zu Kaiserlichen oder Reichstruppen während einem Reichskriege in Ansehung der . . . Landesherrlichen Festungen*, etc. (n.p., 1794), pp. 17–18.

11. Ibid., pp. 19–20, 24–25.

12. Anon., *Beiträge zur richtigen Beurtheilung der Kapitulation von Mannheim* ([Frankfurt], 1796), pp. 3–52 passim.

13. Cited in Aretin, *Heiliges Römisches Reich*, I, 104, from J. J. Moser, *Neues Teutsches Staatsrecht*, 20 Parts (1766–75), VI, 810.

14. W. A. F. Danz, "Deutschland," etc., *Neues Patriotisches Archiv für Deutschland*, 2 (1794), 142.

15. See above, pp. 35–39, for a general description of the constitutional procedures for calling up the *Reichsarmee*.

16. After Rossbach, where the equipment of the Imperial Army was so poor that hardly one fifth of the available muskets fired at all, it was known among Prussians and some others as the *Reissausarmee* (runaway army), a word play on *Reichsarmee*. Jähns also cites the following doggerel (my translation) as a verse current after the battle:

> And when great Frederick doth appear,
> And claps hands upon his flanks,
> Then off the Imperial Army scoots,
> Along with Pandours and Franks.

Jähns, "Zur Geschichte," p. 474. Pandours were South Slavic irregulars attached to the Austrian army.

17. Danz claimed that this force was too ineffective even "to restrain a few collected bunches of rebellious subjects of a small bishopric." "Deutschland," etc., *Neues Patriotisches Archiv für Deutschland*, 2 (1794), 142.

18. Even Aretin, who makes some forgiving comments about the Swabian Circle contingents, for example, seems merely to be saying that the *Reichsarmee* did not fight as badly as it might have under admittedly woeful circumstances. *Heiliges Römisches Reich*, I, 72.

19. For a detailed treatment of Laukhard (1758–1822), see *Allgemeine deutsche Biographie*, XVIII, 42–49.

20. [Friedrich Christian Laukhard], *Schilderung der jetzigen Reichsarmee nach ihrer wahren Gestalt. Nebst Winken über Deutschlands künftiges Schicksal* (Kölln, 1796), pp. 7–19.

21. Ibid., pp. 12–13, 19–24, 26–29, 30–31.

22. Ibid., pp. 59–60, 179–180, 184–187.

23. Ibid., pp. 33–44, 137–138.

24. Ibid., pp. 154–156, 176–177.

25. Ibid., pp. 47–50.

26. Ibid., pp. 81–95. Laukhard's strong disparagement of religion reflects not only his bitter experiences as a young preacher, but also the free, secular, even frivolous spirit that got him in trouble with parishioners and church officials later in his life as well. His comments are important, however, in revealing the extent to which religious differences in the late eighteenth century still played a significant role in German social and political issues. The following quotation is illustrative of the relationship between those differences and the growth of a German patriotism or national spirit: "How shall the Bavarian do something for the Hessian, whom he regards as an arch-scoundrel, a confirmed heretic, and a future inhabitant of hell and consort of Beelzebub? Is that his compatriot? Yea, he would sooner recognize the Spaniard, who tells the rosary, or the Italian, who holds an *agnus dei* with one hand and a thief's dagger in the other, as his brother, and protect him, than the German who goes differently to mass than he." Ibid., p. 93. Laukhard professed to have seen evidences of a real religious hatred among the troops of the *Reichsarmee*, including fistfights after church services in which chaplains of different faiths had made fun of each other's religion. It is worth noting that writers who devoted attention to the problem of German national spirit throughout this period were almost unanimous in seeing religious intolerance as an obstacle to the creation of that spirit, differing only on how serious an obstacle it was.

27. Ibid., pp. 72–79, 199–204.

28. Ibid., p. 82.

29. Ibid., pp. 222–224.

30. Bock's reform ideas are summarized in Anton Ernstberger, "Reichsheer und Reich: ein Reformvorschlag 1794/95," in *Gesamtdeutsche Vergangenheit. Festgabe für Heinrich Ritter von Srbik zum 60. Geburtstag* (Munich, 1938), pp. 179–186. It is interesting to note, as Ernstberger does, that this proposal actually came before the eyes of Emperor Francis II in Vienna through the good offices of the Imperial *Konkommissar* at the Diet in Regensburg. It remained without demonstrable effect, however.

31. Aretin, *Heiliges Römisches Reich*, I, 296 and n. 237. See also Srbik, *Deutsche Einheit*, I, 153.

32. See letters of Carl August to Count Görtz of February 12 and March 21, 1794, in W. Andreas, ed., *Politischer Briefwechsel*, II, 64–65.

33. See John G. Gagliardo, *From Pariah to Patriot: The Changing Image of the German Peasant, 1770–1840* (Lexington, Ky., 1969), pp. 165–166.

34. [Georg Franz Edler von Blum], *Patriotische Gedanken und Vorschläge zur Vermehrung der teutschen Reichs-Armee, zur Regulirung des Aufgebots und Herbeyschaffung baarer Mittel zu deren Unterstützung* (Frankfurt and Leipzig, 1794), pp. 98–108.

35. Ibid., pp. 141–145.

36. Ibid., pp. 110–120.

37. See above, pp. 36–37.

38. Blum asserted optimistically that if his proposals were carried out he foresaw the likelihood that the Empire could force the French to abdicate not only Alsace and Lorraine, but the bishoprics of Metz, Toul, and Verdun as well, thus

recovering a substantial share of its territorial losses to France in modern times. Ibid., p. 147.

39. For all these financial proposals, see ibid., pp. 161–186.

40. Among the important princes of the Empire, none recognized the need for a separate Imperial Army more clearly than Elector Max Franz of Cologne, who in the spring of 1794 instructed his ambassador to the Westphalian Circle to employ all his energies to awaken patriotism among the Estates of the Circle and to urge them to put aside their "chicaneries": "It is not a matter here of a fortuitous war, like the Seven Years' War, or as in previous times of keeping the Netherlands for the House of Austria, but of the preservation of the existence of every single state and almost of every single individual; here it is not so much the obligation that should be debated as the necessity and consequently the possibility of the support to be given. The German Empire, left to its own protection, must summon all possible forces to avoid destruction." Cited in Max Braubach, *Maria Theresias jüngster Sohn*, pp. 297–298.

41. Gerhard Anton von Halem, "Etwas über die möglichen Vortheile der Deutschen Kreisverfassung" (1797), in *Schriften*, IV, 256–260.

42. Ibid., pp. 265–269.

43. Cited in Wolfgang von Groote, *Die Entstehung des Nationalbewusstseins in Nordwestdeutschland 1790–1830* (Göttingen, 1955), p. 28.

44. Halem, "Etwas," etc., *Schriften*, IV, 260–261.

45. For the preceding account I have relied chiefly on the detailed narrative and interpretation of Aretin, *Heiliges Römisches Reich*, I, 301–318.

46. Ibid., pp. 307–308.

47. Since his own government was involved in the decisions which led to the conference, as well as in the conference itself, Gagern obviously had knowledge of the proposed league; yet it is unlikely that his writing was officially sanctioned, though Aretin points out that it was held to be so in some places, among them Vienna. Ibid., p. 306.

48. Hans Christoph Freiherr von Gagern, *Ein deutscher Edelmann an seine Landsleute* (n.p., 1794), pp. 3–16. Gagern's idea that the assembly he proposed should flood Germany with popular propaganda—*Volksschriften*—in order to awaken the enthusiasm of the nation for the common cause, while somewhat visionary, was shared by Edelsheim, Botzheim, and Bürgel, ministers of Baden, Nassau, and Hessen-Kassel, respectively, who devoted a considerable amount of discussion to it at Wilhelmsbad. The reaction of their masters, on the other hand, was probably best expressed by Wilhelm IX of Hessen-Kassel, who wrote in his diary: "In the four- to five-hour sessions, it was only with difficulty that I could control my impatience at the absurd proposals that Edelsheim, Botzheim, and Bürgel made. The talk was only of newspapers, popular appeals, and admonitions to subjects, instead of about a well-organized army and the means for its support against the common enemy." Cited in Aretin, *Heiliges Römisches Reich*, I, 307.

CHAPTER TEN

1. Carl Friedrich Häberlin, "Geschichte der Entdeckungsversuche des Verfassers der Germania," etc., *Staats-Archiv*, 1 (1796), 498–502.

2. Anon., "Uiber Preussens StaatsInteresse und Politik, von dem Hubertusburger Frieden (1763) an bis zur Reichenbacher Convention (1790)," *Europäische Annalen*, Siebentes Stück (1795), esp. 11–12, note.

3. This was above all visible in the promise Prussia received that the peace would be valid not only for herself but for other northern German Estates of the Empire as well; and, as Huber has pointed out, "Insofar as they declared their agreement with the Prussian action, they too renounced their constitutional duties to the Empire." *Deutsche Verfassungsgeschichte*, I, 30.

4. For Müller's views, see Stauffer, *Die Idee*, esp. pp. 50–51.

5. [Carl Christian Graf zu Lippe-Weissenfeld], *Nichteinigung, ein Bruchstück des Zeitalters. An meine Mitstände* (Vaterland, 1796), pp. 55–56.

6. Anon., *Soll das deutsche Reich der politischen Auflösung nahe seyn?* (n.p., 1795), pp. 1–20.

7. Christian von Bentzel, "Teutschlands Weh und Wohl," *Der teutsche Merkur,* 1795 (April), 425–436.

8. Anon., *Vorstellungen über den gegenwärtigen Krieg an die Völker Deutschlands, von einem Freunde der Wahrheit und des Vaterlandes* (n.p., 1795), p. 42.

9. See Ernstberger, "Reichsheer und Reich," p. 186.

10. Cited from an undated letter, probably of March, 1797, in Beaulieu-Marconnay, *Karl von Dalberg,* I, 219.

11. The depth of the hostility between Austria and Prussia which had so quickly reasserted itself may be seen in the proposals for a declaration of war against Prussia which circulated for a time in Vienna following the Peace of Basel. In Prussia, similarly, once Austria's determination to continue the war was known, Frederick William II's minister Karl von Hardenberg went so far as to suggest that Prussia force northern Germany into subordination, raise Ansbach, Bayreuth, and Silesia to a war footing against Austria, and then proceed to secularize and annex the territories of ecclesiastical princes as well as of Imperial Cities and Imperial Knights in the south. These actions, for which Hardenberg foresaw the assistance of Bavaria, were designed virtually to exclude Austrian influence from the rest of the Empire. Srbik, *Deutsche Einheit,* I, 155.

12. Aretin, *Heiliges Römisches Reich,* I, 339–340.

13. Gerhard Anton von Halem, for example, upon hearing the news of Leoben, rejoiced that the Empire had survived intact, and spoke of a "dusted off" Pütter celebrating the event—suggestive of a conviction that the Empire would now return to its old condition. "Lied bey der Nachricht von der gehofften Integrität des Deutschen Reichs" (1797), in *Schriften,* V, 173.

14. See above, p. 152.

15. Immanuel Kant, *Perpetual Peace: A Philosophical Essay,* trans. M. Campbell Smith (New York and London, 1972), p. 123.

16. *Allgemeine deutsche Biographie,* XI, 778–780.

17. [August Hennings], "Ein kleiner Beitrag zur Beförderung des Reichsfriedens," *Der Genius der Zeit,* 6 (September-December, 1795), 216–222; and "Europens politische Lage und Staats Interesse," ibid., 8 (May-August, 1796), 731–737.

18. There has been some disagreement about the date of publication of the work. The *Deutsches Anonymen-Lexikon,* ed. Michael Holzmann and Hanns Bohatta, 7 vols. (Weimar, 1902–28), VI, 209, which identifies Krug as the author, gives the actual date of publication as 1782, but this is clearly impossible, given the dates of Krug's life (1770–1842). Hermann Schulz, *Vorschläge zur Reichsreform in der Publizistik von 1800–1806* (Dissertation, University of Giessen, 1926), on the other hand, not only states that the place of publication (Altona and Vienna) is faked, but that it was published in an unspecified later year. Schulz gives no reason for this judgment, however, and there is no internal evidence to suggest that it could not have been published in 1797. For more on Krug's career, see *Allgemeine deutsche Biographie,* XVII, 220–222.

19. [Wilhelm Traugott Krug], *Grundlinien zu einer allgemeinen deutschen Republik gezeichnet von einem Märtyrer der Wahrheit* (Altona and Vienna, 1797), pp. 21–23.

20. Ibid., pp. 28–33.

21. Ibid., pp. 53–56, 64–65.

22. Ibid., pp. 15, 54.

23. Ibid., p. 5.

24. Anon., *Kritik der deutschen Reichsverfassung,* 3 vols. (Germanien, 1796–98), I, 57.

25. Ibid., II, 56.

26. Ibid., I, 70–95, 138–139, 263.
27. Ibid., 76, 181–188, 267.
28. Ibid., II, 131.
29. Ibid., 157.
30. Ibid., 189–190.
31. Ibid., 149–151, 215–220. Following Kant, this writer also subscribed to the notion that a republic was unlikely to wage offensive wars, because the representatives who decided questions of war and peace shared the burdens of war: "Their war can and will be only a defensive war." Ibid., 143–144.
32. Ibid., III, 72–74.
33. Ibid., 108.
34. Ibid., 39–46.
35. Ibid., 227–283 passim.
36. Kant, *Perpetual Peace*, pp. 124–125.

CHAPTER ELEVEN

1. The frustrations and uncertainty which gripped the whole Empire through most of 1798 can be seen in the shifting moods of Elector Max Franz of Cologne, whose confidence in the integrity of the Empire was at one point—probably early in the year—so badly shaken that he seemed prepared to accept an immediate partition of the Empire into a few powerful states as preferable to the continuation of an imperial system that offered no protection to its members and to their subjects. Braubach, *Maria Theresias jüngster Sohn*, p. 342. Toward the end of July, however, at a moment when the possibility of renewed war between France and Austria was being rumored, he expressed himself in favor of the conferral of a kind of dictatorial power on the Emperor by the whole Empire for a specified period of time. Oldenhage, *Kurfürst Erzherzog Maximilian Franz*, p. 355.

Karl von Dalberg, whose assumption of the throne of Mainz was now only four years away, also vacillated in his views of the proper course the Empire should take in this uncertain situation. In March, he suggested that the abdication of the Left Bank to France might be stopped by a plan whereby Archduke Charles, as an Imperial General, would be placed in command of the entire *Reichsarmee* and given a virtual dictatorship over the Swabian, Bavarian, and Franconian Circles, while Austria would maintain neutrality in order to hold Prussia in check with her whole power. This proposal, which seems to have assumed that the French would deal more kindly with an Empire from which Austrian influence had momentarily excluded itself, and that the recovery of the Left Bank was therefore a real possibility as long as Prussian meddling was neutralized, stands in strong contrast to the belief he expressed in the summer of 1798, when he earnestly recommended a rapprochement between Berlin and Vienna as the only means of saving both Germany and Europe. See Beaulieu-Marconnay, *Karl von Dalberg*, I, 234, 240–241.

2. See, for example, the anonymous pamphlet entitled *An den deutschen Reichstag. Beim Durchzuge der Russischen Hülfstruppen durch Regensburg* (Regensburg, 1799), esp. pp. 5, 13–18, whose author claimed to be a delegate to the Imperial Diet. Welcoming the Russians to Germany in the common struggle against the French, this writer deplored the fact that the Germans had ceased to be a nation, praised Austria and Russia as the only true nations left on the continent, and insisted that since Francis II was alone responsible for the survival of Germany as a state and of the Germans as a people, he should be given an unconditional obedience. Without the full assistance of the rest of Germany, he continued, the Emperor would be entitled to regard a reconquered Left Bank as his own territory rather than the Empire's; and to the argument that such assistance would result in an excessive growth of Austrian power in Germany, he answered that the imperial constitution,

carrying within itself no guarantee of its own preservation, required the protection of an "external power" of the first rank, which, furthermore, had an interest in preserving the integrity of Germany. That power, he concluded, could only be Austria.

3. Jähns, "Zur Geschichte," p. 488. See also Aretin, *Heiliges Römisches Reich*, I, 352.

4. Huber, *Deutsche Verfassungsgeschichte*, I, 44–45. See also Aretin, *Heiliges Römisches Reich*, I, 360, where a strong case is made that Austria's failure to take an active part in discussions about the distribution of compensation, even when approached to do so—a failure that began with Francis II's decision not to act as the Empire's plenipotentiary in the matter, but which was aggravated by disagreements and personal conflicts within the Austrian ministry—destroyed the last real chance for a resolution of the compensation question within a framework commensurate with the imperial constitution by literally forcing some Estates into separate agreements with France. Interpreting Austria's inactivity as a deliberate attempt to evade her responsibilities to the Empire while negotiating secretly with France for her own selfish advantage—a view nourished by Cobenzl's prolonged stay in Paris—these princes turned to Napoleon as a matter of self-preservation. Aretin also sees this period as crucial in the final weakening of the belief among the more powerful Estates that the chief guarantee of their existence lay in the continued integrity of the imperial nexus; from this point on, the striving for full sovereignty became a much more self-consciously pursued objective of the larger and medium-sized states.

5. Probably the best detailed contemporary survey of the changes wrought by the Final Recess is Adam Christian Gaspari, *Der Deputations-Recess: mit historischen, geographischen und statistischen Erläuterungen und einer Vergleichungs-Tafel*, 2 vols. (Hamburg, 1803). A convenient recent summary, including details and statistics on the important territorial changes, can be found in Rössler and Franz, *Sachwörterbuch*, II, 977–979. See also Bornhak, *Deutsche Verfassungsgechichte*, pp. 233–242.

6. For the cases of Augsburg and Nürnberg, see Epstein, *Genesis*, pp. 638–652.

7. The figures are from Huber, *Deutsche Verfassungsgeschichte*, I, 46. The plan also provided generous compensation for all ecclesiastical rulers who now lost their thrones, including not only annual incomes which varied with their rank, but also retention of imperial immediacy for their persons.

8. The *privilegium de non appellando* was granted to all the Electors, as well as to the Landgrave of Hessen-Darmstadt and the various principalities ruled by all the different branches of the House of Nassau. See Bornhak, *Deutsche Verfassungsgeschichte*, p. 237.

9. The figures for the Council of Princes do not take account of the redistribution of votes provided for in the Final Recess, a part of the act which the Emperor did not ratify. It would have created a total of 131 full votes (*Virilstimmen*), of which seventy-eight would have been controlled by Protestants, fifty-three by Catholics. Aretin, *Heiliges Römisches Reich*, I, 456. Of this new distribution, Austria, for example, would have controlled but seven votes, while Bavaria would have twelve and Prussia fifteen! Huber, *Deutsche Verfassungsgeschichte*, I, 50.

10. The figures, converted by me into English miles, are from Rössler and Franz, *Sachwörterbuch*, II, 977–978.

11. Klaus Dieter Hömig, *Der Reichsdeputationshauptschluss vom 25. Februar 1803 und seine Bedeutung für Staat und Kirche* (Tübingen, 1969), pp. 19–21.

12. Aretin asserts that after the Peace of Basel there was no important Prussian statesman who was not at least secretly committed to secularization as a means of territorial expansion; he also notes, however, that Hanover and Saxony, but especially the former, remained opposed to it almost to the end, convinced that it would only serve the interests of the two German great powers of whose motives they were so profoundly suspicious. *Heiliges Römisches Reich*, I, 427–435.

13. Peter Wende, *Die geistlichen Staaten und ihre Auflösung im Urteil der zeitgenössischen Publizistik* (Lübeck and Hamburg, 1966), pp. 9–12. This is the best recent study of the debate over the secularizations as it appeared in public literature, as well as of the previous controversy associated with the prize question. Both are also surveyed briefly in English in Epstein, *Genesis*, pp. 276–285 and 605–615. On p. 277, n. 79, Epstein refers to P. A. von Bibra as a "Reform Catholic," a man of enlightened views interested in strengthening the ecclesiastical states through reform. He was horrified and dismayed at the reaction of his clerical colleagues to the prize question and to the answers it generated; many of them accused him of radical intentions and of being a "traitor to his class."

14. I rely in this and the following two paragraphs largely on the summaries of Wende, *Die geistlichen Staaten*, pp. 15–38.

15. Ibid., pp. 36–38.

16. Josef von Sartori, *Statistische Abhandlung über die Mängel in der Regierungsverfassung der geistlichen Wahlstaaten, und von den Mitteln, solchen abzuhelfen* ([Augsburg], 1787). On Sartori, see the *Allgemeine deutsche Biographie*, XXX, 378.

17. Friedrich Carl von Moser, *Ueber die Regierung der geistlichen Staaten in Deutschland* (Frankfurt and Leipzig, 1787), pp. 39–41, 59–60, 71, 91–92, 108–110.

18. Ibid., pp. 35–39, 42–54.

19. This attitude is revealed, for example, in Moser's pleasure at what he saw as a growing recognition in the Catholic Church that religion was really a matter of the heart and spirit, not of the school, and he rejoiced that the Catholic "even now believes only half what he did two hundred years ago, and in another hundred years the commands of the Roman Curia in Germany will have just as much validity as a decision of the Imperial Aulic Council in Berlin." Ibid., p. 213.

20. The example of Moser once again serves to underline the persistence of deep religious antagonisms in the Empire all the way to its end. Aretin, to be sure, suggests that it is not possible to speak of "a sharp confessional opposition in the proper sense" at the end of the eighteenth century, but even he admits that the Catholic and Protestant factions, as political parties, were "the most important element of imperial politics" during the same period. *Heiliges Römisches Reich*, I, 9. It is quite possible that many modern historians, especially political historians, have come to underestimate the power of religious beliefs in helping to shape political opinions and decisions even in the supposedly rational and secular atmosphere of the later Enlightenment. Indeed, the traditional picture of the late Enlightenment in Germany and elsewhere has been revised in some important respects in recent years, with more attention to its deformation through the explosion of mysticism, irrationalism, and other distinctly "unenlightened" forces. See, in particular, the excellent work of Henri Brunschwig, *Enlightenment and Romanticism in Eighteenth-Century Prussia*, trans. Frank Jellinek (Chicago, 1974); and, for France, Robert Darnton, *Mesmerism and the End of the Enlightenment in France* (Cambridge, Mass., 1968).

21. F. C. von Moser, *Ueber die Regierung*, pp. 160–161.

22. See above, pp. 127–128.

23. F. C. von Moser, *Ueber die Regierung*, pp. 70–71, 136.

24. Ibid., pp. 147–148. The reference is to Heinrich von Brühl, the leading Saxon minister for many years before his death in 1763, whose questionable financial dealings gave him a generally bad public reputation that persisted for generations. The work of more recent historians has rehabilitated him to some degree.

25. Ibid., pp. 165–184.

26. Ibid., pp. 187–192.

27. Moser himself obviously recognized this, for he devoted not a single word in his essay to an exploration of how it might be done; he and his readership were reminded of its lack of feasibility in one of the longest responses to his writing, which in other respects was generally favorable to the criticisms Moser had made of

the ecclesiastical states: Andreas Joseph Schnaubert, *Ueber des Freiherrn von Moser's Vorschläge zur Verbesserung der geistlichen Staaten in Deutschland* (Jena, 1788).

28. F. C. von Moser, *Ueber die Regierung,* pp. 162–163.

29. See below, pp. 211–212, where this point is more fully developed.

CHAPTER TWELVE

1. Wende, *Die geistlichen Staaten,* pp. 58–59.

2. Karl Moritz Fabritius, *Ueber den Werth und die Vorzüge geistlicher Staaten und Regierungen in Teutschland,* 2 vols. (Frankfurt and Leipzig, 1797–99), II, 17–18. It should be noted that many of the ecclesiastical princes, for obvious reasons, supported this view and showed themselves prepared to put forth extraordinary efforts to assist Austria in her renewed campaigning of 1799. The chancellor of the Elector of Mainz, Albini, organized a militia (*Landsturm*) in the Spessart which was able to drive the French out of the Frankfurt area for a time, while the Prince-Bishop of Würzburg contributed 3,500 troops instead of his legal quota of 1,400. Fulda, among others, also did more than its share. Aretin, *Heiliges Römisches Reich,* I, 435 and n. 275.

3. Baron O'Cahill, *Patriotische Gedanken über Deutschlands Integrität* (Frankfurt and Leipzig, 1798), pp. 3–4, 12–15.

4. Dahlberg's view appeared in a short memoir of March 8, 1798, entitled "Patriotische Wünsche," cited in Beaulieu-Marconnay, *Karl von Dalberg,* I, 234.

5. See, for example, the anonymously published work of a certain Fandrich, *Freymüthige Gedanken eines teutschen Staatsbürgers über die Säcularisierung der geistlichen Wahlstaaten Teutschlands in rechtlicher und politischer Hinsicht* (Altona and Hamburg, 1798), pp. 20–22; and Anon., *Noch ein Wort über das Säkularisationswesen. Von einem Freunde der Menschheit und der guten Sache* (Teutschland, 1801), p. 20.

6. Christian Ernst Weisse, *Ueber die Sekularisation Deutscher geistlicher Reichsländer in Rücksicht auf Geschichte und Staatsrecht* (Leipzig, 1798), pp. 162–163.

7. Anon., *Noch ein Wort über das Säkularisationswesen,* pp. 36–38.

8. O'Cahill, *Patriotische Gedanken,* p. 9; Dalberg, "Patriotische Wünsche" (March 8, 1798), cited in Beaulieu-Marconnay, *Karl von Dalberg,* I, 234.

9. [Johann Baptist Graser], *Wie wird es im säkularisirten Teutschlande gehen? Beantwortet in vertrauten Briefen an einen Freund* (Germania [Bamberg], 1802), p. 115; [Johann M. Seuffert], *Versuch einer doctrinellen Auslegung des 7. Freidensartikels von Lunéville* (Germanien, 1801), cited in Wende, *Die geistlichen Staaten,* pp. 55–56.

10. [Karl von Dalberg], *Ueber Bestimmung der Entschädigungsmittel für die Erbfürsten* (Mörsburg, 1801), cited in Beaulieu-Marconnay, *Karl von Dalberg,* I, 249–250; [Graser], *Wie wird es,* pp. 106–107. It should be noted here that there was a considerable degree of agreement among the defenders of the ecclesiastical territories that the preservation of the three ecclesiastical Electorates set absolute limits beyond which secularization must not be permitted to go. See below, p. 216.

11. See, for example, the anonymous work *Unser Reich ist nicht von dieser Welt. Ein erbaulicher Sermon für Geistliche und Weltliche* ([Regensburg?], 1798), pp. 5–7.

12. [Johann M. Seuffert], *Der jämmerliche Prediger mit dem Vorspruche Unser Reich ist nicht von dieser Welt; oder Noch Etwas über die Säcularisirungen besonders nach Grundsätzen der Kantischen Philosophie* (Regensburg, 1798), pp. pp. 16–19.

13. See Wende, *Die geistlichen Staaten,* p. 62. The defenders of the clerical territories were sharply aware of the tide of enlightened opinion against them, as demonstrated by their repeated defensive references to "the spirit of the age," "the

spirit of the times," "the present philosophical times," and so on, and by their attempt to link these to irreligion, impiety, and revolution. See, for example, O'Cahill, *Patriotische Gedanken*, pp. 8–9; [Johann M. Seuffert], *Ueber die Aufstellung grösserer StaatenMassen in Teutschland statt der vielen kleineren, und Organisirung derselben nach dem Geiste des ZeitAlters* (Leipzig, 1799), title and p. 7; and Anon., *Uber die Geistlichen Staaten in Deutschland und die vorgebliche Nothwendigkeit ihrer Säcularisation* (Deutschland, 1798), p. 7. The author of the last work also insinuated in his preface that "ecclesiastical and political Protestantism," which, as distinguished from "the Evangelical religion," he interpreted broadly as a general and destructive spirit of malcontentment, had found in the philosophy of the Enlightenment merely an up-to-date weapon with which to pursue its age-old policy of divisiveness and discord.

14. For the following arguments, see Anon., *Über die geistlichen Staaten*, pp. 13–14, 63; [Fandrich], *Freymüthige Gedanken*, pp. 51–60; and Anon., *Unter dem Krummstab ist gut wohnen, oder Beweis von der Achtung der geistlichen Rheinlande gegen ihre Regenten und politischreligiöse Verfassungen* ([Augsburg], 1801), esp. pp. 8–17.

15. Wende, *Die geistlichen Staaten*, pp. 65–66.

16. Anon., *Noch ein Wort über das Säkularisationswesen*, p. 27. Similar statements from other polemics are too numerous to justify separate citation. Indeed, scarcely an antisecularization tract exists in which the constitutional issue does not appear rather prominently.

17. [Johann Gottfried Pahl?], "Ein Paar Worte von den geistlichen Wahlstaaten," *National-Chronik der Teutschen*, 2 (1802), 12. Another author simply declared, without feeling the need for further clarification, that "The situation of a bishop or prelate can in no way be compared with that of a hereditary imperial prince." Christian Daniel Voss, *Ueber die Schicksale der deutschen Reichs-Staatsverfassung* (Leipzig, 1802), p. 386.

18. Anon., *Ueber die Nothwendigkeit einer allgemeinen Säcularisation der deutschen Erzbisthümer, Bisthümer, Prälaturen und Klöster. Mit Hinsicht auf Deutschlands gegenwärtige Verfassung* (Germanien [Basel?], 1798), p. 50 and note.

19. Voss, *Ueber die Schicksale*, p. 385; Weisse, *Ueber die Sekularisation*, pp. 163–164.

20. Anon., *Unser Reich ist nicht von dieser Welt*, pp. 12–13.

21. [Seuffert], *Der jämmerliche Prediger*, pp. 32–34.

22. Interestingly, however, once this argument from popular sovereignty was accepted, it could be used to try to prove that the ecclesiastical states were more in tune with the times than were the secular principalities. Immanuel Kant, in his *Metaphysische Anfangsgründe der Rechtslehre* (1797), had established the principle that the legal title of all possessions of the clergy rested on "popular opinion" (*Volksmeinung*), and earlier, in *Perpetual Peace* (1795), had also established his preference for republican constitutions. Putting these together, it could be argued, by a rather narrow construction of the meaning of "popular opinion," that the elective system of the ecclesiastical states legitimized their governments as the hereditary principle could not legitimize those of the secular territories. This appears to be the somewhat obscure argument of the author of an anonymously published work entitled *Der Kongress in Rastadt vor dem Richterstuhle der Vernunft* (Rastadt, 1799), cited in *National-Chronik der Teutschen*, 1 (1801), 100. On this whole argument from popular sovereignty, see Wende, *Die geistlichen Staaten*, pp. 81–83.

23. Wende, *Die geistlichen Staaten*, pp. 86–90.

24. Johann Gottfried Pahl penned two statements that are characteristic of this assumption. In one of them, he dismissed the legalities of the whole issue by saying that while the requirement of compensation might well be incompatible with reason, both convenience (the impossibility of a truly equal sharing of sacrifice by all states) and necessity (the French *diktat* on secularization) gave no real choice. "Was sagt die Vernunft über das teutsche Entschädigungsgeschäft?" *National-Chronik der*

Teutschen, I (1801), 241–244. The other statement was even more blunt; terming secularization an emergency measure arising from "our weakness . . . and our — stupidity," Pahl insisted that the question of whether it was just or not was irrelevant: the "Decalog of Politics," said he, teaches that whatever is expedient, appropriate, and advantageous is also right. "Die neueste Lage von Salzburg," ibid., p. 100. Certainly it was this kind of attitude as much as anything else that accounts for the avoidance of the question of legality altogether by so many of the proponents of secularization, though it is also important, as Wende points out, that imperial tradition simply gave no precedent for the sort of extensive transformation in prospect on which its advocates might rely.

25. Weisse, *Ueber die Sekularisation,* p. 166.

26. Ibid., pp. 156–160. See also Wende, *Die geistlichen Staaten,* pp. 76–77, who notes that no work was better known among contemporary publicists than Weisse's.

27. See above, pp. 207–208.

28. Wende, *Die geistlichen Staaten,* p. 84.

29. [Fandrich], *Freymüthige Gedanken,* pp. 73–86. Weisse, part of whose book was devoted specifically to a critical examination of Fandrich's work, disputed the latter's contention that the illegality of secularization would by its example produce a general mood of lawlessness by saying that it was still to be determined whether secularization was, in fact, illegal; he thus insinuated, as in an earlier and similar argument, that the surest way for the Empire to avoid just such results as Fandrich and others gloomily predicted, or worse, was for it formally to declare secularization legal, and by doing so retain a control over its own constitutional law which might otherwise pass to the French. *Ueber die Sekularisation,* p. 166.

30. See, among others, the previously cited anonymous writings *Uber die Geistlichen Staaten,* pp. 121–137, and *Noch ein Wort über das Sakularisationswesen,* pp. 27–33. While it is true that Austrian statesmen believed that the ecclesiastical states did in general provide greater support for the imperial office than did many of the secular states, it is also true, as Aretin points out, that since the period of the League of Princes no one in Vienna reckoned on an unconditional loyalty among the prelates, whose active hostility toward Joseph II clearly demonstrated that they were not prepared to back any Emperor whose actions were perceived as subversive of the imperial constitution. *Heiliges Römisches Reich,* I, 431. On the other hand, the supposedly proverbial devotion of the prelatic states to their constitutional duties is called into some question by allegations such as that of the Austrian *Direktorialgesandter* Egid Joseph Karl Fahnenberg, who in 1797 wrote in disgust and exasperation to Thugut that no less than thirty-three archbishops and bishops, as well as the three prelatic curias, were represented at the Imperial Diet by a total of only nine deputies, all of whom were, furthermore, "drunkards, womanizers, or senile cretins" (*Säufer, Weiberhelden oder senile Trottel*): "To negotiate matters of importance with a collection of such individuals," he wrote, "is nearly impossible." Cited in Wende, *Die geistlichen Staaten,* p. 72, n. 136.

31. J. B. Graser, for example, wanted to save not only the three Electors, but also at least three prelates for the Council of Princes as well as three Imperial Cities. *Wie wird es,* pp. 104, 112. Among the supporters of the idea of retaining the three Electorates, not surprisingly, was Karl von Dalberg, cited in a memoir of March, 1798, in Beaulieu-Marconnay, *Karl von Dalberg,* I, 234. J. M. Seuffert and Josef von Ullheimer (at the time a judge of the Imperial Cameral Tribunal), writing under the pseudonym of Riphelius von Solomel, also worked out territorial proposals to salvage the Electorates. See Epstein, *Genesis,* p. 614 and note 27.

32. Dalberg, who succeeded Elector Friedrich Karl von Erthal upon the latter's death in July, 1802, salvaged his Electorate partly by accepting the principle of wholesale secularization and partly by the argument that his position as archchancellor was necessary to the continued existence of the Empire, something that Napoleon was still prepared to accept at this time. The bribes Dalberg spread so liberally around Paris did not hurt his cause, either, but it was also recognized there

that it could be useful to France to have a grateful archchancellor in the Empire. Aretin, *Heiliges Römisches Reich*, I, 444. Austria, meanwhile, practically guaranteed the destruction of the other Electorates through a fickle policy which first permitted the younger brother of Francis II, Archduke Anton Viktor, to be elected to both Cologne and Münster in the fall of 1801, following the death of Max Franz, but then shrank from allowing him to take office. At the same time, Vienna proved singularly inactive in supporting the plan for the preservation of the Electorates to which the Emperor had supposedly been committed for some time. Aretin believes that Napoleon was probably serious in telling Dalberg in 1804 that Cologne and Trier could have been saved had Austria been willing to forego placing Habsburg archdukes on their thrones. Ibid., pp. 440–441.

33. [Graser], *Wie wird es*, pp. 75–83.

34. See, for example, the two anonymous tracts *Unser Reich ist nicht von dieser Welt*, p. 10; and *Patriotische Wünsche für Teutschland bei dem bevorstehenden Definitiv-Reichs-Frieden. Nebst Verlusts- und Entschädigungs-Tabellen* (Frankfurt, 1801), pp. 6–7, 20.

35. Cited in Hellmuth Rössler, *Österreichs Kampf um Deutschlands Befreiung. Die deutsche Politik der nationalen Führer Osterreichs, 1805–1815*, second edition, 2 vols. (Hamburg, 1945), I, 50.

36. Anon., *Über die geistlichen Staaten*, p. 122.

37. [Seuffert], *Ueber die Aufstellung*, pp. 20–21. This was also the drift of the argument of the Vicar-General of Konstanz, Ignaz Heinrich von Wessenberg, in his anonymously published *Die Folgen der Säcularisationen. Cuique Suum* (Germanien, 1801), cited in Wende, *Die geistlichen Staaten*, pp. 68–69.

38. [Graser], *Wie wird es*, p. 129.

39. [Fandrich], *Freymüthige Gedanken*, pp. 97–99.

40. [Seuffert], *Ueber die Aufstellung*, pp. 36–39.

41. [Seuffert], *Der jämmerliche Prediger*, pp. 8–10.

42. O'Cahill, *Patriotische Gedanken*, p. 10.

43. [Graser], *Wie wird es*, pp. 15–17, 43–51. It might be noted that such views as these contained an unmistakable if oblique admission of one of the major charges leveled against the ecclesiastical states by their critics, viz., that the Enlightenment with its this-worldly emphasis on the study of those things which could improve the well-being of mankind in tangible and material ways, was simply not at home in the clerical states. Friedrich Carl von Moser would doubtless have had great fun with Graser's work had he still been alive.

44. These views, or variations of them, can be found in Anon., *Auf wessen Seite liegt der Vortheil wenn Teutschlands Bissthümer sacularisiret werden?* (n.p., 1802); as well as in [Fandrich], *Freymüthige Gedanken*; Fabritius, *Ueber den Werth*, esp. vol. II; and Anon., *Patriotische Bemerkungen in Hinsicht der Sekularisation und dessen unvermeidlich betrübten Folgen* (Germanien, 1802), esp. p. 34, where the author made a special point of pleading the virtues of a country in which each "little people" (*Völkchen*) could preserve its own physiognomy and "the most pleasing diversity of character."

45. Anon., *Auf wessen Seite*, pp. 12, 70.

46. Ibid., pp. 70, 72. See also [Seuffert], *Ueber die Aufstellung*, pp. 23–24, and Karl Ludwig Woltmann, "Reden über die deutsche Nazion: Erste Rede," *Geschichte und Politik*, 1801 (1), 73–92. Woltmann wrote that the receptivity of some German territories to the troops and ideas of the Revolution was more than balanced by the dogged attachment of others to their traditional rulers and constitutions, and that the passion for republicanization simply lost itself in the labyrinthine toils of the German constitution, which had thus contributed to the security of the whole of northern and eastern Europe: "Through its intricate constitution and its suffering, the German Empire over the last ten years became politically great for Europe." Ibid., pp. 85–86.

47. See above, p. 24.

48. An excellent representative survey of the problems of the cities is [Christian Friedrich Grub], *Ueber einige Reichs-Städte Teutschlands. Ein Wort zu seiner Zeit geredet von einem Staatsbürger* (n.p., 1786). While certainly overdramatizing the moral turpitude of the inhabitants of the cities—their lust, greed, drunkenness and gluttony, the prevalence of illegitimate children, and so on—the author made many shrewd observations about the real social and political troubles that plagued them, and certainly identified what was perhaps their major economic problem: the small size of the territories they commanded, which simply could not absorb their own manufactures. This placed them at the mercy of the surrounding territories whose own policies, however, were often too highly protectionist to provide any real relief. The single remedy Grub proposed for what he saw as the otherwise inevitable disaster that would befall the cities was a voluntarily tighter bond with the imperial court, which would apparently have involved the abandonment of some municipal privileges, especially in the areas of government and administration, to imperial commissioners. This reliance on the higher authority of the Emperor, Grub suggested, would provide the means of establishing better economic relations with other states of the Empire. It would also result in better security for property, a better tax structure, more equitable laws, and an improved administration of justice. These benefits, it may be noted, were precisely the same as those projected for the cities by the later proponents of their absorption by other, larger states. Writing in the mid-1780s as he was, it would not likely have occurred to Grub to recommend such a radical step, which would have involved the extinction of a group of imperial Estates; yet his plan amounted to a kind of partial absorption of the cities by the Emperor, and in any case clearly recognized that the cities were simply no longer viable as fully independent entities.

49. See three articles from the *National-Chronik der Teutschen*, of which the first was probably written by the editor of the journal, J. G. Pahl, while the latter two are anonymous: "Für und über die teutschen Reichsstädte," 1 (1801), 33; "Vorstellung der teutschen Reichsstädte an den Kaiser, ihre Erhaltung und Beschirmung betreffend; dd. Regensburg den 8. May 1801," ibid., pp. 196–197, editor's notes (b) and (c); and "Aus einer teutschen Reichsstadt," 2 (1802), 110–111. The *National-Chronik* was almost unique in the amount of attention it gave to the issue of the abolition of the Imperial Cities; that stemmed, no doubt, from the personal views of Pahl, a strong supporter of the imperial constitution, whose generally favorable attitude toward the cities was probably shaped in part by his experiences in the small Swabian Imperial City of Aalen, where he was born and grew up. See *Allgemeine deutsche Biographie*, XXV, 69–71.

50. Anon., "Vorstellung der teutschen Reichsstädte," etc., *National-Chronik der Teutschen*, 1 (1801), 198, editor's note (g); Anon., "Ueber die Erhaltung der Reichsstädte. (Von einem Reichsstädtischen Patrioten)," ibid., 2 (1802), 145–148.

51. Anon., "Vorstellung der teutschen Reichsstädte," etc., ibid., 1 (1801), 196, editor's note (b).

52. [J. G. Pahl], "Für und über die teutschen Reichsstädte," ibid., p. 34.

53. Anon., *Die freyen Reichs-Städte oder über das Interesse ihrer Verbindung, in nächster Beziehung auf Schwaben* (Reichs-Stadt Kempten, 1801), pp. 6, 14.

54. Ibid., pp. 16–22. There were four of these so-called *paritätische Städte*, of which Augsburg was the most important.

55. Cited in Braubach, *Maria Theresias jüngster Sohn*, pp. 424–425.

CHAPTER THIRTEEN

1. H. Müller, *Der letzte Kampf*, pp. 36–37.

2. The details of the assertion of Prussian sovereignty over the Knights in Ansbach-Bayreuth can be found in ibid., esp. pp. 55–70, as well as in Epstein, *Genesis*, pp. 619–626.

3. According to an article in the *Politisches Journal* in 1804, all the Knights' lands together comprised only about 137 (German) square miles (ca. 630 English square miles), with a population of some 414,000 inhabitants. H. Müller, *Der letzte Kampf*, p. 190, n. 37. It was speculated at the time that the salvation of the Knights in the Final Recess may have been due at least partly to the notion that they, too, were hereditary princes in some sense, and that their abolition would violate the distinction between hereditary and elective princes that was so often cited as justification for the secularization of the latters' territories. See K. S. Zachariae, "Geist der neusten deutschen Reichsverfassung," *Geschichte und Politik*, 1804 (1), 59.

4. These and other common arguments of the time are summarized in Anon., *Resultate mit aller Unpartheilichkeit gezogen aus dem Für und Wider die unmittelbare freie Reichsritterschaft in Schwaben, Franken und am Rheinstrome* (n.p., 1803).

5. Aretin, *Heiliges Römisches Reich*, I, 459.

6. Hanns Hubert Hoffmann, *Adelige Herrschaft und souveräner Staat. Studien über Staat und Gesellschaft in Franken und Bayern im 18. und 19. Jahrhundert* (Munich, 1962), pp. 225–230. In English, see Epstein, *Genesis*, pp. 626–637 for this whole final period of the Knights' independence.

7. H. Müller, *Der letzte Kampf*, pp. 160–161, points out that the Knights attacked by princes in 1803 did not bother to carry their complaints to the imperial courts, but went straight to the Emperor. While this obviously says something about the immediacy of the issue, it also indicates a loss of confidence in the courts, especially in the now much altered circumstances of the secularized Empire.

8. Aretin, *Heiliges Römisches Reich*, I, 465–466.

9. Anon., *Proposizionen bey einem allgemeinem reichsritterschaftlichem Konvent. Träume eines Patrioten* (n.p., 1788), p. 27.

10. See, for example, Anon., *Ein freyer teutscher Edelmann an den Verfasser der Schrift: das teutsche Reich vor der französischen Revolution und nach dem Frieden bey Lüneville* (Germania, 1802), p. 13; and Anon., *Welche Maassregeln kann wohl die Reichsritterschaft in Franken und Schwaben jetzt ergreifen? Ein Gegenstück der Denkschrift: Was für Maassregeln hat wohl die Reichsritterschaft in Franken und Schwaben itzt zu ergreifen?* (n.p., 1803), pp. 55–63.

11. Anon., *Ein freyer teutscher Edelmann*, pp. 7–9.

12. Anon., *Proposizionen*, pp. 13–14.

13. Anon., *Ein freyer teutscher Edelmann*, pp. 14–15.

14. Karl Ernst Adolf von Hoff, *Antwort des Verfassers der Schrift: das teutsche Reich vor der französischen Revolution, und nach dem Frieden zu Lüneville auf das an ihn gerichtete Schreiben eines freyen teutschen Edelmannes* (Gotha, 1802), pp. 6–8, 15–18. Even more abrupt in his dismissal of the Knights' supposedly special relationship to Emperor and Empire was the author who simply reminded his readers that neither Lunéville nor any other recent events gave any reason to believe that much interest in the fate of the Empire or any of its institutions as such existed in any powerful quarters. Anon., "Was wird aus der unmittelbaren freien Reichs-Ritterschaft in Schwaben, Franken und am rechtlichen Rhein-Ufer werden . . . ? Beantwortet von einem teutschen Professor der vaterländischen Geschichte und Statistik," *Europäische Annalen*, 1802 (Siebentes Stück), 204–205.

15. Hoff, *Antwort*, p. 19.

16. Anon., *Was für Maasregeln hat wohl die Reichsritterschaft in Franken und Schwaben itzt zu ergreifen?* ([Würzburg?], 1802), esp. pp. 31–43.

17. Anon., *Welche Maassregeln*, pp. 73–77. This was published specifically as a counterattack on the previous work.

18. Anon., "Einige Gedanken über die Reichs-Ritterschaftliche Verfassung, in so fern daraus eine Beschädigung des Publicums und hoher Reichsstände entstehet," *Reichsritterschaftliches Magazin*, 6 (1785), 447.

19. See, for example, the list of governmental benefits which the Knights' subjects would acquire through the absorption of these territories by larger states according to the anonymous author of "Was wird aus der unmittelbaren freien Reichs-

Ritterschaft . . . werden," etc., *Europäische Annalen,* 1802 (Siebentes Stück), esp. 214–220. In calling attention to the fact that the Knights' lands had long been notorious as refuges for gypsies, beggars, and other undesirables, this writer also provides a clue to the desire of surrounding rulers to eliminate these pockets of independent jurisdiction containing marginally criminal elements whose excursions into neighboring states could neither be prevented by the inadequate policing of the Knights nor punished by their deficient systems of justice.

20. Anon., *Proposizionen,* pp. 28–44, 72–83, 95–99.

21. Ibid., pp. 51–70, 85–95.

22. One author, for example, would· have assigned responsibility for all legislation in public administration to the District Directories, while reserving all general "political deliberations and proceedings" (*Staatsverhandlungen*)—i.e., relations between the Knighthood and the Emperor, the Empire, the Circles, the Estates, and foreign countries—to the General Directory. Anon., *Welche Maassregeln,* pp. 82–83. Another similar proposal would have removed the taxing power from individual Knights altogether, to vest it instead in the District Directories which would then compensate the Knights for their lost revenues on an annual basis. Anon., *Patriotische Wünsche,* p. 37.

23. H. Müller, *Der letzte Kampf,* p. 190.

24. Anon., *Patriotische Wünsche,* p. 37.

25. H. Müller, *Der letzte Kampf,* p. 191.

26. See below, pp. 268–269.

27. H. Müller, *Der letzte Kampf,* p. 194.

28. Epstein, *Genesis,* p. 627.

29. The Knights were scolded for these fantasies in an article of 1802, whose anonymous author not only reminded them of the big difference between the Legion of Honor and the German Knighthood, but also declared groundless· their notion that Napoleon and the French had conceived a great preference for any single group of German nobles. Anon., "Was wird aus der unmittelbaren freien Reichs-Ritterschaft . . . werden," etc., *Europäische Annalen,* 1802 (Siebentes Stück), 202–203.

30. Epstein, *Genesis,* p. 636.

31. [J. G. Pahl], "Bemerkungen über die Auflösung der Reichsritterschaft," *National-Chronik der Teutschen,* 6 (1806), 75–77.

CHAPTER FOURTEEN

1. If one can believe the author—possibly J. G. Pahl—of an article of 1802, there would have been many more except that the furious squabbling over the apportionment and other details of indemnification had obscured the larger issue of basic constitutional reform for many Germans, who seem to have been too preoccupied with gain and loss to think very far beyond the actual territorial changes themselves. "Teutschlands künftiges Schicksal," *National-Chronik der Teutschen,* 2 (1802), 193–196. Certainly it is true of many (though not all) of the works in which compensation was defended that there was remarkably little deliberate speculation on the long-term effects of the enlargements on the structure or operation of the Empire.

2. Before its conquest by Prussia, Silesia had been a dependency of the Kingdom of Bohemia, which had been exempted from Circle membership and therefore also from its responsibilities; this exemption had continued to apply to Silesia under its Prussian rulers.

3. Anon., *Deutschlands Gewinn und Verlust bei der Rastadter Friedens-Basis nebst Vorschlägen zu einer Entschädigungs-Plan und zu einer verbesserten Reichs-Verfassung* (n.p., 1798), pp. 7–9, 119–123, 127–133.

4. Anon., *Auf wessen Seite,* pp. 16–21.

5. Ibid., pp. 65–66; Anon., *Deutschlands Gewinn,* pp. 129–130, note.

6. Anon., *Winke über Teutschlands Alte und Neue Staatsverfassung von einem teutschen Staatsbürger* (Germanien, 1798), pp. 37–38, 40–41, 159.

7. Ibid., pp. 39–40.

8. Anon., *Patriotische Wünsche*, p. 10.

9. These were common arguments even before the Final Recess; they can be found, for example, in ibid., as well as in two articles reprinted from the anonymously published book *Deutschland und Polen: eine historische Parallele* (Frankfurt, 1798), written by Johann Friedrich Reitemeier, a jurist and professor at Frankfurt an der Oder: "Kann Deutschland bey seiner gegenwärtigen Lage hoffen, seine politische Existenz lange zu erhalten?" *Staats-Archiv*, 7 (1802), 360–392; and "Vorschläge, wie die mindermächtigen Stände . . . die Inkonvenienzen einer Theilung Deutschlands verhüten oder doch vermindern können," ibid., 8 (1802), esp. 33–35. After the Final Recess, at least for a time, even more commentators were convinced that a real basis had now been laid for greater strength through concentration and more efficient management of resources. See in particular the work of the Salzburg official and professor Theodor K. Hartleben, *Die deutsche Staatsverfassung nach vollbrachtem Entschädigungssysteme* (n.p., 1803), and that of the peripatetic theologian and cameralist Johann Paul Harl, published anonymously under two titles, the better known of which is *Deutschlands neueste Staats- und Kirchenveränderungen, historisch, politisch, staats- und kirchenrechtlich entwickelt* (Berlin, 1804).

10. [J. G. Pahl], "Ist die teutsche Verfassung nicht mehr die alte?" *National-Chronik der Teutschen*, 3 (1803), 319; [Harl], *Deutschlands neueste Staats- und Kirchenveränderungen*, p. 34; Hartleben, *Die deutsche Staatsverfassung*, pp. 25–26. Harl attributed much of the inactivity of the Diet to the jealousy nurtured by the majority of the Council of Princes against the Electors, but predicted that since the increase in the number of Electors now gave them an absolute majority of votes in the Council of Princes, the wheels of legislative business would now begin to turn again.

11. Such, for example, were the benefits expected from the extinction of the "duodecimo-despotism" of many small states by the author (probably Pahl) of "Frankreichs Absichten mit Teutschland," *National-Chronik der Teutschen*, 1 (1801), 287.

12. Even the most bitterly anti-Austrian writers did admit in fairness that the Habsburgs had on occasion used their dynastic power to defend the legitimate interests of the Empire and even of Europe as a whole. The wars against the Turks were the most commonly cited example, though it was sometimes carefully pointed out that even these wars could hardly be regarded as entirely selfless in view of the territorial gains Austria had derived from them.

13. Most of this argument is from [J. G. Pahl], "Frankreichs Absichten mit Teutschland," *National-Chronik der Teutschen*, 1 (1801), 369–374, but it differs only in detail from most of the analyses of the advantages for peace from the indemnification policy.

14. As seen in earlier chapters, the hoary argument that the European balance demanded the protection of the Empire's integrity as a single, if also decentralized, body appeared with great regularity in German and European political analyses going all the way back to 1648. It had a considerable historical experience to back it up, and has led recent historians such as Klaus Epstein to explain the durability of the imperial structure partly on the grounds that it was "a European necessity." *Genesis*, p. 596. But the many "patriotic" Germans who clung to this point of view right up to the final months of the Empire's existence were given no comfort by one shrewd observer of 1803 who, though as desirous of preserving the Empire as they, blew this whole argument to pieces by drawing a distinction between the positive goal of maintaining the imperial system as it existed and the negative one of preventing that system as a whole from falling under the influence of any single power. "The peace of Europe seems to require only that Germany not fall into the hands

of a single monarch," he wrote; and while he was sure that would not happen, he left the door wide open to a possible partition of Germany which while destroying the Empire could still preserve the balance of Europe by appropriate distribution of German territory among the great powers. Anon., "Was wird aus Teutschland werden?" *Staats-Archiv*, 10 (1803), 45–53.

15. Anon., *Patriotische Wünsche*, p. 13. It is also worth noting that by the time of Lunéville, much of the anti-Prussian sentiment caused by her withdrawal into neutrality in 1795 had evaporated, and her policy was now frequently cited as a model for the rest of the Empire. The defensive tone of pro-Prussian writers of the middle and late 1790s had also disappeared, and was replaced with an unmistakable smugness not only about the success of her "neutrality system," but also about the inestimable services she had performed for the Empire, especially through Frederick II's League of Princes, in frustrating the Austrian policy of converting Germany into the servitor of the House of Habsburg—a policy whose failure was seen as particularly fortunate in light of the recent war and its results. See Voss, *Ueber die Schicksale*, p. 387; and Gaspari, *Der Deputations-Recess*, I, 80. Later, in 1805, the editor of the *Nordischer Merkur* continued to sing the praises of Prussia's peace policy: "What has Prussia not done, in the ten years since it retired from the theater of war, for the expansion of its [territory], for the glory and dignity of its throne, for the concentration of its political resources, for the benefit of its subjects, for the arts, sciences, trade, manufactures, and factories." Cited in Siegmund Satz, *Die Politik der deutschen Staaten vom Herbst 1805 bis zum Herbst 1806 im Lichte der gleichzeitigen deutschen Publizistik* (Dissertation, Berlin, 1908), p. 73.

16. [J. G. Pahl], "Ist die teutsche Verfassung nicht mehr die alte?" *National-Chronik der Teutschen*, 3 (1803), 317–319.

17. Austria, Prussia, Bavaria, Mecklenburg, Nassau-Orange, Württemberg, Baden, Hessen-Darmstadt, Hessen-Kassel, Hanover, Braunschweig, Holstein, Saxony, and Anhalt.

18. [J. G. Pahl], "Vorschlag zu einer Veränderung der teutschen Staats-Constitution," *Staats-Archiv*, 6 (1801), 94–107. This article was reprinted from Pahl's longer book *Patriotisches Appel an den Friedenscongress in Lüneville* (Osnabrück and Münster, 1801), which was actually published, anonymously, at Nördlingen.

19. [Karl von Soden], "Zugabe zu dem in dem Staats-Archiv, Heft 21, Nr. V concentrirten Vorschlag zu einer Veränderung der deutschen Staats-Constitution," *Staats-Archiv*, 7 (1802), 81–103.

20. [Heinrich Gottlob Heinse], *Der Deutsche Fürstenbund nach den Forderungen des 19. Jahrhunderts, von Hieronimus a Lapide dem Jüngeren* (Leipzig and Gera, 1804), summarized in Hermann Schulz, *Vorschläge zur Reichsreform*, pp. 36–38.

21. Anon., *Vorschläge zur Verbesserung der Deutschen Reichsverfassung bey Gelegenheit des Congresses zu Rastadt den Ständen des Reichs gewidmet* (n.p., 1798), esp. pp. 15–31.

22. Niklas Vogt, *Die gescheiterten Projekte dieses und des vorigen Jahrhunderts* (Frankfurt an der Oder, 1803), summarized in Schulz, *Vorschläge zur Reichsreform*, pp. 46–47.

23. This was doubly true of the smaller surviving secular princes and Imperial Counts and Knights, who felt themselves threatened not only in the macrocosm of European power politics but even within the microcosm of German politics following the disproportionate expansion of some of their fellow Estates as a result of the Final Recess. It was this fear for their continuing survival that the author of a plea for a "mini-league" of the smaller Estates was referring to when he remarked that no period of the history of Germany could present clearer or simpler motives and goals for such an association. He felt that an alliance could make these princes and the danger to which they were exposed more visible to the great powers, which would then offer them protection against the depredations of the larger states. J. B., *Ueber*

die Unionen kleinerer Reichsstände. Ein Sendschreiben eines ritterschaftlichen Consulenten in Schwaben an seinen Kollegen in Franken (Am Bodensee, 1804), pp. 36–51.

24. Georg Wilhelm Friedrich Hegel, *Die Verfassung des Deutschen Reichs. Eine politische Flugschrift von Georg Wilhelm Friedrich Hegel,* ed. Georg Mollat (Stuttgart, 1935), pp. 1–6, 9. The title is that of the editor, since Hegel himself gave it none.

25. Ibid., p. 14.

26. Ibid., pp. 16–26.

27. Ibid., pp. 118–120.

28. Ibid., p. 118.

29. Ibid., p. 119.

30. Ibid., pp. 120–121.

31. Recent scholarship has concluded that the individual to whom Hegel looked for Germany's salvation was not Napoleon, as some earlier scholars had assumed, but Archduke Karl as a more worthy successor to Francis II on the imperial throne. See Henry S. Harris, *Hegel's Development: Toward the Sunlight* (Oxford, 1972), pp. 475–476, who follows the arguments earlier laid down in Franz Rosenzweig, *Hegel und der Staat,* 2 vols. (Munich, 1920), I, 125–127.

32. One author, for example, after discussing various categories of political structures, concluded that Germany was indeed a state because there existed a central authority with powers that extended to the internal affairs of the member territories, thus indicating a subordination of the parts to the whole. The notion that the Empire might be a federation was rejected because of the existing inequality of rights of the members in terms of their influence on the affairs of the Empire— something that could not, according to him, exist in a true federation, where the rights of all with respect to the whole had to be exactly equal. He then went on, however, to criticize the Empire for wanting to be something that according to its present "nature and situation" it could not be, and thus wound up in the not altogether logical position of having asserted that while it was indeed a state it also could not be a state. He went on to propose the dissolution of the imperial constitution, involving full sovereignty and independence for all the German states, and calmly accepted the probability that many of these states would sooner or later be absorbed by others. Anon., *Sollte man die Vernichtung der teutschen Reichsverfassung wünschen?* (Frankfurt and Leipzig, 1798), pp. 27–41.

33. Hegel, *Die Verfassung,* p. 46. This brief formula, which cut like a razor through the lengthy and tortuous discussions of the political nature of the Empire contained in formal treatises on public law, is one of several evidences of the impatience with which Hegel viewed what he regarded as the hopelessly naive efforts of the learned to make a state of the Empire by means of verbal definitions alone. At one point, he declared scornfully that even in the face of the utter political collapse of Germany and the plundering it would bring with it, the scholars of public law would know how to demonstrate that all of this was exactly as it should be according to both formal rights and practice, and that all misfortunes whatsoever were mere bagatelles against the preservation of the basic principle that the state should have no power. Ibid., pp. 9–10.

34. Gaspari, *Der Deputations-Recess,* I, 61–64.

35. Summarized from works published by Gönner in 1804 by Gross, *Empire and Sovereignty,* pp. 465–475.

36. Gaspari, *Der Deputations-Recess,* I, 68–69.

37. Ibid., pp. 70–90.

38. Karl S. Zachariae, "Geist der neusten deutschen Reichsverfassung," *Geschichte und Politik,* 1804 (1), 34–66.

39. Ibid.

40. He also regarded the many complaints among the traditionalists about the present deficiencies of the Empire as stemming from their fundamentally incorrect

view of it as a single state, suggesting that while improvements were needed in any case many of the supposedly faulty institutions and procedures of the Empire would not look quite so bad if they were seen in the context of Germany as a league rather than as a state. Ibid., pp. 60–61. Confusion of the two concepts in the literature of the time was frequent, even though it often shows up only in lamentations about the disparity between the ideal and the reality expressed by the imperial constitution. Occasionally, however, it was patent, as in the work of one author who in 1803 defined the Empire as "a very limited elective monarchy made up of numerous subordinate states," but who in the next paragraph found that it resembled more than anything else "the so-called states-system," a similarity he found even more pronounced as a result of the Final Recess. Hartleben, *Die deutsche Staatsverfassung,* p. 23.

41. Karl S. Zachariae, "Geist der neusten deutschen Reichsverfassung," *Geschichte und Politik,* 1801 (1), 66.

42. Julius Frey, *Die neuen und alten Churfürsten und Fürsten der Entschädigungsländer als Mitglieder des deutschen Reiches, als Regenten und als Menschen geschildert* (Leipzig and Gera, 1804), pp. 301–302.

CHAPTER FIFTEEN

1. Aretin, *Heiliges Römisches Reich,* I, 457.

2. This was most clearly obvious in Vienna's handling of the so-called *droit d'épaves,* whereby Austria confiscated the property and capital sums of secularized ecclesiastical foundations which lay on Austrian soil. The bishoprics of Bamberg, Passau, and Freising, for example, all of which had been absorbed by Bavaria, had previously had valuable properties in Austria; the government now took them over. With these new riches, Vienna then approached a number of small princes and Imperial Counts in Swabia, who had been rather poorly compensated for their Left Bank losses, and offered them these more lucrative Austrian properties in return for their little territories. Many of them accepted gladly. Austria's intention in acquiring these lands was to encircle as many territories of Imperial Knights and others as possible in order to absorb them if in the future their mediatization should prove unavoidable or even simply desirable, and thus to gain a stronger position in the Swabian Circle. Ibid., pp. 466–467.

3. Schulz, *Vorschläge zur Reichsreform,* p. 13.

4. See, for example, the proposal of Karl Heinrich von Bernkastell, who linked the progressive weakening of the Empire to the elective system that had forced every candidate for the imperial office to agree to a steadily increasing series of restrictive conditions, through which the entire imperial system became constantly looser and more deficient. Bernkastell felt that the essential character and balance of the constitution would not be affected by making the imperial crown hereditary in the House of Habsburg, especially if the present Electoral Capitulation were fixed for all time as a "hereditary constitution" (*Erblichkeits-Konstitution*). *Gedanken über die Frage: Verliert, oder gewinnt vielmehr Deutschland, wenn es der herrschenden Familie das Erbrecht zu seinem Kaiserthron überlässt?* (Basel, 1806), iii–v, 19–45.

5. A more detailed analysis of these events can be found in Epstein, *Genesis,* pp. 656–660, whose own work is based largely on Heinrich Ritter von Srbik, *Das österreichische Kaisertum und das Ende des Heiligen Römischen Reiches 1804–1806* (Berlin, 1927), and on two studies by Hellmuth Rössler: *Österreichs Kampf um Deutschlands Befreiung,* already cited; and *Napoleons Griff nach der Karlskrone: Das Ende des alten Reiches 1806* (Munich, 1957).

6. Hanover had also been promised to Prussia, thanks to Russian mediation, as the price for participation in the coalition against Napoleon—a promise rendered nugatory, of course, by Berlin's failure to enter the war.

7. Aretin believes that "sovereignty" was interpreted by the rulers who received it—and especially in Baden and Württemberg—as conferring on them essentially the same free hand in domestic matters that Austria and Prussia had long since obtained, and that it therefore corresponded to an "unlimited *Landeshoheit*," a term for which there was no French equivalent and which was therefore translated as *souveraineté* in the treaties, which were composed in French. It speaks for this interpretation that King Frederick of Württemberg declared himself opposed to the dissolution of the Empire in May, 1806, because he believed that thereafter the states of second rank in Germany would have no external guarantee. *Heiliges Römisches Reich*, I, 478.

8. See Anon., "Ueber den Ausdruck Souverainität," *Staats-Archiv*, 15 (1806), 341–350; and [Heinrich Alois Graf von Reigersberg], *Ein Wort über die Lage des Kayserlichen Reichs-Kammergerichts nach dem Pressburger Frieden. Geschrieben von einem deutschen Patrioten* (n.p., 1806), pp. 1–25. Reigersberg, president of the Cameral Tribunal, seems to have had as much concern to preserve the threatened jobs of the judges and employees of the imperial courts as to provide a continuing source of arbitration for the conflicts of the Estates. On his career, see *Allgemeine deutsche Biographie*, XXVII, 696–697.

9. Anon., *Winke an's Vaterland* (n.p., 1806), esp. pp. 10–17.

10. [Georg Heinrich Kayser], "Von den höchsten Interessen des teutschen Reiches, mit besonderer Rücksicht auf den Einfluss welchen Baiern gegenwärtig auf jene behauptet. Heilbronn, 1806," *Staats-Archiv*, 14 (1805), 431–450; 15 (1806), 153–186. The content of this work approximates very closely that of the anonymous book *Beiträge zum neuen deutschen Staatsrecht* (Heilbronn, 1806), which is summarized in Schulz, *Vorschläge zur Reichsreform*, pp. 38–40, and is almost certainly the same.

11. [Kayser], "Von den höchsten Interessen," *Staats-Archiv*, 15 (1806), 351–392.

12. Anon., "Einige Betrachtungen über die in dem vorigen Heft des Staats-Archivs befindliche Schrift: Von den höchsten Interessen des teutschen Reichs," ibid., pp. 97–98.

13. [Freiherr von Rhaden], *Zufällige Gedanken eines Hannoveraners beym Lesen des IV. Heftes der Schrift: Von den höchsten Interessen des Teutschen Reichs* (Regensburg, 1806), pp. 16–17. As a Hanoverian, needless to say, this writer was also much exercised about Kayser's acceptance of the destruction of the former Electorate through its absorption by Prussia. See pp. 7–8.

14. Ibid., p. 17.

15. [J. G. Pahl], "Betrachtungen über den XIV. Artikel des Friedens von Pressburg," *National-Chronik der Teutschen*, 6 (1806), 49–51.

16. Fridolin Wurmsamen [pseudonym], "Ueber die künftige Verfassung Teutschlands," ibid., pp. 137–139; and Anon., "Noch mehr über die künftige Verfassung Deutschlands," ibid., pp. 220–223.

17. This proposal, almost certainly that of someone with a great sense of confidence in the political future of post-Pressburg Bavaria, is contained in the anonymous work *Politische Gedanken über den jüngst geendeten Krieg und seine Folgen in Hinsicht auf Bayern* (Deutschland, 1806), summarized in Mathys Jolles, *Das deutsche Nationalbewusstsein im Zeitalter Napoleons* (Frankfurt, 1936), p. 99. It is worth noting that a significant proportion of the works which in this period called for the dissolution of the imperial nexus without at the same time suggesting a basis for another kind of union of some or all of the German states appear to be of Bavarian origin. This fact reflects the very ambitious political visions of King Maximilian I Joseph and his able minister Montgelas who, unlike the more traditionalist and still largely dynastically oriented rulers of other enlarged states, were modernizing the government of Bavaria with an eye to attaining the position of a European power of at least second rank. See Aretin, *Heiliges Römisches Reich*, I, 477–478.

18. Rössler, *Napoleons Griff*, pp. 26–27.

19. Aretin, *Heiliges Römisches Reich*, I, 499.

20. Beaulieu-Marconnay, *Karl von Dalberg*, II, 36–39. See also Aretin, *Heiliges Römisches Reich*, I, 500.

21. Cited in Beaulieu-Marconnay, *Karl von Dalberg*, II, 46–47.

22. The archchancellor's attitudes and initiatives in these matters have been judged quite differently by historians. A nineteenth-century biographer has suggested that Dalberg's concern for the preservation of the imperial constitution, though genuine enough, arose largely from his awareness that such power as he had or ever might hope to have stemmed not from the territory he ruled after the Final Recess, which was so absurdly small as to make him far and away the puniest of the Electors, but from the office and dignity of archchancellor, with its associated functions as director of the Council of Electors and of the Diet, and guardian of the laws. If the Empire and its constitution were dissolved, so was his only claim to any substantial influence on public affairs; he was therefore prepared to work towards its preservation at almost any cost, including handing its German throne over to a foreigner. Ibid., pp. 93–94.

This interpretation, which sets a high priority on naked self-interest as Dalberg's chief motivation, has been largely rejected by more recent scholars. Aretin, for example, sees Dalberg as a true and time-tested *Reichspatriot*, who settled upon a Napoleonic emperorship only after events had overwhelmed all other alternatives, and as the last chance of saving a thousand-year-old edifice, which he truly admired and believed in very deeply. The argument that the archchancellor somehow betrayed the German national interest in soliciting a foreign prince for the imperial dignity, Aretin suggests, neglects not only the political and cultural cosmopolitanism of the times, which Dalberg shared with almost all other German princes, but also the fact that for him to have predicated his imperial politics on a national basis would have required an adequate national prop, or stay, in the form of a strong German guarantor. With Austria in a state of apparently irremediable defeat and disarry, and with no other candidates either clamoring for the role or capable of fulfilling it, his choice reduced to one: "The lack of a power in Germany (sufficient) to guarantee order forced Dalberg into Napoleon's arms." Aretin admits that Dalberg suffered from a chronic lack of political realism—from a "naively credulous idealism," as he puts it—but he is not prepared to see this fault as of such magnitude as to outweigh the merits of the sincerity with which he pursued his patriotic goals. *Heiliges Römisches Reich*, I, 484–485, 502.

23. The best studies of the formation of the Confederation are by Theodor Bitterauf, *Geschichte des Rheinbundes. Band I: Die Gründung des Rheinbundes und der Untergang des alten Reiches* (Munich, 1905), and Satz, *Die Politik der deutschen Staaten*. Convenient shorter summaries can be found in Bornhak, *Deutsche Verfassungsgeschichte*, pp. 277–309, and Huber, *Deutsche Verfassungsgeschichte*, I, esp. pp. 68–84.

24. Aretin, *Heiliges Römisches Reich*, I, 502.

25. Cited in Rössler, *Napoleons Griff*, pp. 55–56.

26. Aretin, *Heiliges Römisches Reich*, I, 479. King Frederick openly opposed the idea of the Confederation until it was made clear to him that his territory would be occupied by French troops and that he would lose out to Bavaria and Baden in the future mediatization of neighboring Imperial Counts and Knights. Even thereafter, he protested privately against his separation from the Empire and the loss of his electoral title, and reserved to himself for the future all his rights as Estate and Elector of the Empire. Montgelas' attitudes, too, were not nearly as friendly to the creation of the *Rheinbund* as Talleyrand supposed. The Bavarian minister declared openly to his king that "I see the days coming when we will yearn for the mild governance of the Roman Emperor in Vienna. But there was and is no other way." Cited in Rössler, *Napoleons Griff*, p. 65.

27. Schmidt, *Preussens deutsche Politik*, pp. 80–101.

28. Helmut Tiedemann, *Der deutsche Kaisergedanke vor und nach dem Wiener Kongress* (Breslau, 1932), pp. 27–28. Both the *Dictatum* and the French note are

reprinted in Ernst Rudolf Huber, *Dokumente zur deutschen Verfassungsgeschichte*, 2 vols. (Stuttgart, 1961–64), I, 32–35.

29. Epstein, *Genesis*, pp. 663–666; Rössler, *Napoleons Griff*, pp. 44–51.

30. Huber, *Deutsche Verfassungsgeschichte*, I, 71–73.

31. Rössler, *Napoleons Griff*, p. 64; Tiedemann, *Der deutsche Kaisergedanke*, pp. 35–36.

32. As described, for example, in Epstein, *Genesis*, p. 669.

33. Cited in Satz, *Die Politik der deutschen Staaten*, p. 71.

34. Cited in Wilhelm Koppen, *Deutsche gegen Deutschland. Geschichte des Rheinbundes* (Hamburg, 1936), p. 132.

35. Srbik, *Deutsche Einheit*, I, 164.

36. Kemiläinen, *Auffassungen*, p. 75.

37. Anon., "Patriotische Reflexionen eines teutschen Bürgers," *National-Chronik der Teutschen*, 4 (1804), 369.

38. Anon., *Winke über Teutschlands Alte und Neue Staatsverfassung*, pp. 163–164.

39. Anon., "Was wird aus Teutschland werden?" *Staats-Archiv*, 10 (1803), 39, note, and 52–55.

40. Anon., "Wahrer Abriss des neuesten practischen teutschen Staatsrechts," ibid., 12 (1804), 33.

41. [J. G. Pahl], "Teutschland im Laufe des Jahres 1806," *National-Chronik der Teutschen*, 6 (1806), 6–7: [Pahl], "Betrachtungen über den XIV. Artikel des Friedens von Pressburg," ibid., pp. 50–51.

42. Anon., *Winke an's Vaterland*, pp. 4–5.

43. Quoted in Meinecke, *Cosmopolitanism and the National State*, p. 46. The translation is by Robert B. Kimber.

44. [J. G. Pahl], "Patriotische Phantasien. Am ersten Morgen des Jahrs 1802," *National-Chronik der Teutschen*, 2 (1802), 2.

45. Quoted in Bitterauf, *Geschichte des Rheinbundes*, I, 99.

46. The quotation from Schiller is from Meinecke, *Cosmopolitanism and the National State*, p. 46; those of Novalis are from the same work, p. 55. All are the translations of Robert B. Kimber except the first quotation from Novalis, which I have translated for what I believe to be greater accuracy from the original German in Meinecke's *Weltbürgertum und Nationalstaat*, ed. Hans Herzfeld (Munich, 1962), p. 66.

47. Christoph Martin Wieland, "Was ist zu thun?" (1798), in *C. M. Wielands sämmtliche Werke*, ed. J. G. Gruber, XLII, 131.

48. Quoted in Jolles, *Das deutsche Nationalbewusstsein*, pp. 265–266.

49. Kemiläinen, *Auffassungen*, pp. 253–255.

50. [J. G. Pahl], "Sind die Teutschen nun noch eine Nation?" *National-Chronik der Teutschen*, 6 (1806), 340–342.

51. The reference to Dalberg in the last line of the poem was intended to recall the venerable custom of the coronation ceremony of the German Emperors since the time of Maximilian I, whereby the imperial herald would invite the senior Dalberg out of the crowd of attending dignitaries for the first renewal of knighthood after the coronation with the words: "Is no Dalberg at hand?" (Ist kein Dalberg da?)— thus calling attention to the special relationship between the Emperors and the Dalbergs as the "first family" of Imperial Knights. Halem's poem, "Der Rheinbund" (1806), is in *Schriften*, V, 359.

52. Napoleon's attitude is neatly summed up in a comment he made to Metternich in 1807. After an audience with Dalberg, the Emperor turned to the Austrian diplomat with these words: "That man [Dalberg] is a numskull. He keeps tormenting me to reconstitute what he calls 'la patrie allemande.' He wants to have his (Regensburg), his imperial Chamber, with all its traditions of the old German Empire. He has just been trying to talk this nonsense to me, but I cut him short."

Quoted in Herbert A. L. Fisher, *Studies in Napoleonic Statesmanship: Germany* (Oxford, 1903), p. 165.

53. Gross, *Empire and Sovereignty*, p. 465.

54. Nikolaus Thaddäus von Gönner, *Ueber den Umsturz der deutschen Staats-verfassung und seinen Einfluss auf die Quellen des Privatrechts in den neu souverainen Staaten der rheinischen Conföderation* (n.p., 1807), pp. 10–11.

55. [J. G. Pahl], "Der Rheinische Bund," *Chronik der Teutschen*, 7 (1807), 81; and [Pahl], "Blicke auf Europa in den ersten Tagen des April, 1807," ibid., p. 130. Pahl shortened the title of his journal in late 1806, reflecting his conviction that while a periodical which devoted its attention more or less exclusively to German cultural affairs could still be termed "national," one that intended to discuss the political life of Germany, as he did, no longer could be.

56. Koppen, *Deutsche gegen Deutschland*, p. 237.

57. One of the strengths of Bitterauf, *Geschichte des Rheinbundes*, is that it recognizes contemporary perception of the Confederation in terms similar to these, and at a time—1905—when German historiography was almost uniformly hostile to the policies of the south German states. See Epstein, *Genesis*, p. 661, n. 26.

58. Quoted in Eckhart Klessmann, ed., *Deutschland unter Napoleon: in Augenzeugberichten* (Düsseldorf, 1965), p. 80.

59. Rössler, *Napoleons Griff*, p. 65.

60. Cited in Fisher, *Studies in Napoleonic Statesmanship*, p. 163.

61. Rössler, *Napoleons Griff*, p. 64.

62. Ibid., p. 165: "In broad circles of the people the grief for the deceased and the hope and belief in the resurrection of Emperor and Empire lived on, and many now glorified the great, proud past of which they had earlier scarcely taken notice." Helmut Tiedemann refers to the stubborn rejection by many of the notion that the great and sublime German crown, "with which the first dignity of the world had been associated," could ever be irretrievably lost to a people for whom it had so long been the very essence of their political being. *Der deutsche Kaisergedanke*, p. 41.

63. Quoted from Arndt's *Geist der Zeit* (1807) in Kemiläinen, *Auffassungen*, p. 21.

Bibliography

PRIMARY SOURCES

Anon. *An den deutschen Reichstag. Beim Durchzuge der Russischen Hülfstruppen durch Regensburg. Von einem Komitial-Gesandten.* Regensburg, 1799.

Andreas, Willy, ed. *Politischer Briefwechsel des Herzogs und Grossherzogs Carl August von Weimar.* Bearbeitet von Hans Tümmler. 2 vols. Quellen zur deutschen Geschichte des 19. und 20. Jahrhunderts, vols. 37 and 38. Stuttgart, 1954–58.

Anon. *Auf wessen Seite liegt der Vortheil wenn Teutschlands Bissthümer sacularisiret werden?* N.p., 1802.

[Bauer, Conrad Alois]. *Reichsverfassungsmäsige Betrachtungen über die Fortsetzung des Reichstags unter der hohen Reichsvikarien Autorität, und über die Nothwendigkeit und Gesetzlichkeit ihrer Befugnisse. Angestellt von einem Verehrer der deutschen Konstitution.* N.p., (April) 1790.

Anon. *Beiträge zur richtigen Beurtheilung der Kapitulation von Mannheim.* [Frankfurt], 1796.

Anon. *Bemerkungen bey Gelegenheit des neuesten Fürstenbundes im Deutschen Reiche.* Berlin and Leipzig, 1786.

Berg, Günther Heinrich von. *Ueber Teutschlands Verfassung und die Erhaltung der öffentlichen Ruhe in Teutschland.* Göttingen, 1795.

Berlinische Monatsschrift. Edited by Friedrich Gedike and Johann Erich Biester. 28 vols. Berlin, Jena and Dessau, 1783–96.

Bernkastell, Karl Heinrich von. *Gedanken über die Frage: Verliert, oder gewinnt vielmehr Deutschland, wenn es der herrschenden Familie das Erbrecht zu seinem Kaiserthron überlässt?* Basel, 1806.

Anon. *Betrachtungen über die Frage: Ob Deutschland durch die Säcularisation der Bisthümer und Abbteyen gewinne oder verliere?* N.p., 1803.

Anon. *Betrachtungen über die Freiheit und Wolfarth des deutschen Reichs, und über die Mittel zu deren Erhaltung von einem Patrioten.* N.p., 1789.

Anon. *Betrachtungen über den deutschen Reichstag.* N.p., 1789.

[Blum, Georg Franz Edler von]. *Patriotische Gedanken und Vorschläge zur Vermehrung der teutschen Reichs-Armee, zur Regulirung des Aufgebots und Herbeyschaffung baarer Mittel zu deren Unterstützung.* Frankfurt and Leipzig, 1794.

[Bretschneider, Karl Gottlieb]. *Teutschland und Preussen oder das Interesse Teutschlands am preussischen Staate. Von einem Nicht-Preussen.* Berlin, 1806.

[Bülau, Johann Jakob]. *Noch etwas zum Deutschen Nationalgeist.* Lindau am Bodensee, 1766.

Conrad, Hermann, ed. *Recht und Verfassung des Reiches in der Zeit Maria Theresias: die Vorträge zum Unterricht des Erzherzogs Joseph in Natur- und Völkerrecht sowie im deutschen Staats- und Lehnrecht.* Cologne and Opladen 1964.

Dalberg, Karl von. *Von Erhaltung der Staatsverfassungen.* Erfurt, 1795.

Anon. *Das wahre Interesse des Deutschen Reiches bey dem gegenwärtigen Krieg zwischen den Häusern Preussen und Oesterreich.* [Berlin], 1761.

Der Deutsche. Published by Commercien Rath Hechtel. 8 vols. Magdeburg, Frankfurt a. d. Oder, Hamburg and Itzehoe, 1771–76.

Der Genius der Zeit. Edited by August Hennings. 21 vols. Altona, 1794–1800.

Der neue deutsche Zuschauer. Oder Archiv der denkwürdigsten Eräugnisse, welche auf die Glückseligkeit oder das Elend des menschlichen Geschlechts und der bürgerlichen Gesellschaft einige Beziehung haben kann. Published by Freunde der Publizität. 4 vols. Zürich, 1789–90.

Der teutsche Merkur. Edited by C. M. Wieland et al. 131 vols. in 76. Weimar, 1773–1810.

Der Weltbürger. Oder deutsche Annalen der Menschheit und Unmenschheit, der Aufklärung und Unaufgeklärtheit, der Sittlichkeit und Unsittlichkeit für die Jetztwelt und die Nachwelt. Edited by Theophil Friedrich Ehrmann. 3 vols. Germanien [Zürich], 1791–93.

Deutsche Monatsschrift. Edited by Gottlob Nathanael Fischer. 15 vols. Berlin, 1790–94.

Deutsches Magazin. Edited by Christian Ulrich Detlev von Eggers. 20 vols. Hamburg, 1791–1800.

Anon. *Deutschlands Gewinn und Verlust bei der Rastadter Friedens-Basis nebst Vorschlägen zu einer Entschädigungs-Plan und zu einer verbesserten Reichs-Verfassung.* N.p., 1798.

Die Chronologen. Edited by Ludwig Wekhrlin. Nos. 1–12. Frankfurt and Leipzig, 1779–81.

Anon. *Die freyen Reichs-Städte oder über das Interesse ihrer Verbindung, in nächster Beziehung auf Schwaben.* Kempten, 1801.

Dohm, Christian Wilhelm. *Ueber den deutschen Fürstenbund.* Second edition (?). Berlin, (December) 1785.

D. W. R. *Ueber den Patriotischen Vorschlag zu einem Frieden zwischen Bayern und Oestreich. Die Austauschung Bayerns gegen die Niederlande betreffend.* N.p., 1743 and 1786.

[Eberhard, Johann Heinrich]. *Freie Gedanken über einige der neuesten Staats-Streitigkeiten.* Geschrieben in H. R. Reich Deutscher Nation. [Frankfurt], 1767.

Anon. *Ein freyer teutscher Edelmann an den Verfasser der Schrift: das teutsche Reich vor der französischen Revolution und nach dem Frieden bey Lüneville.* Germania, 1802.

Anon. *Einige patriotische Blicke auf die jetzige bedenkliche Lage des teutschen Reichs im Zwischenreiche.* N.p., 1790.

Ephemeriden der Menschheit, oder Bibliothek der Sittenlehre, der Politik und der Gesetzgebung. Leipzig, 1776–86.

Anon. *Etwas vom Patriotismus im deutschen Reiche. Von einem Deutschen Mit deutscher Freiheit.* N.p., 1788.

Eudämonia oder deutsches Volksglück, ein Journal für Freunde von Wahrheit und Recht. 6 vols. Leipzig, Frankfurt and Nürnberg, 1795–98.

Europäische Annalen. Nos. 1–52. Tübingen, 1795–1820.

Fabritius, Karl Moritz. *Ueber den Werth und die Vorzüge geistlicher Staaten und Regierungen in Teutschland.* 2 vols. Frankfurt and Leipzig, 1797–99.

[Fandrich]. *Freymüthige Gedanken eines teutschen Staatsbürgers über die Säcularisierung der geistlichen Wahlstaaten Teutschlands in rechtlicher und politischer Hinsicht.* Altona and Hamburg, 1798.

F. D. *Ist die teutsche Kaiserkrone für das Haus Oesterreich wichtig? und Wie verhält sich dabey das Interesse des teutschen Reichs? freymüthig beantwortet von einem Patrioten.* Vaterland, 1790.

[Frank, Peter Anton]. *Etwas über die Wahlcapitulationen in den geistlichen Wahlstaaten.* Frankfurt, 1788.

Frey, Julius. *Die neuen und alten Churfürsten und Fürsten der Entschädigungsländer als Mitglieder des deutschen Reiches, als Regenten und als Menschen geschildert.* Leipzig and Gera, 1804.

Anon. *Freye Gedanken über die Vereinigung der Deutschen als Grundlage der allgemeinen Wohlfahrt, von einem deutschen Sklaven.* N.p., 1802.

Anon. *Freymüthige Anmerkungen zur Schrift des Freyherrn Otto von Gemmingen über die Königl. Preussische Association zu Erhaltung des Reichssystem.* Teutschland, 1785.

Gagern, Hans Christoph Freiherr von. *Ein deutscher Edelmann an seine Landsleute.* N.p., 1794.

Gaspari, Adam Christian. *Der Deputations-Recess: mit historischen, geographischen und statistischen Erläuterungen und einer Vergleichungs-Tafel.* 2 vols. Hamburg, 1803.

Anon., *Gedanken über die Berichtigung des Lüneviller Friedens durch die hohe Reichsfriedensdeputation.* N.p., 1802.

Gemmingen, Otto von. *Ueber die königl. Preussische Assoziazion zu Erhaltung des Reichssystems.* Deutschland, 1785.

Gerstlacher, Carl Fridrich. *Anmerkungen über Ihro regierenden kaiserlichen Majestät Josephs des IIten Wahlcapitulation, sonderlich, wie eine künftige Wahlcapitulation zu verbessern seyn möchte.* Stuttgart, 1789.

Geschichte und Politik. Edited by Karl Ludwig Woltmann. 12 vols. Berlin, 1800–5.

Gönner, Nikolaus Thaddäus von. *Ueber den Umsturz der deutschen Staatsverfassung und seinen Einfluss auf die Quellen des Privatrechts in den neu souverainen Staaten der rheinischen Conföderation.* N.p., 1807.

Görtz, genannt von Schlitz, Johann Eustachius Graf von. *Memoiren eines deutschen Staatsmannes aus den Jahren 1788–1816.* Leipzig, 1833.

[Graser, Johann Baptist]. *Wie wird es im säkularisirten Teutschlande gehen? Beantwortet in vertrauten Briefen an einen Freund.* Germania [Bamberg], 1802.

[Grimm, Friedrich Wernhard]. *Umfang und Gränzen des Reichsständischen Bündnissrechts nach dem wahren Sinn der Reichsgeseze. Nebst damit verbundenen Betrachtungen über den Teutschen Fürstenbund.* Berlin, 1786.

[Grub, Christian Friedrich]. *Ueber einige Reichs-Städte Teutschlands. Ein Wort zu seiner Zeit geredet von einem Staatsbürger.* N.p., 1786.

Halem, Gerhard Anton von. *Schriften.* 7 vols. Münster, 1803–10. Volumes 6 and 7 never published.

[Harl, Johann Paul]. *Deutschlands neueste Staats- und Kirchenveränderungen, historisch, politisch, staats- und kirchenrechtlich entwickelt.* Berlin, 1804.

Hartleben, Theodor K. *Die deutsche Staatsverfassung nach vollbrachtem Entschädigungssysteme.* N.p., 1803.

Hartmann, Karl Joseph. *Ueber den Ursprung und das rechtliche Verhältniss der Landstände in Teutschland.* Nürnberg, 1805.

Anon. *Hat der katholische deutsche Reichstheil im Lüneviller Frieden Vorrechte verloren die der protestantische Reichstheil im westphälischen Frieden gewonnen hat und noch besitzt? Eine Frage deren Erörterung in unsern Tagen wichtig wird.* N.p., 1805.

Hegel, Georg Wilhelm Friedrich. *Die Verfassung des Deutschen Reichs. Eine politische Flugschrift von Georg Wilhelm Friedrich Hegel.* Edited by Georg Mollat. Stuttgart, 1935.

Heinrich, Christoph Gottlob. *Teutsche Reichsgeschichte.* 9 vols. Leipzig, 1787–1805.

[Hendrich, Franz Joseas von]. *Freymüthige Gedanken über die allerwichtigste Angelegenheit Deutschlands.* Third edition. 3 vols. Germanien [Zürich], 1795–96.

Herder, Johann Gottfried. "Idee zum ersten patriotischen Institut für den Allgemein-geist Deutschlands" (1787). In *Sämtliche Werke*, edited by Bernhard Suphan, 33 vols., Berlin, 1877–1913, XVI, 600–616.

———. "Ueber die Verbindung der Deutschen Völker und Provinzen zum Anbau der Humanität" (1793). Ibid., XVII, 25–28.

———. "Warum wir noch keine Geschichte der Deutschen haben?" (1795). Ibid., XVIII, 380–384.

Anon. *Herrn Pfeifers verunglückter Versuch den teutschen Fürstenbund wieder zu zerstöhren, aus den eignen Worten des Herrn Pfeifers klärlich gezeigt von einem Layen in Reichssachen*. Cöthen, 1787.

Hertzberg, Ewald Friedrich Graf von. *Sur la forme des gouvernemens, et quelle en est la meilleure? Dissertation, qui a été lue dan l'assemblée publique de l'Acad-emie de Berlin le 29. Janvier 1784*. Berlin, 1784.

Hoff, Karl Ernst Adolf von. *Antwort des Verfassers der Schrift: das teutsche Reich vor der französischen Revolution, und nach dem Frieden zu Lüneville auf das an ihn gerichtete Schreiben eines freyen teutschen Edelmannes*. Gotha, 1802.

Humboldt, Wilhelm von. "Ideen zu einem Versuch, die Gränzen der Wirksamkeit des Staats zu bestimmen" (1792). In *Gesammelte Schriften*, edited by Albert Leitzmann, 17 vols., Berlin, 1903–36; reprinted, 1968, I, 97–254.

I. I. S. P. G. [Johann Jakob Schmauss, Professor Göttingen]. *Patriotischer Vorschlag zu einem Frieden zwischen Bayern und Oesterreich, . . . neu aufgelegt im Jahre: 1785*. N. p., 1785.

Anon. *Ist es rathsam, den deutschen Kayser in der neuen Wahl-Capitulation noch mehr einzuschränken, als er es jetzt schon ist? Und welche Veränderungen sind bei der Wahl-Capitulation überhaupt zu treffen?* Frankfurt and Leipzig, 1790.

J. B. *Ueber die Unionen kleinerer Reichsstände. Ein Sendschreiben eines ritter-schaftlichen Consulenten in Schwaben an seinen Kollegen in Franken*. Am Bo-densee, 1804.

J. E*** zu M***. *Sendschreiben des Hofkammerkanzlei-Dieners J. E*** zu M*** an Herrn Otto von Gemmingen Reichsfreiherrn, als eine einfältige Antwort auf desselben Gedanken über die Königliche Preussische Assoziation zu Erhaltung des Reichssystems*. N.p., 1786.

Kant, Immanuel. *Perpetual Peace: A Philosophical Essay*. Translated by M. Camp-bell Smith. New York and London, 1972.

[Kayser, Georg Heinrich]. *Von den höchsten Interessen des teutschen Reichs mit besonderer Rücksicht auf den Einfluss, den Baiern gegenwärtig auf jene be-hauptet*. 5 Hefte in 3 vols. Heilbronn, 1806.

Anon. *Kritik der deutschen Reichsverfassung*. 3 vols. Germanien, 1796–98.

[Krug, Wilhelm Traugott]. *Grundlinien zu einer allgemeinen deutschen Republik gezeichnet von einem Märtyrer der Wahrheit*. Altona and Vienna, 1797.

[Kruse, Karl Friedrich Freiherr von]. *Freimüthige Betrachtungen über die Gesezge-bung der Teutschen bey Gelegenheit der Wahl eines römischen Kaisers*. [Wies-baden], 1790.

Anon. *Kurzer Entwurf und Uebersicht einer Freystaatsverfassung*. Frankfurt, 1793.

[Laukhard, Friedrich Christian]. *Schilderung der jetzigen Reichsarmee nach ihrer wahren Gestalt. Nebst Winken über Deutschlands künftiges Schicksal*. Kölln, 1796.

Leuchtholz, Hanns. *Keine Säkularisation der Geistlichen Stände sondern Eine Modi-fication des ganzen Reichs*. Sarmatien, 1802.

Linden, Franz Joseph von. *Sind die Stände des deutschen Reichs verbunden an dem gegenwärtigen Kriege Frankreichs gegen den König von Ungarn und Böhmen Theil zu nehmen?* Mainz, 1792.

[Lippe-Weissenfeld, Carl Christian Graf zu]. *Nähere Beleuchtung des Nichteini-gung-Systems. Ein Bruchstück für die Geschichte der Zukunft. An meine Mit-stände*. Vaterland, 1798.

[———]. *Nicheinigung, ein Bruchstück des Zeitalters. An meine Mitstände.* Vaterland, 1796.

Litteratur und Völkerkunde. 9 vols. Dessau and Leipzig, 1782–86.

Minerva. Ein journal historischen und politischen Inhalts. Edited by Johann Wilhelm von Archenholz et al. 261 vols. Leipzig, Berlin and Hamburg, 1792–1857.

Möser, Justus. *Justus Möser's sämmtliche Werke.* Edited by B. R. Abken. New edition, 10 vols. in 7. Berlin, 1842–43.

Monzambano, Severinus von [Samuel von Pufendorf]. *Ueber die Verfassung des deutschen Reiches.* Translated by Harry Bresslau. Berlin, 1922.

[Moser, Friedrich Carl von]. *Buntschäkiges Gemählde verfertiget von einem Teutschen Biedermanne.* N.p., 1766.

[———]. *Patriotische Briefe.* N.p., 1767.

———. *Politische Wahrheiten.* 2 vols. Zürich, 1796.

———. *Ueber die Regierung der geistlichen Staaten in Deutschland.* Frankfurt and Leipzig, 1787.

[———]. *Von dem Deutschen national-Geist.* N.p., 1765.

[———]. *Was ist: gut Kayserlich, und: nicht gut Kayserlich?* Second edition. Vaterland, 1766.

[Moser, Johann Jacob]. *Betrachtungen über das Gleichgewicht von Europa und Teutschland in Rücksicht auf den Umtausch von Bayern.* Frankfurt and Leipzig, 1785.

———. *Von Teutschland und dessen Staats-Verfassung überhaupt.* Stuttgart, 1766.

Müller, Johannes von. *Darstellung des Fürstenbundes* (second edition, 1788). In *Sämmtliche Werke,* edited by Johann Georg Müller, 27 vols., Stuttgart and Tübingen, 1810–19, XXIV, 8–258.

———. *Teutschlands Erwartungen vom Fürstenbunde* (1788). Ibid., 259–284.

———. "Zweierlei Freiheit" (1786). Ibid., 1–7.

National-Chronik der Teutschen. Eine politische Zeitung. Edited by Johann Gottfried Pahl. 8 vols. Gmünd and Ellwangen, 1801–8. Title changed to *Chronik der Teutschen* in 1807.

Neue Litteratur und Völkerkunde. 5 vols. Dessau and Leipzig, 1787–91.

Neues Patriotisches Archiv für Deutschland. 2 vols. Mannheim and Leipzig, 1792–94.

Neueste Staats-Anzeigen. Edited by Freunde der Publizität und der Staatskunde. 6 vols. Germanien, 1797–98.

Anon. *Noch ein Wort an Teutschland.* N.p., 1800.

Anon. *Noch ein Wort über das Säkularisationswesen. Von einem Freunde der Menschheit und der guten Sache.* Teutschland, 1801.

Novalis [Friedrich von Hardenberg]. *Novalis' Werke.* Edited by Hermann Friedemann. Berlin, Leipzig, Vienna and Stuttgart, n.d.

O'Cahill, Baron. *Patriotische Gedanken über Deutschlands Integrität.* Frankfurt and Leipzig, 1798.

Ortmann, Adolph Dieterich. *Patriotische Briefe zur Vermahnung und zum Troste bey dem jetzigen Kriege.* Second edition. Berlin and Potsdam, 1759.

P., J. R. R. v. [Johann Freiherr von Pacassi]. *Betrachtung über die Berliner Beantwortung der Königlich Preussischen Association: Darin die Stärke von Preussen gezeigt, und die eigentlichen Absichten des Berliner Kabinets unter dem Scheine der grosmütigen Beschüzung der Rechte Deutschlands aufgesucht werden.* Munich, 1786.

Anon., *Patriotische Bemerkungen in Hinsich der Sekularisation und dessen unvermeidlich betrübten Folgen.* Germanien, 1802.

Patriotisches Archiv für Deutschland. Edited by Friedrich Carl von Moser. 12 vols. Frankfurt, Mannheim and Leipzig, 1784–90.

Anon. *Patriotische Wünsche für Teutschland bei dem bevorstehenden Definitiv-Reichs-Frieden. Nebst Verlusts- und Entschädigungs-Tabellen.* Frankfurt, 1801.

Pfeiffer, Christoph Ludwig. *Die teutsche Reichsverwirrung im Grandrisse. Oder: die Staatsgebrechen des heiligen Römischen Reichs teutscher Nation.* Mannheim, 1787.

————. *Was ist teutsche Volksfreiheit, teutsche Reichsfreiheit, und teutscher Fürstenbund? Eine teutschpatriotisch-staatsrechtliche Betrachtung.* [Heilbronn?], 1786.

Plant, Johann Traugott. *Schon wieder ein Kaiser aus dem Oesterreichischem Hause? Warum wählte man Ihn? Warum keinen Andern? Was gewinnt Oesterreich durch die Kaiserwürde? oder freimüthige Aufklärung über die Kaiserwahl Leopolds II.* N.p., 1790.

Anon. *Politische Betrachtungen und Nachrichten.* 2 vols. N.p., 1785.

Anon. *Proposizionen bey einem allgemeinem reichsritterschaftlichem Konvent. Träume eines Patrioten.* N.p., 1788.

Anon. *Prüfung der Ursachen einer Assoziazion zu Erhaltung des Reichssistems welche in der Erklärung Seiner Königl. Majestät von Preussen an Dero hohe Reichsmitstände und andere Europäische Höfe sind vorgelegt worden.* N.p., 1785.

Pütter, Johann Stephan. *Historische Entwickelung der heutigen Staatsverfassung des Teutschen Reichs.* 3 vols. Göttingen, 1786–87.

[————]. *Patriotische Abbildung des heutigen Zustandes beyder höchsten Reichsgerichte, worin der Verfall des Reichsjustizwesens sammt dem daraus bevorstehenden Unheile des ganzen Reichs . . . erörtert werden.* Frankfurt and Leipzig, 1756.

Anon. *Reichsgesetzmässige Erörterung der Reichsständischen Verhältnisse zu Kaiserlichen oder Reichstruppen während einem Reichskriege in Ansehung der in ihrem Gebiete liegenden Landesherrlichen Festungen zur Beantwortung einer dem Publikum darüber vorgelegten Frage.* N.p., 1794.

Reichsritterschaftliches Magazin. Edited by Johann Mader. 13 vols. Frankfurt and Leipzig, 1780–90.

[Reigersberg, Heinrich Alois Graf von]. *Ein Wort über die Lage des Kayserlichen Reichs-Kammergerichts nach dem Pressburger Frieden. Geschrieben von einem deutschen Patrioten.* N.p., 1806.

Anon. *Resultate mit aller Unpartheilichkeit gezogen aus dem Für and Wider die unmittelbare freie Reichsritterschaft in Schwaben, Franken und am Rheinstrome.* N.p., 1803.

[Rhaden, Freiherr von]. *Zufällige Gedanken eines Hannoveraners beym Lesen des IV. Heftes der Schrift: Von den höchsten Interessen des Teutschen Reichs.* Regensburg, 1806.

Riesbeck, Joahnn Caspar. *Travels through Germany.* Translated by the Rev. Mr. Maty. 3 vols. London, 1787. Originally published anonymously as *Briefe eines reisenden Franzosen über Deutschland: An seinen Bruder zu Paris.* 2 vols. N.p., n.d.

Rössig, C. G. *Ueber deutsches Staatsinteresse, Ländertausch, und das Schuzbündnis deutscher Fürsten. Zur Widerlegung der Schrift des Freyherrn von Gemmingen.* Leipzig, 1786.

[Sartori, Josef von]. *Leopoldinische Annalen. Ein Beitrag zur Regierungsgeschichte Kaiser Leopolds II.* 2 vols. in 1. Augsburg, 1792–93.

————. *Statistische Abhandlung über die Mängel in der Regierungsverfassung der geistlichen Wahlstaaten, und von den Mitteln, solchen abzuhelfen.* [Augsburg], 1787.

Schnaubert, Andreas Joseph. *Ueber des Freiherrn von Moser's Vorschläge zur Verbesserung der geistlichen Staaten in Deutschland.* Jena, 1788.

Schulze, Friedrich, ed. *Die Franzosenzeit in deutschen Landen, 1806–1815: in Wort und Bild der Mitlebenden.* 2 vols. Leipzig, 1908.

[Schweighofer, Johann Michael]. *Unpartheyische Betrachtungen über die Vorrechte und Vortheile der Kaiserkrone.* N.p., 1790.

Anon. *Sendschreiben an die Kurmaynzische Akademie zu Erfurt über die von derselben ausgesetzte Preisfrage: Welches sind die Mittel dem teutschen Bürger den Werth und die Vortheile der Reichs-Konstitution recht fühlbar und ihn derselben noch anhänglicher zu machen?* N.p., 1792.

[Seuffert, Johann M.]. *Der jämmerliche Prediger mit dem Vorspruche Unser Reich ist nicht von dieser Welt; oder Noch Etwas über die Säcularisirungen besonders nach Grundsätzen der Kantischen Philosophie.* Regensburg, 1798.

[——]. *Ueber die Aufstellung grösserer StaatenMassen in Teutschland statt der vielen kleineren, und Organisirung derselben nach dem Geiste des ZeitAlters.* Leipzig, 1799.

[Soden, Julius Reichsgraf von]. *Teutschland muss einen Kaiser haben.* N.p., 1788.

Anon. *Soll das deutsche Reich der politischen Auflösung nahe seyn?* N.p., 1795.

Anon. *Sollte man die Vernichtung der teutschen Reichsverfassung wünschen?* Frankfurt and Leipzig, 1798.

Solomel, Riphelius von [Josef von Ullheimer]. *Auch ein Entschädigungsplan an den Friedenkongress zu Rastadt.* N.p., 1798.

Staats-Archiv. Edited by Carl Friedrich Häberlin. 16 vols. Helmstedt and Leipzig, 1796–1808.

Staatswissenschaftliche Zeitung. 2 vols. Leipzig, 1789–90.

[Strube, David Georg]. *Rechtliche Ausführung von erlaubten und unerlaubten Kriegen der Teutschen Reichs-Stände wider einander.* Frankfurt and Leipzig, 1758.

Anon. *Teutschlands neue Konstituzion. Ein Bruchstück. Entworfen von einem teutschen Staatsbürger.* Edited by Erdmann Weber. Frankfurt and Leipzig, 1797.

[Troeltsch, Johann Friedrich Freiherr von]. *Unpartheyische Gedanken über die Anmerkungen des teutschen Hippolithus a Lapide.* Cölln, 1762.

[Truchsess zu Zeil und Trauchburg, Franz Anton Reichsgraf]. *Bedenken eines oberdeutschen Patrioten über den Tausch von Baiern.* Mörsburg, 1785.

Anon. *Über die Geistlichen Staaten in Deutschland und die vorgebliche Nothwendigkeit ihrer Säcularisation.* Deutschland, 1798.

Anon. *Über die Lage und Bedürfnisse des deutschen Reichs. Oder braucht Deutschland einen mächtigen Kaiser?* N.p., 1790.

Anon. *Ueber die Nothwendigkeit einer allgemeinen Säcularisation der deutschen Erzbisthümer, Bisthümer, Prälaturen und Klöster. Mit Hinsicht auf Deutschlands gegenwärtige Verfassung.* Germanien [Basel?], 1798.

Anon. *Unpartheiische Gedanken über die Unabhängigkeit einzelner deutscher Reichsstände in Beziehung auf auswärtige Mächte, und über ihr Recht mit denselben Krieg zu führen.* Frankfurt and Leipzig, 1792.

Anon. *Unser Reich ist nicht von dieser Welt. Ein erbaulicher Sermon für Geistliche und Weltliche.* [Regensburg?], 1798.

Anon. *Unter dem Krummstab ist gut wohnen, oder Beweis von der Achtung der geistlichen Rheinlande gegen ihre Regenten und politischreligiöse Verfassungen.* [Augsburg], 1801.

Anon. *Untersuchung der Frage: ob es Teutschland nützlich sey, dass das Haus Oesterreich die Kayserliche Würde behalte?* Frankfurt and Leipzig, 1752.

Anon. *Vorschläge zur Verbesserung der Deutschen Reichsverfassung bey Gelegenheit des Congresses zu Rastadt den Ständen des Reichs gewidmet.* N.p., 1798.

Anon. *Vorstellungen über den gegenwärtigen Krieg an die Völker Deutschlands, von einem Freunde der Wahrheit und des Vaterlandes.* N.p., 1795.

Voss, Christian Daniel. *Ueber die Schicksale der deutschen Reichs-Staatsverfassung.* Leipzig, 1802.

Anon. *Warum soll Deutschland einen Kayser haben?* N.p., 1787.

Anon. *Was für Maasregeln hat wohl die Reichsritterschaft in Franken und Schwaben itzt zu ergreifen?* [Würzburg?], 1802.

Weisse, Christian Ernst. *Ueber die Sekularisation Deutscher geistlicher Reichsländer in Rücksicht auf Geschichte und Staatsrecht.* Leipzig, 1798.

——. *Von den Vortheilen der teutschen Reichsverbindung. Nebst einem kleinen Beytrage zum Staatsrecht des Mittelalters, nach Anleitung der schwäbischen Dichter.* Leipzig, 1790.

Anon. *Welche Maassregeln kann wohl die Reichsritterschaft in Franken und Schwaben jetzt ergreifen? Ein Gegenstück der Druckschrift: Was für Maassregeln hat wohl die Reichsritterschaft in Franken und Schwaben itzt zu ergreifen?* N.p., 1803.

Wieland, Christoph Martin. "Betrachtungen über die gegenwärtige Lage des Vaterlandes" (1793). In *C.M. Wielands sämmtliche Werke,* edited by J. G. Gruber, 53 vols., Leipzig, 1818-28, XLI, 283-333.

——. "Patriotischer Beytrag zu Deutschlands höchstem Flor, veranlasst durch einen im Jahr 1780 gedruckten Vorschlag dieses Nahmens" (1780). Ibid., XL, 135-160.

——. "Ueber deutschen Patriotismus. Betrachtungen, Fragen und Zweifel" (1793). Ibid., XLI, 334-353.

——. "Vorrede" to Schiller's *Historischer Kalender für Damen* (1792). Ibid., XLII, 449-462.

Anon. *Winke an's Vaterland.* N.p., 1806.

Anon. *Winke über Teutschlands Alte und Neue Staatsverfassung von einem teutschen Staatsbürger.* Germanien, 1798.

Wolfter, Peter. *Geschichte der Veränderungen des teutschen Reichsstaats.* Zürich, 1789.

SECONDARY SOURCES

Because the number of works treating one or another aspect of the history of the Holy Roman Empire in modern times is enormous, the following listing is designed chiefly to contain only those titles which were of immediate importance to the author in the writing of this book. For a much larger group of secondary (and some primary) sources, the reader is perhaps best referred to the 2,233-item bibliography in the work, listed below, of Karl Otmar Freiherr von Aretin, *Heiliges Römisches Reich, 1776-1806: Reichsverfassung und Staatssouveränität,* II, 349-424.

Allers, Ulrich S. *The Concept of Empire in German Romanticism and its Influence on the National Assembly at Frankfort, 1848-1849.* Washington, 1948.

Allgemeine deutsche Biographie. Published by the Historische Commission bei der königlichen Akademie der Wissenschaften. 56 vols. Leipzig, 1875-1912.

Aretin, Karl Otmar Freiherr von. *Heiliges Römisches Reich 1776-1806: Reichsverfassung und Staatssouveränität.* 2 vols. Wiesbaden, 1967.

Aris, Reinhold. *History of Political Thought in Germany from 1789 to 1815.* London, 1936.

Bassenge, Edmund. *Der nationale Gedanke in der deutschen Geschichte.* Leipzig, 1921.

Beaulieu-Marconnay, Karl Freiherr von. *Karl von Dalberg und seine Zeit. Zur Biographie und Charakteristik des Fürsten Primas.* 2 vols. Weimar, 1879.

Beck, Karl. *Zur Verfassungsgeschichte des Rheinbunds.* Dissertation, University of Giessen, Mainz, 1890.

Becker, Friedrich Wilhelm. *Die Kaiserwahl Leopolds II, 1790: eine Untersuchung zur Geschichte des alten Reiches und der Nachwirkung des Fürstenbundes.* Dissertation, University of Bonn, 1943.

Benecke, G. *Society and Politics in Germany, 1500-1750.* London and Toronto, 1974.

Berdahl, Robert M. "New Thoughts on German Nationalism," *American Historical Review,* 77 (1972), 65-80.

Bernard, Paul P. *Joseph II and Bavaria: Two Eighteenth-Century Attempts at German Unification.* The Hague, 1965.

Berney, Arnold. "Reichstradition und Nationalstaatsgedanke (1785–1815)," *Historische Zeitschrift,* 140 (1929), 57–86.

Bitterauf, Theodor. *Geschichte des Rheinbundes.* Band I: *Die Gründung des Rheinbundes und der Untergang des alten Reiches.* Munich, 1905.

Bog, Ingomar. *Der Reichsmerkantilismus: Studien zur Witschaftspolitik des Heiligen Römischen Reiches im 17. und 18. Jahrhundert.* Forschungen zur Sozial- und Wirtschaftsgeschichte, I. Stuttgart, 1959.

Bonjour, Edgar. "Die Idee des europäischen Gleichgewichts bei Johannes von Müller," *Historische Zeitschrift,* 182 (1956), 527–547.

Bornhak, Conrad. *Deutsche Verfassungsgeschichte vom Westfälischen Frieden an.* Stuttgart, 1934.

Bosl, K., and Möckl, K. *Der moderne Parlamentarismus und seine Grundlagen in der ständischen Repräsentation.* Berlin, 1977.

Braubach, Max. *Maria Theresias jüngster Sohn Max Franz, letzter Kurfürst von Köln und Fürstbischof von Münster.* Vienna and Munich, 1961.

Brunschwig, Henri. *Enlightenment and Romanticism in Eighteenth-Century Prussia.* Translated by Frank Jellinek. Chicago, 1974.

Crämer, Ulrich. *Carl August von Weimar und der Deutsche Fürstenbund, 1783–1790.* Wiesbaden, 1961.

Deutsches Anonymen-Lexikon. Edited by Michael Holzmann and Hanns Bohatta. 7 vols. Weimar, 1902–28; reprinted, Hildesheim, 1961.

Droz, Jacques. *L'Allemagne et la Révolution Française.* Paris, 1949.

Epstein, Klaus. *The Genesis of German Conservatism.* Princeton, 1966.

Ernstberger, Anton. "Reichsheer und Reich: ein Reformvorschlag 1794/95." In *Gesamtdeutsche Vergangenheit. Festgabe für Heinrich Ritter von Srbik zum 60. Geburtstag,* pp. 179–186. Munich, 1938.

Feine, Hans Erich. "Zur Verfassungsentwicklung des Heiligen Römischen Reiches seit dem Westfälischen Frieden," *Zeitschrift der Savigny-Stiftung für Rechtsgeschichte,* Germ. Abt., 37 (1916), 131–260.

Fischer, Ernst. *Carl Friedrich Haeberlin, ein braunschweigischer Staatsrechtslehrer und Publizist, 1756–1808.* Dissertation, University of Göttingen, 1914.

Fisher, Herbert A. L. *Studies in Napoleonic Statesmanship: Germany.* Oxford, 1903.

Gagliardo, John G. *From Pariah to Patriot: The Changing Image of the German Peasant, 1770–1840.* Lexington, Kentucky, 1969.

Glas-Hochstettler, Thomas J. "The Imperial Knights in Post-Westphalian Mainz: A Case Study of Corporatism in the old Reich," *Central European History,* 11 (1978), 131–49.

Gollwitzer, Heinz. *Europabild und Europagedanke: Beiträge zur deutschen Geistesgeschichte des 18. und 19. Jahrhunderts.* Second edition. Munich, 1964.

Gooch, G. P. *Germany and the French Revolution.* London, 1920; reprinted, New York, 1966.

Grolle, Joist. *Landesgeschichte in der Zeit der deutschen Spätaufklärung: Ludwig Timotheus Spittler (1752–1810).* Göttinger Bausteine zur Geschichtswissenschaft, XXXV. Göttingen, 1963.

Groote, Wolfgang von. *Die Entstehung des Nationalbewusstseins in Nordwestdeutschland 1790–1830.* Göttinger Bausteine zur Geschichtswissenschaft, XXII. Göttingen, 1955.

Gross, Hanns. *Empire and Sovereignty: A History of the Public Law Literature in the Holy Roman Empire, 1599–1804.* Chicago, 1973.

Gschliesser, Oswald von. *Der Reichshofrat: Bedeutung und Verfassung, Schicksal und Besetzung einer obersten Reichsbehörde von 1559 bis 1806.* Vienna, 1942.

Harris, Henry S. *Hegel's Development: Toward the Sunlight.* Oxford, 1972.

Heller, Hermann. *Hegel und der nationale Machtstaatsgedanke in Deutschland: ein Beitrag zur politischen Geistesgeschichte.* Leipzig, 1921.

Hertz, Frederick. *The Development of the German Public Mind: A Social History of German Political Sentiments, Aspirations, and Ideas.* Vol. II: *The Age of Enlightenment.* London, 1962.

Hömig, Klaus Dieter. *Der Reichsdeputationshauptschluss vom 25. Februar 1803 und seine Bedeutung für Staat und Kirche.* Tübingen, 1969.

Hofmann, Hanns Hubert. *Adelige Herrschaft und souveräner Staat. Studien über Staat und Gesellschaft in Franken und Bayern im 18. und 19. Jahrhundert.* Munich, 1962.

Huber, Ernst Rudolf. *Deutsche Verfassungsgeschichte seit 1789.* Band I: *Reform und Restauration 1789 bis 1830.* Stuttgart, 1957.

——. *Dokumente zur deutschen Verfassungsgeschichte.* 2 vols. Stuttgart, 1961–64.

——. "Reich, Volk und Staat in der Reichsrechtswissenschaft des 17. und 18. Jahrhunderts," *Zeitschrift für die gesamte Staatswissenschaft,* 102 (1942), 593–627.

Jähns, Max. "Zur Geschichte der Kriegsverfassung des Deutschen Reiches," *Preussische Jahrbücher,* 39 (1877), 442–490.

Jastrow, J. *Geschichte des deutschen Einheitstraumes und seiner Erfüllung.* Berlin, 1885.

Joachimsen, Paul. *Vom deutschen Volk zum deutschen Staat. Eine Geschichte des deutschen Nationalbewusstseins.* Revised and continued from the second edition of 1920 by Joachim Leuschner. Göttingen, 1956.

Jolles, Mathys. *Das deutsche Nationalbewusstsein in Zeitalter Napoleons.* Studien zur Geschichte des Staats- und Nationalgedankens, I. Frankfurt, 1936.

Kaegi, Werner. *Historische Meditationen.* Erste Folge. Zürich, 1942.

Kaufmann, Hans-Heinrich. *Friedrich Carl von Moser als Politiker und Publizist (vornehmlich in den Jahren 1750–1770).* Quellen und Forschungen zur hessischen Geschichte, XII. Darmstadt, 1931.

Kemiläinen, Aira. *Auffassungen über die Sendung des deutschen Volkes um die Wende des 18. und 19. Jahrhunderts.* Suomalaisen Tiedeakatemien Toimituksia, Series B, CI. Helsinki, 1956.

Kleinheyer, Gerd. *Die kaiserlichen Wahlkapitulationen: Geschichte, Wesen, und Funktion.* Karlsruhe, 1968.

Klessmann, Eckart, ed. *Deutschland unter Napoleon: in Augenzeugberichten.* Düsseldorf, 1965.

Koppen, Wilhelm. *Deutsche gegen Deutschland. Geschichte des Rheinbundes.* Hamburg, 1936.

Krieger, Leonard. *The German Idea of Freedom: History of a Political Tradition.* Boston, 1957; reprinted, Chicago, 1972.

Masur, Gerhard. "Deutsches Reich und deutsche Nation im 18. Jahrhundert," *Preussische Jahrbücher,* 229 (1932), 1–23.

Mathy, Helmut. *Franz Georg von Metternich, der Vater des Staatskanzlers: Studien zur österreichischen Westpolitik am Ende des 18. Jahrhunderts.* Meisenheim am Glan, 1969.

Meinecke, Friedrich. *Cosmopolitanism and the National State.* Translated by Robert B. Kimber from the 1962 reprint of the seventh edition of 1928. Princeton, 1970.

Mittelberger, Herta. *Johann Christian Freiherr von Hofenfels, 1744–1787.* Münchener Historische Abhandlungen. Erste Reihe: Allgemeine und Politische Geschichte, Heft 8. Munich, 1934.

Müller, Heinrich. *Der letzte Kampf der Reichsritterschaft um ihre Selbstständigkeit (1790–1815).* Historische Studien, LXXVII. Berlin, 1910.

Oldenhage, Klaus. *Kurfürst Erzherzog Maximilian Franz als Hoch- und Deutschmeister (1780–1801).* Quellen und Studien zur Geschichte des Deutschen Ordens, XXXIV. Bad Godesberg, 1969.

Rall, H. *Kurbayern in der letzten Epoche der alten Reichsverfassung, 1745–1801.* Munich, 1952.

Randelzhofer, Albrecht. *Völkerrechtliche Aspekte des Heiligen Römischen Reiches nach 1648.* Schriften zum Völkerrecht, I. Berlin, 1967.

Ranke, Leopold von. *Die deutschen Mächte und der Fürstenbund. Deutsche Geschichte von 1780 bis 1790.* Leipzig, 1875.

Renner, Bruno. *Die nationalen Einigungsbestrebungen Friedrich Carl von Mosers (1765–1767).* Dissertation, University of Königsberg, 1919.

Ritter, Gerhard. *Stein: eine politische Biographie.* Third edition. Stuttgart, 1958.

Rössler, Hellmuth. *Napoleons Griff nach der Karlskrone: Das Ende des alten Reiches 1806.* Munich, 1957.

——. *Österreichs Kampf um Deutschlands Befreiung. Die deutsche Politik der nationalen Führer Österreichs, 1805–1815.* Second edition. 2 vols. Hamburg, 1945.

——, and Franz, Günther. *Sachwörterbuch zur deutschen Geschichte.* 2 vols. Munich, 1958; reprinted, 1970.

Rosenzweig, Franz. *Hegel und der Staat.* 2 vols. Munich, 1920.

Roth von Schreckenstein, Karl Heinrich, Baron. *Geschichte der ehemaligen Reichsritterschaft in Schwaben, Franken und am Rheinstrome.* 2 vols. Freiburg im Breisgau, 1871.

Rürup, Reinhard. *Johann Jacob Moser: Pietismus und Reform.* Veröffentlichungen des Instituts für europäische Geschichte Mainz, XXXV. Wiesbaden, 1965.

Satz, Siegmund. *Die Politik der deutschen Staaten vom Herbst 1805 bis zum Herbst 1806 im Lichte der gleichzeitigen deutschen Publizistik.* Dissertation, University of Berlin, 1908.

Scheel, Heinrich. *Süddeutsche Jakobiner: Klassenkämpfe und republikanische Bestrebungen im deutschen Süden Ende des 18. Jahrhunderts.* Deutsche Akademie der Wissenschaften zu Berlin. Schriften des Instituts für Geschichte, Reihe I: Allgemeine und deutsche Geschichte, XIII. Berlin, 1962.

Schick, Johannes. *Der Reichstag zu Regensburg im Zeitalter des Basler Friedens, 1792–1795.* Dissertation, University of Bonn, 1931.

Schlie, Ulrich. *Johann Stephan Pütters Reichsbegriff.* Göttinger Rechtswissenschaftliche Studien, XXXVIII. Göttingen, 1961.

Schmidt, Wilhelm Adolf. *Geschichte der preussisch-deutschen Unionsbestrebungen seit der Zeit Friedrich's des Grossen.* 1 vol. in 2. Berlin, 1851.

——. *Preussens deutsche Politik.* Second edition. Berlin, 1850.

Schulz, Hermann. *Vorschläge zur Reichsreform in der Publizistik von 1800–1806.* Dissertation, University of Giessen, 1926.

Sieber, Eduard. *Die Idee des Kleinstaats bei den Denkern des 18. Jahrhunderts in Frankreich und Deutschland.* Basel, 1920.

Smend, Rudolf. "Zur Geschichte der Formel 'Kaiser und Reich' in den letzten Jahrhunderten des alten Reiches." In *Historische Aufsätze, Karl Zeumer zum 60. Geburtstag als Festgabe dargebracht von Freunden und Schülern,* pp. 439–449. Weimar, 1910.

Srbik, Heinrich Ritter von. *Das österreichische Kaisertum und das Ende des Heiligen Römischen Reiches 1804–1806.* Berlin, 1927.

——. *Deutsche Einheit: Idee und Wirklichkeit vom Heiligen Reich bis Königgrätz.* Third edition of vols. I and II. 4 vols. Munich, 1940–42.

Stauffer, Paul. *Die Idee des europäischen Gleichgewichts im politischen Denken Johannes von Müllers.* Basler Beiträge zur Geschichtswissenschaft, LXXXII. Basel and Stuttgart, 1960.

Tiedemann, Helmut. *Der deutsche Kaisergedanke vor und nach dem Wiener Kongress.* Untersuchungen zur Deutschen Staats- und Rechtsgeschichte, Heft 143. Breslau, 1932.

Valjavec, Fritz. *Die Entstehung der politischen Strömungen in Deutschland, 1770–1815.* Munich, 1951.

Vann, James A. *The Swabian Kreis: Institutional Growth in the Holy Roman Empire, 1648–1715.* Brussels, 1975.

——, and Rowan, Steven W., eds. *The Old Reich: Essays on German Political Institutions, 1495–1806.* Brussels, 1975.

Vierhaus, Rudolf. "Land, Staat und Reich in der politischen Vorstellungswelt deutscher Landstände im 18. Jahrhundert." Published paper of the XIV International Congress of Historical Sciences. San Francisco, 1975.

Waechter, Eberhard Baron von. "Die letzten Jahre der deutschen Reichsritterschaft," *Württembergische Vierteljahrshefte für Landesgeschichte*, 40 (1934), 243-289.

Wahl, Adalbert. *Uber die Nachwirkungen der französischen Revolution vornehmlich in Deutschland*. Stuttgart, 1939.

Walker, Mack. *German Home Towns: Community, State, and General Estate, 1648–1871*. Ithaca, N.Y., and London, 1971.

Weigel, H. *Die Kriegsverfassung des alten Deutschen Reiches von der Wormser Matrikel bis zur Auflösung*. Erlangen, 1912.

Wende, Peter. *Die geistlichen Staaten und ihre Auflösung im Urteil der zeitgenössischen Publizistik*. Historische Studien, CCCXCVI. Lübeck and Hamburg, 1966.

Zorn, Wolfgang. "Reichs- und Freiheitsgedanken in der deutschen Publizistik des ausgehenden achtzehnten Jahrhunderts." In *Darstellungen und Quellen zur Geschichte der deutschen Einheitsbewegung im neunzehnten und zwanzigsten Jahrhundert*, edited by Paul Wentzcke, II, 11–66. Heidelberg, 1959.

Index